LON

All The Best

Ron Anders

LONG TATERS

A Baseball Biography of George "Boomer" Scott

Ron Anderson

Foreword by Bill Jenkinson

McFarland & Company, Inc., Publishers
Jefferson, North Carolina, and London

LIBRARY OF CONGRESS CATALOGUING-IN-PUBLICATION DATA

Anderson, Ron, 1942–
    Long taters : a baseball biography of George "Boomer"
Scott / Ron Anderson ; foreword by Bill Jenkinson.
      p.   cm.
    Includes bibliographical references and index.

    ISBN 978-0-7864-4976-7
    softcover : acid free paper ∞

    1. Scott, George, 1944–   2. Baseball players — United
States — Biography.   I. Title.
GV865.S39A53 2012
796.357092 — dc23
[B]   2011037387

BRITISH LIBRARY CATALOGUING DATA ARE AVAILABLE

Front cover: Scott swings away in a 1979 early-season game
(courtesy Boston Red Sox)

Manufactured in the United States of America

McFarland & Company, Inc., Publishers
  Box 611, Jefferson, North Carolina 28640
  www.mcfarlandpub.com

For Mom and Dad

Contents

Acknowledgments

My greatest debt of gratitude I owe to my wife, Gail, who endured with me the many long and tedious hours, which eventually stretched to four and a half years, that I spent at work on this project. When, on occasion, the task seemed more than daunting, it was her persevering faith in me that kept this project on track.

There are so many other individuals who made invaluable contributions to this work and whom I gratefully acknowledge, from George Scott's boyhood friends, acquaintances, teammates, neighbors, coaches, mentors, town historians to numerous baseball historians, SABRites and the many former major league teammates, or opponents, who kindly gave their time to be interviewed.

I owe special thanks to Hodding Carter III for his sage perspective on the history of Greenville, Mississippi, his insightful views on the political and social structure of the town and its relevance to the boyhood days and challenges confronting George Scott and African American athletes like him; to Dorothy Williams, Ph.D., for her likewise articulate description of what it was like for an African American growing up in Mississippi in the '50s and '60s; social justice activist Betty Jo Boyd for her perspective on the town, its people, the all-black institution known as Coleman High, and the times in the racially conflicted Mississippi Delta; and Beverly Gardner for his views on historical Greenville, its racial climate, and the history of venerable Sportsman's Park, the seat of semipro baseball in the Delta, where major league and Negro League baseball, The House of David, and the likes of Roy Campanella, Jackie Robinson, Bob Feller, and Don Newcombe once played.

My heartfelt thanks go out to the late Ed Scott, the Red Sox scout who signed George Scott, for his hours of interviews with me delving into the history of his time and experiences with the Red Sox, his Negro League days, his discovery of George Scott and Henry Aaron, and the numerous stories he shared with me about his life in baseball.

Carlos Fragoso was of enormous help to me with Scott's Mexican League years, scouring the newspaper stories of the day, interviewing key Mexican

League baseball people, and altogether helping with many loose ends on Scott's five seasons south of the border. Edward Almada helped with information on the Mexican and Mexican Pacific [Winter] Leagues; Almada's father, Mel Almada, was the first Mexican national to play in the major leagues (1933–1939).

My thanks also to Dan Desrochers, my dedicated companion on several trips we made to Boston to meet with Red Sox, *Boston Herald* and Boston Public Library personnel, to identify, assemble and organize photographs for the book project. His editorial experience and expertise was invaluable.

Contributors

George Scott
Jay Acton
Mike Babcock
Stan Block
Mike Kardamis
Jim Mudcat Grant
Marty Pattin
Gene Martin
Whitey Herzog
Frank Sanders
Diego Segui
Lenny Green
Rico Petrocelli
Jim Gosger
Mary Haynes
John Provenza
Davis Weathersby
Sam McDowell
John Wathan
Joseph Barthell, Jr.
Ed Scott
Bob Veale
Eddie Dennis
Edsel Neal
Bobby Doerr
Fred Beene
Jonathan Fleisig
John Thomas
Zelma Kelly
Bill Slack
Elijah Moore
Andrew Jackson
E. T. Davis
Beatrice Scott

Bob Scranton
W. C. Gorden
Beverly Gardner
Betty Jo Boyd
Alex Grammas
Clark Viegas
Darrell Brandon
George Digby
Merv Rettenmund
Luis Tiant
Tommy Harper
Gloster Richardson
Hodding Carter III
Fred Patek
Leonia Collins Dorsey
Doctor Dorothy Williams
Doctor Robert Young
John Hawkins
A.C. Thomas
Willie Richardson
Charles "Chuck" Prophet
Doctor William Ware
Carlos Fragoso
Debbie Matson
Bill Nowlin
Dan Desrochers
David Laurila
David Vincent
Martha Reagan
Greg Rybarczyk
Mary Dayle McCormick
Princella Nowell
Elisabeth Keppler
Aaron Schmidt

Noel Workman
Charlie Blanks
Brenda Fulton-Poke
Thomas Van Hyning
Edwin Fernandez-Cruz
Alfredo Ortiz
Alfonso Araujo
Manuel Cazarin
Porfirio Mendoza
Jose Pena
Tommy Morales
Benjamin "Papelero"
  Valenzuela
Lee Sigman
Jose Luis Gutierrez
Jacob Cruz
Edward Almada
Leonte Landino
Jorge Colón-Delgado
Tom Larwin
Bill Jenkinson
Phil Lowry
Miles Wolff
Pam Ganley
Doug Adams
Mary Russell Baucom
Arthur Pollock
Pat Kelly
Allison Midgley
David Smith
Milt Bolling
Sam Mele
Dan Osinski
Dina Wathan

Foreword

by Bill Jenkinson

When I published my book about the history of "tape measure" home runs in 2010, I was pleased and proud. Yet, even then, I knew that the book had a drawback. There simply wasn't enough space to honor everyone who had distinguished themselves as truly great long distance hitters.

Literally hundreds of millions of males have tried their hand at bashing baseballs, and choosing only sixty-three for specific recognition by way of "mini-chapters" would result in the exclusion of some truly powerful hitters. I dreaded the prospect of disappointing the men who rightfully expected to be honored for their exceptional prowess, but who were not even mentioned in my treatise. And for those who had already passed, I hated the thought of compromising the cherished memories of friends and descendents.

So, when I wrote my book, I tried to remind readers that there were bound to be some omissions and oversights. This is where George "Boomer" Scott entered the scene. Shortly before publication, I was coincidentally contacted by author Ron Anderson who was working on a biography of Scott. He asked me if I was aware of Boomer's massive clout into Yankee Stadium's towering left field upper deck.

I acknowledged that I had heard about it, but admitted that I didn't know any details. That home run was belted on April 26, 1966, and was one of twenty-seven recorded by Boomer in his first Major League season. A subsequent study of all those 1966 homers convinced me that Ron had a great story to tell. However, by that time, there was no way that I could honor George Scott in my own book. That bothered me.

As readers will learn in subsequent pages, young George was a poor kid with a very powerful body. As often occurs with true athletic prodigies, he completely overmatched his childhood peers, and eventually became a hugely successful multi-sport athlete in high school. As an African-American child growing up in rural Mississippi in the 1940s and 1950s, it seemed that his destiny, like his peers of the Delta, was to labor in the cotton fields picking cotton under the broiling southern sun.

Yet, despite the hardship, those experiences created a powerful inner resolve that inspired George to do better, and helped motivate him to strive for athletic excellence. Scott passionately wanted to make it to the Big Leagues ... and stay there. When he arrived in Boston in 1966, at age twenty-two, George was a six-foot-two-inch, 217 pound juggernaut who radiated power with his every move. That epic 500 foot homer in New York was only one of several of his tape measure shots that left witnesses gaping in awe.

It is an historical fact that most successful Major League sluggers hit the ball harder and farther in their early to mid-twenties than they do as older players. They usually become better all-around performers later in their careers, and that evolution often includes the ability to hit more home runs. However, they tend to hit them farther as younger men. That appears to be the case with Boomer.

There are two reasons for this phenomenon: The first is physiological. Many baseball athletes simply generate greater bat speed when they are in their twenties. The second factor is more complicated, but, in my opinion, more interesting from a biographical standpoint. Oftentimes, power hitters simply reduce the force of their swings in order to make more consistent contact.

That appears to be happening now with such noteworthy contemporary sluggers as Albert Pujols, Adam Dunn and Ryan Howard. They are each immensely strong men who have the capability to launch baseballs prodigious distances. Yet, as they have proceeded through their respective tenures in Major League Baseball, they have tended to hit the ball slightly less far.

In the entire history of the sport, there have been extremely few players who have steadfastly swung as hard as they could, and still succeeded in the Majors over extended periods of time. Babe Ruth, Mickey Mantle and Willie Mays come to mind, but let's be honest. Those legends were three of the most extraordinarily and implausibly gifted physical marvels that America has ever produced.

If you want to stay in the Big Leagues, you need to repeatedly center the bat on the ball. When you're competing against men of roughly equal talent, who focus on the art of making you miss the ball, it is an extremely daunting challenge. Only roughly one man in every half million is up to the mark. And remember this: George Scott badly wanted to be a successful ballplayer. He was willing to do whatever he needed to do to keep earning those Big League paychecks. Who could blame him?

Accordingly, when those gifted Major League hurlers identified the flaws in his swing (and they always do), Boomer had to cut back just a little in order to survive. Plus, as Ron will relate in the full story, there were sometimes managers and coaches who, although well intended, provided too much advice. George needed only minor adjustments; his natural swing was suited to his personal capabilities, and major alterations worked against him.

But he endured. When the final tally was made, George "Boomer" Scott had played fourteen memorable seasons (1966–1979) of Big League ball. During that time he slugged 271 home runs and drove in 1,051 runs. It should also be recalled that George compiled those numbers during an era that was dominated by many of the greatest pitchers in baseball annals.

Plus, due to his athletic virtuosity, Scott won eight Gold Gloves for his outstanding defensive work at first base. Almost as importantly, he also became a fan favorite in both Boston and Milwaukee. Everybody seemed to like Boomer; his smile and demeanor were infectious.

I remember George Scott well. Despite his willingness to dial down his vast power a notch or two, he still struck the ball with savage force until the day that he ultimately retired. Although his rookie season of 1966 was his best as a tape measure hitter, Boomer left a trail of memorable "taters" everywhere he played for as long as he played. The guy just brutalized baseballs.

We rarely get the chance for "do-overs" in life, but this is one of them. I am sincerely grateful to both McFarland and Ron Anderson for the opportunity to share my conviction that George Scott was one of the most powerful men to ever swing a baseball bat. If there is a second edition to my book, I promise to find a way to include him.

Bill Jenkinson • Baseball Historian

Preface

When a man has established his superiority for as long as Scott has, he is in danger of being taken for granted. I believe this is what happened to Scott last year. When he fielded in sensational style down the stretch, it only was viewed as a return to his normal level of proficiency. Anyone else would have been hailed as the new Hal Chase. — Bob Ryan, *Boston Globe*, 1978

Statements like Bob Ryan's 1978 comment in the *Boston Globe* caught my attention and helped inspire me to write this story, for it was often George Scott's conviction that he was held to a different standard than the rest.

I met George Scott for the first time in the summer of 1996 when he was the manager of a very successful independent-league baseball team, the Massachusetts Mad Dogs. It was a brief encounter but a memorable one. George signed some bats and balls for me and we talked for a long while about his baseball career. He was open with his views, unassuming (a characteristic I was not expecting), frequently of good humor, and altogether a pleasure to talk to.

Since then a friendship has formed and I have come to learn much more about George Scott, the man. Far more than an ex-ballplayer, Scott is a complex individual who encountered numerous obstacles on his way to the major leagues. He was a black athlete contending with the racial turbulence of the '60s; he lived and grew up in serious poverty; and he was a product of the Mississippi Delta, a hotbed of racism, from which he would emerge only to find himself at the door-step of the Boston Red Sox, notably the last team to integrate.

What is not well-known about George "Boomer" Scott — a much-loved Boston sports figure of the '60s and '70s — is the extent to which he confronted a compendium of racial challenges throughout his baseball career. He was treated by the occasional fan with racial hostility, was an anathema to some teammates, dealt with disapproving managers and a tough Boston media laced with racist tendencies, and altogether confronted a baseball hierarchy whose expectations and standards set for him at times seemed different — if

1

not greater — than what was expected of teammates. Because he had such an unmitigated passion for the game and a desire to succeed in the only profession he knew, and believed would sustain him, he sought to avoid controversy. Unlike his counterparts, that approach did not always serve him well personally; but it was a means to job survival, especially while in his formative years in Boston.

Distrustful of baseball management, George learned early in his career to accommodate his feelings, finding the path of least resistance, common to the black man of the times and of his own locally assimilated culture. And yet he was, as well, frustrated by this false sense of acceptance and unnatural restraint as he progressed in the majors. He became more vocal, spoke loudly in his own behalf and in defense of the underdog ballplayer leading to eventual clashes with baseball authority that likely sealed his fate from later reentering major league baseball.

It was often a precipitous journey for George "Boomer" Scott, from the disastrous nearly career-ending '68 season to his American League MVP-candidate season of 1975. He was an intense, prideful man — sometimes rubbing teammates the wrong way — whose natural athletic skills swiftly propelled him from the harshness of his Mississippi roots to the highest levels of professional achievement in a Northern white man's world. But his Southern black culture held him in its grip: he was accustomed to being the "outsider," a self-appointed role he would not — could not — shed throughout his baseball career.

He was a loner, often "misunderstood," said a teammate. During his youthful years when the Boston press took him to task, he would vigorously fight back, exclaiming, "but I'm from Mississippi," as if by assumption everyone must realize he came from cultural depravity, warranting their forgiveness. His instincts compelled him to succeed with a team heretofore known for its racial intolerance, and in a city built around racial boundaries once described by Boston Celtics great Bill Russell as "a flea market of racism."

Howard Bryant in his book *Shutout* quoted former New York Yankee Willie Randolph's description of the city of Boston: "We knew Boston's reputation and as a player you always look for that something extra ... It was the reputation of the city that made me want to beat them that much more."

This story is not merely to illustrate the ascension of a talented young athlete to his ultimate success in the professional baseball world — a home run slugger, major league All-Star and eight-time Gold Glover; it is instead a tale of the rare triumph of a young black man of the racially turbulent '50s and '60s, the product of an infamous Mississippi, who emerged victorious from immense poverty, the madness of segregation and a dehumanizing Mississippi-style racism, to reach the big leagues, where he flourished for fourteen seasons.

Scott encountered elements of racism and personal rejection throughout his career culminating in a snub from major league baseball upon his attempt to re-enter the game following retirement, and after years of slogging around independent and Mexican League baseball cities in an effort to establish his coaching credentials. He aspired to ultimately manage in the big leagues, remaining in the game that he loved, but Major League Baseball turned its back on him.

1

Pee-tuck

I wanted to be a great major league ballplayer like Willie Mays. He was my favorite. That was one dream. The other was about a day I would come home, set my mother down at the kitchen table and put a pile of money in front of her. Then I'd tell her that she would never have to work hard again. I can't wait for that day to come.— George Scott[1]

In the spring of 1944 George Charles Scott Jr. entered the world, a product of the Mississippi Delta, born unto a climate beset by a racially divided social and political system that was the plight of the African American of the Deep South. It was a time of profound racial segregation rooted in Southern behavior of the harshest kind that would leave its ugly mark forever on the history of the country.

World War II was raging in Europe and the Pacific, with America heavily engaged in both military theaters. Inherent in this was a powerful sense of national identity. Americans, in great numbers — prominent citizens and celebrities, including many notable professional athletes — were leaving their jobs and enlisting for military service. A keen national spirit and pride of country was evident and pervasive; at the same time civil disturbance was brewing on the home front — especially in the South — between white and black Americans of a dimension that would eventually lead to great turbulence and tragedy in America.

In the South, state and local *Jim Crow Laws,* built upon a theme of racial segregation and discrimination, were still in effect and widespread, a legacy of the post–Civil War *Reconstruction* period. For the African American it was their moment of terror to find their own way — a story of survival — in a hostile land. Lynching, political disfranchisement, social humiliation and economic impoverishment were the plight of the Southern black that transcended into the '60s. But Mississippi stood even further apart from its neighboring Southern states: Mississippi "is something different ... something almost unspeakably primal and vicious; something savage unleashed there that has yet to come to

5

rest," wrote African American historian Anthony Walton.[2] Mississippi's contempt for blacks seemed to be of an even greater intensity, a more virulent hostility of a style all its own.

In the early 1960s Mississippi, "the absolute nadir of racism, violence and poverty,"[3] was the poorest state in the nation with 86 percent of the non-white population living in poverty. In 1961 less than 7 percent of Mississippi blacks were registered to vote largely due to the efforts of the Ku Klux Klan and white Citizens' Councils who were opposed to blacks establishing a foothold in the state. Segregated black schools received little funding for education compared to their white student counterparts, with a consequence of low graduation rates and few young blacks going on to college.[4]

Martin Luther King intensified his effort for civil rights with the advent of *Freedom Rides* in the South in 1961 following the Supreme Court decision (*Boynton v. Virginia*) banning segregation in interstate transportation. Spurred by Doctor King and his supporters the *Freedom Movement* blossomed throughout the South. James Meredith became the first black admitted to the University of Mississippi, a sacrosanct institution of Southern white rule, in October 1962, amidst the turmoil and violence inspired and led by the opposition of segregationist governor Ross Barnett.

This was the social and political climate into which George Scott Jr. was born and raised. There were rigid rules — racial mores, in truth — he would be obliged to steadfastly follow as a young black man growing up in a racially divided community, knowing that any misstep would likely bring harsh retribution. It was simply understood. He would have to fall into line — as the black community was accustomed — to the "rules" laid down to him by family and a neighborhood support system to avoid repercussions certain to follow from any breach of "good and acceptable" behavior. Survival for the African American of the South meant assiduously following the accepted standards of black-white decorum, which was that "everybody knew their place."

The youngest of three children of Magnolia and George Scott Sr., George Jr. was born on March 23, 1944, "out in the country," a popular expression of the times, in Longwood, Mississippi, a small hamlet in the southwest part of the state bordering the Mississippi River that was actually part of a plantation where young George's father worked driving trucks, picking and chopping cotton. The little community, named after the plantation, was established on 3000 acres originating with Thomas Jefferson Wilkerson, in 1835, and then by one Ben Smith, a Delta planter, whom Wilkerson deeded a portion of the land to in the same year. It was an antebellum period "working farm" in a geographic district that once supported slave labor, similar to other plantations in the South of that time preceding the Civil War, but where many emancipated black laborers lived and toiled — often a wretched existence — following the war.

By all accounts George Sr. was most likely a common day laborer on the plantation. It was possible, however, though less likely, that he could have been operating as a tenant-farmer — a sharecropper — which was a post–Civil War reciprocal arrangement between landowner and freed slave known as the tenant-credit system, a form of economic slavery. George Sr. lived on the plantation with his wife, Magnolia, "in a very small house," relates his daughter, Beatrice, where they bore their children.[5]

When George Jr. was just one year old his father collapsed suddenly and died while working in the fields. It was a very hot day which, it was felt, led to "heatstroke" precipitating his untoward demise. According to accounts of that day George Sr. was found lying beside his truck and never regained consciousness. Being so young, George Jr. would not remember his father. His mother was suddenly alone, confronted with full responsibility for the care and welfare of her young family.[6]

Left with responsibility for three young children and without a job or government benefits to survive on, the widow, Magnolia, departed Longwood soon after for the nearby town of Greenville, situated twenty miles up the road. There she took up residence with her small family and found greater opportunities for work. She settled into a three-room *shotgun* style house[7] on Clay Street in the poorest section of town, the south end, and an even poorer section of the south end known to the locals as *Booker Town*. "It was a tough part of town," said George's high school teammate and friend John Hawkins. "You didn't come to the south side unless you had your parent's permission."

The Mississippi Delta in the '50s and '60s has been described as the "epicenter of the national struggle over civil rights."[8] Greenville, the county seat of Washington County, a port on the banks of the Mississippi River, was the largest municipality in the Delta. Known as "The Queen City," Greenville was made up of various manufacturing trades but its primary industry was cotton farming. It was also a racially divided city, situated in the middle of the Delta described by James C. Cobb as "the most southern place on earth."[9]

White landowners and other prominent white businessmen — whose mansions, by their sheer opulence and charm, stood out on Washington Avenue and Main Street in the heart of Greenville — were a privileged class. This was not so, however, for the black residents; their social status, if not their plight, was the antithesis of the white gentry and agrarian elite aristocracy of Greenville. It was a society of white and black coexistence, where skin color distinguished and a racial caste system was firmly in place; it was where a young George Scott would quickly come to know and learn the ways of survival in a white man's world.

The Ku Klux Klan remarkably lacked footing in Greenville, unlike other Mississippi towns, but *Jim Crow* segregation nevertheless was firmly in place;

the town had a certain racially tolerant moderateness about it that irritated hard-line white segregationists of adjoining communities. Journalist Hodding Carter, Jr., a rare "Southern liberal," majority owner and editor of Greenville's local newspaper and a progressive journalist, among a rich tradition of Greenville writers and artists, spoke for racial tolerance and against the mistreatment of blacks that sufficiently aroused the state NAACP field director in 1965 to inexplicably proclaim the town "the heaven of Mississippi."[10]

Carter followed the lead of his confidant and patron William Alexander Percy, acknowledged "cultural tsar" and legendary figure of Greenville, and a champion of *noblesse oblige*, who persuaded him to come to their city in 1936 and start a newspaper of "courageous and incorruptible" quality, and to flush out the excesses of white mob rule. Carter created what would eventually become the *Delta Democrat-Times*, in which he wrote scathing editorials dealing with race and bigotry. He won the Pulitzer Prize in 1946, bringing him publicity and corresponding national attention to the Delta and Greenville. This was more than unsettling to the white establishment, which found themselves in constant flux as they attempted to preserve their "way of life" as a *right way* to handle the race question.[11]

Greenville's all-white constituency of lawyers, planters and businessmen of the Citizens' Council conducted practices and passed down rules largely to preserve white class control in the name of making a "smooth transition to integration," that lasted well into the 1960s. Carter, and later his son, Hodding Carter III, who ran the *Delta Democrat-Times*, strenuously resisted the efforts of the Citizens' Council and neutralized their subversive initiatives. This favored a young George Scott and other blacks of Greenville, allowing them more of an opportunity to be educated and ultimately achieve as opportunities were less available to blacks in surrounding towns.

"[Greenville was] the most urbane and progressive city in Mississippi ... an oasis in the racial strife and obsession that smothered the rest of Mississippi," wrote Mississippi congressman Frank Smith. "Strict segregation prevailed, but there was an atmosphere of harmony and respect for basic rights that did not exist elsewhere. It was a main ingredient of the economic progress of the town. The moving force behind the spirit of Greenville was Hodding Carter, and his newspaper the *Delta Democrat-Times*." But this perception was not always shared by members of Greenville's black community, who felt the yoke of racist policy by the town too burdensome to bear. As one resident of Greenville described the times: "This seemingly benign living scheme was only a facade because the lines of segregation were tightly drawn and everyone knew his or her place in the racial pecking order.... We wanted to be free but ultimately there was no hiding place from the *ism* of race."[12]

Segregation of whites and blacks was clearly defined in Greenville. There were white and black schools, businesses, one black motel, and "colored only" designated facilities throughout the town; neighborhoods were distinctively segregated. The insular black community was supportive of their youth, encouraging them to pursue their goals while at the same time reminding them often of the dangers that surrounded them if they strayed from racially acceptable behavioral patterns. George Scott grew up in poverty at a subsistence level, depending nearly as much on the moral support and occasional funding he received from members of the black community and his teachers as he could expect from his bereft mother. "He came from nothing," said former Greenville resident and Baltimore Colts football standout Willie Richardson.[13]

It was nothing less than daunting for Magnolia to keep her family afloat upon their arrival in Greenville, amidst a white-rule society, but Mag[14] would do all within her power and control to keep her family together, mostly performing domestic work for white residents. She also worked a second job as a cook in a small restaurant, and sometimes worked as many as three jobs to make ends meet.[15] This would be a compelling reason why George would ultimately make professional baseball his career choice over basketball or football — his best sports — to rescue his mother from the hard labor and servitude in which she had been toiling for so long. He could not see himself spending four years in college despite his potential for football or basketball scholarships, when baseball offered him what he needed foremost — money — to help support his struggling mother.

George exhibited a speech impediment at an early age, "tie-tongue" the locals called it, felt to be a manifestation of his culture and the environment in which he was raised, Greenville residents who were close to him explained.[16] This he would eventually overcome following his arrival in Boston in 1966, resulting from his contact with major leaguers, sports journalists and a Northern culture generally, acquiring an acculturation of new behavior, speech and, quite remarkably, even semblance of a New England accent.

Former Red Sox teammate Rico Petrocelli said about Scott when he first met him in the Red Sox Ocala, Florida, minor league training camp in 1962: "His speech wasn't very clear, you know, he kind of mumbled, and people like myself would say — when he'd say something — 'What? What'd you say?' He was a kid from the Deep South — you know small towns. He was a great athlete, and this was probably the first time he came to a more ... obviously a professional organization and some of the other [metropolitan] areas around."[17] Petrocelli added that after awhile Scott made great improvement in his speech and, when he wanted to, "could speak the King's English!"

Like so many other young blacks of Greenville and surrounding towns, at the young age of nine George went to work in the fields in the summer around Greenville picking and chopping cotton. "That's all we knew," he related. "When I was a kid working on my hands and knees all day in the sun — the money I earned I couldn't even spend to buy a shirt or a pair of pants. It had to go to my mother so she could buy food for us."[18] He received $2.50 for every 100 pounds of cotton he picked. George picked an average of 200 pounds a day, "but that's really pickin'," he said. Although pickers wore gloves because of the thorns, George would not because he felt it slowed the "pickin'" process, and his hands — still showing the scars — were bloodied because of it.

The Collins Cleaners, a black dry-cleaning establishment four houses down from where George grew up, on Gum Street, was a refuge of a kind for young George, who came by the house daily to read the paper and take in an occasional meal. "Every day my mother knew that he was going to be there to read the sports page ... I mean he would be right at it, I mean religiously and so serious about it. You know I don't know who he was rootin' for or what but that was his page," explained Leonia Collins Dorsey, daughter of owner Fred Collins. The Collins Cleaners would become more than an occasional refuge for George, as an important life-line later on.[19]

Greenville had separate — segregated — public school systems for whites and blacks. Scott began his education at the south end's all-black Lucy Webb Elementary School, a short walk from his childhood home. George Crawford, the 6th grade teacher, was his first coach, introducing George and other students to "all sports," recalled high school teammate Hawkins, from softball to basketball and football. All the elementary schools had football teams and "we would play each other."[20]

Among a wide assortment of sporting activities and events proffered by schoolmaster Crawford was boxing, beginning in the 5th grade and continuing into the 10th, when Scott competed in amateur Golden Gloves tournaments. The young pugilist took to the sport readily, winning all eighteen bouts in which he competed. There was no weight class. "We just competed according to age and going from school to school, town to town," said Scott. "A lot of things as kids parents did not know about it ... if I had told my momma that I had played football [or boxed], there's no way that she would have let me play," Scott chuckled.

The thrill of playing team sports and a strong desire to be competitive began to percolate in the young and impressionable George Scott during these early years at Lucy Webb, where he began to visualize personal goals for himself of athletic accomplishment and achievement. He loved to compete, exhibiting athletic skills from the very beginning that were quickly recognized and eventually nurtured by the adult black community. Big for his age and standing taller than most of his peers, George stood out wherever he played.

One of George's earliest childhood memories was watching a televised game that featured future Hall of Famer Willie Mays. Scott was mesmerized by Willie's athleticism and made up his mind then-and-there he would learn to be just like him. "That might have been the day I fell in love with baseball," said Scott to *Boston Globe* reporter Will McDonough. "I don't know for sure. But I love baseball more than anything else in the world, and nothing's going to change it."[21]

His passion for baseball soon escalated to a level where he played it almost daily. As he explained, "People in my town thought I was crazy. The other kids in my town played basketball and football but didn't really care for baseball." He had a bike and rode around the neighborhood looking for friends who would go with him to play ball at nearby Frisby Park. Most of the time they wouldn't join him so he went there on his own and proceeded to hit baseballs from one end of the park to the other, retrieve them, and then hit a slew of pop-ups to himself. He also went to nearby railroad tracks, sometimes with his friend E.T. Davis, where he would hit rocks with a baseball bat "for hours in different directions."

Frank Sanders, starting halfback on the 1957 Big Eight state champion football team at Coleman High School,[22] and a boyhood chum, remembered George playing with him and friends on the Lucy Webb playground when George was about ten to twelve years of age. George didn't live too far from the playground so when he heard the crack of a batted ball he would come running full-speed eager to play. He recalled Scott's constant chatter — a harbinger of *trash talk* before it was fashionable — which he found "annoying," and his superb defensive skills. He was "talking his noise ... you didn't always know what he was saying sometimes but he'd keep talking; he just always talked baseball. We would let him play, put him on third base and we would just try our hardest to knock his head off, but he would just come up with that ball just like he was paying no attention," said Sanders. "It was because of his chatter and his dominancy at his age. He was dominant and he was good at it. You just couldn't get no balls by him no matter how hard you was trying ... he just handled them like you didn't know what you were doing but just trying to hit the ball [normally]."[23]

George often walked across town to Sportsman's Park, a state-of-the art baseball stadium at the time, on the corner of Union and Wilson Street in the north end to take a peek at the pro team playing there, the Greenville Bucks, a minor league club in the Class C Cotton States League. Black residents were not allowed to go inside the stadium nor sit on or look over the park's fences; the games were restricted to whites. But they could catch an occasional glimpse through fence-openings and knot-holes. George and his playmates shagged balls that were hit out of the park, would return them to park authorities and receive twenty-five cents a ball in compensation, or "take 'em home so we would have something to play with." He set his sights on a left-handed batter for the Bucks, Luther Tucker, who often lofted baseballs out of the park over the right-field wall, which George would chase down. His peers soon recognized Scott's affinity for the slugger and anointed him with a nickname, "Tuck," which in time changed to *Pee-tuck*. The nickname stuck with him even after his high school years.[24]

Like other racial components of Greenville culture, Little League teams were also distinctly segregated; there were numerous black and white teams but they were restricted to play within their own leagues, never to compete with each other or share the same field at the same time. Black teams, however, did receive sponsorship support from local businesses, a reflection of the moderate political and social attitude of the town that was not shared by many of the surrounding towns in the Delta. But they often played on inferior fields compared with their white counterparts, who received the community's full attention and support.

Elbert Foules, who became George's high school baseball coach and steadfast mentor, first laid eyes on the

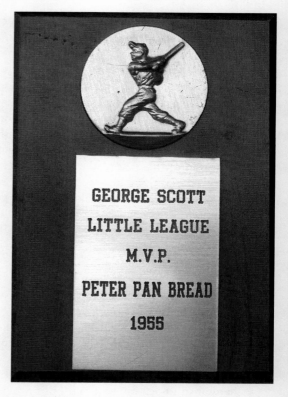

GEORGE SCOTT
LITTLE LEAGUE
M.V.P.
PETER PAN BREAD
1955

Little League Most Valuable Player, age 11. George Scott was bigger than most kids his age and was clouting home runs at a prodigious pace; in one stretch of six games he rapped out two to three homers per game. He was temporarily dropped from the league because he was considered "too good" (author's collection).

budding protégé playing Little League baseball at age 6 with boys twice his age. "He was catching and though he didn't look too much like a catcher, I noticed he moved around pretty easily."[25] Scott was a part-time catcher, but mostly a shortstop in Little League, a position he played predominantly through high school. Supervisor of the league Davis Weathersby remembered him as the "top ballplayer in the league," which awarded George with Most Valuable Player designation in 1955. T.B. Holloway, his Little League coach, remembered George for his glove: "We didn't know he could hit."

In his final year of Little League George put on more bulk, was stronger, taller and became a force to be reckoned with. He was hitting the ball with authority, slamming home runs and overwhelming some of the smaller players attempting to catch his line drives and hard-hit ground balls. In one stretch of six games, he hit either two or three home runs in each game. It was a level of performance and athleticism confounding the league authorities that led them to question whether he was too old to play. His "reward" for being "too good" was to be thrown off the team, but he was later reinstated.[26] Scott found refuge from his critics after Little League by playing ball in town sandlot games with older boys and grown men who seemed more willing to accept the hazardous duty of catching his line drives laced to the right side of the diamond and through the pitcher's box. Except for pick-up games and weekend sandlot ball, following Little League Scott did not again participate in organized baseball until his junior year of high school.

Scott demonstrated leadership qualities at an early age that would suit him well later on in baseball, basketball and football at all-black Coleman High School. His closest boyhood friend, E.T. Davis, recalled being impressed by George at a young age leading his tattered troop of neighborhood ballplayers from the south end of town like the Pied Piper midst his minions. "All the guys had to walk to the park, and I can remember him bringing the guys in from the south end and he was leading 'em across the field. I will never forget that. They was following him and he was their leader," said Davis.[27]

It was customary for the black students of Greenville to enter Coleman High in the 7th grade where they received their education over a six-year span. George was thirteen at the time and already showing signs of varsity level potential. Weathersby, Coleman High's athletic director and varsity head football coach, saw the young talent blossoming and proceeded to organize a seventh-grade football team in an effort to nurture it. Recognizing his leadership qualities early-on Weathersby assigned George the quarterback role. "At that time I knew that he had the potential, so I was just waiting until he got into the upper grades so we could move him onto the B team and the varsity," said Weathersby.[28]

Former Coleman High football co-captain John Hawkins explained that George had natural advantages "with his size, he was always ahead of us. He played with us, but he played with the older kids, too." George had a presence about him because of his stature, matched with his exceptional talent, that attracted coaches as well as athletes who were much older than him. Although not on the football varsity roster when he was in the 7th grade, George was frequently asked to participate in practice scrimmages with the varsity team. He was a captain "in all sports," said Hawkins, including Coleman High's three major team sports — football, basketball and baseball — beginning in the 10th grade.[29]

When local industrial and town teams, such as the Chicago Mill Browns and Greenville Blues, were playing Scott was often invited to play with them with guys much older than him, in their twenties and thirties. It was a melting pot of very talented baseball men, mostly locals, many of them active or former professional ballplayers, minor leaguers and Negro Leaguers. They would join these teams on a game-by-game basis as opportunity presented itself. This brand of baseball was commonly referred to around Greenville as "semipro," but they really were pickup teams — "bush leaguer," related Hawkins — that played weekends, mostly on Sundays, traveling by car to towns within a 100- to 200-mile radius that sometimes took them to nearby Arkansas. As was their custom, "We would take our spikes and put 'em out in our glove on the steps on Sunday, and Saturdays, and just wait for someone to come along and pick you up," exclaimed Hawkins.

The Browns and Blues played most of their games on a large field behind the Garrett Hall School, on Nelson Street, a *chitlin' circuit* stop made famous by the Second Whispers Restaurant in the early days of the Blues. They also played in an "open area" on Clay Street near the railroad tracks, in the black residential district, as well as "down on the Levee," a popular spot near Lake Ferguson in the south end of town bordering the Mississippi River. They were nothing but "open fields," said one Greenville citizen that they would make into a makeshift ball diamond suitable for playing baseball. On occasion black and white teen-age youngsters assembled at the Levee to play informal games of pick-up baseball together. "We didn't play any teams that had whites at that time. Now the only time we did … the Etheridge boys. We played against them. We played against all the whites that didn't mind playing. They didn't see the color; all they wanted to do was play," said Hawkins.[30]

Beginning in the summer of 1959, at the young age of fifteen, Scott could be found playing weekends for the Browns, Blues, and occasionally the Barnes All-Stars, an all-black team composed of several talented brothers, the Barnes boys, and some other nifty ballplayers that competed against quality local ball clubs including Negro League teams, such as the Birmingham Black Barons and Memphis Red Sox. Thirty-three-year-old Frank Barnes, progenitor of the team, a pitcher in the St. Louis Cardinals organization, occasionally competed in these games when he was free of his pro ball commitments. It was high caliber baseball and George was right in the middle of it. His reputation then was that he couldn't hit a curve ball, but his coach of the '59 Barnes All-Stars team noted, "I knew way back there he was gonna be a star someday … he had a good pair of hands."[31]

One memorable game, played on June 11, 1961, pitted the local industrial team, the Chicago Mill Browns, against the Barnes All-Stars. George was playing for the Browns on this day, remembered as an intense pitching duel between two ace hurlers, Hughie Jefferson of the Browns and Mack Johnson of the All-Stars. Jefferson and Johnson pitched no-hit ball until the fifth inning when George walloped a two-run homer that would turn out to be the only hit and runs of the game. "He broke up the ball game," said Elijah Moore, a

Greenville resident and former Coleman High coach. "He [Johnson] had been throwing smoke." Moore said the home run — hit with authority — off Johnson, a much better-than-average pitcher, was unexpected where he seemed in total command of the Browns batters. "Everybody was talking about it," said Moore.[32]

Greenville chums and former teammates remark about the challenges George Scott had to confront coming from poverty as he did, and how resourceful he had to be to keep up with his peers and to just get by. He was affected in more challenging ways than were many of his friends, some who had the ability and resources to buy gloves and balls. Hawkins remembers the tattered baseball glove George used, which was appalling: "That was the ugliest glove you ever seen in your life! I don't know what that thing was," laughed Hawkins. When players would come off the field and customarily lay their gloves on the sidelines or in the dugout, Scott "rolled that thing up and put it in his back pocket ... he was practically barehanded out there, but, hey, his hands were so quick." George would often borrow a glove to play with from his teammates in his teen years, but before that his "glove" was a paper bag rolled up as close to the shape of a baseball mitt as he could make it; it was all that he could afford.

Red Sox scout Ed Scott (no relation), who would ultimately sign George to a Red Sox contract, described one of his first encounters with the young slugger: "He used to joke. He used to tell me, 'you know, when I was a kid, see I was poor. I didn't have no money [so] I got me a paper bag. That's what I used catchin' all those balls. I got me a paper sack. See the kids loaned me their glove and I got out there with that glove and started pickin' it.' He used the word 'pickin'.' 'I started a-pickin' it, and they'd get jealous of me pickin' it with their glove and come and take the glove away from me. I'd get me a paper bag and pick it right on,'" related an amused scout Scott.[33]

Mathematics teacher and high school basketball coach Andrew Jackson saw George Scott for the first time as a freshman when he came out for the Coleman High basketball team. "He had unusual athletic ability which I would term 'God's gift,'" said Jackson. Jackson described Scott, a shooting guard and sometime forward, as an extraordinary athlete and basketball star. "George was an exceptional player," said Jackson, adding that he averaged 33 points a game his senior year. "He was just an outstanding player. He was an outstanding shooter. If three point plays had been set up then like it is now he would have had all kinds of records because he could really shoot the long-distance ball and the short ball ... that last year [1962] was really an outstanding year because without him we couldn't have won that Big Eight championship. He led that team all the way. Players used to try and intimidate him. They would bump him and knock him out of the court and against the wall, but he still would drill that ball right through the hole."[34]

Asked what it was like to play against George Scott, former Greenwood, Mississippi, athlete Chuck Prophet answered simply: "Hell." Said Prophet: "He talked a lot. He did a lot of bragging. We were in a sense wanting to try to shut him up, but you couldn't shut him up! Whatever he said they was going to do, they did it! He was just running his mouth all the time and he was big enough that you couldn't get mad at him ... he was just a tough, aggressive ballplayer." Greenville's Hawkins compared Scott's trash talk to Muhammad Ali: "He wasn't loud and boisterous like Ali was, but he talked all the time. He talked the game and he played the game, because whatever he talked about, he backed it up." Prophet added, "In the Spring we find out that he was supposed to be an [even] better baseball player than he was anything else! We all wanted to know 'where did he come from?'"[35]

During his freshman year Scott suddenly dropped out of school. His mother, living at the poverty level, could barely make ends meet trying to support her three kids, and had to reach out to them to help bring in family income. Coach Jackson was alarmed at the circumstances and appealed to the school principal, G.P. Maddox, and athletic director Davis Weathersby to find a solution that would bring George back to school and at the same time help resolve the Scott family dilemma. They worked with teachers and George's mother, Magnolia, to arrange a work schedule for George at the Collins Cleaners that would earn income they needed, so he could remain in school. George also found work at the Pepsi-Cola Bottling Company of Greenville during the summer to earn extra money, where they accommodated him with flexible work hours. It was a crucial moment in Scott's young life, a turning point enabling him to stay connected with high school sports and, ultimately, a long and successful career in professional baseball.

This was momentous for the Scott family, but more than that it was the personification of something even greater: the rallying strength of the black community to reclaim one of their own. Coleman High's teacher force led by principal Maddox, an enlightened educator who imagined opportunity for blacks through their athleticism and their success as a positive reflection on his school, strived diligently to bring out the best in their students whatever their individual strengths. It was a trait that the black community learned and performed well. While Coleman High was a sports powerhouse, its legacy was not confined to sports, graduating many students who went on to earn degrees in medicine, education, philosophy and other comparable areas. Betty Jo Boyd, a self-described "social justice" activist and resident of Greenville, effusively spoke about the all-black high school: "Coleman in its heyday had wonderful teachers, a wonderful athletic system and the facility was just absolutely grand ... if you were black, [it] would have been that you had a great school and [it was] much better than surrounding communities. It would have been just an absolutely great place to go to school."[36]

Hodding Carter III, former editor of the *Delta Democrat-Times* during the early 1960s and Assistant Secretary of State in the Jimmy Carter administration, described the phenomenon in this way: "The *talented tenth* actually worked. The old black doctrine is that in the face of total repression the necessity is to nurture the *talented tenth*. The one-tenth [of the black population], you know, that gave extra push and pull whatever their talent might be. It was a long-time black thesis so there was in the context of an utterly impoverished society a group of people who were constantly educators and the like [who] were constantly trying to nurture [by] that vest that this lousy system was producing and to help them in every way they could."[37]

Elbert Foules, Coleman High's science and chemistry teacher, defensive back coach of the football team, and Coleman's first baseball coach, arrived at the school in 1960. Foules was a Coleman graduate himself, went to all-black Central State University [Ohio], and played some baseball in the Negro Leagues during summers as a shortstop with the Memphis Red Sox and the Birmingham Black Barons. Soon after his arrival Foules organized the formation of a baseball team, a first for the school. The turnout was overwhelming with some 50 or more applicants, including seventeen-year-old George Scott.

Their first "uniforms" consisted of white tee-shirts and jeans. The most distinguishing of their apparel was a maroon cap with a white "C" emblazoned on it. Their shoes were pre-worn, "got 'em from the local Army surplus store here called Barney Brill for fifty cents or a quarter," said Hawkins. "You had to furnish your own shoestrings, though." For inner soles they cut out cardboard to the shape of the foot and placed them inside the shoe to protect the feet from being cut "because the iron cleats would come through." Meanwhile the all-white Greenville High received full baseball uniforms and cleats courtesy of money appropriated from town taxes.

Coleman's first game of the new baseball program was against Shelby High, which Coleman lost, 5–3. But they would win many contests that year under coach Foules, capping a successful inaugural season and the beginning of countless strong Coleman baseball teams. There was no baseball championship held that year, or the next, as it was also the beginning of baseball programs for other Delta schools. Greenwood and Clarksdale had teams, but "to get real competition we had to go to Jackson," recalled Hawkins. "Any time we played Jackson schools that was competitive in any sport." Reminiscing, William Ware, former athletic director and coach of Coleman High's archrival Broad Street High of Greenwood, expressed his view that "Coleman High was one of the finest baseball schools in the area."

Occasionally the Coleman baseball team competed with colleges since there were so few high school teams around. One such occasion was a game played against Jackson State in which George "hit some long *taters*," said Hawkins, the team's second baseman, who played adjacent to Scott, the short-

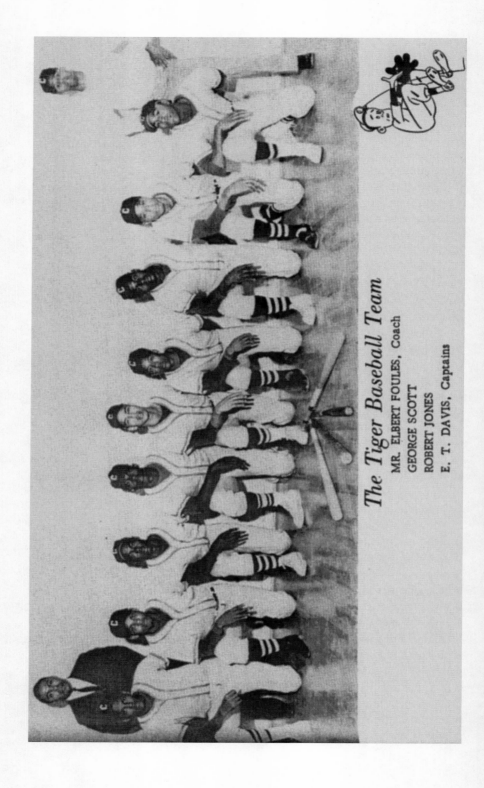

The Tiger Baseball Team

MR. ELBERT FOULES, Coach

GEORGE SCOTT
ROBERT JONES
E. T. DAVIS, Captains

stop. "They were shots," laughed Hawkins. Since the black teams usually played on fields with no outfield fences, players had to "leg-it" to make home runs. On this day Scott hit more than one tater that the Jackson State players "had to go do triple relays on" to get the ball back into the infield.[38] "That [nickname *taters*] came from growing up back home in the Delta," said Scott. "I ate me a bunch of taters and I hit some, too. I liked 'em both ways."[39]

Although Scott was never credited with being a strong academic student, his athleticism was superior, fostering a belief among the coaches that it needed to be nurtured determinedly; this was especially the case with coach Foules. Elbert "was his mentor [and] taught him the game," reported Beverly Gardner, a self-taught Greenville historian and acquaintance of Scott's and Foules. "Elbert worked to polish him up in terms of speech and what have you. Some people think he did a terrific job; some still felt he didn't do a good job. But George is George. He [Elbert] worked a lot in terms of getting him ready and acclimated for the big time because he felt that George had the potential to go on and become a major leaguer ... he sort of mentored George and tried to prepare him for living and working in the big city so to speak," said Gardner.[40]

Coleman High launched a strong football team in the fall of '61 under coach Weathersby, with Scott as its quarterback, defensive back and co-captain. One of several schools of the Delta making up the North Zone district of the Negro Big Eight, Coleman proceeded to win their first six contests, dominating the opposition and giving up no points. "No team had ever crossed our twenty yard line," said Hawkins. Confidence high after such overwhelming victories, Coleman traveled to Monroe, Louisiana, to meet Carroll High, who had a 5–1 record yielding only 13 opposition points. Coleman was humiliated, 34–12. "That bad memory has always been there," recalled Hawkins, Coleman's starting halfback and a co-captain. "The irony is it got us ready for the next ball game," which was a big one and possibly a deciding game for the North-Zone Big Eight title against a tough foe from Jackson, whom Coleman had not beaten since 1958 when they won the Big Eight state championship.

The Lanier Bulldogs of Jackson, bringing a 5–1 record into Coleman's home turf in Greenville, had three big linemen and two backs of all-state caliber to contend with. Venerable Sportsman's Park had undergone some renovations and the playing surface was mostly dirt. It rained for three straight days prior to the game, and "mud was up to your ankles," said Hawkins. It worked to Coleman's favor, helping neutralize the Lanier team. The three Coleman co-captains, Scott, Thomas and Hawkins, excelled, beating the formidable Jackson opponent, 20–6.

Opposite: The 1961 Coleman High baseball team, the inaugural season for the Coleman Tigers. Coach Elbert Foules, standing to left, developed Coleman's baseball program and coached the team. George Scott is fourth from left (courtesy of Andrew Jackson).

Davis Weathersby (left), George Scott's (right) high school football coach, mentor and a surrogate father (author's collection).

They followed with a 14–0 win over Louisville the next week. Resolute to bring home a championship, Coleman then edged neighboring Broad Street High of Greenwood, a traditionally difficult opponent, on Thanksgiving Day, 12–7. The win gave them the North Zone Big Eight championship.

It was on to Hattiesburg to meet undefeated (10–0) Rowan High, the South Zone Big Eight champions, for the all-around Negro Big Eight state football championship. Rowan was another big team led by two all-state tackles, Willie Townes at 6'6" and 246 pounds (Dallas Cowboys 1966–1970), and Eddie Pope at 6'4" and 243. Their halfback was a talented Taft Reed at 6'1" and 185 pounds. The consensus was that Coleman was overmatched. But the upstart team from Greenville surprised the talented Hattiesburg eleven with Scott playing his heart out, passing for two touchdowns and taking the lead over Rowan, 13–7, at the end of the third quarter. But Rowan couldn't be contained, scoring a final touchdown toward the end of the fourth quarter to win the game and Negro Big Eight state championship, 20–13.

Despite winning the title the Rowan team, big pre-game favorites, and their supporters were shocked by the resistance put up by Coleman High, containing their team in a way that was perceived as nothing less than "disrespectful." As the defeated Coleman players were crossing the field and getting onto their bus for the drive back to Greenville, they were met with gun fire from Rowan fans. "They actually shot on the bus," said Hawkins. "The driver had

George Scott (left) with coach Andrew Jackson holding the Negro Big Eight State Championship trophy won by Coleman High in 1962. Coleman was led by co-captain Scott, who averaged 33 points per game (author's collection).

to lean down under the seat and hold the wheel on the road ... the bullets pierced the windows."

Recognized as the team leader by his coaches and teammates, the young quarterback was also noted for his defensive prowess. He was a fierce competitor — a two-way player — and, as one Coleman coach put it, "You better hope you have a blocker in front of you when George Scott was bearing down on you."

Coach Weathersby reminisced about "Tuck," his all-around star athlete. Keeping him "out-of-the gym" and focused on his school work was always challenging. "He was a 'gym rat,'" he said. Weathersby became a father-figure, helping George with money for lunches when he needed it and also applying discipline as the occasion warranted because "he didn't have a dad at home. He had his mom at home and George needed some help along the way. George would miss a class if you didn't stay on top of him." Following one such class-skipping incident Weathersby decided to make a point once-and-for-all for his young athlete at the risk of causing him great embarrassment. Coleman High had new football uniforms George's senior year, with maroon and white colors. Coach Weathersby issued thirty-three uniforms, but one uniform — designated for George Scott — was all white, because Scott had missed a class. Consequently he played one of his high school games adorned entirely in white. It was an object-lesson he would not soon forget.

Following in the shadow of a near-perfect football season, Coleman High would reach even greater heights in their basketball season, led by guard and co-captain George Scott who averaged better than 33 points a game. They won the North Zone Big Eight title beating Jim Hill of Jackson 89–68, and on February 28 triumphed over Eva Gordon High of Magnolia, 68–50, for the overall Negro Big Eight state championship. George Scott was the leading scorer in both games, with 26 and 29 points, respectively.

Reflecting on his favorite Mississippi sports memory upon his 2007 induction into the Mississippi Sports Hall of Fame, Scott said it was basketball — not baseball — that was uppermost in his mind: "Winning the Big Eight championship in basketball in 1962, my senior year. That was my last opportunity, obviously, to win a championship; go out on top," said Scott.[41]

In spite of championship Coleman sports teams, award-winning bands, chorales and altogether outstanding academic achievement, there was little to no news in the local paper, the *Delta Democrat-Times*, written about the school in recognition of their accomplishments or even existence. "Greenville High School got all the coverage even though they weren't winning anything ... they [whites] knew we were there but it was like we weren't there," exclaimed a frustrated Hawkins. "That's the way it was," said Hodding Carter III, formerly of the *Delta Democrat-Times*. "To run any news at all about black folk was considered to be an assault on the established way of life, and covering Coleman High would have only barely occurred to anybody, no matter who [distinguished themselves] from the publisher, editor right on down," said Carter.

That effrontery was perpetuated by the actions of white-ruled Greenville when in 1970, upon the court-ordered integration of public schools, all-black Coleman High was summarily dismantled to merge with all-white Greenville High. "The whole tradition and everything associated with Coleman went out the window," said Boyd, remembering how black students were suddenly stripped from their beloved school as if it had never existed, like it had no tradition, or that it even had a purpose since it was black. "It was as though the whites were the ones that were giving up ... they were accommodating [the blacks]." Mysteriously, not only were the black students uprooted, but the hundreds of academic and athletic championship trophies were also ripped from the school, and have never been seen again.

The matter of racial censoring had a more unfortunate and far-reaching effect on the black community, especially on its athletes, who strived to be noticed with aspirations of professional careers. Absent any write-up in local papers or by news media around the state, their chance of being noticed by national media and colleges was minimal. At the very best they depended on word-of-mouth if they hoped to be spotted at all.

Scott's good fortune was growing up in a town that displayed a certain amount of racial tolerance, though certainly restrained by the oppressive Southern-style racist rule of *separate but equal*.[42] Were it not for journalists like the Carters, William Hodding Carter Jr. and III, and their paper the *Delta Demo-crat-Times*, Greenville was likely to have been bereft of news from Coleman High or the black community. As it was news of them, when published, was scanty, usually spotted on back pages; coverage of Coleman sports teams, frequently of championship caliber, was sparse, often in the form of post-scripts at the bottom of interior sports pages, reflecting the racial climate of the times and life in the Delta in the '50s and '60s. White teams and white society received the spotlight; it simply was understood.

"If it was today's baseball [where everyone has equal opportunity], we would have had at least half of the team go to professional ball. And I know we would have had guys playing Division I college baseball. That's how good we were," exclaimed a bitter Scott. Former teammate Hawkins concurred: "It was difficult ... I'll put it to you like this: if a lot of these [Coleman High] guys had been white with the kind of skills that they had they could have gone on to the professional level easily, really easily."

According to a 1973 *Los Angeles Times* article written by a sportswriter with a flair for hyperbole, Dave Distel, Scott was offered "152 scholarships" upon graduating from Coleman High School.[43] Although there were scholarship opportunities for George, they were well short of the number quoted by Distel. Foremost, Scott had to contend with the unfortunate racial climate of the South. He had two strikes against him: news of black athletes, no matter how distinguishing they were, was scarce, and mainstream Southern colleges were strictly segregated and steadfastly refused to recruit black high school athletes. He needed a few breaks and he would get them, some the lucky sort, through an altruistic coaching staff, and especially from George's mentor and coach, Elbert Foules, who had connections and some influence outside of the Delta.

The University of Oklahoma had its eye on Scott for its basketball program. The Oklahoma coach who came to watch George, according to Jackson, said "he'd never seen an athlete with that kind of desire. He wanted to recruit George and George had his mind on baseball." Michigan State was also interested in him for football, as was coach John Wooden of UCLA, who promised him a four-year basketball scholarship, according to Scott, but this was never confirmed. Wooden claimed that Scott "was a better shooter than Pete Maravich, and this was when Maravich was at LSU," said Scott.

Every top Southern black college wanted him for their football program, in particular Jackson State. But when Scott refused their attempts, Jackson State's John Merritt, according to the story, was upset over the rebuff and wrote to several major league baseball scouts encouraging them to come down to Greenville to see the boy wonder. Scott reminisced that may have been a turning point for him when pro scouts began to show up in Greenville, even though he was disgruntled by the way in which it was handled. He later accused Merritt of "setting me up" by interfering with the recruitment process.

Though baseball became Scott's primary love, he also had thoughts of one day going on to professional basketball, a sport he excelled in, that would require a four-year major college basketball career. But he knew ultimately that college was not a realistic choice for him. "I felt that if my mom had been well off where I could have gone to college, I felt I would've got 70, 80, 90, 100 thousand dollars when I got out of college to sign. But my mother was poor, and I just didn't feel I could leave her in a position [of impoverishment] and go to college," said a resigned George Scott.

2

When the Going Gets Tough, the Tough Gets Going

Well I'm sitting with these here men one day, and someone says: "There's a kid in Greenville, Mississippi, who can hit that ball out of the world...." He's at shortstop when I see him and he has great hands and he's fielding everything easy, and I say, "I wanna see this kid hit the ball," and I know he's only a kid of 17, mind you. Now he comes to the plate in the first inning and this kid from Lanier has a fair curve ball and he lays one on this kid's bat — and brother, that's my first look at George Scott from Greenville, Mississippi. He lost it. — Ed Scott[1]

In 1962, Scott's senior year at Coleman High School, the buzz surrounding the young baseball star of the Mississippi Delta had reached the major leagues and scouts were making frequent stops in Greenville to size up the lauded Coleman shortstop with the sure hands and big bat. Foremost among the scouts were ex-major leaguer George Crowe of the St. Louis Cardinals and Ed Scott of the Boston Red Sox. Also in hot pursuit were the Los Angeles Angels, Pittsburgh, Chicago White Sox and Houston.

Coleman had another winning season bolstered by the play of young Scott and several talented teammates whom George felt had major league potential, hindered only by their skin color in making it to the pro level. "They wasn't letting blacks in as easy," Scott said. He described that year as winning the equivalent of a state title, "We won the title, but we lost more games [than the previous year]. We had a lot of good baseball players in Greenville, Mississippi at the time. I'm the only one that made pro. There were a lot of guys, that if they were operating the same system that they have today, at least five or six more guys would have made pro ball."[2]

Crowe, a highly-regarded clutch power hitting first baseman of the Negro Leagues and major league baseball, was the first of the scouts with any interest in Scott to appear in Greenville. The belief is that Scott's high school coach, Elbert Foules, with ties to former Negro League ballplayers and baseball author-

25

ities, tipped off Crowe to the young phenom.[3] Crowe took a personal interest in the young ballplayer, spending time with him to polish his skills and develop him to full major league potential.

"Scotty had been a right field hitter," said Foules in a 1966 interview with Roger Birtwell of the *Boston Globe*. "In fact, his first year with me, I batted him number two because he could hit to right without trying. But Scotty had power — not power like he has today — but so much power that I wanted him to pull, and I had trouble teaching him. George Crowe came out to the park and he really helped Scott. He got him hitting the ball a bit to the left center, and sometimes he'd pull it to left."[4]

Crowe spent the better part of a month with young Scott, watching him play competitively for Coleman and working with him on finer points of hitting. After the high school season ended Crowe approached Foules, advising him he had arranged for "two more scouts" to come down and see Scott. They were St. Louis' head scout, Walter Shannon, and ex-major leaguer Buddy Lewis, a veteran of eleven seasons with the Washington Senators and a .297 lifetime hitter.

Fate was in the air that summer day in Greenville with Shannon and Lewis that would ultimately determine Scott's future in the major leagues. Foules recounted the occasion as a turning point for the young slugger, expressing mild surprise why there was even further need for more Cardinals scouts to come down when George Crowe had been watching Scott for weeks. But Crowe was black, one of a few major league black scouts at the time, and had little to no authority to sign prospects. He was obliged to solicit the "help" of higher authority in the organization to make the decisions.

Upon realizing that more scouts were coming down to Greenville, Foules found himself scurrying around for a pitcher suitable for the occasion to pitch to Scott. Since the town was rich in baseball talent the task should not have been difficult, but whether by quirk or momentary circumstance brought about by late notice beyond his control, Foules came up with a challenge for his young charge. "I drove around town looking for someone to pitch to Scotty, and the fellow I found was a right-handed sidearm pitcher," said Foules. "Crowe knew Scotty could hit, but the other two men had to be shown. This sidearm pitcher made things tough for Scotty. He was stepping in the bucket a little, and he wasn't meeting the ball very well. Finally the scouts had a talk. Lewis said he thought Scotty would make a good minor league player, that was all. Shannon seemed to think the same way. Crowe knew better, but there wasn't anything he could say," said Foules. The Cardinals duo turned lukewarm on Scott, frustrating George Crowe who felt unduly slighted.

Scott powered several balls of home run caliber during the tryout that day, but the scouts felt because he failed to pull the ball enough that he would "never be a big leaguer." They returned to St. Louis without signing Scott, to the disappointment of Crowe. Scott later alluded to "race" being a likely factor in the non-signing, a view he believed was shared by Crowe. The Cardinals of the 1940s and 1950s were a racially intolerant organization. It wasn't until August Busch, Jr., took over the team in 1953 that attitudes began to change. In the early '60s they not only began the serious task to integrate, but they worked at the more problematic issue of racial acceptance. Stars like Bob Gibson, Curt Flood, Bill White and Lou Brock began to emerge. "It was not a smooth transition," though, wrote Howard Bryant. "The Cardinals, like the Red Sox and many other clubs, had powerful strains of racism that ran throughout each segment of the organization."[5]

Whether the decision by the Cardinals not to sign Scott was racially motivated remains problematic; but there was little doubt in Crowe's mind, and Scott's, that the Cardinals scouts were disingenuous about signing him. They were indifferent to Crowe who had scouted George for months, ignoring his opinion, and disregarded the clouts Scott hit that spring day in Greenville. Crowe left the St. Louis organization not long after; he would point to the Scott non-signing among his reasons.[6]

Reeling from the flak owing to the Pumpsie Green episode in 1959 when Green — the first black to play for the Red Sox — was suddenly and unceremoniously dumped to the minors after a strong spring, the Red Sox elected in 1961 to deflect further criticism by hiring their first black scout, Ed Scott. Hired by Red Sox senior scout, and former Bosox shortstop, Milt Bolling, Scott brought scouting depth to their ranks, having himself played Negro League ball and as a scout for the Negro League's Indianapolis Clowns. He discovered future Hall of Famer Hank Aaron, signing him to the Indianapolis Clowns in 1952, Aaron's first professional baseball contract.

Ed Scott's arrival with the Red Sox was done "in a moment of brilliance," reported *Boston Globe* sportswriter Clif (Clifton, aka Cliff) Keane. He was immediately assigned to investigate black baseball talent in the South, a wide berth of geography for the new 44-year-old Red Sox recruiter. But there can be little question this hiring move by the Red Sox was to further mitigate criticism by the NAACP and Massachusetts Commission Against Discrimination (MCAD) who claimed discriminatory practices by the Boston club, and to overcome remarks made by Red Sox brass, such as GM Joe Cronin, club owner Tom Yawkey, and legendary Boston sportswriter and Yawkey crony Will McDonough absurdly decrying that the only reason for their not playing blacks was in their not finding blacks who could play.[7]

His indoctrination with the Red Sox and major league scouting held its challenges in the beginning of his assignment. He recalled a moment in an empty Fenway Park when he and other Red Sox scouts were assembled for a meeting, and was accosted by one of his own. "I think he was a [Red Sox] scout out of Pennsylvania," said Scott. "I was standing up. There wasn't nobody in the stands or anything like that, but us scouts. Another scout was sitting with him, and I was standing up and he looked around at me [and yelled] to 'sit down, everybody sees you!'" Scott said in anger, remembering that day and the racial implications contained in the rancorous remark.[8]

During the Red Sox rookie camp held in Ocala, Florida, in the early '60s, scouts were expected to be there with the newly signed players. Ed Scott remembers being approached by Neil Mahoney, Boston's scouting and farm director, at his first rookie camp and being told that because he was black where he stayed and ate his meals had to be apart from the rest of the ball club. "Neil told me the first time I was in a meeting. They got ready to have a meeting and he says, 'Scott, this is hard for me to tell you, but where we're going you can't go,' because I was the first black and they [had already] made hotel reservations, it wouldn't be alright for black people to come [to a white only hotel]. And he said, 'you know, I wouldn't [ordinarily do this to you].' He said he was sorry that happened. I said to myself, 'you know, they didn't have to have [the Red Sox] stay there, you know.'"[9] Mahoney gave Scott some meal money along with a reassuring pat on the back, saying, "But here's ten dollars. You can go and get your dinner." Not a lot had changed with the Red Sox in three years following the arrival and debacle surrounding Elijah Jerry "Pumpsie" Green.

Feeling frustrated after a few months of knocking around small Southern towns and coming up with talent of little note, Scott got a break during a casual moment in his hometown of Mobile, Alabama, sitting around with a bunch of guys engaged in small talk. One fellow piped up that there was an extraordinary kid from Greenville, Mississippi, who was a baseball phenomenon with a power stroke. Scott perked up upon hearing this. "I'm all ears," said the now roused Red Sox scout. "Now I don't say nothing, but while I'm sitting [here] in Mobile I know I should get to see this kid," said Scott. "I had been Florida'd out — running all over Florida and around Texas, and I hadn't seen anybody. That was my first year [scouting for the Red Sox]. I was kind of really [particular]. When I had to go see a guy he had to really show me something.

"It was George Scott. He was playing in Jackson, Mississippi. And so when I was in Jackson, I goes over there and I see this guy at shortstop. And George, boy he's just pickin' it," laughed Ed Scott. "He [was] showing me those good hands, you know? And I said [to myself] ... gee, look at that guy. Boy he's just handling himself and playing that short [like a pro] and, the field was terrible! And he was pickin'. He was really fielding, you know, good hands, soft hands. And I said to myself, I bet he can't hit a bull in the butt with a handful of oats. So the first time he comes up to the plate, he hit that ball ... oh, he hit the ball out of the park way over to another field. [I said to myself] Umm, that guy can hit.' So I go along to the phone that night calling Mr. Neil [Neil Mahoney]."

At the risk of being accused of misjudgment, especially after just attending a Red Sox scouts meeting and being warned not to prejudge talent, Scott phoned Mahoney in haste to point out he had found his man. "Well Mr. Neil I saw a ball player today," Scott said. "How many times did you see him?" Mahoney inquired, since he liked a scout to see a man several times before turning in a report. Scott didn't even send him a report. "Just one time," Scott said. "You like him that good?" Mahoney asked. "Mr. Neil, if he's not a major league prospect you can give me my walking papers," Scott replied. "I moved right into that town of Greenville for 10 days, and I tracked that kid down like mad," said Scott. "But the second time I see George Scott he only hit two homers and a triple in a double-header and I'm getting more excited all the time."[10]

Ed Scott was later quoted by many scribes describing George as a better hitter when he graduated from high school than Aaron was at the same age and stage of development. "I got Aaron started, and I said about George to myself, 'This kid's got more 'n Aaron, 'cause Hank had the bat only and this kid's got all the tools,'" said Scott in an interview with sportswriter Clif Keane of the *Boston Globe*.[11]

"I liked his makeup," said Scott. "I liked his soft hands, and I liked his power. And I knew he was a student of the game and a hard worker because the first time I saw him he had his hands way down kind of low, and he would hit everything to right field. You know his power and everything was to right field. He didn't hit much of anything to left and center. So I told him, 'you know I probably can help you hit the ball more to center and to all fields.' But I said, 'I'm not going to bother you now. You just go ahead and do what you want because I might mess you up.' He just kept on saying, 'Come on. I wouldn't change, I wouldn't change.' I took him to dinner this particular day and we're sittin' down eatin', and man, he just kept on pinning me down about hitting ... he is such a student of the game."[12]

As word got around scouts began to descend on the town of Greenville and Coleman High in the spring of '62. The Cardinals were still watching, though less exuberant, employing a "bird dog for Buddy Lewis out of Memphis" to follow the team, said Scott. Houston was also at the games and would later make a bid for the young slugger. But with George Crowe's departure the Red Sox scout saw an opportunity to pounce, by approaching George's mother, Magnolia. Fortuitously, because there was only one black hotel in the town, and not a very good one, Ed Scott stayed with the family off-and-on while scouting George. It was common practice then for black families to take in black ballplayers passing through their towns, since there was nowhere else to stay in a white-only ruling society.[13]

Red Sox head scout George Digby, who traveled to Greenville on more than one occasion to take a look at the young ballplayer prospect, told of the practice by blacks in the South of hosting visitors in their homes on occasions such as these: "I taught Ed Scott how to go in a house and stay with 'em when he couldn't get into the hotels. [They] couldn't get into the motels. In those days blacks couldn't get into either restaurants or hotels in the South," said Digby.[14]

Though a native of Louisiana, Digby had not personally spent time scouting black ballplayers in the Deep South. Historically and unofficially the practice was generally "off limits" by the Red Sox until Ed Scott was hired. Recalling his first swing through Greenville to see Scott play, Digby was startled by his experience there being the only white person at an all-black sporting event. "Well he played in a little town. It was an all-black community up in somewhere in Mississippi. I can't think of the name of it. It was an all-black community," said Digby. "They played there. I remember driving up in my car to see him play and I saw all these buses coming along with black people in it. I went to the coach and talked to him, and I said to the coach, 'Is my car going to be safe out there?' He said, 'Oh yeah, you won't have to worry about it.' And it was safe. And that's when I first saw him play at shortstop."

Ed Scott spoke about George's mother, "Mag," as she was known in the community: "She didn't have much and I used to help her, too, you know. I used to help her when I would go there [to Greenville]. I had him [George

Scott] dreaming that he was playing with the Red Sox. His mother, she was a fine person. I figured I had him all but signed because I used to go there to his home and just help them all, and help George with anything they'd need," said Scott fondly. It was a tactic that often paid dividends in the days before the draft was implemented, as scouts used their own

18-year-old George Scott signing his Red Sox contract in the office of principal G.P. Maddox, minutes after his high school graduation on May 28, 1962. Left to right: Red Sox scout Ed Scott, George Scott, and Coleman High baseball coach Elbert Foules (A.C. Thomas collection).

ingenuity and tactics to capture their prize prospect. "We made an agreement for a small bonus, not much, mind you and I wait for the graduation day to come," said Scott.[15]

In this case it worked. Although he had confidence he would sign the young phenom, Ed Scott knew he had to employ an innovative strategy to be certain the youngster would join the Red Sox. This included establishing leverage with Elbert Foules, George Scott's baseball coach and mentor, and, as fortune would have it, a friendship he had established with Foules. "I knew Elbert well," exclaimed Scott. But the rookie scout lacked financial authority, for one he was a new scout, but mainly because he was black. He had to solicit help from senior scout Milt Bolling and head scout Digby, who had final say and control of the money.

George Scott made a point later on that "I never would have been with the Red Sox if George Crowe had been in a position to sign me, because George Crowe would have signed me," speaking in tones of gratitude for all the time Crowe had spent with him. Crowe was well-liked, enjoying good standing with the Coleman High coaching staff— especially Foules — and Greenville's black community. It was a surprise to everyone in Greenville that the Cardinals failed to sign their high school standout. The St. Louis club's folly ultimately proved to be a stroke of luck for Ed Scott and the Red Sox, who seized the opportunity to fill the breach left by the Cardinals and quickly sign the high school senior.

On the day before the signing Bolling was sitting with Ed Scott in Scott's car, plotting strategy on how they would handle the next-day's events, when they were approached by a Greenville policeman who was not pleased with the appearance of a black man associating with a white. His complaint to them was of little substance other than for the sole reason that they — a black and a white — were together, which was neither customary nor acceptable behavior in the town, or within the Delta. Both were concerned that further trouble was about to occur to interfere with their plans, but level heads prevailed and the officer went on his way.

Realizing that Houston's scout was in town on May 28, 1962, the day of George Scott's high school graduation, the same day they planned to approach him with a contract, the two Red Sox scouts decided to plant themselves on the Coleman High School steps and seize upon the young graduate right after he accepted his diploma. "And them kids went up and got their diplomas, and I waited for Scotty to get his, and the next thing I did was to take him right into the principal's office before he could get them fancy clothes off and I signed him to the Red Sox right in that room," explained Ed Scott. "The day I did [sign him], I said to the world, 'George Scott will be in the Hall of Fame' in baseball; the most dedicated kid I ever saw. A real leader, baseball, quarterback in football, star in basketball. He loves this game of baseball."[16]

Recalling that memorable day, George expressed astonishment at how the signing went down: "The night I graduated the principal came to me right after I walked off the stage with my gown on, he told me he needed me in his office. A couple of gentlemen wanted to talk to me. I went in there and it was Ed Scott and Milt Bolling."

Bolling described the occasion of the signing with amusement. "Don't give me any credit because it belongs to Ed Scott," said Bolling. "I was there the night we signed George, though. We sat on his high school steps all through his graduation exercises and signed him as soon as he got his diploma. The Houston scout was there also, but the rest of the scouts didn't arrive until the next morning. It was too late by then because we had him."[17] Quite by surprise, among the clubs who made a belated attempt to sign him were the Cardinals who apparently reconsidered their original position on Scott. "The morning after Scott was signed by the Red Sox, the Cards called me long distance," said [Elbert] Foules, "but by then the die was cast."[18]

The contract was for $8,000 with bonus incentives. "I think they had the incentive bonus which is $7500 once you made different levels — Double A $1,000, Triple A $1,500, major leagues $5,000. But I'm not sure he got that, but I think he did. That was pretty decent money back then. It was more than anybody else offered him, let's put it that way," recounted Bolling.[19]

George pointed out his reasons for signing with Boston, explaining: "[It] was because I knew that Boston did not have no blacks. I knew that they were looking for good black ballplayers, and I felt if I could go there I could go through their organization pretty fast if I showed 'em that I could play, and that's exactly what happened."

Houston, a first-year National League expansion team, did meet with George Scott — the only team besides the Red Sox to talk money — but the kind of money they had in mind was less than Boston's proposal. As Ed Scott would later explain, major league teams were accustomed to exploitation of black athletes of the '50s and '60s, who were satisfied for the mere opportunity to play pro ball, and desirous of lifting themselves and their family from poverty. "There wasn't no draft then," said Scott, "and black guys just wasn't getting any money for signing, you know, in those days. They were so glad to get in the majors to play baseball; you know ... they wasn't giving no bonuses in those days to no blacks."[20] The Red Sox contract with George Scott, a black, had to be viewed as nothing less than a magnanimous, if not uncharacteristic, gesture by the organization at the time.

The day after the signing Bolling took George to downtown Greenville to their local sporting goods store to buy him a glove and accessories. With Scott "flipping a baseball in the air" while they were walking, Bolling asked the young man some challenging questions about adapting to life in professional baseball and how he would handle himself when confronted with those bad days. "George, have you ever been 0-for-4?" Bolling asked him. "Oh, no sir," said Scott. Bolling followed with, "What about 0-for-8?" Alarmed at the suggestion Scott bellowed, "Oh no, no." Bolling went on, "When you go to play pro ball it's a little different and you might have some days where you go 0-for-16." Appalled at the very thought of such an unthinkable possibility, Scott ranted, "Oh no — oh sir, my saying is 'When the going gets tough, the tough gets going.'" Bolling was taken aback by the youngster's supreme self-confidence and maturity. "This was something [extraordinary] for an eighteen-year-old kid," laughed Bolling.[21]

Not long after this, during Scott's first year in the minors, Red Sox owner Tom Yawkey, whom Bolling had apprised of his experiences with the newly-signed and astutely confident rookie, became aware that George had a streak where he had gone 0-for-16. He called up Bolling, suggesting that he might want to needle Scott with a reminder about his slogan, and maybe ask him directly what he planned to do under the circumstances. It was a comical moment and one they would relish, helping the ebullient young ballplayer realize pro ball would not be as easy as he once thought. Bolling wrote Scott a letter reminding him of his "rallying-cry" slogan. Scott wrote him back, embarrassingly acknowledging ownership of the statement, assuring Bolling he would plan to "get tough."

Slated to report to the Red Sox' minor league affiliate Waterloo, a Class D Midwest League club, on June 3, plans were quickly altered and George was reassigned to Olean — also a Class D club — of the historic New York-Penn League. The Midwest League was viewed as slightly faster in makeup with more senior baseball talent, drawing larger crowds. The club settled on the idea that a more junior league would be better for George.

"I started with Tony Conigliaro. Tony and I went up to Olean, New York, the same year (Tony Conigliaro made his debut in 1963 in Wellsville), and Tony Conigliaro came out of high school the exact same year I came out," said an endearing George Scott. "It was all kids out of high school and out of college," continued Scott. "That year I did pretty good. I didn't do anything to set the house on fire. I did probably what I expected coming out of my high school environment. I hit for a decent average; I don't know the exact number."[22]

Alluding to his lack of playing time between Little League and the introduction of a baseball program in his junior year of high school, as well as playing more softball than baseball in Greenville (few wanted to pitch to him), George felt hindered by a confessed lack of experience. It took him his first season in the New York-Penn League to acclimate to pro-level baseball.

Arriving at Olean on June 3 — a mere six days after he graduated from Coleman High School — Scott joined the team already a month into the season, under the tutelage of 28-year-old manager Hal Holland, in his second season at the helm. Holland was a hard-hitting player-manager from Mitchell,

Ontario, Canada, of the Basin League, the equal of the Cape Cod League as the best summer amateur baseball leagues in baseball.

On June 8 George Scott made his first appearance as a pro, for Olean, before 400 fans in a contest against the Batavia Pirates. He was stationed at third base, a position he would occupy for most of his minor league career. It was an inauspicious beginning for the young rookie, going 0-for-4, though scoring two runs, helping Olean beat Batavia, 10–7. There were eight errors in the nine-inning contest, one by Scott. George also participated in a double play.

The highlight of the Olean victory was the performance of another rookie, Bob Guindon, a left-handed-hitting slugger who walloped his 7th homer in a span of three consecutive days, establishing a pro ball record.[23] Guindon excelled throughout the year finishing with 36 homers — a record for the Olean club — and taking Rookie of the Year honors and "Player to Go the Farthest" award.

The struggling Scott couldn't establish a rhythm, going 0-for-12 in his first three games with 4 strikeouts in the third game against Hank LeMoine of Batavia, who struck out 16 Olean batters. But on June 15 George walloped his first professional home run — and first base hit — a long smash over the right-center-field wall off pitcher Pete Sierra of Erie. He went 2-for-5 in the game won by Olean, 8–1, and played sensationally in the field.

But his struggles continued. By June 21 he was at the bottom of the league in hitting with a .111 batting average and only 4 hits to his name. But starting with a July 2 game against Jamestown, George began a streak of six games going 8-for-24 with a home run, a triple, 7 RBIs and hitting at a .333 clip. He managed to raise his average slightly and by July 11 was batting .223. He was being shifted around the infield defensively between third, short and second base, and at times used sparingly by manager Holland.

George was discouraged by his poor performance and thought about quitting. "Things ahead looked tough. Neil Mahoney of the Red Sox talked me out of giving up," Scott later told *Chicago Tribune* reporter David Condon.[24] But he credits his mother the most, who in a stern manner convinced the young ballplayer he was as good as the rest of them and he should not give up, but battle like a man. "I was 18 years old, just getting out of school. I knew I could play, but I didn't know about playing professional ball. I called my mom one day and said, 'I'm coming back home.' She said, 'Why?' I said 'I'm outclassed. They're better than me.' She then asked, 'Don't they have two eyes, two arms and two legs?' I answered, 'Yes.' She said, 'Then you better get to work.' Without her advice, I would have probably packed up and gone home. My baseball career would not have gotten off the ground," said Scott, fondly recalling his mother's admonishment of him and her encouraging words.[25] That was convincing enough for George and he stuck it out, finishing the season playing in

June 1962 — Red Sox signee George Scott, fresh out of high school, arrives at Olean, New York, to play for the Class D Olean Red Sox. Left to right: Bob Guindon, the league's Rookie of the Year, manager Hal Holland and Scott (courtesy of *Boston Herald*).

63 games with a .238 batting average and a modest 5 home runs, but committing 18 errors in the field.

Hall of Famer Bobby Doerr, who was a "roving coach" and instructor for the parent Red Sox club, recalled going down to Olean to help the frustrated first-year player: "The first time I saw him, I guess it was at Olean, he had his bat down, kind of in front of him and quite low, down almost to his belt.... I think he was copying some major league ballplayer that he liked pretty much, and he was of course conscious of trying to hit home runs, and he was missing good pitches all the time. We finally got him to get his hands up a little bit higher, more over his shoulder — right shoulder — and he did improve as he did that."[26]

Olean was in pursuit of its second successive Governor's Cup league title, finishing in fourth place during the regular season to qualify for the playoffs. They met their season-nemesis Erie in the first round and swept them in two games without the services of Guindon, who was ill. But the Auburn Mets were too much for Olean, sweeping the Red Sox two straight in the finals. George Scott did not play in either series.

The year 1963 brought change for minor league baseball: competition from television, new leisure pursuits, popularity of other sports like football, major league baseball's expansion and relocation to minor league cities, and the beginning effects of an unpopular Vietnam War served to erode the fan base. Attendance dropped precipitously, and with it numerous minor league teams. Major League Baseball intervened to protect its player source, and formed the Player Development Plan in 1962. It was a sweeping change that called for minor league affiliations aligning with major league teams. Major league clubs would now pay portions of player salaries and provide other forms of assistance to minor league affiliates.

Along with the decline in cities which once supported minor league teams was the elimination of the Class B, C, and D leagues. Olean was one of the victims of the destabilization and restructuring. With the lowest attendance (11,104) of the six New York–Penn League teams in '62, Olean was targeted by the now-vested Boston Red Sox as unable to sustain the franchise and they looked elsewhere for a suitable replacement. The little town of Wellsville, New York, once a member of the New York–Penn League, stepped up to rejoin the league for the '63 campaign. Olean's franchise and many of its players — including George Scott — moved to Wellsville in the revamped Class A league, under manager Bill Slack.

It was a year highlighted by the arrival of 19-year-old and future Red Sox standout Tony Conigliaro, who started late because of an injury but had a sensational season at Wellsville, batting a solid .363 with 24 home runs, and winning the New York–Penn League Rookie of the Year. "Tony had a phenomenal year," said Scott, "and Tony was called up to Boston. I struggled a little bit and when Tony left, I struggled even more because not only did I lose my best friend on the team but I also put a lot of pressure on myself to perform so I could get called up too. Bobby Doerr came down and worked with me and I was struggling up until the time he came there. The day he left, I hit two home runs [on] the day he left, and I never stopped hitting from that day on. I ended up hitting 23 or 24 home runs [15 HRs officially] in that league," said an enthusiastic Scott. "Then the next year, of course, I went to Winston-Salem in the Carolina League, and I almost led that league in home runs."[27]

Doerr remembered the time he spent with Scott in Wellsville as a turning point for the young ballplayer, who was continuing to struggle through the first half of the season. He worked with George "quite a bit," said Doerr. "George had a tendency to be home run conscious, makes him pull off the ball a lot [and] was missing a lot of his good pitches. I went into Wellsville one time and the manager of the club had taken him out of the lineup. He was playing third base, I think, at that time, and when I went in the clubhouse George was sitting there with tears coming down his eyes, and I said, 'What's the matter, George?' He says, 'Well I'm not playing.... I haven't been doing very good.' So I went to the manager [Matt Sczesny, who replaced Bill Slack on July 5] of the ball club and I said, 'Let's have George come out at batting practice tomorrow and see what we can do with him.' We got him to move his hands up a little higher and he got hitting the ball pretty good. He [Sczesny] played him — I don't know whether he played him that night, or not, but he played him. He started playing him and George ended up being the most valuable third baseman in the league that year. I think he ended up hitting .290 or something. But he really made a big improvement when he started to be a little bit more cautious of not hitting home runs, but [just] hitting the ball," said Doerr.[28] Doerr not only worked on his mechanics, but he "worked on your psyche," said George. "He could mentally get to you. Ted Williams was the same way."[29]

"We had a really good hitting club," recalled Slack, pointing out a nucleus of future Red Sox stand-outs in Conigliaro, Joe Foy — with whom Scott would compete for a roster position on the Boston Red Sox — and George Scott. "George had a great glove. There was no hole between short and third because George had that long arm and somebody'd hit a ball in the hole — and I'd be in the dugout — and I could see that long arm going out into the hole and grabbing the ball," laughed Slack. "He was a good hitter; he did everything pretty good…. It was a tossup who was going to hit the longest home runs, either Homer Green or George Scott."[30]

Wellsville finished the 1963 season in second place with a 73–57 record, three games behind the Auburn Mets, establishing a new league home run mark of 153 round-trippers as a team. But they were swept in two games by Jamestown in the playoffs. Scott meanwhile fell short of the leader boards throughout the season based on his poor start. Bolstered by a significant improvement in confidence and batting skills, aided by the beneficent Bobby Doerr, Scott had an eye-opening second half, finishing the season with a .293 average, 12 doubles, 9 triples and 15 homers. He was named starting third baseman of the New York–Penn League all-star team.

Emphasizing player development, the parent Boston club invited several of their promising young minor leaguers to attend the Florida Instructional League which opened its season on October 8. Among the Red Sox invites was George Scott, who for the first time met Red Sox Instructional League manager Eddie Popowski, who became like a father to him and would later be profoundly influential in George's further development in the minors and on the parent club. Based in Sarasota the Red Sox had a uniquely cooperative arrangement with the Houston Colt .45's, combining their camps and splitting a 50-game schedule; the Red Sox group of twelve players finished the short season with a 16–9 record under Popowski.

All eyes were on young Tony Conigliaro. Boston had set their sights on the first-year 19-year-old minor league slugger out of Wellsville, along with outfielder-first baseman Tony Horton, also a first-year rookie out of Waterloo, who was not at the Instructional League camp. Johnny Pesky, manager of the parent club, effusive over the two, was asked by a reporter if there were "any other Boston prospects that have made impressions in Florida?" Pesky's response was Dick Wohlmacher, a Wellsville teammate of Scott's, "who also looked improved." No mention was made of George Scott; he didn't appear to be on Boston's radar.[31]

His second-half performance at Wellsville earned Scott a promotion in 1964 to Winston-Salem of the Carolina League — Single A, but a faster brand of baseball. But he was damaged goods, owing to an off-season right knee injury incurred in the winter playing an informal game of basketball in his hometown of Greenville. In spite of the injury Scott did appear in six games early in the season with the damaged knee, playing third base and pinch-hitting, going 7-for-17 at a .412 clip. He was placed on the disabled list on May 14, flown to Boston on May 18 for knee surgery that week, and was expected to be out for most of the remainder of the season.

Scout Ed Scott, who had signed George to a Red sox contract, was made aware of his young protégé's injury and decided to check on him. "I caught up with him in my travels," complained the concerned scout to a local reporter at the time, "and I saw him playing in that splint, and I got so mad and told him he'd be ruined. But he played [anyway]. I say again, this man is maybe even more dedicated than Willie Mays ever was."[32]

Remarkably in just over four weeks since his surgery George was back with Winston-Salem and participated in batting practice before an exhibition game on June 22 in Winston-Salem with the parent Boston team. George's friend, Tony Conigliaro, was now in his first year with the Bosox, and spoke well of Scott to his major league teammates, who were anxious to see the young slugger whom they had heard so much about. But the risk of stepping into the batting cage was akin to being cross-examined, as the Boston players began to chide Winston-Salem players like it was a fraternity hazing, distracting them as much and as often as they could.

Boston's slugger Dick Stuart, the penultimate prankster, did the most needling, provoking even Conigliaro as he took his practice swipes. But it was young George Scott they wanted to see, especially. Up to then there was casual bantering going on between the players on both sides, but when Scott stepped up, the last Winston-Salem batter to hit, the major leaguers quickly swarmed around the cage to watch, ranting good-natured taunts mixed with words of encouragement. Scott had been in Boston earlier in the year for treatment of his knee injury, taking the opportunity to visit the Red Sox clubhouse while there, and connect with the big league players. But according to Boston shortstop Eddie Bressoud, 20-year-old George Scott showed little humility: "He did a lot of talking," said Bressoud with a grin, who, along with other Boston players, indoctrinated him to a stern measure of major league razzing. This reached a crescendo of guffaws, resonating in George's own prophetic words: "When the going gets tough, that's when the tough get going," being cried by the Boston players derisively. They slammed him at every swing and reminded him of the confident words that he likely had crowed about earlier to them when he was in the Hub city.[33]

But George was undaunted, sensing this was his supreme moment, his opportunity to show off his batting skills and raw power to the Boston elite. His first swing was a grounder to short, a certain double play razzed the onlookers; the next was fouled back ricocheting around the cage and striking him on the back of the head; and the third was again hit to shortstop, a weak ground ball that he was reminded by Boston players a bat boy could handle. Then he lifted a high drive out of the ballpark in left-center, and another closer to the foul line. The Boston players mellowed as George found his rhythm and hit one pitched ball after another out of Ernie Shore Field. "We came down here to see George swing and the trip was worth it; he's got some sweet swing," said one of the Boston players to reporters as he left the batting cage after Scott's power display.[34]

"You talk about somebody putting on a show," said Bill Slack, then the Winston-Salem manager, describing Scott's performance that June day in Ernie Shore Field. Slack went on to say that George was the last of his players to take batting practice — purposely arranged by Slack over Scott's objections — because he knew George would put on a hitting display that would get the attention of Pesky and his Boston club. Slack, a former pitcher, was pitching batting practice. "I threw it right there [into Scott's wheelhouse] and he hit one after another over that left-field fence, center-field fence, left-center-field fence. I mean it was like — I don't know how many [home runs] it was but [Dick] Stuart and Yaz and all them guys were over there warming up and when George got finished hitting they were all back around the cage watching him ... he put on one of the best shows. I've thrown a lot to a lot of hitters — Ted Williams and everybody — but he put on one of the best shows I've ever seen. I don't know how many balls he hit out of the ballpark. He just kept hitting 'em and I just kept throwing 'em," said Slack.[35]

It may well have been a defining moment for George, who remembers drawing the attention of Red Sox manager Pesky, who liked the young infielder's stroke and impressive power. Except for the reports volunteered by Conigliaro, no one of the parent club had any idea they had a future star in their midst, and who in three short years would play such an important role on the '67 "Impossible Dream" team that would force a richly talented and World Series favorite St. Louis Cardinals to a full seven games in the Fall Classic.

Scott came off the disabled list on June 27 and was used in pinch-hit roles for most of July. Slack commented that he introduced Scott to fielding some first base during early stages of his recovery, though not as a starter. This was

George's initial exposure to the position that would eventually lead to eight Gold Gloves as a major leaguer.[36] "He didn't play much at first base; he played mostly at third base," said Slack. "He had a good glove; he could 'pick-it' pretty good ... the guy'd hit a ground ball pretty good in the hole and I'm saying, 'Oh the shortstop's not going to be able to throw him out,' and George would get the ball ... he'd go out and get the ball [in front of the shortstop] and throw him out at first," laughed Slack. "He was pretty soft on his feet for a big guy ... he was good, he just had good hands. He could make all the plays at third and first ... he made all the plays at third base. He was one of our best hitters [too]. We had some good hitters but he was probably as good as anybody we had."

Laboring in his first few games back at third base after returning full-time from the disabled list, he committed two errors in his first three games and through July 27 Scott was batting an underwhelming .261. But then he caught fire on July 30 clouting two home runs — his first two for Winston-Salem — one a 440-foot wallop clearing the D.D. Bean sign over the center-field wall and landing on a high embankment well behind it, for which he won a $200 cash award from the local merchant who said such a feat was not possible.

Misfortune struck again on August 3rd in the first game of a doubleheader against Peninsula when Scott tripped over the first base bag trying to beat out an infield ground ball, and reinjured his right knee. It was a bruise just above the surgical site according to team officials, who announced that Scott "will be ready to return to the lineup tonight," as reported in the *Winston-Salem Journal* on August 4. But he didn't return until a week later, on August 10.

In spite of the nagging injury, George hit for a .305 average from July 30 to the end of the regular season, closing out the final twelve games at a .415 pace and clouting 7 of his 10 homers, four in the last five games, helping his club win the Carolina League pennant — Winston-Salem's first in 14 years — on the last day of the season.[37] Scott hit a decisive home run in the final game against Greensboro, a tape-measure shot that "was one of the longest home runs of the season; it went high over the 390-foot fence in left-center," according to *Journal* reporter Frank Spencer.

Winston-Salem took the league title, winning four straight games, two contests against Greensboro and two against Portsmouth, for the playoff championship. Scott went 1-for-15 in the championship series. He finished the regular season batting a solid .288 with 30 RBIs and a .551 slugging percentage.

George had his first professional encounter with racist vitriol and personal threats while playing for Winston-Salem. Racism was rampant amongst the fan base and teams in the league. Racial epithets were common in almost all the cities, especially Rocky Mount, Wilson and Raleigh. On one occasion, in Raleigh, Scott remembers opposing team players bringing a black cat to the game, holding it for all to see, claiming it to be his sister, and yelling "obscene racist things" at him from the dugout. Though he does not recall any problems in the home city, racial overtones were in place. The local paper, the *Winston-Salem Journal and Sentinel*, reporting on new roster players for Winston-Salem, profiled Scott disdainfully as "another Negro" arriving in the city. It was an all-too familiar refrain by the local media to unceremoniously set Scott, and other black members of the team, apart from white teammates preferring to classify him as a "Negro" infielder.[38]

On one occasion during the season while the team was traveling, manager Slack recalled an event — designed to be humorous — involving George and his teammates. His teammates realized George's sensitivity to racial matters coming from Mississippi and decided to play a prank on him by dressing up in Ku Klux Klan type garb, to scare him. "They said George jumped about ten feet in the air and when he landed he was in the bathroom," chuckled an amused Slack. Scott was so upset at the prospect of Klan members pursuing him that he refused to leave the restroom. The players called the manager to come down and help extricate the petrified ballplayer. "So I knock on the door and I said, 'George, this is the skipper, your manager, Bill.' He said, 'No, I'm staying in here, they ain't going to get me.' I said, 'What do you mean? George everything's alright, open the door.' Finally we got him to open the door," said Slack. The caper nevertheless reminded him — a Canadian — of the gravity of what was occurring in the South at the time and how this borderline prank, in reality, actually appeared to the unsuspecting and wary young Scott, whom all of his life had lived in the presence of paroxysms of rage in a racially violent Mississippi. Scott was in no way amused.[39]

"Even some of the guys on your own ball club [were racist] — they were from the South, right? That's the way they were brought up.... George, he'd be playing third base. When we got past Raleigh — Raleigh was sort of bad enough because the stands were right on the field, and so was Rocky Mount and Wilson, North Carolina. First time I'd go over to Rocky Mount, they'd have that one section right back of third base there, and, oh God, I mean they were calling him everything, and I'm saying, 'What's the matter with these people? That's bad; what are they doing?' They'd say [to me], 'Well that's the South.' They were calling him 'jungle bunny' and 'nigger' and 'black boy' and 'Sambo.' I couldn't understand it coming from Canada," said an irritated Slack.

Ball clubs arranged with black residents — many of them lawyers and doctors — to take black ballplayers into their homes, since they were unwelcome in the local hotels. They would bus them to the games each day and pick them up when the games were over. It was an accepted practice that was never questioned by the league, individual ball clubs or residents of the towns and cities where they played. It left a lasting impression with George Scott, who had not seen the level of racial hatred in his hometown of Greenville displayed the way that it had during his one season in the Carolina League; it was palpable.

Scott's boyhood friend from Greenville, Mississippi, E.T. Davis, who had a trial with the Red Sox in the spring of '67 and was assigned to the Greenville Red Sox of the Western Carolinas League, sadly remembers the racial hatred permeating the Carolina's even after Scott was there. "It was rough then in Carolina," said Davis. "Blacks were not welcome there ... it was just the atmosphere there ... the [anti-black] atmosphere there; you could cut it with a knife." Davis was being ignored by the media and the team, and soon found himself sitting at the end of the bench and no one was talking to him. "I think it was the management," said Davis, who points a finger at the organization for its unseemly behavior. As he explained later to his friend George Scott, who was trying to get him a shot with the Cincinnati ball club, "I told George, 'I don't want this hurt again, man. I don't want to get hurt like that again.'"[40]

Many black ballplayers of the '60s found intolerable the challenges of racial abuse and the barriers confronting them in the minors, especially in the South, and dropped out of baseball. The difficulties of just making the grade to a major league level added to the pain of racism was an unbearable mix. But some hung on in the face of it; George Scott was among them.

3

Great Scott

The rapid rise of Scott has had something of a fictional ring to it ... even though there have been elements of unreality embroidering most phases of his career. Everything seemed to happen so fast for him that the big fellow still is in something of a whirl. He was a nobody in spring training and the Boston brass expected nothing of him. Their prize rookie — or so they thought — was Joe Foy, the youngster they had designated as their regular third baseman. — Arthur Daley, *New York Times*[1]

Believers in development of their young ballplayers, the Red Sox put together another team in the Florida Instructional League in the fall of 1964, inviting Scott along with other select rookies and some veterans. Their sights were on Joe Foy and Tony Horton as most likely to become Red Sox regulars. Horton was already on Boston's roster, but in need of seasoning. Foy was rapidly winning favor with the Boston brass as heir-apparent to third baseman and perennial All-Star Frank Malzone, whose 1965 season would be his last with Boston. Both Foy and Horton, it turned out, were challenged by a young upstart, George Scott, for roster spots on the '66 Red Sox team in a way that no one had imagined.

The instructional league season began on October 8 under the watchful eye of manager Eddie Popowski and his coaches, Mace Brown and Bobby Doerr. Six days later, on October 14, Scott clouted a grand slam home run — his first as a pro — to break up a tight pitching duel, giving the Red Sox farm team a 6–4 win over their counterparts with the Tigers. By the end of October Scott was hitting .400 with two home runs, but he was not among the leaders by the end of the short season (December 2). Joe Foy, however, against whom Scott would compete for the Red Sox third base slot, was among the leaders, finishing sixth in batting with an impressive .325 average.

Before the 1965 minor league season got underway, an assemblage of select Red Sox minor league Double-A and Triple-A players, some coming off the recently concluded FIL season, joined for a one-game exhibition on March 25,

43

playing for Boston's Toronto affiliate against Rochester. Scott was on the Toronto club that day and powered a home run blast of well over 400 feet that got everyone's attention; it was the beginning of a memorable career-making year for the young slugger from Mississippi.

But Red Sox management's attention was on Foy, who was rising quickly in the organization, elevating him to the newly-formed Triple-A Toronto team of the International League for the 1965 season under their new skipper, Dick Williams. Foy played well for Williams at Toronto that year, winning the International League MVP, and Horton was nearly as good, factoring into Williams' loyalty for the two who helped him win the IL championship in his first year at the helm. Horton would have an even better year in '66, clouting 26 home runs that led to Williams' second straight International League title; the young manager was soon drawing the attention of the parent club. Williams' desire to favor his Toronto players, especially Horton, set the stage for early conflict with George Scott, a relatively unknown to Williams when the youthful manager was eventually promoted to lead the parent club in 1967.

Scott was promoted to the newly established Pittsfield Red Sox of the Double-A Eastern League. Pro baseball returned to the city of Pittsfield, Massachusetts, in 1965 after the city's attempts at organized baseball in the old Eastern League during 1919–1930, and the ill-fated Canadian American League with stints during 1941–1942 and 1946–1951. Franchise owner Joe Buzas brought his Eastern League Red Sox farm club from Reading, Pennsylvania, to the Shire City. It was a risky move. Pittsfield had a reputation for being a "novelty community," showing support at first but quickly losing interest.[2] But Buzas, a former New York Yankee infielder (1945), had visions of a successful venture if promoted properly, as well as strategically operating in a town only 150 miles from the doorstep of Fenway Park in Boston.

Buzas and his team were welcomed by the city and its civic and business organizations led by 32-year-old executive Fred Rubin of the Association of Business and Commerce of Central Berkshire County. He established the hype with Buzas, leading to significant season ticket sales, and selling out advertising space on park fences and in baseball scorecards and programs. Mayor Robert Dillon proclaimed the opening week of the season as "Baseball Week" to honor the city's reclamation of baseball after a fourteen-year absence. On the day before the opening game, a street parade was held on a raw, rainy night and 1,000 attended ceremonies at a local gymnasium to honor the team. Excitement was high among the town folk to see good quality baseball again. Buzas' expectations were met: the new team drew over 79,000 fans in its first season, nearly 12,000 more than at Elmira, second highest in league attendance.

Pittsfield was managed by diminutive Eddie Popowski, who was Scott's manager in the Florida Instructional League and came to be an important role model for the young ballplayer from Mississippi. George Scott would thrive on the leadership qualities and energy of the little manager, all 5'4" of him, once a member of the House of David semipro barnstorming baseball team, whose job it was to develop young ballplayers into major league prospects. He performed the task skillfully, sharing his passion for the game and showing patience to nurture the best in his players, especially if "Pop," as he was affectionately known, realized potential in a player. "If it wasn't for 'Pop' I doubt if I would have played in the major leagues," said a respectful George Scott. "He taught me how to play ... and if you could play, he really made you work."

Ironically George received some of his greatest support in his young career from two baseball men, whom he credits with teaching him valuable lessons about baseball, who couldn't have been more different: Hall of Famer Ted Williams and Popowski. This was the tallest and shortest duo of baseball mentoring one could possibly imagine, with Williams at 6'4" and Popowski a whole foot shorter. Both men could see that George was a diamond in the rough, with much promise. They uniquely complemented each other with their individual strengths and skills to help mold raw talent into the ballplayer they knew Scott could be. It all began to take shape in Pittsfield.

A larger-than-life Ted Williams, brash and irrepressible, who often sought the spotlight during his long career as a Red Sox outfielder, began to work with young George in the Florida Instructional League. George was eager to learn, soaking up every word of advice from the great slugger about hitting technique and, importantly, how to read pitchers. And as long as George showed an eagerness to listen, Ted would share his baseball wisdom with him. Scott later on would credit Ted as the person responsible for maintaining his batting style that manager Dick Williams was threatening to change.

Popowski, on the other hand, was of a different nature than the colorful and sometimes bombastic "Splendid Splinter." Smaller in stature and mellow by nature, Pop was looked upon endearingly by so many of the young players whom he tutored. He worked tirelessly with them hammering endless assortments of ground balls, fly balls, and preached fundamentals. Humor was a tool — forever the prankster — to keep his players loose and to get the best from them. He was also a tough critic when he had to be, but by all accounts he was the consummate baseball man, prepared at all times.

This worked for George who looked upon Pop as a man in whom he could completely place his trust. He credits Popowski with teaching him invaluable lessons about fielding and about life. "I had my best year ever in baseball playing for Pop," said Scott. "He was a great man. He never showed any racism or prejudice with any of the black players.... It is a thing where as a black ballplayer playing for white coaches you would not get well-liked anyway. I did not get close to anybody, but Pop. He was like a father to me. He taught us a lot of baseball. He loved me, man. He loved George Scott.... I loved the man so much."[3]

Venerable Wahconah Park was to be the new home of the minor league Red Sox. Built in 1919 amidst the mountains of Berkshire County in a working-class neighborhood of Pittsfield, it held all the charm of an old-time baseball facility with its wooden grandstand and vintage design. Plastic owls hung from rafters to keep the pigeons at bay, and the peculiar park dimensions and angles frustrated many a player. Outfield fences were 334 feet to left field, 345 feet to center and 333 feet to right. But the park's most unusual feature was its placement. Built before the advent of night baseball when most day games finished well before sunset, home plate faced due west directly into a setting sun, forcing "sun delays." Games were stalled for several minutes until the angle of the sun was more favorable for batters, catchers and the umpires to see the ball.

On April 25 Wahconah Park swelled with over 3200 fans for the Red Sox' opening game, an afternoon contest against Springfield. It was the largest opening day turnout of any of the Eastern League teams that year. There was a cold mountain chill in the air on that early spring afternoon which may have affected performance, as it was a sloppily played contest with five errors between the two teams, including one by George Scott at third base. But George atoned for that in the third inning, his second time at bat, by stroking a decisive two-run homer to please the partisan crowd and help Pittsfield win their inaugural game, 5–1.

On May 26 Scott collected three hits in a twelve-inning game, including a homer, for the seventh time in the young season won by Pittsfield over Springfield, 5–4. By the end of May the club was tied with Williamsport for first place with a 23–14 record. Scott was batting .319 and leading the league with 7 home runs, one more than teammate Owen Johnson, who kept pace with Scott along with another teammate, Chris Coletta, throughout the season.

"Great Scott! He's Holy Terror, Eastern Loop Hurlers Testify," was a headline in the *Berkshire Eagle*, Pittsfield's local paper, in June of that year describing Scott's abuse of Eastern League pitchers. By June 13 he led the league in base hits with 56. He was hitting the ball with authority and even his outs, hit just as hard, were the talk of the league. By July 18 he slipped in average, but was among the leaders batting .283 with 12 home runs and 51 RBIs. His teammate Johnson, a 27-year-old seasoned minor leaguer who was having a career year batting .320 with 15 homers and 64 RBIs, and Chris Coletta, who was batting a solid .323, were ahead of him. Pittsfield was in first place by a half-game over Elmira, managed by future Hall of Famer Earl Weaver.

Sportswriters, sensing stiff competition looming between Joe Foy and Scott to replace the perennial All-Star and Gold Glover Frank Malzone, rumored to be in his final year with Boston, unhesitatingly put Pop on the spot as the season progressed to explain whom he favored. Both Foy and Scott were having remarkable years. Pop took pride in having coached and mentored both of them, and before that Malzone. He also knew that Foy was on Boston's fast track as designated heir-apparent for the third base job; it would be his to lose. So Pop responded cautiously, but realized that the kid from Mississippi was going to give Foy a run for his money.

Popowski sought a balance with reporters when speaking about his protégés, explaining that Foy would hit for a higher average, but that Scott had more power. Using greater diplomacy he described their fielding in a manner to appear comparable: Foy had the stronger arm, but Scott was more accurate. Foy did have a strong arm, but tended to be wild with throws over to first, averaging 29 errors in his first four seasons of minor league ball. It was enough to sooth the writers' curiosity, however, though Pop knew that George was the better fielder, which he was to prove in the major leagues.

Elmira, the previous year's champion, Pittsfield and Williamsport jockeyed for first place through the first half of the season. But by August 1 Elmira had slipped into a stronger position leading Pittsfield by four and one-half games, and it appeared they would run away with the title again. The Red Sox went into Elmira on August 1 for a doubleheader, expected to be the fatal blow that would stretch the Pioneers' lead to six and one-half games. But Pittsfield won them both with two pitchers, one just called up from Winston-Salem and the other a so-so performer all season, to close the gap between the teams. It was the turning point for Pittsfield, said Popowski, and the team kept pace with the Elmira club, until September 2 when they vaulted over them into first place by a full game.

Going into the final day of the season, Pittsfield held onto its one-game lead. The pennant was on the line as Elmira, which had two games washed out late in the season, could have won the championship with a .601 percentage over Pittsfield by winning their last game, had Pittsfield lost. The Red Sox hung tough calling on their workhorse pitcher, Pete Magrini, 17–8 overall, to face the Springfield Giants in their final game of the season, at home. It was a close contest through eight innings until George Scott launched a home run in his final at-bat to ice the game, and the pennant, for Pittsfield. Springfield pitcher Thomas Arruda hung a curve ball into Scott's wheel-house and he got all of it. It sent the packed stadium of hometown fans into a delirium, not only for their team that won the first professional pennant for Pittsfield in 44 years, but also for their young hero, George Scott, the hitting star of Pittsfield's stretch run, taking 11 of the final 14 games.

It was as dramatic an ending as any Hollywood writer could ever dream of for putting together the perfect script. George's home run blast on his final at-bat of the season not only captured the 1965 pennant for Pittsfield, but he accomplished much more: it catapulted him into the league lead in several categories and over teammates whom he had been pursuing since the beginning of the season. The homer, his 25th, won him the home run title, beating Johnson who had 24; it also earned him the Triple Crown, finishing with a league-leading .319 batting average over Coletta who finished second at .318, and 94 RBIs. Johnson finished with 93 RBIs. In addition George led the league in total bases (290), base hits (167), doubles (30), at-bats (523) and games played (tied with one other player at 140). He was named Most Valuable Player by the league and received a unanimous vote from the National Association of Baseball Writers that named him to the Double-A All-East All-Star team. Popowski took honors of his own by being named the Eastern League's Manager of the Year.

George Scott, 1965 Eastern League MVP and Triple Crown winner.

Over the course of 52 games from mid–July until the end of the season, Scott rapped out 74 base hits, 43 RBIs and 13 home runs, and raised his batting average by 36 points. With this phenomenal performance, George was coming into his own as a premier ballplayer and serious contender for the big club's third base slot. "That's when my minor league and [baseball] career took off," said Scott about his year in Pittsfield. Reminiscing about the "last six weeks" of the season there when he had his amazing run, George unabashedly pointed out the difficulty to raise a batting average so dramatically when you've got more than 400 at-bats. "I'm telling you, man, you've never seen anything like it. I was averaging two and three hits every game for six weeks," boasted Scott, and then further emphasizing that a pennant, Triple Crown and MVP was accomplished "all with one swing."

It was a banner year for George, assuring him a spring trial with the big club in '66 after only three and a half seasons of minor league ball. Following his electrifying performance Boston's new general manager, Dick O'Connell, promptly picked up Scott's contract from Pittsfield at season's end and began to make plans to groom him for the big leagues. The timing couldn't have been more fortuitous. Not only was George deserving of a shot at the big leagues, after his unexpected meteoric rise in the minors, but he was assured of it due to another event at the time in the Red Sox organization.

Mike "Pinky" Higgins, a long-time crony and drinking buddy of Red Sox owner Tom Yawkey, and a reputed racist, who, while managing the team in the 50s, was quoted by writer Al Hirshberg as saying, "There'll be no niggers on this ballclub as long as I have anything to say about it."[4] Higgins was the GM from 1962 to 1965 at the end of a line of Red Sox administrators alleged to have resisted the influx of black ballplayers. The black press of the day called the Red Sox "the living symbol of racism in baseball."[5] On September 16, 1965, Yawkey fired Higgins. On the same day he replaced him with the unknown O'Connell, neither a Yawkey crony nor drinking buddy; unlike previous management types, O'Connell had no roots in the South. He wasted no time signing George Scott as one of his first moves following his appointment.

The nation's escalating military buildup in the Vietnam war took its toll on baseball, especially in the minor leagues. Where once a minor league contract encouraged dropping out of school to play ball, young men now chose to remain in school under the protection of a college deferment from the military draft, available to them as long as they remained in school. The pool of college players dried up.

Once again, for a third consecutive fall season, George joined his mentors Popowski and Doerr on the Red Sox entry in the Florida Instructional League, based in Sarasota. He played there briefly, and then departed for winter ball in Nicaragua where the Red Sox wanted him to face a steadier diet of quality pitching that the league was noted for. George signed with a Managuan team, the Boer Indians, who were the defending Nicaraguan League champions, arriving there the end of November just before the conclusion of the first half of play that ended December 13. It was a faster brand of baseball with a mix of minor league prospects, rookie and first-year major leaguers as well as former major leaguers to challenge the 20-year-old youngster.

Boer finished in second place behind the Leon Melenudos in both the first and second half races, but emerged the overall league champion after beating first-place winner Leon in a best-of-seven series, four games to one. "We won the championship that year and I led the league in home runs," said Scott.[6] Actually, he finished second with 13 home runs behind Jim Hicks of Leon, who led the league with 18.[7] George's enthusiasm laced with hyperbole is pardonable after continuing unabated his batting heroics in Nicaragua following his sensational run in Pittsfield to be a major factor in Boer's surge for the league championship.

By December 9 Scott had hit three home runs, the last of these a ninth-inning three-run blast that iced a win for Boer. Meanwhile Joe Foy was doing damage of his own in an even faster winter league, filled with established major leaguers, playing for Caguas of the Puerto Rican League. In one game he knocked in all five runs of a 5–0 win over Santurce that included a two-run homer, and was among the batting leaders. Boston continued to keep their focus on Foy while Scott remained only in their long-range plans.

In a span of several games from late December into early January, Scott was rapping out key base hits, and hit two homers, one estimated at 490 feet. By the end of the regular season, January 23, Boer was tied with Estrellas for second place. Scott finished with a .307 average, the only Boer player to hit above .300. His last three base hits of the regular season were home runs, producing 6 RBIs. On January 24 Boer and Estrellas competed in a one-game playoff to determine who would qualify for the championship series. Scott triggered the attack in that game by hitting two homers and Boer won, 9–1, earning the right to play against the season's first-place finisher, Leon.

It was a memorable championship series for George, this time leading what some considered only an "average" ballclub to a remarkable finish. In addition to Boer having only one .300 hitter — Scott — only one Boer starting pitcher posted better than a .500 won-loss record. Scott and teammate Bob Oliver swung big bats, George connecting for three home runs in the second game of that series, and five homers altogether in the first three contests starting with the January 24 one-game playoff against Estrellas. Boer's victories over Leon ended in 1–0, 8–2, 10–2 and 5–1 scores, with a 3–2 loss mixed in when Leon pushed across a run in the bottom of the ninth inning of a tightly-pitched fourth game.

It was a performance of a magnitude quite the same as Scott's heroics only a few short months before in Pittsfield. In nine weeks of baseball, including the playoff and championship games, Scott clouted 18 home runs. During eight weeks that he played in the regular season, he was a steady performer amassing 51 base hits, 13 home runs and 32 RBIs. Nicaraguan League pitching, notably of higher quality than he had faced before, didn't faze him. The "Great Scott" was on a roll and he was not going unnoticed by Red Sox brass in Boston.

Nicaragua during this time was in political turmoil. The Somoza regime, led by Luis Somoza Debayle and his brother Anastasio, sons of the late notoriously corrupt Nicaraguan president, Somoza Garcia, had complete control of the political machinery and National Guard. Taking a leaf from their father's book they assumed greater power in nefarious ways by installing trusted friends in government, maintaining control of the military, and conducting their affairs exploitatively whenever the opportunity presented itself. Fierce political opposition was emerging amongst considerable unrest. Guerrilla groups were beginning to form and there was fighting in the streets.

American ballplayers approached their playing time in Nicaragua with mixed feelings. It was a good brand of baseball, philosophically supported by several major league teams including the Red Sox; it was also perceived as a means of expediting their rise to the major league level. But it also had a dark side. There were concerns about players safety as gun-toting rebels roamed the Nicaraguan streets. George Scott saw it only as an opportunity; to him there was little risk if it meant advancing to the big leagues. "It was a very good league," remembered Scott. "It's funny because they was having a war in Nicaragua at the time. About two miles down the street from the ballpark you'd hear all these guns being fired, and it was the strangest damn thing. They said that they was having war. And of course the Americans got scared, but we didn't get scared enough to quit. We went on and played"[8]

During a 1966 interview with *New York Times* sportswriter Arthur Daley, who wrote about the young slugger's tape-measure home runs and his rapid rise to baseball stardom, Scott emphasized his play in Nicaragua as a main reason why he was in the big leagues so soon. Describing the importance of playing against good pitching there and the value of maintaining his timing, he told Daley, "Without it I would have been farmed out and never lasted long enough to get the chance to stay in the big leagues."[9] Nicaragua was his launching pad for his arrival with the Red Sox.

4

Mind's Made Up — He's Staying

In all my years in baseball I have never seen a player have a debut like Scott.
He's amazing. — Rick Ferrell, Hall of Fame catcher[1]

Until Mike Higgins was fired as GM in September 1965, the "color line"
still played a role in the Red Sox organization under owner Tom Yawkey.
Esquire's writer-at-large, frequent contributor to National Public Radio, and
award-winning sportswriter, Charles Pierce, wrote a piece called "The Dead
Zone," a satire of the times focusing on the many ills and indiscretions of the
Boston Red Sox, in which this excerpt appeared: "Then there was the day on
which I insisted on being Earl Wilson when I pitched, which caused some consternation, because Earl was, as you know, a colored player. In fact, the curse
of these particular years was not the imaginary Curse of the Bambino but,
rather, the very real Curse of Tom Yawkey — a.k.a. the Curse of Jackie Robinson — which also had very much to do with the continued employment of the
horror that was Pinky Higgins, who died in prison after drunkenly plowing
his car into a Louisiana chain gang."[2]

Surprisingly, as if by default, Yawkey replaced Higgins with a local guy,
Dick O'Connell. It was an uncharacteristically peculiar move by Yawkey, who
had always relied on hard-bitten baseball men such as Eddie Collins, Joe
Cronin, Bucky Harris and Higgins to run his baseball operations. Things were
about to change. O'Connell was nothing like his predecessors; he was more
the suit-and-tie kind of fellow with a keen business sense but inexperienced
in baseball operations. Whatever the reason behind Yawkey's appointment of
O'Connell, it turned out to be a magnificent move for the Red Sox. O'Connell
began for the first time the task of seriously signing, developing and integrating
black players for the parent club. But overcoming years of Red Sox racial intolerance would prove more than difficult. It would be disquieting as well for
George Scott, who was about to make his entry into the pro ranks with the
heretofore racially troubled team. The task was made more difficult when the
Red Sox decided to make a change in their spring training location.

In 1966, wooed by a contingency of town fathers, the Chamber of Commerce and local citrus growers, the Red Sox left Scottsdale, Arizona, for a new spring training site in Winter Haven, Florida. Almost immediately there were problems. On February 26, Earl Wilson, the Red Sox' talented black pitcher and Red Sox 1965 MVP as voted by the Boston chapter of the Baseball Writers' Association, was refused service at the Cloud Nine, a Winter Haven lounge-bar. He was refused service a second time that same night at another Winter Haven bar. The Red Sox brass seemed to stumble over how to respond at first with manager Billy Herman informing Wilson to simply "forget the incident." Red Sox management did everything they could to keep the matter quiet, as if it never happened.

Wilson followed the company line for awhile but his anger could not be contained; upon being confronted by *Boston Herald* sportswriter Larry Claflin, who heard about the incident, he revealed the story. Consistent with instructions from the Red Sox, who appeared to have more concern for their own image in a new southern baseball town, Wilson cautioned Claflin to remain quiet, but he was later confronted by other sportswriters as the incident was leaked and a story began to unfold. Wilson was now at a boiling point. His pride was hurt and he felt degraded, particularly knowing that the team would not stand behind him. He made up his mind that the truth had to be known, and reported the incident to the press. His fate was sealed with the Boston club.

Confronted with a swirling press corps on the cusp of a hot scoop, and the NAACP who was quickly at their doorstep, the Red Sox reversed direction by eliciting an apology from the lounge's management; but the effort seemed half-hearted at best. New GM Dick O'Connell even attempted to make light of the incident using humor, by remarking that the bartender who refused Wilson a drink was, absurdly, from Massachusetts. His attempt at levity was insensitive, amateurish and clearly a mistake that did nothing to ease the tension.

Seething with contempt for the Red Sox since the Cloud Nine fiasco, and then later with more Red Sox indiscretions, Wilson erupted. He was the senior black player on the team, and without hesitation took the lead by defiantly registering his objections to management. Scott reasoned that the other black players, though alarmed about these matters, were reluctant to do anything that might upset their chances since they were mostly either rookies or first-year Red Sox players fighting for jobs. Wilson's reward for his intractability was to be traded to Detroit on June 14 for Don Demeter, a mediocre ballplayer at the end of his career, and little-known Julio Navarro. Wilson, who had pitched a no-hitter in '62, went on to win 64 games in five seasons for the Tigers, winning 22 games in '67, and playing in the 1968 World Series.

Scott was a raw-boned rookie at the time of the Wilson incident with total focus on making the team; he simply wanted to keep his nose clean. But in later years he would remark that there were other incidents of racial intolerance attributable to the Red Sox that year that played a part in Earl Wilson's departure from the team. Scott stated that when the Red Sox held barbecues and other family social functions, only the white players and wives were invited. Wilson would not accept this and challenged the team. Manager Billy Herman responded by alleging Wilson to be a drinker and "troublemaker," showing no sensitivity or remorse by sending his talented and promising black ace to Detroit.[3]

William Jennings Bryan "Billy" Herman, a former Cubs and Dodgers star and future Hall of Famer, was at the helm in his second full season as Red Sox manager after taking them to a disappointing ninth place finish in '65. He had been hired at the end of the '64 season by general manager and personal friend Higgins, who unceremoniously dumped Boston favorite Johnny Pesky.

Herman seemed to fit in well with a prevailing team mood of indifference and contentment with mediocrity. His penchant for golf, which he preferred discussing with the media — and even with his ballplayers — more often than he did baseball, was a distraction. Being frequently dressed in golf wear instead of a baseball uniform during spring training practice sessions did not settle well with established players such as Carl Yastrzemski, who was overheard to say, "It just seemed to me that if you're trying to turn a team around, the team should be thinking about baseball. So should the manager."[4] He did not give the appearance that his mind was on the team, but rather on a quick golfing getaway as soon as practice sessions were over.

Perhaps it was out of frustration that Herman appeared content with the status quo and open to distraction, since he realized no genuine effort was being made by management to improve their standing, or by his players, no doubt victims themselves to the lethargy, who were lackadaisical and renowned bunglers. The team was the laughing stock of major league baseball.

At the same time, however, Herman had his own shortcomings. He had no patience with young ballplayers favoring veterans instead, whom he felt were more capable of bringing him a championship. He took an immediate dislike to rookie shortstop Rico Petrocelli that sportswriter Al Hirshberg called "almost pathological." He felt the same about Tony Conigliaro, who had such rawboned talent along with considerable home run power that in spite of how Herman felt about the young slugger personally, Conigliaro simply couldn't be ignored. Tony was confident if not brash and it didn't sit at all well with Billy Herman and some of his veterans, including future Red Sox manager, bench jockey and quick-tempered tough guy Dick Williams.[5]

But when Dick O'Connell replaced Higgins, a youth movement was initiated by the new general manager, including the assimilation of black ballplayers onto the parent club from the farm system, and through trade. This would not have been tolerated by Higgins who had a hand in demoting their first black player, Pumpsie Green, to the minors in 1959 three days before the season opener, after Green had had a great spring training. He was instrumental in keeping the even more talented and successful minor leaguer, Earl Wilson, down on the farm as well. Wilson was brought up to the parent club for the first time at the end of July 1959 only after Yawkey replaced Higgins as manager in mid-season. Higgins was reinstated as manager in mid-season 1960, and once again quashed a promising Earl Wilson by shipping him to the minors for the 1961 season. There was little opportunity for black players in Boston until the arrival of Dick O'Connell.

In the winter of '65 talk had been growing around Boston and in the media that Joe Foy, a black player, coming off an MVP season at Triple-A Toronto and *The Sporting News'* minor league player of the year, was a hands-down favorite to replace veteran third sacker Frank Malzone who was released by the Red Sox on November 20. Toronto's manager, Dick Williams, had nothing but praise for the 22-year-old from the Bronx who played a key role for Williams in their 1965 International League championship season. "Foy is ready to play in the major leagues right now," voiced Williams, asserting that Foy was prepared in all aspects of the game, especially hitting and fielding.[6] Foy did hit impressively in Toronto, batting .302 with 151 base hits, 14 home runs, a .381 OBP and slugging at a .460 pace; but his glove work was mediocre, making 26 errors — the most on the team — and a less than spectacular .941 fielding percentage. Williams may have been overstating his case for Foy, but winning the International League MVP could hardly be ignored.

Along with Foy, O'Connell called up two other promising black rookies from the Red Sox farm system, Reggie Smith and George Scott, who joined black utility players Lenny Green, George Smith and Joe Christopher, who were picked up by the Red Sox in '65; Smith and Christopher were traded for by O'Connell. In June O'Connell traded for two additional black players who would become important members of the '67 team, Jose Tartabull and John Wyatt. The Red Sox were hardly recognizable from the all-white teams preceding them. O'Connell drew no distinctions between black and white; his goals were two-fold: finding baseball talent, no matter the color, and establishing a team built around youth. He set out in earnest to build a competitive ball club, no matter what it took.

George Scott was looked upon as nothing but a long shot to make the team in 1966. His invitation to join the club in Winter Haven was complimentary at best. With Joe Foy standing in his way, and already labeled Malzone's replacement, George was predestined for assignment to Toronto for more seasoning. Since the Red Sox could hardly pass him by so easily after Scott's sensational MVP year in Pittsfield, they needed to take a look at the young slugger from Greenville, Mississippi.

On March 1 Boston's all-time great slugger and soon-to-be-enshrined Hall of Famer, Ted Williams, arrived in camp to share spring coaching honors with another all-time Red Sox great, Bobby Doerr. Always the crowd-pleaser and larger than life, Williams immediately made his presence known to the crowd and the ballplayers. As was his spring custom, Williams announced his intent to play a game of pepper with some of the new players, choosing George Smith and George Scott. It did not go unnoticed that both players were among the few black prospects in a Red Sox camp of mostly whites.

It was a fast game of pepper, by design, with Williams slapping ground balls at the two infielders at a rapid pace. He declared it would be a contest: if the players won they would get a Cadillac; if they lost it would be cokes. They didn't have a chance. Ted hit a sharp grounder between the players that Scott snared with his quick glove hand. He then rapped another ball to Smith's opposite side while he was off-balance, and Smith muffed it. The game was over. Williams was pleased with what he saw in young Scott, his home run power, fielding skills and especially his penchant to learn, and went out of his way to help George acquire major league skills. Young George soaked up every minute of it.

Williams made a powerful statement at his Hall of Fame induction later that summer in behalf of black ballplayers, insisting that the great Negro Leaguers, the majority whom had been barred from major league baseball, be recognized by the National Baseball Hall of Fame. Ted's statement was said to have irritated his former boss and friend, Tom Yawkey, who was in attendance. The unprecedented gesture led to the first Negro Leaguer Hall of Fame inductee in 1971, Satchel Paige. Hall of Fame inductions of numerous former Negro League stars soon followed. The Hall of Fame has formally credited Ted Williams with "getting the ball rolling."[7]

On March 3, the first full day of 1966 spring practice for all Red Sox players, Scott walloped two impressive home runs that immediately got manager Herman's attention. "He's going to give Foy quite a tussle," said Herman to a batch of New England sportswriters, who were keeping an eager watch on the new rookies, and sensing the drama that was about to play out between them contending for the vacated third base job. "The kid certainly looked good up there," commented Herman in astonishment over the power displayed by the young but clearly untested batsman.

On March 6 Herman held his first intra-squad practice game which they named "Meet the Red Sox Day," designed for the new Winter Haven fans who paid a dollar a look. One sportswriter, Pres Hobson of the Quincy *Patriot Ledger*, saw some humor in this event saying that the "Sox played their favorite opponents: themselves!" His intent was that if they expected to win a game, it would probably have to be against their own team; otherwise there was little hope. Manager Herman hit a sour note when, speaking over the public address system while the game was in progress, commented on a slick demonstration by his players of a double play: "I wish it was that easy all summer," said the skipper. His cynicism did not escape some of his ballplayers, and several of the fans and writers who were in attendance.

Realizing how they were being perceived and the embarrassment it brought them, on March 8, just prior to the start of the spring exhibition season, some of the Red Sox players reacted by making an open public "confession" that they were sick of losing, and that the reason for this was due to their own poor attitudes. So public a pronouncement was a revelation that would haunt them throughout the spring and into the '66 season, leading to fan and player ridicule. They were a joke in the eyes of other teams and their players.

Led by star player Carl Yastrzemski and senior reliever Dick Radatz, a press conference was held with the writers that day to explain that attitudes had to change, including their own. Self-confessing his own misdemeanors of previous seasons, Yaz admitted he overthrew cutoff men, wouldn't run out ground balls hit to infielders, and continued to do these things knowingly to the detriment of the team. But he was going to change, he said, and with the help of the rest of the Red Sox players they were about to do their own self-policing. "We're going to watch these situations, including the racial situation," exclaimed Radatz to an eager Boston press corps salivating over such hot news.[8] Herman meanwhile, during a weak moment, and speaking out of frustration, was quoted by a wire service reporter that this shift in attitude "came several years too late." He later denied the statement.

From the start of spring training the battle was on between Joe Foy and George Scott that became a media playground and had the full attention of Red Sox brass. Foy was a designated shoe-in for the third base job. Scott knew he faced an uphill battle even to make the team. As one Boston sportswriter sized up the situation, "Only a sensational spring training could land Scott a job with the big club sooner than '67."[9] Local and national news media were exuberant in their support of Foy, splashing his name in sports news headlines and featured spring-training articles. A March 14 *Patriot Ledger* cartoon profile of Foy described him as "the big noise down here in Winter Haven." Just before the start of the major league season the United Press International picked three rookie infielders "who have earned regular jobs" as their "top rookie prospects for 1966." They were Bobby Murcer of the Yankees, Tommy Helms of the Reds and Joe Foy of the Red Sox. Foy tied with Murcer receiving the top number of votes. George Scott was nothing but an afterthought.[10]

"Joe Foy was ahead of me, and they really should have given him the job," explained George Scott in a 2006 interview. "I had no quarrel with that, but I wasn't going to settle for that. I was going to try to be on that roster come Opening Day. You know, it wasn't actually that I was trying to take Joe Foy's job. I was trying to win a roster spot for Opening Day," Scott said.[11]

Coach Eddie Popowski, who knew both rookies, and who was assigned to work with them along with other rookies on the spring roster, constantly

Contenders: Scott's competition for a roster spot was Joe Foy (left), the Triple-A MVP, who was a shoe-in for the starting role at third base. Scott had a sensational spring with the Red Sox, upsetting Foy's plans, and was the starting third baseman for Boston on Opening Day (courtesy of Boston Public Library).

needled both men to get the best from them. But he targeted Foy particularly. "Pop" applied constant pressure on the young third sacker to help him avoid complacency and realize his full potential with the Red Sox. It was good motivational strategy, basically the party-line approach in behalf of the Red Sox who were fixed on Foy as their choice to fill the third base slot. On one such occasion Pop was overheard barking at Foy in the batting cage: "Led the league in hitting, Joe? Well so did Scott. And he led the league in homers and runs batted in." And digging further into Foy, he continued, "Minor league player of the year, huh, Joe? *The Sporting News* made you a big man. Well you better start hitting because they tell me Scott is whacking the ball all over the lot across the street."[12]

Although Popowski clearly had Foy's best interests at heart and was nurturing him for the big-time, his fondness for George was undeniably genuine. "He loved me man; he loved George Scott," said Scott endearingly in a 2006 interview, disclosing a special bond between the two.[13]

The Red Sox began their spring exhibition season on March 10 in Sarasota against the Chicago White Sox, losing 4–3. Joe Foy started at third base and went 1-for-2 at the plate. Scott subbed for him in later innings — his first appearance in major league level competition — and went hitless in his one at-bat. Contrary to manager Herman's charge made before the game that this year's team would be better defensively and offensively, old habits were evident from the start. Smith, their new second baseman, booted the first ball hit to him. Yastrzemski misplayed a fly ball into a hit and made a poor throw, and Conigliaro threw to the wrong base. There was a sense of comic relief when, shortly after the misplays, an announcement was made over the public address system: "Attention please: will the Red Sox bus drivers please report to their buses." Everyone in the stands felt Herman was going to stop the game before any further damage was done. Though never the manager's intention, it was nonetheless an amusing moment reflecting the sad state of the hapless Red Sox.

Scott banged out his first spring base hit, a double, in another Red Sox losing cause, their third in succession, on March 12 against the Kansas City A's. It earned him a shot at a starting assignment at third base the next day, replacing Foy who had gone 2-for-8 and looked ragged in the field. The Red Sox were playing their first spring game at their new home park, Chain O' Lakes, in Winter Haven, and a near-capacity crowd of 3,009 turned out to see their new ballclub.

Despite home-field advantage and the hoopla surrounding the inaugural game, the Red Sox lost their fourth straight Grapefruit League contest, 8–4, to the Athletics; but George Scott was a standout and became an immediate fan favorite. His enthusiasm for being in the lineup was electric, palpable to the crowd; they could sense it, and reacted in adulation of the young ballplayer. He wasted no time responding to the fan fervor building around him, one of the bright spots on an otherwise hapless group of unremarkable downtrodden ballplayers. He became the darling of the fans.

In his first at-bat Scott proceeded to crush a tape-measure home run off of Aurelio Monteagudo. It was a towering blast sailing high over the left-center-field wall, landing 450 feet from home plate, drawing gasps and shouts of ecstatic chants from the Winter Haven crowd. It was the first home run hit at the new ballpark. It was also the beginning of many such prodigious blasts that Scott would hit during his professional baseball career, colossal shots hit with concussive force that sailed to the outer reaches of ballparks that would become his hitting trademark.

As George later expressed in an interview, "the ball was hit high over the water tower [behind the left-center-field wall], damned near hit that dome," laughed an enthusiastic Scott describing the clout and the exhilaration he felt from hitting such a monstrous homer for the home crowd. Cartoonist Leo White of the *Patriot Ledger* memorialized the blast by depicting the ball flying

Spring 1966, Winter Haven — George Scott hustles to first as Tommy McCraw of the White Sox takes the throw (courtesy of Boston Red Sox).

high over the Chain O' Lakes Park outfield wall. His hyperbolic caption read: "They're still talking about his first home run at Chain O' Lakes Park, it traveled almost 600 feet."[14]

General Manager O'Connell later on explained the importance of that home run to a Red Sox organization that had little to crow about: "He could be a tremendous drawing card. He hits the ball a mile, he plays hard every minute and he has that something that appeals to the fans."[15]

Scott also got a two-base hit that day and played superbly on defense, making slick plays and displaying fielding skills that impressed manager Herman. But it was Scott's hustle in breaking up a double play at second base in the sixth inning that captivated the crowd, and even more so Billy Herman. Rico Petrocelli hit a routine grounder to Sal Bando at third, who threw to second for the start of an easy double play. Scott, who was on first, got a good jump on the pitch and launched himself into the A's classy second baseman Dick Green, effectively taking him out of the play and preventing a relay throw to first. It was an aggressive heads-up pro move, making George an instant fan-favorite and more than a pleasant surprise for manager Herman.

Whenever he was not playing, Scott was constantly on the move, whether it was warming up pitchers, doing wind-sprints with them, or waving a bat around in the dugout to get Herman's attention that he was ready for action. He was dubbed by the media and fans as one of the hardest workers in camp.

On March 14, Herman put Scott in the lineup again against the New York Yankees. Once more he was productive, stroking two of four base hits made by the Red Sox, with two RBIs, in a 5–4 losing effort. Herman realized through Scott's well-rounded performance that day that he had in him the ingredients of the ballplayer type he was looking for; ironically he was not the seasoned veteran he preferred, but a raw-boned rookie. Given the chance, Scott proceeded to display multiple baseball skills, offensively and defensively, including significant home run power, but above all an attitude of "team" and a clear desire to win. It was a melting pot of skills and attitude that spelled success. Herman was about to be challenged by the two minor league MVPs in ways he never imagined, the envy of American League managers, deciding on a position that he and the rest of the Red Sox brass, at the start of spring training felt unquestionably was Joe Foy's right of inheritance.

A one-time major leaguer himself and a field supervisor for major league baseball's Scouting Bureau, Art Gardner, familiar with Scott's talents, described him this way: "He could just kill the high fastball," Gardner said, "take it 440 feet to right-center, going the other way. But he was a line drive hitter, a lot like Dick Allen back then."[16]

In spite of Scott's impressive three-game performance going 5-for-10 at the plate with a home run, double, three RBIs, and slick fielding, Herman persevered in his strategy with a rambunctious press corps, who relished the thought of conflict, that he would continue to split the third base duties between Scott and Foy. He didn't let on that he was already thinking of other infield options for both men if Scott continued his hot hand.

On March 17, with the Red Sox heading for their 7th spring training loss in eight games, and his first baseman, Tony Horton, continuing to underperform in the field, Herman pulled Horton and replaced him with Scott late in the game. It was an experimental move by the manager, sensing that Horton, though a good hitter, might ultimately not make the grade because of his deficiencies in the field. Scott, however, with little more than some instructional league experience at the position, displayed good form and skills around the first base bag that day to the excitement of the Winter Haven crowd, which continued in their praise and overall clamor for the young Mississippian.

In the next three games Scott was 3-for-7, with one of his hits a timely game-tying double ripped to left-center in the eighth inning against the Cincinnati Reds, which the Red Sox went on to win. But Scott's bat went silent in another stretch of three games that he had started at third base. Herman sat him down, favoring Foy who only managed one base hit himself during this span. The Red Sox had now lost seven consecutive games with a dismal spring training record of 2 wins and 14 losses. Manager Herman was none too pleased, especially after his players had embarrassed themselves earlier with "true confessions" about their various transgressions and how determined they were to turn over a new leaf and play winning baseball. He was aware that the only way they could redeem themselves now was to win, and winning they were not. In fact they became the laughing stock throughout spring training. After an 8–6 loss to the Yankees on March 23, their fifth straight defeat, Herman had had enough, declaring there would be no further "morale" meetings by the players and that he was "going to do the managing of this club" from here-on-out.[17]

Tony Horton had by now made four fielding errors along with a handful of misplays and misjudgments around the first base bag. He also had difficulty chasing balls hit to his right, line drives hit right at him and he was weak starting the 1–6–3 double play. In the March 25 game against the Minnesota Twins in Puerto Rico, Horton made his fifth error, but it was a misjudgment play that aroused manager Herman's ire the most. The Twins' Ted Uhlaender rapped a grounder to Horton's right that was fielded by second baseman George Smith. When Smith poised himself to throw the runner out at first, for the third out, Horton was out of position; the Twins went on to score six runs in the inning. Herman was losing even further confidence in Horton and sat him down for the second and third games of a series, replacing him again with George Scott and playing Joe Foy at third base. Scott was 1-for-8 with a double and RBI, and the Red Sox split the last two games with the Twins, winning their third contest of the spring. But once again Scott was flashy around the first base bag, figuring in a double play, to the delight of Billy Herman.

On March 30, in Winter Haven, the Red Sox were preparing to meet the St. Louis Cardinals, a very sound good-hitting ball club with strong pitching. Scott, once again relegated to the second unit, was noticeably upset upon leaving the practice field that day, proclaiming that he had had enough of the "second infield stuff" and wanted to play. He got his wish.

The Red Sox hung tough against the Cardinals but were on the short end

Rookie and his music. George Scott enjoying some quiet time (courtesy of Boston Public Library).

of a 3–2 score with two out in the bottom half of the ninth. Herman called upon left-handed batter Dalton Jones to hit against Tracy Stallard. But manager Schoendienst countered with Joe Hoerner, a crafty southpaw, who would have a strong season for the Redbirds with a 1.54 ERA in 57 appearances. Herman used some strategy of his own by pulling Jones and replacing him with Scott.

It was a defining moment for George, who in dramatic fashion proceeded to blast a tape-measure game-tying home run off Hoerner high above the eight-foot center-field fence, landing 420 feet from home plate. Herman,

On the big league roster. Rookie George Scott looks over the bats he'd use against American League pitchers (courtesy of *Boston Herald*).

quickly taking to his rookie with the powerful batting stroke and exemplary work ethic, cheered along with the crowd delirious with excitement as his young slugger rounded the bases in triumph, clearly a happy man.

The moment was short-lived when a struggling Dick Radatz served up a game-winning two-run homer to the Cards' Curt Flood in the 10th inning. Manager Herman, however, could not overlook two key throwing miscues by Joe Foy, one leading to two unearned runs in the sixth inning when he bobbled a ground ball, then threw wild to first base, as a primary reason for their losing. Foy's less-than-stellar performance that day seemed to convince the oft-frustrated manager to take a much harder look at Scott, who still seemed destined for assignment to Toronto.

Moreover, on March 31 Tony Horton made his sixth exhibition season error (he would make seven errors that spring) creating further opportunities for Scott, who could play well at either third or first base. His future with the Red Sox was beginning to come together much earlier than even he had imagined. Herman and the Red Sox now had their eyes on the slugger from Greenville to possibly supplant Joe Foy as their season-opener third baseman.

Scott was given the starting third base assignment for the remainder of the spring season, and began a run of torrid hitting that opened the eyes of every fan, coach, manager and Red Sox brass, sealing the fate of his rival, Foy, from earning a starting role. Between March 30 and April 9, a stretch of eight games, Scott rapped out 14 base hits — hitting safely in every game — including four home runs, three doubles, two triples, and 5 RBIs; a phenomenal .452 clip. He just missed hitting another home run on April 10, the final exhibition game against the Senators, when he stroked a ball 430 feet to dead center that would have been out of most ballparks, but was caught by Don Lock. He finished the exhibition season batting .291 with five home runs, six doubles, three triples and 23 base hits.

The word on young Scott and his achievements in Winter Haven had reached the Hub and hype soon seized the city that this kid was the greatest Red Sox revelation since Ted Williams. But toward the end of the spring season another kind of buzz began to emerge, and take hold, that the young phenom may indeed be shipped back to the minors just like the Red Sox had done with Pumpsie Green. It was an ill-conceived notion, at least for the reasons they believed, but Boston fans had seen this happen before. They were starving for a winning team, and especially for the chance to see new talent that would break the mold of Red Sox mediocrity and in whom they could at last find reason, for a change, to celebrate; they simply could not tolerate the idea that they would not be able to see their new kid slugger, who had set Florida afire, playing in Fenway. But rumor of Scott's imminent departure to Toronto had the fans in its grip and the Red Sox were soon being assaulted with panicked phone calls and letters from the fan base announcing their strong disapproval.

Scott explained that a week before they broke camp for Boston, manager Billy Herman asked to see him following his wind sprints. George was convinced he was going to be told he was being sent down to Toronto, since Toronto manager Dick Williams was strongly recommending Foy and Horton for the major league roster, and the Sox brass had programmed it that way. Scott recalled that Herman was under great pressure from the Red Sox to send him down to Toronto "no matter what I did." Herman, however, saw it differently, convincing management the young slugger was ready.[18]

Washington Senators manager Gil Hodges, a once great power hitter, perennial All-Star and Gold Glover for the Brooklyn Dodgers, remarked about Scott as the two teams were barnstorming north: "I haven't seen anybody swing a better bat in Florida."[19] On April 7 following an intra-squad game wrapping up the Florida exhibition season — and Scott's phenomenal performance in seven straight games — Billy Herman announced that George Scott would be his starting third baseman on Opening Day. Scott was ecstatic exclaiming, "This is a very wonderful thing!" and then confidently announced that he planned to become Rookie of the Year. "That's what I'm aiming for," he barked to a bunch of reporters standing nearby.[20] He felt as if he was standing on top of the world.

Although finishing the spring exhibition season with a dismal 8–19 record, manager Herman was enthusiastic about a new-found energy visible on his team that was not apparent before. Five of those wins came during the final ten games when Scott was in the lineup tearing up opponents. When discussing the attributes of his players and Red Sox chances for playing winning baseball, Herman always seemed to come back to the subject of his big rookie slugger, George Scott. "That kid at third has given me the biggest encouragement," proclaimed the exuberant skipper.[21]

5

Tape Measures to Goin' Fishin'

The Red Sox have had some startling rookies over the years, but even Babe Ruth, Tris Speaker and Ted Williams never started more impressively than has George Scott. — Harold Kaese, *Boston Globe*[1]

Toward the end of 1966 spring training when George Scott, the rookie, was ripping the ball all over Florida, smashing extra-base hits and tape-measure home runs, he acquired his trademark sobriquet "Boomer," by which he would be lastingly identified. For many he was no longer just George Scott the ballplayer; he was of insuperable stature, he was the "Boomer." The nickname took on a life of its own that stayed with him throughout his baseball career.

Ironically, it was his closest competitor, rookie Joe Foy, whom Scott credits with originating the distinguishing appellation, after watching him smash baseballs out of ballparks. "Man you put a boom on that ball," was the remark made by Foy reacting to Scott's prodigious home run drives during those spring games of '66, said Scott, that evolved into a life-long nickname. Although initially described as "The Bomber" and "The Great Scott" by the media scribes, these nicknames soon transformed into the "Boomer." Scott was the first of a handful of athletes to take on this moniker.[2]

Boston Globe reporter Bud Collins wrote his own endorsement of the nickname in his April 12 Opening Day column by describing Scott as "Boomer," as if, by birth, it was his middle name. Eager to align with a new hero labeled as the next Babe Ruth and the most exciting Red Sox rookie to come along since Ted Williams, Red Sox fans, most who had never seen Scott, excitedly picked up on Collins' column. They wasted no time in raising their new "Boomer" to celebrity status. The thought of watching exciting baseball for a change and even the possibility of actually winning, with new talent, was compelling.

Though Collins was mindful of a Red Sox organization of underachievers who settled for mediocrity, which he reminded readers of in his column, he wasn't entirely pessimistic. Herman, looking for leadership on and off the field,

Instructions on hitting from one of baseball's all-time best. George Scott, the student, and Ted Williams, soon to be inducted into the National Baseball Hall of Fame (courtesy of Boston Public Library).

called a team meeting on April 11 to elect a team captain, and a reluctant Carl Yastrzemski was their choice. Collins couldn't resist a jab of cynicism, describing Yastrzemski's task as one "to lead the Reformation at Fenway Park." But his focus was one of optimism placed on a young George Scott, whom he described as "more welcome on a cold April day than a squadron of robins."[3] He had set the mood for the Boston fan base and they were prepared to respond.

The big rookie infielder, who had upset Triple-A MVP Joe Foy to dispossess him of the third base job and was taking the city by storm, whacked two home run balls into Fenway's center-field bleachers, and put another off the left-field wall, in his first batting practice swings upon his arrival in Boston. He was the real deal.

The Red Sox opened their season with sixteen new players on the roster. "Six of the players who checked in at Fenway Monday were Negroes. The Red Sox are joining the 20th century," wrote Bud Collins, emphasizing a dramatic shift from previous club anti-black sentiment and the racist views of a recently departed GM Mike Higgins.[4]

George later recounted how few minor league black players were in the Red Sox system at the time and how difficult it was for them to make the club in the early '60s, and even more so how difficult it was to stay: "I was the first black position-player to come up in Boston [from their farm system] and be productive in baseball. All the rest of the black guys that they had up there before me, they was just bench guys, or guys that played every now and then."[5] It was true, except for Joe Foy, who was also in the Red Sox farm system at the same time as Scott, but who had an unremarkably brief six years in the major leagues; he was never the "productive" player that Scott was. Another player who was also in the system, Reggie Smith, who became a solid ballplayer and All-Star, came up briefly with Scott in '66, but was sent down after six games; he returned to stay in 1967.

Sizing up "differences" among white and black players and how they were viewed and treated by Red Sox management was immediately apparent to a young George Scott upon his arrival in Boston. Scott said, "I could fawn with Mr. Yawkey all I wanted to, but if I didn't play baseball I was gone." Some of the white players could do the same with Yawkey, he lamented, and the owner would show them favor. Scott perceived of himself to be an anomaly to Red Sox brass; either he performed or he was on his way back to Mississippi.[6] "Color" was a likely factor, believed Scott.

On April 12 the new-look Red Sox opened their season against the Baltimore Orioles before 12,386 jubilant and very hopeful Fenway fans. It was a chilly 44 degrees, more like football than baseball weather. Scott strode across the diamond to the cheers of the fans and took his position at third base. Barely 22 years old and only four short years since his graduation from Coleman High, he was in the big leagues. He was nervous at first he said later, but his manner of play belied any feeling among the fans that he was anything but confident.

Baltimore took an early lead by scoring two runs in the first. Then in the top of the second they threatened again, loading the bases with two out and a fast runner, Paul Blair, standing on third. At the plate was the speedy Luis Aparicio, who was an adept bunter. Little Luis tried to surprise the rookie Scott and dropped an Earl Wilson pitch perfectly on the ground about a foot

April 12, 1966 — Red Sox rookie George Scott obliges Fenway Park fan Bob Preston of East Boston with an autograph on Opening Day in Boston against the Baltimore Orioles. It was a chilly 44 degrees at game time (courtesy of *Boston Herald*).

inside the third base foul line. Blair raced for home. Looking every part the veteran, Scott had noticed that Aparicio had dropped his left shoulder, appearing to bunt, and charged toward home plate. In one fluid motion he picked up the ball bare-handed and threw a strike to Horton at first for the out, ending the inning. It was Scott's first play in the majors and he looked much like his predecessor, Frank Malzone, who mastered the art of fielding bunts. The Fenway fans roared their approval; they had something here.

Scott lined out to left field in his first major league at-bat, getting good wood on a Steve Barber pitch, that settled his jitters, he said later. But in the third inning the Red Sox rallied to tie the score. The bases were loaded with two out, and rookie Scott was at the plate. Remembering a recent spring game against the Red Sox when the big rookie pummeled Orioles pitching, Barber pitched to him carefully, and walked in a run on a 3–2 count for Scott's first major league RBI.

The next time up, in the sixth, with the score tied, 3–3, Barber started off with a pitch high and tight and directly at Scott's head. He managed to get out of the way. The next pitch was again inside, this time striking George in the left ankle. The big rookie was hurt, a deep bruise, but he stayed in the game. (He later claimed that Barber was throwing at him.) He wasn't about to leave the contest, a frame of mind he would carry with him for the remainder of his playing career, to his detriment he would often say after leaving base-ball — playing hurt.

In the eighth inning Scott crushed a Moe Drabowsky pitch on a line to the deepest outfield reaches of Fenway, striking the top of the center-field wall and caroming back toward the infield. Center fielder Blair had to run at top speed to chase the ball down as it rolled away from him, as Scott wound up at third easily, standing up. (Scott also hit a triple off Drabowsky a week earlier in a spring game after being knocked down by the pitcher.) It was his first major league base hit. He later scored. "The ball missed by about six inches from going out of the ballpark in dead centerfield," lamented a disappointed George Scott, who was hoping his first major league hit would be a homer.[7]

The Red Sox lost their opener to the Orioles, 5–4, in thirteen innings. They lost their second game as well against future Hall of Famer Jim Palmer, who shut down the Red Sox on five hits and a single run. Scott got one of those, a hard-hit single, in a pinch-hit role. George Scott had made his mark during those two days, much to the delight of the Boston fans.

And then it happened — just as George's confidence was at its peak the Red Sox traveled to Cleveland and proceeded to play terrible baseball, shades of the '65 team, the scribes wrote. They were up against the Indians left-handed flame-thrower, "Sudden Sam" McDowell, in game one of the three-game series; Scott wilted under his pitching mastery, striking out three times. He then proceeded to strike out against two other Indians pitchers — going 0-for-5 on the day, whiffing in every at-bat. He also committed an error among five Red Sox errors, as the Sox lost in twelve innings, 8–7.

He proceeded to strike out in his first

George Scott was struck in the ankle by Baltimore's Steve Barber in his first major league game. Scott later hit a triple off Moe Drabowsky, his first major league hit (courtesy of *Boston Herald*).

at-bat the next day against Gary Bell, but settled down with three hits in his next four plate appearances. "I remember Leon Wagner [Indians centerfielder] making fun of me. Every time I struck out he would hold a finger up, and he told me he was glad I made contact because he was beginning to run out of fingers," Scott lamented.[8]

Herman had had enough of the team's poor defensive play and by the third game came to Scott, appealing to him to take over first base, in spite of George's big league inexperience there. Tony Horton was not hitting and had also hurt his knee in the first game by a line drive hit directly at him that he should have caught. An incredulous Herman approached coach Pete Runnels, a former first baseman, asking him, "Can a line drive hit a first baseman on the knee when he is 100 feet from home plate?" Runnels replied, "I didn't think so, but now I do." Herman also displayed little confidence in Joe Foy by substituting his new guy, Eddie Kasko, a newly acquired veteran, at third in place of the rookie. "I'm putting some leather into the lineup," exclaimed the frustrated manager. Scott played the final game of that series at first base, going 2-for-4 at the plate with two assists and initiating a double play.[9]

Although George played well enough in his first official major league assignment at first base, the team continued the charade they called baseball, losing the contest, 6–0. As the weekend debacle drew to a close, with two outs in the eighth, shortstop Rico Petrocelli and left fielder Yastrzemski collided chasing a Rocky Colavito pop fly, as the batter reached second on the error. The next batter singled to left. Yastrzemski fielded it cleanly and made a strong throw to the plate attempting to get the runner, but instead the ball went through the catcher's legs. As the batter rounded second, the pitcher, Sadowski, backing up the catcher, picked the ball up and threw wildly to third, allowing the batter to score.

The Sox were playing atrocious baseball, committing ten errors in the series, thirteen in their first five games; Scott with two of them. They missed at least a half a dozen fly balls that should have been caught and were picked off base twice. Further, they set a major league all-time team record for strikeouts in two consecutive games, whiffing 33 times, and a major league record of 42 in three games. Manager Billy Herman was becoming apoplectic: "We can't run, we can't hit, we can't catch a pop fly," bellowed the enraged skipper.[10]

In the meantime in just a few short days from Opening Day the improbable had occurred. Rookie Scott had effectively dismantled the pre-season plans of the Boston brass by realigning half of their infield, first, by upending their top choice, Joe Foy, at third base, and then in a move bordering on impertinence dispossessing another Boston management favorite, Tony Horton, their $138,000 highly regarded prospect, of a job at first base. Scott was playing so well that Horton was destined for the bench; he was sent down to Toronto for further seasoning under manager Dick Williams after playing in only six games.

"Joe Foy was my best friend," said a solemn George Scott. "There was one job open going into the season and that was third base, and we both happened to be [competing for] third base. Tony Horton opened the season at first base. Tony Horton had a lot of trouble, not only trouble hitting, but he had trouble catching the ball." Scott, startled by the suddenness of the manager's move, found himself scrambling around the dugout and amongst teammates to borrow a suitable first base mitt. "I went to first base and I stayed there the rest of my career," Scott proudly exclaimed, winning several Gold Gloves along the way.[11]

The Red Sox returned to Boston with a disappointing 0–5 record and had little to be pleased about, except for their pitching which deserved a better fate. Scott was batting .294 with 5 hits to his credit, going into an April 19 doubleheader with Detroit.

Ex–Red Sox pitching star Bill Monbouquette, a Hub fan-favorite let go by Boston to Detroit in the offseason, was the starter in the first game; he was rudely treated by his ex-teammates, who scored six runs off him in two innings. In the third Joe Sparma came on in relief and was promptly greeted by George Scott's first official major league home run, a blast that sailed high over the Fenway Park left-field wall — the "Green Monster"— and the big screen atop it, onto Lansdowne Street. The crowd was abuzz at the sight of such a mighty poke that was both towering and traveled so far. It was the first of many prodigious blasts by George. The home crowd knew they had a gem in this new kid from Mississippi, and the more than 25,000 Fenway rooters shook the ballpark resoundingly with their cheers of approval as the big rookie rounded the bases.

The talk among Boston fans following the game was that Scott's home run was very likely the highest they had ever seen hit in Fenway — a "rainmaker." It "scraped the clouds" reported George Bankert of the *Patriot Ledger*. Red Sox third base coach, Billy Gardner, a seasoned baseball veteran, exclaimed that he had never seen a home run before in the major leagues that was hit with such height. Belting towering shots out of ballparks would become a George Scott signature that he fondly called "taters," a term that caught on with baseball fandom and its media and became a household word memorialized in baseball lexicon to this day.

The Red Sox did not make an official error, nor, importantly, did they make any judgment miscues, during the three-game Detroit series, and they turned four double plays. Herman was pleased with his new rookie first basemen, whose hitting stats were among the Red Sox leaders. He made a symbolic gesture of his approval by rewarding Scott with a new uniform number, a low No. 5 — usually among the numbers reserved for Red Sox regulars — from his previous No. 39. He was going to stay at first "from now on" declared the manager; he planned to move Foy back to third, dispelling any rumors he was going back to Toronto.

On April 23 at home against Cleveland Scott clouted another tape-measure home run, off Gary Bell, his second, clearing everything in left field and tying the score. It was still climbing as it left Fenway. *Boston Globe* sportswriter Will McDonough, describing Scott's blast in his next-day column, said that it was "mammoth," and that it made the Indians home runs that day "look puny." George's day was not done, however, when in the ninth inning he participated in a rare baseball moment, a triple play. With Bell on third base and Davalillo on first, Max Alvis rapped a short-hop liner to second baseman Smith who whirled and threw out the runner at second; Petrocelli relayed to Scott at first for an apparent double play. When Bell hesitated and then broke for home, Scott alertly rifled a perfect strike to the catcher Bob Tillman who tagged out Bell. Once more the Fenway throng went wild over the baseball savvy displayed by the young Mississippian from Greenville; there was something and someone, indeed, to cheer about once again in Boston.

Boston went into New York on April 25 for two games against a struggling Yankee club at 1–9, and took the first game, 8–5. Scott, in his first look at fabled Yankee Stadium, pasted the ball all over the lot, going 3-for-4 and nearly hitting for the cycle, with a single, double and triple. The Yankees avoided that from happening and eliminated any chance for further embarrassment by the rookie by intentionally walking Scott in the ninth, who had come up with the tying run on third and two out. The Yankees meanwhile established a team record for the most losses at the start of the season, losing 10 of their first 11 games.

Whitey Ford, the venerable Yankee southpaw and future Hall of Famer, was slated to start the next game; it would be one of George's most memorable ballgames. Not only did he have the opportunity to compete against the likes of such a skillful pitcher, he also hit a shot off the left-hander that may be remembered as one of the longest home runs in the history of Yankee Stadium.

The rookie first baseman was hitting nearly everything being thrown at him, going 5-for-11 in his previous three games, and batting .333 for the young season. The buzz around the league was that Scott had no weaknesses, was abusing pitchers and hitting home runs out of sight. He put on a show for the fans and Yankee ballplayers, who were watching him intently from the top of the dugout steps while he took his pre-game batting practice cuts. Scott put three balls well out of the park, each one estimated at 450 feet or better, leaving the reporters and ballplayers aghast at the performance as they stood around the batting cage. Tillman announced as he followed Scott into the batting cage that it would be a tough act to follow, shaking his head in disbelief.

The Red Sox scored a run in the first and were threatening to score more. With Yastrzemski perched on third base, Conigliaro on second, and one out, Ford looked over to the dugout and manager Johnny Keane as George Scott strode to the plate. They would have nothing to do with the dangerous rookie, and intentionally walked him. But the next time he came up, in the third inning, the Yankee pitcher dealt with him, to his chagrin. He later explained that the best way to pitch to George Scott was to "pitch him four balls in a row, and then he won't be able to hit it."[12] On Whitey's first pitch Scott hit a blast that was labeled home run, but it went foul. He then fouled a couple more off, and Ford worked the count to 1-and-2. He had him now, Ford thought, and then threw him a high inside fastball. The young Red Sox slugger put his full weight into the pitch and got all of it, propelling the ball to the highest reaches of Yankee Stadium, landing well up in the third deck. It was "territory hitherto explored only by Jimmie Foxx," reported Arthur Daley of the *New York Times*, referring to a memorable blast once hit by the future Hall of Famer that landed in approximately the same spot as Scott's homer.[13]

It was a colossal wallop struck with such concussive force that it seemed as if to jolt the partisan Yankee fans, whose collective gaze was riveted on the high-flying missile that appeared headed for outer space. "I'll never forget it," exclaimed former teammate Rico Petrocelli, laughing robustly and admiringly about the memorable home run during an interview. "It was the longest home run I've ever seen ... when he hit that ball it was such a loud crack ... it seemed like it never [would] come down."[14] Mouths dropped open throughout the ballpark. Ford appeared in a trance watching the still-rising baseball ricochet against the concrete steps adjacent to the exit ramp of the uppermost deck. He later confessed it was one of the longest home runs he ever surrendered. Reluctant to publicly declare it the longest, stating that both Walt Dropo and Frank Howard had hit similar shots off of him, he sheepishly admitted that if Scott's blast had been hit toward the bleachers, "it would have come close to the last row." Until then only 16 men in the history of the Stadium had ever hit a ball in the bleachers; anywhere near the last row would be the longest. Ford gave Scott his due, but it was at best a back-handed compliment.

After the game the New York sportswriters flocked around Ford who was standing just outside of the players' lounge, a little retreat spot behind the Yankee clubhouse that was out-of-bounds to reporters, and quickly picked up on the heckling he was receiving from his teammates over the Scott home run. Ford was noticeably embarrassed. Pressed by reporters to guess how far the ball was stroked, Ford looked to Mickey Mantle standing beside him, and raising a speculative eyebrow asked if it might have traveled 490 feet. Mantle laughed, "Why don't you round it off to 500 feet." Ford reeled at the incriminating thought declaring, defensively, "No that will ruin my image. Why don't you say it was 183 yards? That sounds better," said Ford in an obvious moment of personal anguish.[15] But, according to Larry Claflin of the *Boston Record-American*, Ford conceded shortly after that, "I believe that was the longest home run ever hit off me." It has been estimated that Scott's home run ball traveled between 500 and 505 feet.[16]

"That's the home run that never was talked about, and is never talked about today," expressed a disappointed George Scott, lamenting over how inexplicably little reporting or sports media commentary there was, or is today, of his monster home run hit off of Whitey Ford. The *New York Times* failed to mention it at all in its April 27 game summary, emphasizing, instead, the Yankees' first win after seven straight losses. "They always come up with other guys," exclaims Scott, when the subject of who hit the longest home run in Yankee Stadium comes up with sports media, or amidst sports talk shows and their fans. Scott relates that even today, "every time" he meets up with the guileful Hall of Famer, Whitey Ford, at autograph shows or other baseball events, Ford, in fun, will cover his hand over his mouth, gesturing to Scott not to speak about *the* home run to anyone.[17]

The Red Sox were limping along at a 4–11 pace, nine and one half games out of first, heading into a two-game series with Detroit beginning May 3. Rookie Scott was batting a solid .302 with 12 RBIs and 5 home runs, four in the previous seven games. Boston lost the first game to Tiger ace Mickey Lolich, Scott managing one base hit. But then he erupted for 20 base hits over the next ten games at a .432 clip, launching 6 home runs — two of them monster shots — two doubles, a triple and 13 RBIs, adding to a hitting streak of 14 games.

On May 4 Scott hit two long home runs, the first off Bill Monbouquette, with one runner on base, that sailed into the center-field lower deck of Tiger Stadium, around 415 feet from home plate. But he was just warming up. The second was struck in the ninth inning with two on base off of former World Series hero, right-hander Larry Sherry, helping the Red Sox to a rare victory, and a 7–0 shutout. This one was of a magnitude approaching the blast he had hit off of Whitey Ford, except that this one left the ballpark in a hurry, said former teammate Jim Gosger who was perched on second base at the time. It was another spectacular shot that left the 3,965 fans, and the players, speechless. "I remember *that* one," shouted Gosger with enormous enthusiasm as if the game had just concluded. "There's only one other kid that I ever saw that was probably as strong as him [Scott], and that was Reggie Jackson ... the ball jumped off their bat," said an admiring Gosger.[18] Hall of Famer Rick Ferrell, then a Tigers vice president, commented that Scott had wonderful bat control, and "that's why I'm already convinced he's no flash in the pan."[19]

The ball narrowly missed going onto the roof of Tiger Stadium and completely out of the ballpark in left field toward the power alley, finally settling halfway up in the upper deck, a drive of about 510 feet and some 90 feet above field level when it landed. Left fielder Gates Brown, who was watching the ball from field level and positioned closer to its trajectory, said he was certain the ball was leaving the park, and felt that it would have hit the roof had there been any kind of wind that day. In fact it barely missed striking the rooftop and then dropped just inches below its overhang, sailing deep into the upper rows of empty seats.[20]

Following the game, a Detroit Tigers club official stated that he knew of only two ballplayers who had hit home runs on the roof of Tiger Stadium. One was by Harmon Killebrew that was pulled much closer to the left-field foul line (340 feet) than Scott's drive, hitting the roof and bounding out of the park; the other was by Tiger pitcher Jim Tobin in 1945.

Then it was on to Minnesota and spacious Metropolitan Stadium for a four-game series. Scott was becoming the toast of the town wherever he went and in hot pursuit by sportswriters as they contended with each other to get a look — and a first-hand story — at this new baseball sensation, who was now being compared to a young Babe Ruth and Jimmie Foxx. Twins players were asking a multitude of questions right along with the reporters as they anticipated the young slugger's arrival. Scott once again was lacing batting practice pitching to the outer reaches of the ball field as players, fans and the media gaped at his display of power. One such long-distance drive that got them buzzing struck the facing of the second-deck left-field bleachers that even Harmon Killebrew, who was asked by sportswriters to comment about, had not accomplished. Killebrew remembered hitting the "batter's eye" for a 475-foot drive to center field at the Met, but never the second deck. Scott's drive was the first ball ever to strike the second deck, and would have traveled more than 500 feet had it not struck its facing.

Scott then proceeded to stroke two homers in the first game of the series, neither tape measures but well hit, and went 3-for-4 in the second as the Red Sox lost both. Awe-struck Red Sox pitching coach Sal Maglie claimed that Scott's first seven homers had traveled more than 3000 feet, a prodigious feat by anyone's standards. In the final game, the second of a doubleheader, he was confronted by Minnesota's wily two-time All-Star pitcher, Jim Mudcat Grant, who had the previous year posted a 21–7 record, and stood at the peak of his career.

In the eighth inning with Yastrzemski on first base and two out, Scott leaned into a Grant fastball and launched it high and deep to dead center field over the eight-foot-high wire fence, landing 443 feet from home plate. Partisan fans notwithstanding, it was what they came to see, and he didn't disappoint them, crushing another "tater" out of sight. The Red Sox had won both ends of the doubleheader and their first wins at Metropolitan Stadium in almost two years.

Later on Scott recounted his before-game conversation with Grant, who phoned him the night before to invite him to his place for dinner. Scott explained that he refused the invitation, stating he would see him on the mound, whereupon Grant admonished him with a promise that he was going to throw him nothing but smoke. Grant expressed the view years later in an interview that because of his power, George Scott could quickly change the momentum of a game with one swing of the bat, and was looked upon by American League pitchers apprehensively. "We were always careful with George ... he hit balls [pitched] away from him very hard and very far. We feared George Scott," said Grant.[21]

Detroit pitcher Hank Aguirre, after seeing Scott's prodigious home runs in Tiger Stadium, announced somewhat abstrusely that "he [Scott] could be the best Negro player ever to come into the league." It was said, perhaps, as a well-meaning effort to reconcile some of the racial wrongs of baseball's past, but it was a superficial gesture, patronizing at best; the old racial lines were still in evidence with that utterance that merely defined the times.[22]

Not only did the young slugger wear out Minnesota pitching with his bat by clubbing three home runs, a double and triple, and hitting safely in seven of his sixteen plate appearances, but he also performed magnificently in the field by displaying sure handedness with the glove, a strong arm and, remarkable nimbleness afoot for a big man. Yastrzemski marveled later that he had never seen such agility for a man of Scott's size.

It was becoming delightfully easy for him, this game of major league baseball, the rookie slugger thought. Wielding a 36-ounce bat, the longest and heaviest on the club, he was becoming a regular menace to American League pitchers and their speedball deliveries, and he loved every minute of it. In fact young George Scott from Greenville, Mississippi, his confidence building, was beginning to feel quite invincible. By mid–May he was among the American League batting leaders, hitting .332, trailing only Tony Oliva and Frank Robinson; he led the pack with 10 home runs and 3 triples.

With complete confidence that his rookie sensation had no clear weaknesses, manager Billy Herman, in a moment of indecorum, answered questions of a zealous press about Scott, suggesting that moving the ball around the strike zone, or making him chase bad pitches might possibly work to get him out. Otherwise, as Red Sox pitching coach Sal Maglie and opponents were to speculate, only the infamous beanball may be the ultimate solution for him. It appeared that young Scott was being put on notice. As Scott left the friendly environs of Minnesota's Metropolitan Stadium he joined his teammates for a trip to Kansas City, brimming with confidence. If perhaps displaying even a bit of cockiness, he asked: "Nice place to hit. What's Kansas City like?"[23]

In spite of the young phenom's heroics the Red Sox continued to struggle and were mired at the bottom of the league with an unimpressive 7–17 record. Their pitching was falling apart; at one low point manager Herman asked in a moment of desperation, "I wonder if Scotty can pitch?" that was overheard by the press crew. The joke among the media and Red Sox followers was to keep as close to the opposition as possible and then let George Scott hit the ball into tomorrow; he usually did.

May 13, 1966, Anaheim Stadium — Tony Conigliaro (left), the American League's 1965 home run leader, and George Scott, the rookie sensation who had already hit 10 homers, peer over the new Anaheim Stadium, home of the California Angels. Scott hit his 11th homer there on May 14, extending his hitting streak to 14 games (courtesy of Boston Public Library).

The Red Sox were swept in Kansas City, losing two of the three games in extra innings, much to the consternation of manager Herman who was about to crack down on some of his players for curfew violations, and a team malaise the players themselves had declared in the spring would never be repeated. Scott, meanwhile, continued his assault on American League pitchers going 7-for-14 in the three-game series. He was finally stopped in California on May 15, going hitless after hitting safely in 14 straight games, in which he batted .377 with 23 hits, 17 RBIs, and stroked 8 home runs.

In the California series Scott began to slump for the first time since his major league debut a month earlier. Whether coincidental or not, but appearing to follow up on Billy Herman's earlier unfortunate outspoken assumptions that "bad pitches" might do the trick, pitchers were beginning to throw him curve balls and off-speed stuff outside of the strike zone that the young slugger was reaching and flailing for. In a stretch of ten games he uncharacteristically mustered but six base hits, batting a meager .167 with one home run. He whiffed

12 times, culminating in his first-ever ejection on May 22 when he slammed his helmet onto home plate after a questionable third-strike call. He was clearly frustrated with himself and disappointed for his behavior; but he later quipped that umpire Bill Haller, who did the ejecting, had not made his life any easier by making some rather unusual and most peculiar calls on him in other games, as well.

The buzz going around baseball circles and in the media was that George Scott had "gone fishin'," nibbling at "bait" outside of the strike zone. Defending him was an unlikely source, American League president Joe Cronin, whose reputation with the Red Sox was a longstanding refusal to racially integrate, reputedly had passed on signing Willie Mays, and was one of the infamous Red Sox men behind the 1945 sham "tryout" of Jackie Robinson. Cronin spoke up in Scott's defense by generously comparing him with Ted Williams and Walt Dropo as rookies. Each had to learn the strike zone, he said, and Dropo (AL Rookie of the Year in 1950), much like Scott, "was a swinger — not a waiter." Cronin expounded on Scott's good hitting range, strength and remarkable agility as qualities that would keep him in the major leagues, maybe "he could even be a great one," he said.[24]

But the 22-year-old rookie continued to flounder at the plate — and, as long as he did, American League pitchers continued to serve him junk — over the next 19 games, hitting only two home runs on 14 base hits, and batting an anemic .203; his strikeouts began to mount with 17 during the stretch. American League pitchers seemed to have him figured out. "Arthur Fiedler [Boston Pops Orchestra conductor] could get him out on a curve ball," wrote *Boston Globe* columnist Ray Fitzgerald.

Scott caught fire again on June 11 stroking his 14th home run in Baltimore, and five more after that, but one of them, hit against Cleveland on June 13, was officially cancelled due to a rain-shortened contest. During the stretch he batted .382 with 14 RBIs, but the sorry state of the Red Sox continued with the team losing 10 of the 14 games. Sportswriter Bud Collins mocked that the Boston club was on a pace for achieving the rare "Grand Slum": finishing last in the standings, batting, fielding and pitching.

On June 14, in a controversial trade that alarmed Boston fans, the Red Sox unceremoniously dispensed with their starting pitcher, Earl Wilson, along with utility outfielder Joe Christopher, for Detroit outfielder Don Demeter. Herman was purportedly looking for more outfield depth and, where Demeter could also play first base, possibly subbing for Scott. Boston fans were not pleased. There seemed to be far more to the trade with the sudden and inexplicable departure of Wilson, a bonafide major league pitcher who once pitched a no-hitter, than was being explained by the Red Sox, whose pitching was the worst of the ten American League clubs.

The majority choice of his peers based on his early-season performance, by a vote of 141 to 62 over Detroit's Norm Cash, Scott was named the starting first baseman for the 37th All-Star Game, the only rookie named to either the American or National League squads. He was the fourth Red Sox rookie to achieve the honor, in addition to Walter Dropo (1950), Frank Malzone (1957) and Don Schwall (1961). Despite being in esteemed company, tied for third in the league with Mickey Mantle with 18 home runs going into the Summer Classic, George was once again not hitting in the remaining games leading up to the All-Star Game, with no home runs and only seven RBIs, and his batting average had dropped to .279. He was slumping badly; a season of paradox for Scott after beginning so sensationally. Meanwhile the Red Sox were mired in last place.

Seizing on the unfortunate timing of Scott's precipitous nosedive and adding a sour note of his own, New York's outspoken three-time All-Star first baseman Joe Pepitone, who placed third in the 1966 All-Star balloting, having hit 19 home runs himself, boasted that he was a better ballplayer than either Scott or Cash and deserved to be the starting All-Star first baseman. Pepitone was a Gold Glove first basemen the previous year and won it again in 1966 and 1969.

July 12 in St. Louis was a scorcher, registering 103 degrees in the city, and, at one point, 123 degrees on the field of the new Busch Stadium where the All-Star Game was played. The heat was a distraction with many fans leaving their seats seeking the shade under the stadium, and some were carried to first aid stations due to heat prostration. But as George Scott put it years later remembering the occasion, "I thought it was an ice box. It was just the thrill of being there my rookie year. I didn't worry about no heat," he quipped.[25] Scott played six innings of the contest, the only member of the Red Sox to participate (Yastrzemski sat out), and was 0-for-2 against future Hall of Famers Sandy Koufax and Jim Bunning, popping out both times. The National League won the game by a 2–1 score in 10 innings.

When the regular season reconvened, the American League hurlers continued to bait George with tantalizing pitches off the plate, and he continued to struggle. "I kept looking for fastballs and they wouldn't give them to me," lamented Scott during a later interview. "What happened is the pitchers and teams adjusted on me, and I didn't adjust to them; I didn't adjust quick enough," Scott went on to say, explaining that he wasn't even sure if he was capable of making the adjustment then, as he saw very few curves and change-ups during his minor league seasons. He was confident he could hit any fastball thrown him, but so were American League pitchers.[26]

Billy Herman, whose team was floundering in last place, felt that he might have to bench Scott because of his mid-year batting swoon. But he was reluctant to do it because Scott's fielding was arguably the best on the team, one bright spot on an otherwise poorly performing ball club; they needed him to stabilize an infield that was the worst in the league.

Irked over his team's failure to perform well on a western road trip, and with George Scott going 0-for-7 in a two-game split with Kansas City, and not hitting a home run since June 19, Herman announced he would bench the first baseman on July 19 upon their return trip to Fenway against the Angels. George's batting average had dropped to .270, and he had fallen off the hitting leaderboards.

Herman had no idea what was percolating back in Boston in reaction to his decision as the team took a long and tiring two-day train trip from Kansas City, because of an airline strike, arriving in Boston mid-afternoon of the 19th. Herman's announcement on Scott appeared to galvanize the Hub city into action, reverberating amid mixed cries of fans and media as they came to the young Red Sox slugger's defense. It was a remarkable display of support, a rallying cry, for the young slugger whom Red Sox loyalists had adopted as their new bright light and a perfect reason, if not an excuse, to show support for a team that seemed to be going nowhere. They loved the big rookie, who showed them so much energy and determination to do well, this aberration from Mississippi, unassuming, so likeable, and who could hit a baseball out of sight.

They actually had a name for it: they called it "The George Scott Case," as reported in a July 25 *Boston Globe* feature article. Scott was devastated at the news, the fans were confused, and Herman's back was to the wall to justify benching his rookie sensation. It made the local sports headlines for days. Speculation was rampant whether George was being treated fairly. Scott complained that both Red Sox management and even his teammates had largely turned their backs on him, a circumstance that when it occurred, he alluded to in later years as being possibly racially inspired. As he expressed to *Boston Globe* reporter Clif Keane, "I get the feeling that nobody wants me around here, and I can't say why. I try hard, I'm a rookie. I got lots to learn about this game. I don't make people think I know it all." Keane, revealing a bias of his own, reasoned that Scott being young and from the South, didn't have much going for him in a Northern city like Boston and also knew little about human nature, "since he comes from a part of the country where they don't acquire it: Greenville, Mississippi."[27]

Contrary to Herman's avowal that he would sit Scott down, he was in the lineup for the opening game with the Angels on the 19th. Before the game was cancelled and the Red Sox players were standing around in their dugout, Scott began to openly question himself why he wasn't hitting well, which was overheard by Red Sox pitching coach Sal Maglie. Maglie seized the moment, going into great detail with Scott on being selective about major league pitching, and to look for his pitch. Scott responded comically, though he meant it in perfect seriousness. "I'll tell you something," said Scott. "I just go up there looking for the baseball."[28]

Years later in an interview, Scott blamed the Boston media as main culprits for being underrated, he felt, because of their manner of not crediting him when he thought it was due, but were the "first ones" to seize and embellish on his mistakes and momentary lapses when he was not doing well. "I don't know why, but I think I do," said an anguished Scott, remembering his days in Boston dealing with the sports writing fraternity there, stated with a perceived awareness that some of them may have been racially intolerant. "Well they weren't used to me," said Scott disdainfully of the Boston press, who for the first time had to deal with a black Red Sox starter.[29]

While waiting for a plane out of Boston, Carl Yastrzemski made an odd appeal to the Boston press, asking them if they might help Scott in some way. Jerry Nason of the *Boston Globe* responded, humorously, with a remedial help column written on Scott's behalf, in his article "How to Cure Scott's Sl — p," citing a need for a "borrowed bat" to remedy his misfortunes. Nason listed several players, among them Willie Mays and Joe Adcock, who resolved their batting slumps by borrowing another's bat, usually of someone who was hitting poorly.

Manager Herman had stated, defensively, that it was up to George himself to straighten his situation out, not the manager or the Red Sox. He accused Scott of refusing to listen to advice. *Boston Globe* reporter Harold Kaese rose to Scott's defense in his July 20 column, by pointing out Red Sox past history when scouts and the front office often did not see eye-to-eye over the development and handling of their young players. The Red Sox were quick to point their finger at the scouts alleging they were not getting good prospects; the scouts were just as quick to point out that it wasn't their fault, but the fault of the Red Sox for not developing their players properly. Kaese even questioned whether the Red Sox were capable of developing young players like Scott. Having once been referred to as a successor to Babe Ruth, and with a sense that prospect was now in jeopardy, the enormous flock of Red Sox fans directed their angst over Scott squarely at Herman and the Red Sox.

George Scott was not about to languish over his poor performance. He took action, watched film, made adjustments to his stance, and talked often to teammate Lenny Green who helped him the most. He began to emerge from his slump; on July 29 he hit his 19th home run, and the next day his 20th. But he struggled again for several games until manager Herman decided, after a doubleheader against Detroit when George was 1-for-7, to bench him. But Don Demeter, who was to replace him, came up lame with a bad back and Scott was reinserted into the lineup, playing against the Indians on August 8. In a fog-shrouded game Scott hit his 21st home run, a game-winner, so Herman kept him at first base.

He then struck for two more home runs in that series including a monstrous clout, one of the longest ever hit in the park, estimated at 500 feet that came a few feet from clearing the back wall of the center-field bleachers. Larry

Claflin of the *Boston Herald* wrote that the blast off Scott's bat struck the top of the wall about thirty feet to the right of the center-field flag pole, and stunned the Fenway crowd as it nearly left the park. The *Boston Globe* captured the astonished gaze of center fielder Vic Davalillo as he looked up, in a trance, at where the ball landed. Scott launched his 24th against Blue Moon Odom of the Kansas City Athletics, another of his many tape-measure shots that landed on the roof of a building across the street from Fenway's left-field wall.

Although he was to continue to hit for power — an attribute favored by the Red Sox — he did not hit for the high average that had accompanied his slugging during the first half of the season. He finished the year with 27 home runs and 90 RBIs, but batted a mere .245. The team finished in ninth place, only one-half game better than the last-place New York Yankees.

On September 9, 1966, Billy Herman was fired by the Red Sox. He lacked the "pedagogic drive" to instruct and lead a team, especially young players, reported *Boston Globe* scribe Harold Kaese. The Red Sox wasted little time in replacing Herman with little-known Dick Williams — described as a tough no-nonsense type of leader — of the club's Triple-A Toronto affiliate, hiring him on September 28.

During the offseason, major league players, coaches and managers honored George Scott with the most votes (532) in their selections for the 8th annual Topps All-Star Rookie Team, ranked the best of both leagues. Tommie Agee — who would later cop the Rookie of the Year award — placed second with 517 votes.

Scott was an early season favorite for American League Rookie of the Year, and may have won the award (Scott finished third in the writers' poll, tied with Dave Johnson of Baltimore, behind Tommie Agee of the White Sox, and Jim Nash of the A's, who finished second) had he not had such a disappointing second half. Some people, including George Scott himself, felt that Scott may have won it if he had not been playing for a 9th place club. "I

Another home run for the big first baseman, George Scott (courtesy of Boston Public Library).

thought I had a better year than Tommie Agee had," said Scott in answer to an interview question. "I just think the reason that I did not get more votes was because the White Sox was going for the playoffs, and the Red Sox finished last," he said.[30] Scott finished in second place, again to Agee, in an independent players' poll held only days before.

Among Scott's accomplishments, he was a leading fielder, the only rookie listed among veteran first basemen, with a .991 percentage. He was also among the leaders in game-winning "clutch" hitting, described then as base hits producing either tie-breaking or come-from-behind winning runs. He set an American League record for a rookie of 13 intentional walks.[31] He played in all 162 games, more than any other Red Sox player, in spite of a few very close moments when he was all but written out of the lineup by a perplexed Billy Herman.[32]

The Boston baseball writers elected George Scott and Joe Foy as co-winners of the Harry Agganis Memorial Award as Red Sox rookies of the year.

Pete Runnels, Red Sox acting manager who took up the reins upon the departure of Billy Herman, voiced a precautionary note that Scott needed to learn the strike zone to become the complete ballplayer he had confidence he would become, respectfully comparing him to future Hall of Famer Harmon Killebrew. "They've got the same strength and stroke. Killer used to swing hard, too," said Runnels, referring to Scott's outsized swing.[33]

Refining his overall baseball skills and playing winning baseball, to be certain, would not be without its challenges for young George Scott playing for a manager like Dick Williams, who sportswriter Will McDonough once described as a man of complex moods and personality with a quick and explosive temper. He was to be an anomaly to Scott quite unlike any baseball manager he had ever seen.

6

An Irascible Sort

We didn't tell it to the press, but we agreed with them. We couldn't understand why Williams was playing Scott in the outfield. Boomer was a great athlete, but he wasn't an outfielder. In fact, he went on to play 2,034 games in the major leagues and not one of them was in the outfield.— Rico Petrocelli[1]

With the Herman era ended, the Red Sox and George Scott were about to experience a transformation of managers they never could have imagined — from an uncommunicative sort in Billy Herman to an ultimate autocrat in Dick Williams. Carl Yastrzemski, whom Herman steered into a captainship that Yaz never wanted, and who had once attempted to persuade a reluctant Tom Yawkey — who loved his celebrated outfielder — to trade him to the hated Yankees after several clashes with the star, soon realized his life with Williams would fare no better. In fact Williams, who was once a Red Sox teammate of Yastrzemski's, ridiculed the Boston standout, claiming he ran the bases like Jackie Robinson, but "only you get caught," ranted the consummate heckler. It was a sign of things to come.

Having wrapped up his playing career as a utility man with Mike Higgins' country-club Red Sox in 1963–1964, then managing the club's Triple-A Toronto club to two consecutive International League championships, Dick Williams wasn't about to inherit a team that he couldn't control; he had a clear understanding about this with the Red Sox brass right from the beginning. Williams was from the old school of Dodger training (1951–1956) which preached fundamentals, and he was bound to instill this form of baseball prowess into his young players, no matter what he had to do, how extreme, or how tough he had to be to achieve the desired results. In 1965 this unorthodox method of dealing with subordinates became confrontational when Mickey Sinks, one of his Toronto players, punched him in the eye after resenting the pugnacious young manager's brazen and wholly insensitive manner. Boston sportswriters began to speculate, days before Williams was actually named the new manager,

86

what might happen if he took such a line with Red Sox players, but then reasoned it could be just what they needed.

Williams took the team by storm; untested, sarcastic, and fiery by nature he was unlike any recent Red Sox skipper Boston fans had ever laid eyes on. He was loath to the idea of working in a "country club" atmosphere, a Red Sox anomaly; he would dismantle it at once. It was a rude awakening to Red Sox players, especially the veterans, reaching shock proportions for second-year man George Scott whose next few years under Williams were turbulent and, at times, disheartening for the young slugger.

Barely had the ink dried on Williams' Red Sox contract, he began posturing and making noises around town that he would be, unquestionably, the boss. On September 29, the day after he was hired, he announced to an eager but somewhat spellbound Boston press that he was eliminating the captain role established by Herman. There would only be one "chief," he declared, and that would be Dick Williams. It had the effect of a direct assault on Yastrzemski who held the position, though reluctantly, all through the 1966 season. The announcement stunned the city; it seemed almost in the form of a violation of something sacred. Tom Yawkey's fair-haired boy, Boston's darling, and the only real star to come along since Ted Williams retired was suddenly being manhandled by this brash new and completely inexperienced upstart from Toronto who was already an enigma to them. Williams insisted there would be no player meetings of any kind without his coaches and himself present. "This team won't quit on me," he said, stating that he wouldn't be a baby-sitter, but if someone needed a "boot," he would be happy to deliver the remindful blow, a prophesy of things to come. Williams was accustomed to saying, "We'll win more games than we lose," a safe retort to reporter's questioning on his team's chances, but a promise, nevertheless, he planned to keep.

There was considerable talk in the offseason between the Red Sox brass and Dick Williams that no one was an untouchable, including Carl Yastrzemski, if the right trade offer was made to them that might improve the team. Furthermore Williams strongly suggested that Scott did not have a foothold on first base, and that it was up for grabs between George and Tony Horton in Winter Haven. He was very high on Horton, even claiming that the heretofore mistake-prone infielder, who appeared so unsteady in the field the first part of 1966, was a "good fielder" and wished to give him every chance he could to win the position. He knew that Scott was more versatile, could play third base and possibly other positions, while Horton, he felt, was capable of only one — first base — but he wanted Horton's prolific bat in the lineup. Williams made the point many times, frequently posturing with the press about first base asserting that Horton would be given "every opportunity" to strip the job from George Scott. What was astounding about that statement was that it sounded more like it was Horton's post to lose than to win, enough so that the media began to speculate that this might be the new skipper's way of using psychology on Scott.

Moreover, acting more like a plant put there by Williams, Boston's Florida Instructional League coach Mace Brown spoke freely to the sportswriters about the first base situation, remarking that "George will have to find somewhere else to play," he said, because "Tony Horton will chase George Scott off that first base bag next spring." The challenge was on; the tone and climate was set for spring training, far more likely to be a "boot camp" than a training ground.[2]

Amidst all the hoopla taking place in Boston over Dick Williams and his frequent threats to rearrange the team, his demand for discipline, and the fact that no one, but no one was immune to trade, George Scott had shuffled off to the winter ball circuit. The Red Sox were anxious for him to get a close look at good major league level pitching and to cut down on his strikeouts (152 in '66). But George's arrival there was fraught with complications. The Managuan club alleged to have had a working agreement with the Red Sox for Scott to return to Nicaragua, where he had been a batting star for the champion Boer team the previous winter. George, in fact, had pulled off a coup of sorts by convincing the Boer club to accede to his salary demand of $1,700 a month, that was the largest salary ever paid a Nicaraguan League ballplayer.[3] The deal therefore was struck and their general manager, Isaac Gorn, made the announcement to the league of the Red Sox player's acquisition.

It was to be short-lived, however, when Scott suddenly reversed direction by leaving the Boer club for more money and greener pastures in Venezuela, joining the Aragua Tigers and Red Sox teammate Jim Lonborg. Boer GM Gorn put forth an immediate protest to baseball commissioner William Eckert, alleging that the Red Sox were behind the maneuver in violation of their agreement with the team. The complaint lacked substance, no more than a cry of foul, and never got off the ground.

What followed a few months later, however, was a more formal complaint of "illicit financial arrangements" raised by the Licey club of the Dominican League, protesting that the Venezuelan League teams were raiding the other Latin-American teams of imported players who had already come to terms with them, but then left for a better offer in Venezuela. They pointed to an "agreement" between Organized Baseball and the four Latin Leagues that limited a player's salary to a maximum of $1,000 plus $350 in expenses; in effect the Venezuelan clubs, it was alleged, were paying their imported players additional money under the table. This got the Venezuelan government's attention since "some players," it was alleged, who were participating in this scheme — whether they even knew it was a scheme — were not paying taxes on that money.

George Scott was the "most prominent" of these players according to a December 10, 1966, article in *The Sporting News*. Scott, it was believed, was pulling down the highest salary of $2,000 per month. He was named among twelve or so imported players to be probed by the government. But due to a very loose and unregulated arrangement between the Latin winter leagues and Organized Baseball, this complaint had little support, so the investigation fell flat.[4]

Venezuela was a hot-bed of hostility at the time, inspired by Cuban dictator Fidel Castro, who instigated communist terrorist activity and anti–American sentiment throughout the country. His support for guerrilla warfare and armed revolutionary tactics produced violence that occasionally reached the walls of ballparks, and was even felt inside the stadiums by the presence of heavily armed soldiers who stood guard with their machine guns in each team's dugout. Terrorist activity broke out in December when Venezuelan president Raul Leoni, fearing an overthrow of the government, suspended all constitutional agreements; tourists hurriedly left the country. Violence reached the doorstep of major league baseball that spring when the Twins and Athletics played an exhibition game in Caracas; student rioting erupted around the stadium and in the ensuing gunfight two students and a policeman were wounded.

Whether Scott decided to leave because of the unrest and violence is unclear, but he did say that it was troubling: "They were at war and there was shooting going on all around us," he growled, at a level that expressed the gravity of the times. He, along with Red Sox teammate Jim Lonborg, quit the team at the end of December due to fatigue from playing so much, he said, and explained further that his mother was ill and he needed to be home. He had been playing baseball almost steadily since he was signed by the Red Sox out of high school in 1962. Scott was batting .276 with 6 home runs when he left winter ball, third behind the leaders.

Joe Foy, who had been playing in Puerto Rico, began to get quite a ribbing from teammates when they heard Dick Williams posturing that Scott was at risk of losing his first base job with the Red Sox. Future Hall of Famer Earl Weaver, then a manager in the Baltimore farm system, who was doing some managing in Puerto Rico, believed he knew the value of George Scott to the Boston club. Always the jester Weaver began to needle Foy unmercifully, asserting that if Tony Horton were to win the position then Foy was the more expendable, and would lose his job outright to Scott. "There goes your job," ranted the pesky Weaver. It was a friendly exchange between the two, but a frank reminder that George Scott's overall value to the team, especially his extraordinary fielding skills, appeared indisputable to the astute baseball eye.

But Dick Williams was not of a mind to share Weaver's view, announcing at the traditional manager's press conference held at Fenway Park in January that the only certainty about the '67 season was that Carl Yastrzemski, Tony Conigliaro, Rico Petrocelli and Joe Foy would be in the opening day lineup. Scott's name was noticeably absent in his discussion of Red Sox starters. When asked by a reporter about the obvious omission of George Scott, Williams snapped back that Scott's club record-setting 152 strikeouts in '66 was a factor in his thinking. He later appeared to change direction by remarking that with Scott's fielding skills, he could play anywhere, but Horton was only capable of the one position, first base. Playing the outfield or, astonishingly, even second base was a possibility for Scott, declared the new manager, revealing that he planned to give Horton, his protégé from Toronto, more than a fair shot at the first base slot, but also implying, surprisingly, his unwillingness to lose a good glove like Scott's. There was skepticism among the sports scribes whether Williams was being honest with them. They were not happy with the manager's apparent disparate treatment of Scott, whom they saw as a solid first baseman and believed deserved more respect than Williams appeared willing to give.

Curiously, Williams pointed out on more than one occasion in his discourse with the sportswriters that he had no plans for employing "Gestapo tactics," which by the mere mention of the words was unsettling. The Boston writers realized that they were about to experience a Red Sox spring camp quite unlike any they had witnessed before. It was certain to be newsworthy, with a leading storyline being George Scott's survival at the hands of Dick Williams in the battle to be Boston's first sacker.

On January 26 at the Boston baseball writers dinner, a drama unfolded. At the moment that toastmaster Curt Gowdy was handing George Scott his Red Sox Rookie of the Year trophy, a distinction he shared with Joe Foy, and explaining that Foy, who was playing ball in Puerto Rico, couldn't make the dinner, Foy walked in. His sudden unexpected arrival couldn't have been more symbolic — he was not about to play second fiddle to Scott again.

In Dick Williams' autobiography *No More Mr. Nice Guy*, written with Bill Plaschke in 1990, he recounted his early days as manager in Toronto, the importance of winning, and the rage he felt for ballplayers that appeared indifferent and showed a lackluster attitude toward the game. Losing was anathema to him, and if he sensed it in a player "I'd damn near kill him," declared an irascible Williams. Losses that were based on judgment errors or casual play "made me a deadly weapon," he said. Elaborating on how he defined himself as a manager and the reason behind his being such a fierce competitor, was an underlying "hate" factor. Williams reasoned that athletes give 100 percent because "they hate something," not because they want something. If what it took to win was instilling some hate into the equation of baseball, the Dick Williams way, then that's what he instilled in his players, in whichever manner it had to be executed, to get the "best" performance from them. For those who appeared nonchalant in their ways and tolerant of losing, for them he gave another reason to hate: It was "Me," he said. Armed with this philosophy as a man to be reckoned with, Dick Williams was about to embark on his first major league role as a manager with the Red Sox. It was to be a year to remember.[5]

Williams' method of dealing with his players was one of resolute toughness. He seemed impervious to ballplayers' feelings, having no favorites, treating everyone the same, "miserably," said one player. But as hard as he was on the team, he was especially tough on young Scott.[6] For reasons not always clear to his teammates, Scott was the object of Williams' derisiveness, bordering on racial implications, some cautiously reasoned; he became a poster child for the scorned in the face of acerbic behavior and sometimes contentious leadership. But Scott, surprisingly, would later credit the inexorable Williams for using this technique to motivate and get the best from him, an attribute that held no greater importance to Scott who was desirous of being "a great major league ballplayer like Willie Mays."[7] There was no mistaking that this encounter between the two, whatever its composition, was to become a love-hate relationship of a most peculiar kind.

Peter Golenbock carried the theme in his book *Red Sox Nation*, in his description of Dick Williams: "He was a bastard every day, giving no ground, accepting nothing less than perfection, and railing at the players and in the press when he didn't get it."[8] This was his method of inspiring his players, to shed them of old habits of complacency — the "country club" phenomenon — in pursuit of his most inalterable goal: winning.

During the offseason, Scott declared publicly that he was going to have to adjust and no longer be a "dumb hitter," by not chasing bad pitches as he did the latter half of the '66 season. He was intent on reducing his strikeouts and going with the pitch to right field instead of trying to pull the ball toward Fenway's inviting left-field wall. Will McDonough of the *Boston Globe* summed up the state of George Scott this way: "Successful teams — winners — are built around super-stars. Scott can be a super-star. He has all the credentials — the necessary tools. His problem, and he knows it, is to get his mind in the same orbit with his body."[9] An ungentle critique, perhaps, but tinged with elements of prophecy, as well, that would eventually play out in one form or another throughout his baseball career.

The Red Sox opened their spring camp on February 25 amid a group of notable and familiar former Red Sox stars who assembled in Winter Haven along with the team to work with the young ball club. Appointed special coaches for the spring campaign were Dominic DiMaggio, Frank Malzone, Bobby Doerr and the inimitable Ted Williams. In a humorous moment Dick Williams, in a self-effacing manner, dubbed himself "the wrong Williams," as if to acknowledge that he knew he was standing in the shadow of a Boston legend. But it was spoken purely for humor; he had no plans to stand in anyone's shadow for very long, which the Red Sox elder statesman, Ted, was about to find out.

Upon their arrival in Winter Haven each player was informed by the new manager that maintaining a proper "weight" and the need for good conditioning would be an important part of his spring program as well as in the regular

George Scott getting ready to start 1967 spring training in Winter Haven in preparation for his second year with the Red Sox (courtesy of Boston Red Sox).

season. He had developed a chart listing each player's desired playing weight, threatening if they failed to attain the goal by the end of spring training that they might remain behind when the team went north. He was a stickler about this, insisting that to win he needed more than just good hitters. He needed well-conditioned athletes, who could steal bases, take the extra base, hit-and-run, run-and-hit, execute squeeze plays, have more speed in the field, and have the stamina to play extra-inning games, and win them. It was a Dodger brand

Spring 1967, Winter Haven — The consummate teacher Dick Williams, rookie Red Sox manager, "teaching" finer points of playing first base to pupil George Scott, who would win his first of eight Gold Gloves in 1967 (courtesy of *Boston Herald*).

of baseball that Williams cut his teeth on — "National League baseball" style — small ball, which involved surprise and stealth. Home runs would take care of themselves he would say.

In addition to this Williams required his pitchers to play volleyball (also position players when nothing formal was scheduled) when they weren't pitching to gain footwork skills, which drew a surprise response from the sportswriters and the ire of their vice president and special instructor, Ted Williams, who charged this was more like a "boot camp" than anything resembling baseball. The "wrong Williams" did not hesitate to openly admonish Ted when he was seen kibitzing with his players, having pulled them aside from their volleyball games for informal dissertations on hitting, when they should have been sticking with the program. Vexed and embarrassed by the affronts of Dick

Williams an upset Ted Williams walked out of camp a few days later; though Williams — the "wrong Williams" — later admitted that he had alienated the "greatest star ever," it had no effect on him; it was his club and he would run it one way only — his way.

To the chagrin of Red Sox management, including a supportive Dick Williams, holdout Tony Horton was the last to report to spring camp, arriving there on March 2, eight days before they were to play their first exhibition game. Clif Keane of the *Globe*, suspecting along with his fellow Boston sportswriters that Horton was a Tom Yawkey favorite, commented in his March 3 column that it would not be unexpected to see Horton entering camp with the Red Sox owner hovering over him. Dick O'Connell had phoned the reluctant ballplayer to work out a deal, possibly at the urging of Yawkey. Red Sox VP Haywood Sullivan spoke disparagingly of the maneuver, stating that he wouldn't have chased the youngster.

Horton worked out for about 15 minutes at first base with an infield group, and then his rival George Scott took over. The contrast in their fielding skills was immediate, with Scott putting on a remarkable display of glove work around the bag that made Horton look overmatched. In the final spring intrasquad game Scott put on a splendid performance, described as "absolutely marvelous" by the *Globe*, exhibiting full range at the position, including scooping up bad throws, and taking three hits away from a frustrated Reggie Smith that made Scott look indispensable. Tony Horton also played well that day but appeared "20 percent as graceful" as Scott, wrote the *Globe*. Horton would have to do extraordinary things with his bat to remove Scott from first base, and it was not likely to happen, the sportswriters conjectured.[10]

Much like the kind of team Dick Williams was hoping for in his young Red Sox, Boston encountered the scratch-and-run offense of the Chicago White Sox in their opening spring season exhibition game, on March 10, at venerable Payne Park in Sarasota, losing 8–3. George Scott was in the starting lineup at first base and went 1-for-4, a single. The White Sox put on a baseball clinic of bunting, including a two-out squeeze play, base stealing, and even some power, in a three-run homer by Tommie Agee. The Red Sox, meanwhile, gave the appearance of the 1966 team by making four errors. It was a bad start for Dick Williams, who abhorred losing, especially through mistakes. He could hardly contain his wrath.

On March 12 Bobby Doerr, adding to the warmth felt in camp for Tony Horton, bolstered Dick Williams' view of him by announcing that he rated Horton in the same class as future Hall of Famer Harmon Killebrew; "put me on record as saying that," he insisted. Athletics manager Alvin Dark, dropping hints before their game with Boston was adamant that he would like either one of them on his team, Horton or Scott. In that game, won by Boston 6–4, Williams' "maiden victory," he declared, Horton couldn't handle a pick-off throw from the pitcher, allowing a run to score, and the runner, who had raced to third on the misplay, eventually scored also.

In the March 13 spring home-opener game against the A's, won by Boston, 8–3, Scott started at third base with Horton at first. George was slick, making some good plays, impressing the Winter Haven crowd; but Horton continued his fielding struggles. In the first inning, with a man on first, he misplayed a line drive hit down the line that glanced off his glove, leading to a run. The batter was given a two-base hit. "He should have had it," said Williams, but in the same breath crowed, "But watch him hit."[11] There were cries from the stands: "Scott would have had it," a fan sneered. Another exclaimed that not only would George have caught it, he would have turned it into a double play. Scott later lined an opposite-field two-run single, highlighting a five-run inning, showing a good batting eye with better bat control than in '66. Horton went 0-for-4. The *Globe* headlined Ray Fitzgerald's article in the March 13 issue: "Horton Wobbly at 1b; Could Be Last Chance."

There was divided opinion among the Red Sox players on the Horton-Scott spring drama. Some, like Doerr, felt he'd be a big star and others were sharply opposed to the idea, thinking it was outrageous Horton was even being given a chance to compete with arguably one of the finest first basemen in all of baseball. They already had the nucleus of a good infield in Petrocelli, Foy and Scott and juggling them around just to find a spot for a one-dimensional player appeared risky, especially when the team for the first time, in a long time, had a decent infield. This was leading into a scoop that the newspaper critics began to follow assiduously.

Both players were struggling at the plate through the first six spring games, Scott batting .222 (four singles), and Horton worse at .158. Williams wasted no time instituting his verbal attacks on Scott, deriding him whenever it seemed the opportunity arose. Former Red Sox broadcaster Ken Coleman in his book *The Impossible Dream Remembered*, a tribute to the '67 Red Sox, recounted that following the March 15 game against the Yankees a reporter asked Williams if Scott had shown improvement laying off low pitches. Williams' response was a sarcastic one, at first saying there was slight improvement, but sneering, "At least he waits until they come up to his shins."[12]

The next day in St. Petersburg against the Mets George exploded with the bat, a symbolic retort to Williams' verbal slam, knocking out four base hits including a long home run in a slugfest the Red Sox won, 23–18. They scored 10 runs in the ninth inning to come from behind. As one press box savant described the fiasco, it was a true test of two ninth-place ball clubs. No one gave Boston much of a chance of winning anything in 1967, including the notable Las Vegas gambler and oddsmaker Jimmy "the Greek" Snyder who rated the Sox 100-to-1 odds to win the AL pennant.

Dick Williams continued to shuffle players around the infield and outfield,

Sluggers Carl Yastrzemski, George Scott and Tony Conigliaro in Winter Haven in 1967, the season of the Impossible Dream (courtesy of Boston Red Sox).

some of it because of injuries, but also to understand the versatility of some members of his team. This was especially true of his experiment with George Scott who had been shifted between first base and third, and their new rookie sensation Reggie Smith, normally an outfielder, who was about to be inserted at second base because of injuries to three of his second sackers. Horton, however, remained a spring-time fixture at first.

Bolstered by a strong 3-for-4 hitting performance by Tony Horton on March 20 against the Pirates, including a long home run, the Red Sox skipper made a move that shook the sanity of the Boston media and hometown followers, when, the next day, he inexplicably assigned Scott to play the outfield. It was a moment of madness, some scribes wrote, but clearly Williams was attempting to find room for Horton because of his bat, feeling he had no other place for him in the field. But it was also cause for some to pause over the strange maneuver, since Horton was originally an outfielder with greater experience in the position than Scott, who had played the outfield only one time in the minor leagues.

His third position in less than two weeks of the spring season, Scott started in right field against the Philadelphia Phillies on March 21. Scott was irate, having had a strong game of his own two days before, going 3-for-4 against the Tigers, but was now being relegated to unfamiliar territory — the outfield. He complained to coach Popowski, arguing that it would "louse up" his hitting. After the lineup was posted and as Scott was heading out to right field, he looked to the manager and blurted, "I'm not a right fielder." Williams was just as quick with his response, shouting back at him, "You are today."[13] The new Red Sox outfielder played five innings in right, and then was shifted to left field in the sixth to replace Yastrzemski. He made a good play behind Horton when a ball was hit down the line past the first baseman into right field, quickly getting to the ball and preventing a double with a strong throw. He also made a good play in left field by charging the ball like an infielder and throwing to third base to prevent the runner from taking an extra base. But Scott was still seething. "I hate it. I'm a first baseman," he insisted.[14]

Trade talk was stirring just before the Phillies game with Red Sox names swirling around spring training sites and major league cities, even including Carl Yastrzemski going to Cleveland. Williams' unwillingness to give the sportswriters what they felt was a reasonable explanation for Scott's recent outfield assignment raised their suspicions that he and the Red Sox had trade in mind. The juggling of Scott at different positions was merely for the benefit of the scouts to look him over, to showcase him, they reasoned. John Ahern of the *Globe* wrote on March 22 that among the few players whom he believed would not be traded, boldly including Scott, was Tony Horton. Ahern puzzled over the idea that someone as inept as Horton could be considered an untouchable; "Somebody in high places likes him very much," wrote the scribe scornfully.

On March 23, George Scott's 23rd birthday, the *Globe* sports page featured this headline: "Red Sox Willing to Trade Scott." They had put him on waivers along with pitchers Jose Santiago and Gary Roggenburk. Adding to the humiliation he must have felt from this surprising maneuver, on the same day Williams put Scott back in right field against the Dodgers, a position he groused about and wanted no part of. It was a horrible day for the young ballplayer, and one that got the attention of fans all the way to Boston. In the sixth inning, with two men on base, John Kennedy hit a slicing line drive to right that Scott misjudged; running at top speed he ran face first into the cinderblock wall. He staggered, and then fell unconscious for a full minute while trainer Buddy LeRoux worked to revive him. Three runs scored as Kennedy circled the bases for an inside-the-park home run. Remarkably Scott suffered only a concussion and a bruised right wrist that kept him out of action for five days and the next three games. "He moved the wall from 330 feet to 332," said second baseman Mike Andrews, in jest, joking about the impact of a big man like Scott crashing into an immovable wall.[15] "We all thought he was dead," exclaimed a bewildered Rico Petrocelli, who, among several of the Red Sox players, couldn't understand why the manager was sticking with his idea of playing Scott in right field when he was a natural first baseman.[16]

Ray Fitzgerald of the *Globe* wrote mockingly on March 25 that "vigilante committees" were organizing and preparing to ride south to string Williams up to the nearest banyan tree. One scout charged that it was the "damnedest experiment" he had ever heard of, noting that the young sophomore sensation, batting .389 at the time and one of the finest first basemen on the diamond, was lucky to be alive. But the youthful manager stood his ground when challenged by the writers, saying he would remove Scott from right field, moving him over to left field instead, where he alleged "it's easier to judge a fly." Williams, obviously angry from the questioning by reporters on whether he felt the left-field wall was as hard as the one in right, added that Scott "won't feel so strange" out there. Summing up the game, Williams, showing little sensitivity to the situation or his young injured ballplayer, went to the immediate defense of his rookie pitcher Billy Rohr, who was throwing a shutout before the wall incident. Putting it bluntly "Rohr threw a six-inning shutout," he shouted, placing blame on Scott for not catching the ball.

Just how bizarre the entire matter was — with the first year manager insisting on continuing to play him in the outfield after the incident — provoked general disapproval from numerous baseball people. One scout scoffed at him for choosing to keep him in the outfield in spite of his near-serious accident there, describing it as pure "foolishness." Critics pointed to the manager's apparent display of favoritism toward his Toronto players: "All organizations have fair-haired boys, the Red Sox more than most. Horton may be one," wrote the *Globe*'s Harold Kaese in his March 24 column, which was headlined: "Is Yawkey Back of Scott Shift?" Kaese presented a forceful argument for management's involvement in "The Horton problem," explaining that as early as the spring of 1966 under Billy Herman, when Herman selected George Scott over Tony Horton, that his number was up with the Red Sox. And, of course, there was the matter of Dick O'Connell signing Horton, the holdout, going over VP Haywood Sullivan to do it, "probably on Yawkey's advice," said Kaese. The "ugly suspicion," he said, was that Yawkey was behind it, wanting Horton on his team. All this he found troubling.[17]

Nothing came of the waiver initiative by the Red Sox. The *Globe*'s Will McDonough speculated in his March 23 article that it could have been a ploy to arouse Scott as a means to motivate him — to "shake up a player," he wrote — where he had been resisting Williams' whimsically appearing tactics. But of course this seemed highly irregular behavior when the young second-year star was batting nearly .400 at the time and fielding magnificently, perhaps the best on the team.

On March 24 the *Globe*'s John Ahern wrote a critique on manager Dick

The starting Red Sox infield in 1967. Left to right: Joe Foy, Rico Petrocelli, Mike Andrews, and George Scott (courtesy of Boston Red Sox).

Williams, summing up his view that "other than the handling of Scott," a view that he shared with others, Williams was shaping up to be a good manager; but he was failing miserably with George Scott. Harold Kaese of the *Globe* followed with a two-part series on Williams on March 26–27 stating that "the signs are good" for him to become a successful manager. He bottomed the second of the two articles with his question of Williams on what the manager planned to do with Scott if Tony Horton were to make the team. Williams was evasive and answered, "I'll wait until it happens, and then I'll have an answer for you. Time will tell."[18]

The *Globe*'s Ray Fitzgerald wrote a satirical column on March 25 on the Williams-Scott spring saga that became the talk of the Grapefruit League: "Should Scott Try Catching?" On the one hand it was written in defense of Williams, but it was also a bit of a spoof on what Fitzgerald called the "current carnival," the new-look Red Sox under Williams, with the juggling of player personnel — especially George Scott — by the new manager like it was a circus act. He emphasized the absurdity of trying Scott in the outfield when they already had a strong outfield. So why not a catcher, he asked, where the Red Sox needed help? "Saints preserve us," he concluded, realizing how ludicrous this would be.

On March 28, with two weeks to go before the opening of the '67 season,

Dick Williams announced he was going to stop his experimenting and establish a set lineup, picking Scott over Tony Horton at first base. Horton was batting only .213 at the time and had shown little in the field. Scott was excited; his manager had turned the pressure off. What pleased him more, however, was his awareness that he was finally acquiring good batting habits by not swinging at bad pitches. He was not "fishing" like before. Never was it more evident than in the April 2 game when he twice worked 3–2 counts against Mets relief ace Jack Fisher, a familiar situation that all too often turned into a strikeout. But this time he went with the pitch, the first time stroking a double, and the second time, catching up with a sidearm slider over the outside of the plate that Scott hit 410 feet over the right-center-field fence. The 23-year-old slugger was jubilant. After the game he exclaimed to teammates and reporters, "This is going to be a helluva year. You watch old George."[19] He was in his comfort zone, in a groove, and never more ready.

In the remaining ten spring games, Scott batted .394 with a home run and 6 RBIs, and in his last three games struck for 8 base hits in 14 at-bats, finishing the spring season with a batting average of .346 on 27 base hits, including 2 home runs and 11 RBIs. A glaring statistic that caught everyone's attention was that he struck out only 9 times in 78 at-bats, a strikeout ratio decidedly improved from the prior year.[20]

7

That Glorious Summer

I don't know if they were afraid of George, I don't know. He was a strapping guy, 210 lbs, a great build and all of that — just a great athlete. If they were afraid [of him], or they maybe used him as a scapegoat, I don't know. But he's right; they seemed to always come out in public about it. Most guys — if they did that now, guys would be screaming. Guys would be like Manny [Ramirez], you know want to get out of here. Like I said he never did that. — Rico Petrocelli[1]

A revamped band of youthful Red Sox and their 37-year-old rookie manager, fresh from a moderately successful spring exhibition season by winning 14 of 27 games — aberrant performance for a heretofore losing ball club — were about to march into Boston. They had a very young team, with a starting lineup averaging less than 24 years of age, the youngest in major league baseball, and a brand new brash no-nonsense skipper in Dick Williams, who boldly promised that "we'll win more than we'll lose." This stirred local sportswriters who found little in the Red Sox to write about since Ted Williams retired in 1960, but it had no affect on an apathetic Boston fan base whose only memory in recent years was of a team with a reputation for losing.

Bud Collins of the *Globe* had added his two cents of pessimism, a safe bet he was right, early in the spring season by writing about the new Red Sox manager and his team: "He won't ask them to do anything hard right away, like catching a baseball. They will have trouble doing that in August, and to ask it of them now would only break their spirits before the season has begun."[2] Though Williams was nothing like Collins described, working his men harder than anyone could remember, the press could not be pacified into thinking that this could be a breakout year for the Red Sox, or that Dick Williams would be any different than the ineffective managers before him once the season was underway.

Celebrated journalistic institutions like *Baseball Yearbook* and *The Sporting News* predicted the Red Sox to finish between seventh and ninth place, and

Baseball Guidebook could see them no better than dead last. The *Boston Globe*, however, raised their sights for the team, figuring a sixth-place finish, but cautioned the public the prediction was made with a sense of cautious optimism. Only the *Globe*'s Will McDonough agreed with Dick Williams that they would ascend to the first division, predicting a fifth-place finish. Bill Nowlin, writing about news coverage of the '67 Red Sox in the book *The 1967 Impossible Dream Red Sox*, wrote of the absurdity of anyone predicting a pennant for the team at the time, calling it nothing more than a "preposterous notion." Who would have thought such an occurrence was even plausible given the history of the team. Not since 1958 had a Red Sox team finished above .500, when, led by a contingency of good hitters in Ted Williams, Pete Runnels, Jackie Jensen and Frank Malzone, they placed third in an eight-team American League.

April 11, Opening Day at venerable Fenway Park, was an inhospitable 35 degrees with wind gusts of 40 mph, and had to be cancelled. The next day was not much better with a temperature of 46 degrees, but the wind had died down some. The Red Sox played before a meager 8,324 robust fans, not the kind of welcome they had hoped for, evoking shades of previous years when few fans sat in the stands. Jim Lonborg won his first outing of the season in a 5–4 victory over the White Sox. Rico Petrocelli was the game's star with a home run on three hits, and four RBIs. Scott got a single in two official trips to the plate, stole a base, and scored. But it was nearly a ho-hum affair, just another Opening Day game for a team of historical ineffectualness, not expected to go anywhere. But it was rookie manager — and future Hall of Famer — Dick Williams' first major league victory, one of 1,571 major league wins he would compile over a span of 21 years with six different teams, including four pennants and two World Series titles.

The next day the Red Sox were back to their customary ways, losing 8–5 to Chicago before a scanty crowd of 3,607, committing five errors in the process and yielding five unearned runs. The skeptics were restored to prominence, sounding their déjà vu rants that this was just another Red Sox team destined for more of the same: ignominy.

On April 14 Williams started his young rookie pitcher, left-hander Billy Rohr, against the New York Yankees in Yankee Stadium. Williams was high on the youngster who had performed well for him in Toronto, and decently in spring training. It was a phenomenal start for the 21-year old southpaw, mixed with a little luck, when Joe Foy picked up a deflected line drive off Rohr's leg in the sixth, preserving a no-hitter, but then losing it when Elston Howard, with two out in the bottom of the ninth, laced a single to right. It was the only base hit the Yankees would get in a 3–0 shutout win for Rohr. George Scott was 0-for-4, striking out twice.

The Red Sox had a 2-3 record by the fifth game of the young season and Dick Williams was not happy. They had a combined 34 team strikeouts, committing 9 errors in the field that led to 7 unearned runs. Scott was reverting back to old habits at the plate again reaching for pitches outside the strike zone, and it got the attention of the skipper. Leaning on the batting cage before the April 16 game against the Yankees, a marathon 18-inning contest won by the Yankees, 7–6, Williams fumed. He was watching Scott taking his batting practice swings, then muttered for all in his immediate vicinity to hear that "talking to George is like talking to cement," adding that he wouldn't listen to the advice of his coaches. Scott must have heard it, too, as he performed poorly that day, hitting safely only once in eight at-bats, making an error, striking out three times and stranding runners in scoring position four times. In one at-bat he missed a take sign on a 3–0 count and grounded out harmlessly with a runner in scoring position, incurring a $50 fine imposed on him by Williams.

He had dug a hole for himself by that performance in New York giving Williams the leverage he needed to bench the young slugger. But the manner in which Williams singularly attacked Scott, openly insulting his intelligence, was received with mixed reaction by the press. Some applauded the manager for being so "candid," while most were critical, feeling that kind of comment was best left in the locker room. It was another of many such verbal assaults directed at George Scott by Williams while with the Red Sox that became legendary in baseball circles. But this vitriolic remark seemed overreaching, if not abusive; it contained all the earmarks of being deeply personal and extraordinarily unfair.

The Red Sox flew to Chicago that night for one game with the White Sox scheduled for April 18. Monday, the 17th, was an off day. Dick Williams ordered a mandatory workout for the afternoon. Some were excused after playing the nearly six-hour game on Sunday, but not Scott, Joe Foy and Jose Tartabull. They were mandated to show up at the ballpark for practice even though all three had played the full 18 innings the day before.

Williams was upset with some of his players, including Scott, for being overweight. He had made it clear in spring training that he would not tolerate players who exceeded the weight standards he had mapped out for them. This, too, was an element that entered into his decision to bench Scott, whom he targeted along with Foy. The *Washington Post* reported with amusement that "Boston Red Sox manager Dick Williams has established a weightwatchers club and set a high membership fee," noting the "charter member" to be Foy with George Scott joining him a day later.[3]

"George is going to the bench," said an irritated Dick Williams, adding that at that pace he was destined to fan 300 times. He was hitting .182 without an RBI, and "he's not that red hot in the field either," he said (Scott had made one error).[4] Things were definitely not going well for Scott. While walking through the Sheraton Chicago Hotel lobby, he was spotted by Williams in a casual sweater instead of the dress jacket Williams required of his players when on the road. Williams swiftly laid into him, ordering the ballplayer to return to his room and to put on a jacket at once. Later in the day Williams called Scott up to his hotel room to inform him he was being benched, and that Horton would take over first base the next day. There's little doubt that Scott also received a severe tongue-lashing, Dick Williams style, for not laying off bad pitches.

There was a "singular toughness of mind," wrote Larry Claflin of the *Boston Herald-Traveler* when it came to Williams' dealings with Scott, quite unlike anything that matched how he associated with his other ballplayers.

Although he was tough with everyone, there was something about George Scott that brought out the worst in Williams. Scott spoke indignantly of Williams during a 2006 interview, when, in response to an initial question about the former manager, he blurted: "He didn't like me and I didn't like him ... Dick Williams and I don't really get along today."[5] Feelings of resentment, the kind he felt for the Red Sox skipper, do not die easily. But he mellowed as he talked, giving Williams what credit he deserved for creating a winning team, explaining that he came up in the Brooklyn Dodgers system and brought the Red Sox a certain "Dodger swagger," a level of confidence they had never known before. "Dick Williams molded us into a team

Dubbed the "Boomer" because of his tape-measure home run blasts, George Scott intimidated pitchers with his powerful bat, culminating in a 14-year major league career in which he hit 271 "taters" (courtesy of Boston Red Sox).

... he taught us how to win," said Scott politely. But his resentment for Williams because of his treatment of Scott and other player personnel, is still palpable.

Interviewed in 2008, former Red Sox teammate and friend Rico Petrocelli remembered the public criticism and verbal assaults brought by Williams against Scott. "It seemed at times he just didn't like George," said Petrocelli, adding that Williams was unusually "tough on him," expressed in a manner highlighting the unpleasantness and uniqueness of these encounters. He was especially displeased with Williams' tactic of making Scott's punishments a public matter. "They could have called him into the office," said Petrocelli, like they did with other players, and kept the matter quiet, but instead "they seemed to always come out in public about it [with George]."[6]

As he had promised Williams benched Scott on April 18 and replaced him with Tony Horton. Scott muttered to himself that he needed to pull himself together, vowing he would win the job back, and when he did, he was going to stay. The Sox won the next three out of five games, but the fielding was sloppy, especially Tony Horton who dropped two foul ball pop flies that he should easily have caught. Williams missed Scott's glove work and presence around first base, his sure-handedness, and his uncanny athletic ability of scooping up bad throws and turning them into outs. Williams inserted Scott back into the starting lineup on April 25 in a game against Washington, won by the Red Sox 9–3. George was 2-for-4, both singles.

Living up to his personal pledge, Scott caught fire with that start against the Senators, stroking 6 base hits in three games at a .462 pace, and by mid–May he had hit safely in 19 of 25 games in which he played, including a ten-game hitting streak, raising his average to .286 along with 13 RBIs. In a May 14 Mother's Day doubleheader against the Detroit Tigers at Fenway, George rapped out four base hits, one a game-winner, made several solid infield defensive plays on errant throws and a riveting heads-up athleticism style of play in the field that all but sent the Fenway crowd into a state of delirium. In the fifth inning of the first game with the score tied, 3–3, two outs, and the bases loaded, Scott came up against Tiger ace Dennis McLain. He worked the pitcher to a full count. It was a dramatic moment, a classic one in baseball: all three runners were now in motion as McLain began his windup and delivered a fastball on the outside part of the plate. Instead of trying to pull the ball, George went with the pitch by rapping it into the right-field corner beyond Al Kaline's reach, the ball ricocheting around the outfield wall's perimeter ahead of the scrambling veteran outfielder. Scott reached third base with a standup triple while all three baserunners crossed the plate, putting the Sox into a lead they never relinquished. The Fenway crowd went into frenzy. Kaline told Scott later on that he was more than confused about how to position himself in the outfield against him anymore because of his recent trend of hitting to right.

But the highlight of the twin bill was, in a manner, not so much Scott's three-bagger that cleared the bases in the first game, but his sensational inning-ending defensive play in the second contest, also a bases-loaded situation that brought the baseball-savvy Fenway crowd to its feet. The Tigers' Don Wert, a right-handed hitter, slammed a ball on the ground directly at Scott whose first instinct was to pivot and throw to second base to begin a double play. But the ball was hit with spin and such a short high-hop that it handcuffed the big Mississippian, forcing him to catch the ball in an awkward position, belt-high. He didn't hesitate. He knew instinctively his play was at home plate, that a throw to second was risky, and he quickly unleashed an overhand peg to the catcher, Mike Ryan, to get the runner coming in from third. Scott's throw was perfect, setting up Ryan for a return throw to Scott who had retreated back to first base to get the batter. It was a brilliant maneuver, performed skillfully, and the 16,436 fans roared their approval.

Boston won both ends of the doubleheader, moving them from eighth place into a virtual tie for third place, and knocking Detroit out of first. The game reached a milestone as well, as it broke a 62-year-old record for extra-base hits in a twin bill, with 28, one more than was set by the Red Sox and Athletics in 1905. But it was Scott's defensive work that was drawing attention of the league and media, and, from manager Williams' standpoint, a necessary ingredient in an infield that was still struggling. They were the worst of the lot, ranked at the bottom of the American League in fielding, having committed 37 errors, by May 16.

Ray Fitzgerald, a third-year sports columnist for the *Boston Globe*, wrote a featured article on Scott entitled "Slugger Scott Turns Artist," reflecting on the fancy glove work of the young slugger, raising his fielding to prominence, whereas previously the emphasis was on his hitting. "The way the man conducts himself around first has become the most exciting part of his game. He saves more errors than a bank examiner," wrote the scribe. Fitzgerald proceeded to describe the essence of Scott's infield acumen and his overall value to the team through his extraordinary ability to overcome the miscues, turning certain errors by his teammates into outs, and making it look easy in the process by scooping up balls in the dirt thrown by infielders or errant pick-off tosses by pitchers, or when he "dives for flighty flings and tags the runner with routine regularity."[7] These serpentine-like acrobatics preventing errors and opponent runs in this way are not typically found in official box scores or on score sheets. There was certain elegance, a natural grace about him stationed there on the first base bag he regularly patrolled. It appeared he owned the position, providing full confidence in the men around him, because George was going to catch the ball they felt, no matter what they threw at him.

This was the stuff of championship-caliber baseball, saving games through defensive prowess that otherwise would be lost. Dick Williams knew it. It was fundamental to his philosophy of winning, it was Dodger ball, the ability to do the little things to win games, and to be able to field a good game most especially. Nick Cafardo in his book *Boston Red Sox: Yesterday and Today* quotes Carl Yastrzemski, who paid homage to George Scott: "In my 23 years in baseball I have never seen a better defensive player. I have never seen a player with the instincts of Scotty." Having come from a man who spent so many years in the company of outstanding ballplayers, many of them future Hall of Famers, and who was a seven-time Gold-Glover himself, it was quite a tribute. It was the "ultimate compliment," said George Scott when he learned what Yaz had to say about him, speaking on the respect he held for the Red Sox Hall of Famer.[8]

Reminders of a history of baseball's and Red Sox racial intolerance suddenly surfaced on May 16 when Jackie Robinson, major league baseball's first black player, spoke at a Lynn, Massachusetts, NAACP dinner that made the front page of the *Boston Globe*. Deeply resentful of Tom Yawkey, whom he once accused of being a bigot and the man behind the team's racial indiscretions, Robinson side-stepped making further accusations against the Red Sox owner but maintained his verbal assault on the institution of baseball, describing it as no better than it was "in the 19th century." Baseball at the player level was fine, he said, because black men could be found on every major league roster. But "the people who run it are not," he declared, because blacks were still being barred from front-office jobs and endorsement opportunities that were still being awarded to whites. This would have implications later on for George Scott, who much later found he was being ignored by major league baseball in his attempts to get back into the game, especially by the Red Sox.[9]

Two of Scott's Red Sox teammates were beginning to put together some fabulous numbers of their own. Carl Yastrzemski, not accustomed to hitting for power before '67 (95 home runs in six seasons), had already stroked 7 homers, many of them of the pulled variety, by May 17. Lonborg was 3–1 and on his way to a Cy Young Award season. Scott said of Yastrzemski after the left-fielder had clouted 5 homers in four consecutive games, "That guy is gonna have some kind of year." It was surely an understatement, as Yastrzemski had the most sensational season of his long career, culminating in a MVP and Triple Crown, the last man to achieve the Triple Crown in major league baseball.

In a May 21 Sunday doubleheader against Cleveland Scott came to bat against Sonny Siebert, a right-handed pitcher with good stuff, who had been throwing a shutout; it ended with Yastrzemski's two-run triple in the eighth inning. With Yaz the tying run on third Cleveland manager Joe Adcock went to the mound to talk with Siebert on how to pitch to the dangerous Scott, a patsy for the low-and-away pitch the previous year. "Throw him tough stuff away," said Adcock, a recipe for a certain out, he thought. But this time the result was different. George popped one out of the park, a high soaring blast, a "mammoth home run into the bleachers," wrote Larry Claflin, that sailed well over the Red Sox bullpen in right-center field. It was on a pitch that Adcock had called for, low and outside. It was Scott's third home run, a game winner, and the second of two that were stroked to the right side of the diamond. "Few right-hand hitters do that," remarked sportswriter Harold Kaese of the *Globe*, mentioning Ken Harrelson and Dick Stuart, the last to do it in 1963. In the second game George hammered a Sam McDowell pitch for a long single off Fenway's left-field wall, vital to a Red Sox go-ahead rally and a lead they never relinquished. He was stroking the ball well, going with the pitch, and showing polish in the field that provoked talk among writers of George's All-Star level of play. Scott showcased a hitting and fielding display in the final eight games of their 10-game homestand, which the Red Sox split with their opponents. He rapped 12 base hits, 6 for extra-bases, including three triples and a home run, and 8 RBIs. For that he won "Player of the Week" honors. Gabe Paul, the Indians general manager, applauded the young ballplayer: "Scott is so young and has so much talent. You look at him now and realize how little actual experience he has, and then you marvel at what he can become in a couple of years — one of the greatest players in the game — if he continues to improve."[10]

Dick Williams was pleased with his troops, who had demonstrated come-from-behind ability in all four games against Cleveland, winning three of them, and eight comeback victories in the month of May. On May 24 in Detroit Jim Lonborg pitched a 1–0 shutout in what his manager described as "the greatest game I have ever seen pitched in my life."[11] But it was done with the help of George Scott who made a fabulous play behind him to preserve the win and the shutout. The second-place Tigers threatened in the seventh inning by loading the bases with only one out. Williams played the infield back looking for a double play, but the batter, McAuliffe, didn't hit into many twin killings. He smacked a hard-hit ground ball directly at Scott who, sensing a double play unlikely, immediately threw a long strike to home, getting the lead runner, Norm Cash, lumbering in from third. Lonborg got the next batter on a foul popup ending the inning. Rico Petrocelli talked about the significance of that play and of Scott later on in his book about the 1967 team, describing George as "one of the greatest instinctive ballplayers I ever played with."[12]

George had a bad day on May 26 against the Orioles, fanning four times. His ignominious reward for this was a quick benching by Williams who sat him down the very next day, replacing him with Tony Horton. But the Sox were abysmal, losing to Baltimore 10–0, four runs unearned on five infield errors, two of them by Horton. It most likely was the coup de grace for Horton. Scott pinch-hit and got a single, and he was back at his familiar station at first base the following day. By the end of the month Scott was batting a respectable .271 and the team was in third place, 4½ games behind league-leader Detroit.

They were barely on the track predicted by Williams of winning more than they'd lose, with a 22–20 record.

After winning four straight on June 1 they ran into Minnesota's ace hurler, '64 Cy Young recipient, Dean Chance, who was to win 20 games in 1967. He shut down the Red Sox on five scattered base hits and 10 strikeouts. George Scott later remarked that Chance was one of the toughest pitchers he faced in the big leagues. "He dominated me pretty good," said Scott, showing annoyance that anyone could intimidate him. He went on to explain with amusement that he ran into Chance in an elevator getting close enough for him to see that "his eyes were crossed. I remember telling a couple of guys at the ballpark, 'do you realize that this guy's throwing that hard and he can't see?'" Scott's memory about having little success against Chance was accurate; of the pitchers he faced 50 or more times (Chance among them), his lifetime batting average against Chance was .143. Only against future Hall of Famer Gaylord Perry did he fare worse, with a lifetime batting average of .043.[13]

On June 2 the Red Sox, at the direction of Williams, arranged a trade with the White Sox for utility infielder Jerry Adair, in exchange for their veteran reliever Don McMahon and a minor leaguer. Adair was hitting only .204 at the time but he had good hands, could play just about anywhere, and was a contact-type hitter, a tough out in baseball parlance; besides, he was a known entity to Dick Williams, who was a teammate of Adair's in Baltimore. Williams viewed him as the "ultimate professional." He would turn out to be a most valuable acquisition for the Red Sox and play a key role with the '67 team.

The Red Sox were still weak in pitching — as a team they were tied for sixth statistically with Minnesota — and needed a first-rate hurler if they were going to be contenders in the American League. GM Dick O'Connell pulled off a slick trade with Cleveland two days after the Adair deal, acquiring a solid performer in right-handed All-Star pitcher Gary Bell by dangling their $80,000 bonus baby, Tony Horton, in front of them, along with utility outfielder Don Demeter. Horton was hitting .308 at the time. The Red Sox until then were reluctant to part with Horton in whom they had a sizable financial stake and, of equal importance, also appeared to enjoy the personal support of owner Tom Yawkey. Williams and O'Connell, however, could see no future for Horton in Boston convinced he would never measure up to the talent of their slick fielder and sometime slugger, George Scott. Bell was excited about the deal, realizing that he was to be inserted immediately into the Red Sox starting rotation, but also knowing that he would not have to contend with George Scott, who in two seasons had rapped him for six hits, five of them home runs, including one the day before the trade (Bell knocked Scott down on the first pitch; he then clouted Bell's fourth pitch out of the park). Scott meanwhile was ebullient about the trade; he knew now that first base belonged only to him.

On June 14, a Fenway doubleheader, the Red Sox encountered the first-place Chicago White Sox and their prickly manager, Eddie Stanky. Stanky had enraged the Boston fan base and Carl Yastrzemski eight days earlier in Chicago when, speaking to the Chicago press, he insulted the Red Sox star by calling him a moody ballplayer and "an all-star from the neck down." Stanky's affront of their star player provoked the Boston fans to action, and they turned out as much to heap their personal abuse upon the Chicago manager as they may have been interested in the outcome of an important series. Stanky could not have realized what his untimely remarks would lead to in Boston, but the aroused Boston crowd went after him with a vengeance, tossing him everything from boos to batteries. Stanky was ejected in the second game after making several appearances to argue calls, to the delight of the Fenway crowd. He later asserted that he would sue if he and his wife didn't receive better protection in Boston.

In the final game of the series on June 15, perhaps the defining moment of the season, the Red Sox upstaged Stanky and his White Sox with a sensational comeback that made Beantown into believers. The White Sox went ahead in the top of the 11th inning when Ken Berry singled home Walter "No Neck" Williams who had doubled. It would have been more than one run had not George Scott, who had crept in from first anticipating a bunt, made a sensational diving play flinging himself in front of Don Buford's smash, on a full swing, that was hit like a bullet down the first base line; Scott miraculously came up with the ball and promptly tagged Buford running up the line as the crowd went wild. Tony Conigliaro then clouted a walk-off homer in the bottom of the inning sending the crowd into complete bedlam. The following day a *Boston Globe* headline applied the phrase "The Impossible Dream," from the hit Broadway musical *Man of La Mancha,* about a Spanish knight who refuses to be defeated, to describe the Red Sox, which quickly caught on with their following.

Scott hit a home run in each game of the doubleheader, his seventh and eighth, with five hits overall in the three-game series, as the Red Sox won two. In a span of 15 games between June 2 and June 15 Scott hit safely in all but one, with 23 base hits to his credit and 5 home runs, raising his batting average to .301. He was in a groove both with the bat and the glove; but especially his glove.

The city stirred again on June 21 when the Red Sox-Yankees game erupted into a brawl at Yankee Stadium. It was another memorable moment among several that year, this incident actually getting the full attention of the press and making the front page of the *Globe*; a photo of the mêlée with a caption describing the 5-minute free-for-all. Jim Lonborg was pitching, seeking his ninth victory, and the second for the Sox of a two-game series. In what appeared to be a clear effort of retaliation for their previous night's loss, Tillotson, the Yankees' rookie right-hander, went after Joe Foy in the second inning with a head-high fastball, beaning the Red Sox third baseman. Foy had broken up the prior night's game, a scoreless pitching duel, with a dramatic fifth-inning grand slam. Lonborg immediately evened the score by hitting Tillotson on his first time at bat the next inning, and the brawl was on. He later calmly admitted he intentionally threw at the Yankees pitcher "to protect my teammates." George Scott added to the Yankee hurler's frustrations by smacking his 10th homer in the top of the third, as the Red Sox went on to win, 8–1. It was the game that "bonded" the Red Sox players into a cohesive unit, the kind of team synergy manager Dick Williams was looking for, said Rico Petrocelli years later.

"I don't aim; I just throw," said Joe Foy laughingly over how he confidently fielded his position, and could take chances, when the sure-handed George Scott was patrolling first base. He was in the clubhouse speaking to the press after a close 3–2 Red Sox win in Minnesota the night of June 27. Gary Waslewski had been pitching a stellar one-run game yielding just three hits; but in the sixth he walked two batters and, with one out, faced a tough foe in Harmon Killebrew. He got the "Killer" to hit the ball on the ground right at Foy, who dashed to third for the force on a fleet-footed Cesar Tovar, and, off-balance, fired to Scott. The throw was low and in the dirt, a certain error that would keep the rally alive, and bring up a dangerous Tony Oliva who had already homered. But Scott deftly flashed his glove and snared the errant throw on the first bounce to end the inning in a terrific display of athleticism. Rico Petrocelli mentioned in his book that Foy was not the best defensive third baseman, and that Scott saved him from numerous errors. "But Foy wasn't alone in that respect; Boomer saved a lot of errors for everyone in the infield," wrote Petrocelli in tribute to Scott.[14]

The Red Sox were catching some lucky breaks as well based on the misfortunes of contending teams: 1966 World Series victors and preseason favorite to win it all in the American League, the Baltimore Orioles, were having an injury-plagued season and lodged well down in the standings. Their perennial All-Star, '66 AL Triple Crown winner and MVP, Frank Robinson, was playing with nagging injuries, principally a brain concussion he received on June 27 in a baseline collision with Chicago's Al Weis; starting pitchers Dave McNally and Jim Palmer were also hurt, and their first baseman Boog Powell was having a poor season. At the same time Detroit's Al Kaline was injured the same day as Frank Robinson in a freak accident, breaking a bone in his hand when he slammed his bat in disgust in a rare fit of anger after striking out. Both Kaline and Robinson were key factors to their teams' chances for a pennant now dampened by injury; both were out of action for a full month. Chicago second baseman Weis meanwhile was out for the balance of the season with a knee injury. This was boding well for the Red Sox. With the most talented team, the Orioles, seemingly out of the running, the remaining contenders, Chicago, Minnesota, Boston, Detroit, and California, fairly evenly matched, were now in a dogfight; the pennant appeared up for grabs, quite astonishingly among five teams.

Talk was circulating around Boston and in the press that George Scott was perhaps deserving of better treatment by his peers who ranked him fourth-best in their balloting for the AL All-Star first base slot, behind Harmon Killebrew, Don Mincher and Mickey Mantle, the latter a sentimental favorite. Killebrew's powerful bat spoke volumes in the voting; he was batting a mere .259 going into the All-Star break, but had hit a robust 22 home runs and was the RBI leader with 62. Mincher was batting .295 with 15 homers while Mantle was at .260 with 16 homers. Mincher and Mantle both made the team. Scott was just behind the AL leaders for average, batting .288 with 10 homers; but

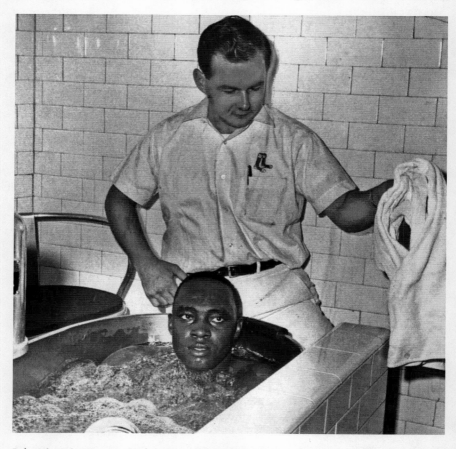

July 26, 1967, Fenway Park — George Scott receives a welcoming whirlpool treatment from Red Sox trainer Buddy LeRoux after a thrilling 9–6 come-from-behind victory over the California Angels. Scott was 2-for-4, hitting a triple and home run. Boston was on a roll winning 11 of their last 12 games (courtesy of *Boston Herald*).

he was far-and-away the best defensive first baseman of the bunch, saving errors and opponent runs with his slick fielding. Harold Kaese of the *Globe,* in his June 28 column, was persuasive in outlining his reasons why Scott should have been an All-Star, distinguishing him from his rivals based upon his superior defensive skills, calling him "the best fielding first baseman in the American League, the best in baseball, and one of the best in the game's history." His defensive play that year, Kaese described as "larcenous" and so very distinguishable from the others, at a palpable level. So why then didn't Scott get the nod by All-Star game manager Hank Bauer, questioned Kaese.[15] It was unques-

Celebrating July 27 win over the California Angels. Left to right: George Scott, Joe Foy, Jose Tartabull and Tony Conigliaro; behind left to right: Rico Petrocelli and Eddie Popowski (courtesy of *Boston Herald*).

tionably about the "bat," not the glove he concluded; but without question the most complete well-rounded first baseman, without peers, was George Scott, reasoned Kaese.

Boston had lost five of the last six games before the All-Star break, and was perched in fifth place six games behind the front-running White Sox. On July 15 the Red Sox picked up journeyman outfielder-first baseman Norm Siebern, in his eleventh major league season, from the San Francisco Giants. The purpose behind his acquisition, it was announced, was for pinch-hitting. But once again it appeared to be another strategic move by skipper Dick Williams to keep George Scott off balance, as a July 17 *Globe* sports front-page feature article was headlined: "Sox Will Use Siebern at 1B." The writer, Harold Kaese, who had listened to Williams explain the situation in the clubhouse, summed it up: "Insurance and pressure are they key words — insurance at first base, pressure on George Scott."[16] On the same day the Red Sox pulled off a triple play, their second in two years, in beating Baltimore, 5–1. It was their second straight victory of a consecutive ten they would win (first time since 1951), including the last six on the road that startled the press to action, and sent the fans into euphoria. The Sox were now 52–40 and within one-half game of first place. Pennant fever was taking over Boston.

The team was greeted by from 5,000 to 10,000 deliriously excited fans who turned out at Logan Airport the night of July 23 to welcome their heroes home. They surrounded the team bus the players had boarded after their plane was diverted to a nearby hangar in an attempt to avoid the mob. But the players decided to acknowledge the madding crowd, anyway, ordering the driver to take them to the gate so they could walk into the terminal in normal fashion and among the welcoming crowd; it was nothing short of chaos. The *Boston Record-American* ran a front-page headline on Tuesday morning proclaiming: "Whole Town Ga-Ga Over Sox." The club had seized the city, hook-line-and-sinker.

Boston's ten consecutive victories, the last six on the road, startled the local press who were so accustomed to writing about losing that they found themselves bewildered over what to say about a winner. This confusion extended to the team as well, finding it unable to cope with the ticket demand. Telephone communications nearly broke down, and then a public relations miscue led the fans to believe the first game of the homestand was sold out; only 21,527 attended the first game which the Sox lost to California 6–4. But Boston bounced back the next day before a throng of 32,403 with a comeback win against the Angels, scoring six runs in the seventh to pull ahead. Scott started the scoring by smashing a triple off George Brunet to drive in Conigliaro; then in the eighth both Conigliaro and Scott surprised a normally steady relief ace, Minnie Rojas, with back-to-back home runs to clinch the win. Rojas had yielded only two homers in 80 innings before that game. The

Sox took the next game as well, 6–5, before the biggest crowd in ten years (34,193) also coming from behind, with a dramatic triple by Reggie Smith in the tenth, and then scoring on an infield error by the Angels. Scott hit his 12th home run in the second inning.

Boston split the twelve-game homestand, including losing three out of five contests to arch-adversary and pennant contender, the Twins. Yastrzemski was having a phenomenal year that would bring him a Triple Crown and MVP, hitting 26 home runs and a .321 batting average through the end of July. They also had an exceptionally talented young right fielder in Tony Conigliaro, 22 years of age and in his fourth season with the Red Sox, batting .303 with 19 home runs; Conigliaro had already hit 84 homers in his first three seasons, winning the home run title in 1965 at the very young age of 20. George Scott, who played with Conigliaro in Wellsville and was a personal friend of Tony C's, was close behind with a .289 average and 13 home runs. He was a nucleus of the Sox infield, making defensive plays the likes of which had not been seen in Boston since Stuffy McInnis of the 1918–1921 Red Sox. He raised his average to .297 with a four-game swat spree during the first part of August and was among the batting leaders in the American League. Playing before 35,469, the largest crowd in Fenway in eleven years, Scott's 13th homer on July 29 against the Twins was, for a man of his size, a remarkable feat. By stroking a hard liner to right field which took an odd bounce high over Tony Oliva's head rolling to the Fenway bullpen wall 383 feet away, the big first sacker "bulled" his way around the bases, just beating the long relay and sliding into home plate in an explosion of dust under the tag of catcher Earl Battey, in an inside-the-park rarity.

Unaccustomed to flattery, or for that matter politeness, particularly when it was about the Red Sox, a feisty Eddie Stanky of the first-place White Sox included Boston with Detroit as his choice for teams most likely to be in the running for a pennant by the end of the season. He pointed to a "tight infield," along with pitching, as the reasons, but primarily a good defense that was more capable of turning the double play; keenly emphasizing the importance of an infield that avoided errors, but, even more importantly, he stressed, one that made "few mistakes." The Red Sox were in that category, he thought, led by their slick first baseman, George Scott.

Typifying that was Scott's glittering infield play on July 28 against the Twins. Roger Birtwell of the *Globe* wrote a feature article highlighting the splendor of a heads-up play made by the first sacker. Birtwell, erstwhile journalist and sportswriter par excellence since 1927 and an experienced baseball writer for most of the previous 30 years, picked up on the unusualness of what Scott had done. With the game tied 1–1 through three innings, the go-ahead run — Ted Uhlaender, a good baserunner — perched on second base, Twins pitcher Dean Chance laid down a sacrifice bunt that went to Scott at first.

Scott, who had edged toward home plate, picked up the ball and in one fluid
motion deftly threw out Uhlaender at third on a tag play. It was a rare baseball
moment, noted Birtwell, who compared Scott to Deadball great Fred Tenney,
the major league record-holder for most assists per season by a first baseman.
Tenney informed Birtwell that he had done it only once himself, in a minor
league game in 1910. Dick Williams would later say: "Until I saw George
Scott, I thought Gil Hodges was the greatest defensive first baseman I ever
saw. But Scott changed my mind."[17]

On August 3 GM Dick O'Connell took some initiative for the stretch
run by picking up 38-year-old catcher Elston Howard, who was placed on
waivers by the Yankees. He was hitting only .196 with New York, but he was
long on experience, including nine All-Star Games and World Series, and the
1963 MVP. Since he was a great defensive player and solid handler of pitchers,
it was a savvy move by O'Connell that would prove immediate dividends for
the Red Sox.

Clinging onto second place two-and-one-half games behind Chicago, the
Red Sox were about to start an important western road swing, where they often
had trouble, and this one would prove to be no different. Going up against an
always-tough Minnesota club they proceeded to lose all three games, two by
shutouts—one of them a "perfect" five-inning game ended early by rain by
Dean Chance—mustering only one run in the entire series. The Twins vaulted
into second behind Chicago, displacing the Red Sox by one percentage point,
.543 to .542. The Sox went into Kansas City for three games, losing the first.
Dick Williams began to juggle lineups and batting orders again, looking for a
solution to their tailspin. Struggling to come from behind in the second game,
utility player Norm Siebern, who had replaced Scott at first base in the seventh
inning, lashed a bases-loaded single to left scoring two runs, and the Sox were
ahead to stay. Roger Birtwell of the *Globe* declared: "Manager Williams rewards
his heroes," following an after-game press session with the Red Sox skipper
who announced he would insert Siebern and Jerry Adair into starting roles for
the rubber game of the series.[18]

Williams maintained pressure on his players, some complained to a fault,
making frequent lineup changes and, particularly, keeping close watch on his
players' personal statistics—their weight (body mass index). It was a rule he
had established at the beginning of the season and one he would strictly adhere
to no matter the consequences, including, apparently, how it might affect the
team, benching any player whose weight was only slightly above the weight
goal set for him. It began for Scott in Minnesota and the Kansas City series,
when Williams alternated him at first base with Siebern; Scott was 2-for-15
through the first five road games.

Upon arrival in Anaheim, on August 9, where the Sox were to play the
Angels—a serious pennant contender—in an important three-game series,

manager Williams quickly went to work determining player weights. Scott tipped the scales at 221 pounds, whereupon the manager unhesitatingly pronounced, "Norm Siebern will play first base tonight!" Siebern was hitting .160 and Scott .290. The Red Sox lost the game, 1–0. The next night the same thing; Scott was not in the starting lineup, and they lost, 2–1. Members of the press were asking pointed questions of Williams challenging him on the propriety — if maybe the sanity — of his decision in the wake of a pennant run, by benching a top hitter and defensive stalwart like George Scott. Moreover Scott was the Red Sox' best hitter against California with a .343 average, four homers and nine RBIs. There was a certain repugnance about this that was not sitting well with the Boston media.

The Sox faced pitcher Jim McGlothlin in the opener, who shut them down on three scattered hits. George Scott was McGlothlin's nemesis, having hit him for three homers in the course of three straight games; in baseball parlance, he "owned" him. In one of his three pinch-hit appearances in the three-game series, Scott was walked by McGlothlin, the only walk he issued. He later said that he was relieved that Scott was not in the lineup, and "happy, too," he exclaimed. And when Scott appeared in the eighth inning to pinch-hit, McGlothlin gave him a wide berth knowing that anything he threw him around the plate was likely to leave the park. Williams snapped back at the reporters: "I have managed this way all season," and he was not about to change his methods, he ranted, "[just] because we are in a tight pennant race."[19] It was a matter of pure principle to Williams, in spite of the cost to the team, but there seemed little sensibility to the decision.

Sliding toward third place in the standings, Red Sox players began to get edgy, feeling this had gone far enough. They desperately needed George's bat, having already lost two low-scoring games and were squandering their chances for a decent pennant run. But Williams, feeling the pressure, stood by his convictions by keeping Scott off the starting lineup for the entire Anaheim series. The Red Sox lost all three games by one-run scores. Rico Petrocelli recalled their frustration with the manager for being intransigent at such a crucial time: "It wasn't like they [Foy was also benched for one game] were grossly overweight; it was just a couple of pounds."[20] Scott was down to 217 pounds before the third game of the series, but Williams wanted him at 215. The less-than-sympathetic sportswriters went after Williams with a vengeance, roasting him to a fare-thee-well.

Boston had lost seven of nine games, six of them to contenders, and slipped precipitously into fifth place, three games behind Minnesota who had taken the lead from Chicago. Remarkably there were three teams between them and first place, in one of the tightest pennant races ever. However, there was no joy felt back in Boston, nor was there any welcome of the team such as had occurred after the previous road swing. Jim Fregosi, the Angels shortstop, who later became a highly successful major league manager himself, mocked the Red Sox manager for his stubbornness: "Are the Red Sox being run by a manager or a dietitian?" he quipped. His admonishment of Williams — a reproof made not by a newsman, but a fellow ballplayer — had a ring to it, and was quickly wrested and put into print by an eager press anxious to get as much journalistic mileage as they could from the unpleasant situation.[21]

The team staggered home for a twelve-game homestand, seven against pennant contenders starting with Detroit that was in third place. Scott was unhappy on the August 13 flight back to Boston, eating the steak he was served but passing up everything else on his tray. On Monday, a day off, when George was down to 213 pounds. Williams quickly inserted him back into the lineup for the Tuesday night opener. The Red Sox skipper knew he was badly in need of a couple of wins at least or the pennant would soon be out of reach. The Sox responded. The leadoff batter, Reggie Smith, promptly jumped on a Joe Sparma pitch for a home run. With two outs, Scott came to bat to a rousing cheer. One of the fans situated behind the backstop yelled out: "C'mon Twiggy, hit one out of here." And that's exactly what he did, lofting Sparma's pitch high into the Fenway left-field net for a home run. He also fashioned a sensational 3–6–3 double play off the bat of former Red Sox outfielder Lenny Green in the seventh that brought the house down. After the game Scott, still angry at the manager, blurted to the press that he should be playing even if he tipped the scales at 500 pounds; he failed to see how his weight should be a factor in determining his qualifications for playing, making that clear to whomever would listen.

The following night Smith and Scott repeated their feat hitting home runs in the first inning, this time off of Denny McLain; and then George did it again, a two-run shot off of McLain in the third inning into the far reaches of the Tigers bullpen. It was enough to win the game for the Red Sox. George also had made another sensational infield play in the sixth by tagging out McAuliffe, unassisted, robbing him of a base hit on a well-executed drag bunt. And the following inning, when Scott appeared safe at first on a relay throw from second base, on a ground ball he had hit that was turned into a double play, Williams got the heave for hotly defending his young slugger. For that he received a standing ovation from the more than 32,000 Fenway throng for showing an uncharacteristic support of his beleaguered first sacker. This time George was a happier man, ebullient over his two-day performance and the mere fact that he was playing again, and maybe because for once he experienced another, better, side of his skipper. He became conciliatory: "Maybe the man was right," Scott said, mentioning that he never felt better at this weight.

August 18 was the first game of a four-game series against the visiting Angels, and one of the most tragic in Red Sox history. Pitcher Jack Hamilton was starting for the Angels. Chronic wildness and inability to spot his pitches had been his affliction and the reason for frequent trips to the minors, until finally sticking with the Mets and Angels in '66 and '67. On this night, before a near-sellout crowd of 31,027, the Sox' young star Tony Conigliaro was felled by a Hamilton fastball, striking him on the left cheekbone just under his eye socket, a crushing blow that could be heard all around the ballpark. When he lay still on the ground for what seemed an eternity, the crowd went still. Blood oozed from his nose and the left side of his face was visibly swollen. The damages were severe: a shattered cheekbone and, later it was determined there was also damage to his eye retina. He remained out of baseball for the rest of the year and the entire 1968 season; although he played a few more seasons after that (in 1970 he hit 36 home runs), he was never quite the same. Vision problems from the injury gradually worsened in 1971 forcing him to leave the game; except for a brief comeback stint in 1975 with the Red Sox, his playing days were over.

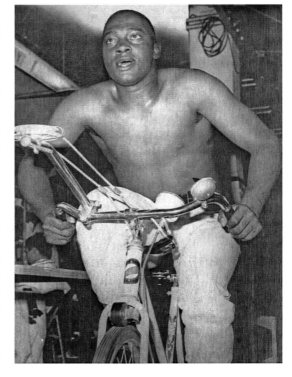

The Red Sox exacted revenge on the Angels for the treatment they received in California by sweeping them in four straight games, the final one a dazzling 9–8 comeback victory after being down 8–0. Scott was 6-for-16 in the series, including clouting his 17th home run, a two-run shot into the center-field bleachers. Carl Yastrzemski was doing some damage of his own having hit three homers in the series, his 31st in the final game; he was hitting .321. Switch-hitting rookie Reggie Smith tied a major league record on August 20 by hitting two home runs in one game, one right-handed and the other left-handed.

The Washington Senators

August 18, 1967, Fenway Park — Boomer was a regular in Fenway Park workout room throughout the season to keep his weight down, abiding by the stringent rules of his manager, Dick Williams. He was 1-for-4 in this day's 3–2 Red Sox win over California. Tony Conigliaro was seriously injured in this game and was out for the remainder of the season (courtesy of *Boston Herald*).

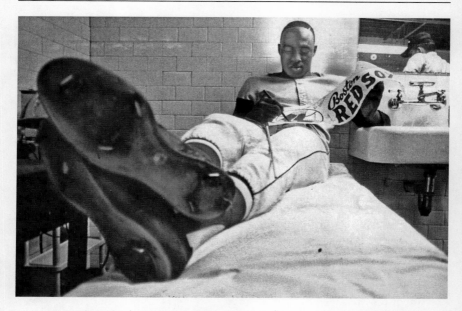

August 25, 1967, Fenway Park — A quiet moment: George Scott signing a Red Sox pennant before game with White Sox, won by Boston 7–1, in which he was 4-for-5. The Red Sox were in 2nd place, half a game behind Minnesota (courtesy of *Boston Herald*).

came to the Hub for a long five-game series to close out the Red Sox homestand, and promptly lost the first three. The Boomer, who had hit safely in ten straight games, became the hero of the second game of the August 22 doubleheader. Trailing 3–2 in the seventh inning, he came to bat with the bases loaded; on a full count he laced a single to right field scoring the tying and game-winning runs sending the Fenway crowd into mass hysteria. With those victories Boston was now one-one-thousandth percentage point behind the White Sox, in a virtual tie for first place.

A showdown was about to happen as Boston traveled to the Windy City on August 24 for a crucial three-day, five-game series, two of them doubleheaders, against Eddie Stanky's front-running White Sox. Stanky, the man who incited the Boston crowd in June accusing their star, Yastrzremski, of moodiness and an "all-star from the neck down," and who was nearly ridden out of Boston on a rail, was about to embark on more of his mischief in the upcoming series. This time he was playing in his own backyard, clearly an opportunity for him to work the umpires — and the Chicago crowd — for advantages and leverage, giving him and his team the upper hand. He was a master of the psychological approach, a needler — from the old school of baseball — and a classic bench jockey, who would do just about anything to garner a win for his team.

The Red Sox made another valuable pickup on August 25, purchasing

August 26, 1967, Chicago — Red Sox celebrate a big win over the White Sox that put them in first place. George Scott was 3-for-5 in the game with an important third-inning RBI. Scott was a key player in August rapping out 41 base hits, including 4 homers, at a .350 pace. Left to right: Reggie Smith, Carl Yastrzemski, Scott and Mike Ryan (courtesy of *Boston Herald*).

25-year-old Ken Harrelson, a right-handed power hitter from Kansas City, who was hitting .305. Dick Williams learned about it in between games of the doubleheader that day and was ecstatic, as it solved his problem of replacing slugger Tony Conigliaro in the outfield and right-handed pinch-hitting which they lacked. Harrelson was also versatile: he could play first base.

The *Herald-Traveler*, Boston's "other" newspaper, announced on Saturday, August 26, that the Boston fan base was in for a "treat" as they were running three-part weekend byline articles authored by one of the Red Sox' key players, George Scott, for his perspective on the vital Chicago series. The first of them, written in advance of the opener, appeared on the 26th, a day after the Red Sox split a doubleheader with the White Sox. George readily acknowledged the importance of the series against Chicago and their speed demons of the basepaths, stressing that the team needed to "make hay," he wrote. He lived up to his prescription for the team with 5 base hits in 9 at-bats in the twin bill which the Sox split with Chicago. Jim Lonborg, destined for the Cy Young Award, won his 17th in the first contest, backed by Scott's four base hits and two RBIs.

On the morning of the 26th Scott wrote his second of three articles, appearing in the August 27 paper, that he had read a disturbing headline in a

Chicago paper: "Stanky — Boston Running Scared." It was another of Stanky's psychological ploys, noted Scotty; summarizing he wrote, "I always try to do my best, but I try harder against these people."[22] Once more he backed up his rhetoric with actions by stroking three consecutive singles in the Saturday game, as well as making a solid inning-ending defensive play, when he threw out Rocky Colavito at second on a tag play after a pickoff attempt by Sox catcher Ryan. The Red Sox, who slipped into first place with the win, now had beaten Chicago for a second time, and were looking for two more over a frustrated Stanky, who bellowed that the Sox would have won all three contests if it weren't for the "stupidity" of Dick Williams in the second game of the series. He got no reaction from the Red Sox manager who refused to take the bait.

By now Stanky's strategy was eroding. The Red Sox had stroked 37 base hits, shredding a strong White Sox pitching staff; George Scott took the honors with 8 hits. The brash little White Sox manager, the "Brat" as he was familiarly known, was clearly frustrated and it showed in the final two games, another doubleheader.

Boston went ahead in the fifth inning by a 3–1 score on Yastrzemski's first of two homers he hit that day. George Scott, the next batter, was promptly hit by a Klages fastball, that Scott felt was deliberate and ordered by Stanky. He later reported in his third newspaper article that "I know he told that Klages to hit me."[24] There were other incidents of Red Sox hit-batsmen and near misses by Chicago pitching that appeared more than just coincidence. The Red Sox won the first game in what may be described as a signature moment of the 1967 season.

Fleet-footed Ken Berry, the fastest man on the White Sox, was planted on third base in the bottom of the ninth with Boston ahead by one run, 4–3. Duane Josephson lifted a soft liner to Jose Tartabull in right, who had a very weak arm. It seemed certain the game would be tied on a sacrifice fly. But Tartabull called upon the depths of his innermost soul to make the peg of his life to home plate. Elston Howard, another role player like Tartabull, made a sensational play by catching the high throw, planting his left foot in front of Berry, and making a sweeping tag to get him. Double play, end of game, Sox win.

The "Baby Bombers," a new moniker hung on the Sox by a Cleveland writer earlier in the season, lost the final contest, 1–0, of the five-game matchup to Stanky's hitless wonders because of a walk by Darrell Brandon that forced in the winning run in the eleventh inning. But they won the series three games to two. George Scott was on fire with 10 base hits and 5 RBIs in 19 at-bats in the series, a .526 pace that wore down Chicago pitching. Yastrzemski stroked a triple and his 33rd and 34th home runs.

By the end of August the Red Sox were in a heated highly intense pennant race in which the four contending teams — Boston, Minnesota, Chicago and Detroit — would, from day-to-day, fluctuate alternately in the standings among first through fourth positions like a Chinese yo-yo for the balance of the season. They went into New York on August 28, winning that game, a 3–0 five-hit shutout by Dave Morehead, and then won the first game of the next day's doubleheader on Jim Lonborg's 18th victory, a 2–1 three-hit gem. The Yankee Stadium throng, unaccustomed to coping with losing teams, was not soothed by the appearance of their beloved former player, Elston Howard, who was now wearing the much-despised Red Sox road grays and ensconced in a key role with the Hub team. It was his first trip to New York since he was picked up by Boston.

In the first game Howard drove in an important run against his old team, called a strong game ending in a shutout, and, for further insult, threw out New York's darling, Mickey Mantle, attempting to steal second base. Boston then lost a 20-inning heartbreaker, 4–3, in the second game of the doubleheader, in which Ken Harrelson made his first appearance for the Red Sox, hitting a homer on his very first trip to the plate. But Minnesota lost, as well, and the exhausted Red Sox were back in first place. They reinforced their lead to 1½ games on August 30 by beating the Yankees again, 2–1, in eleven innings on Carl Yastrzemski's 11th inning game-winning home run, his 35th. The lure of a pugnacious Eddie Stanky and his speedster White Sox coming to Boston for a four-game set and the start of the important September stretch run saw 35,138 fill the Fenway stands opening night, August 31. But the Sox lost the contest, 4–2, and two of the remaining three, as well, dropping them out of first place, one-half game behind Minnesota.

George Scott stroked 41 base hits in the month of August, including 16 RBIs and 4 home runs, at a .350 pace. He was now hitting .305 for the year, third on the leaderboard behind Frank Robinson and on the heels of Carl Yastrzemski who was hitting .310.

On September 6 — a day off for the Red Sox — there was a virtual deadlock for first place in the American League among four teams. The Tigers swept two that day, Chicago won a 13-inning thriller beating California, and the Twins lost, drawing the four teams tightly together with less than one-half game separating Boston and Detroit from the leaders, the Twins and White Sox. On September 7, the beginning of a nine-game homestand starting with New York, Jim Lonborg picked up his 19th victory. However, the credit goes to George Scott, the former Stanford medical student reasoned with the press because of a putout, curiously, that was made by Scott in the second inning. They called him the "Thinking Man's Pitcher," because he was inclined toward intellectual explication rather than directness. Lonborg "hooked the whole game on one play," wrote *Herald-Traveler* scribe Jack Clary, scratching his head along with his peers in his attempt to interpret the musings of the lanky Bosox pitcher. He said it was the "adrenaline" he couldn't seem to muster until Scott, unknowingly, and dramatically intervened, making an extraordinary grab of a Bill Robinson line drive. The crowd responded with thunderous applause, and "Gentleman Jim" was immediately caught up in the Fenway moment. "When Scott caught that ball, that did it," he said, and he went on to win, 3–1, striking out 10 men on three hits.[23]

As often as the subject nearly always revolved around hitting prowess as the formula for winning, the *Globe*'s Ray Fitzgerald, keenly aware of the difference between the bumbling Red Sox of 1966 and a very much–improved '67 club, advanced the notion that a strong defense should not be ignored when measuring a team's success. "There was a time when anything hit on the ground was a deadly weapon," wrote Fitzgerald of previous Red Sox clubs. Not so with this team, he noted, emphasizing their improvement in converting the double play and a generally overall increased ability to execute better defensively. With an emphasis on infield performance, Fitzgerald's tribute could just as easily and more befittingly been meant for their first baseman, George Scott, than the rest of the infield. It was the Boomer, a future Gold Glover, who bolstered an otherwise mediocre Red Sox infield that performed at a level near the bottom of the American League.[24]

The homestand began well enough with the Sox winning five of six — Lonborg winning his 20th against Kansas City — but they were not productive after that, losing all three of the remaining games to Baltimore, dropping them into a tie for third place, one game behind the first-place Tigers. The odds of Boston winning a pennant had tumbled precipitously. The Boomer, meanwhile, was himself productive with 12 base hits in the homestand, concluding in a .302 batting average, one of only four American Leaguers hitting over .300 on the year.

Detroit was the next stop for the Red Sox, a two-game must-win series for Boston. They won them both in nine-inning comebacks against Detroit's toughest, McLain and Lolich. It marked the start of a hitting rampage and clutch performances by Yastrzemski that almost single-handedly vaulted the team to the top of the standings, and into serious contention for the American League pennant. He and Dalton Jones were the heroes of the Detroit opener on September 18, with Yastrzemski hitting his 40th homer to tie the game in the ninth and Jones belting the game-winner in the 10th, tying them with the Tigers and Twins for first place.

The following day George Scott played a key role in their comeback win. Mickey Lolich had allowed but a scant lone run on five scattered hits, and had surgical command of his pitches, striking out 13 Red Sox batters. In the ninth, however, Boomer came up with two runners on base and none out, a classic bunt situation; he tried, but failed to get the ball onto the ground, and was suddenly behind with two strikes. After fouling off Lolich several more times

George rapped a line single to center; the game was tied, and Lolich was dispatched. The Sox scored two more runs that inning that decided the game.

Then it was on to Cleveland where Boston won both contests, remaining in a three-way first-place tie. But there was one man who was not sharing in the excitement of the Red Sox' momentum. The taste of his humiliating 1945 tryout with the Red Sox still on his palate, Jackie Robinson, speaking at a Buffalo, New York, Chamber of Commerce

September 20, 1967, Cleveland — George Scott rewards Yaz with a peck on the cheek after a thrilling ninth-inning 5–4 win over Cleveland. Yastrzemski was 4-for-5 on day with his 41st home run. Scott was 2-for-4, ending the day with a .301 batting average, second best on the team (courtesy of *Boston Herald*).

dinner on September 20, voiced his disgust of Red Sox owner Tom Yawkey, calling him "one of the most bigoted guys in organized baseball." For that reason, he said, he hoped the Red Sox would lose; his money was on the Twins.

As if willed by Robinson, the Sox ran aground in Baltimore where they split four games with the Orioles, leaving the Sox in second one-half game behind first-place Minnesota. On September 25 idle Boston went back into a tie for first when Minnesota lost to the Angels, 9–2. They were now in charge of their own destiny, for once, heading into the final four contests of the season that would be played before a home crowd in friendly Fenway. But any advantage they had hoped for was quickly lost in a two-game series with Cleveland. With their sights locked on the upcoming Minnesota series, the Red Sox performed poorly against the heretofore unremarkable Indians, losing both games, and seriously deflating their hopes for a pennant. Astonishingly neither did the other contenders seem up to the task either, the Twins losing, 5–1, and, shockingly, Chicago losing two games to last-place Kansas City. Detroit, who was idle, vaulted from fourth into second place, a mere .0008 percentage points — 8/10,000th — ahead of Boston, and one game behind league-leading Minnesota. Chicago meanwhile lost yet another game on September 29 to lowly Washington, and after leading the league most of the season, was eliminated from the race. There was still some life left in Boston after all.

Now there were three teams remaining — Minnesota, Boston and Detroit — that had a chance at the pennant. It couldn't have been more dramatic for the

Red Sox. It was down to the final two games of the season and league-leading Minnesota, always a tough opponent for Boston (11–5 season record against the Red Sox), was coming to town. Boston had to win both, and they needed some help in a big way from California in back-to-back doubleheaders with the Tigers in order to cop the pennant.

The 100-to-1 long-shot Red Sox — a team picked unanimously for the second division — were in the fight of their lives in a do-or-die series, and about to contend with two of the American League's toughest hurlers, Jim Kaat and Dean Chance. Kaat had won 16 games; Chance was a 20-game winner, and both had more than 200 strikeouts each on the season, Kaat with 207 and Chance 218. Kaat, a left-hander, was 7–0 in September with a 1.56 ERA. Chance had a 1.58 ERA and two shutouts, including an abbreviated perfect game against Boston. Instead of Lonborg, his ace, Dick Williams went with Jose Santiago in game one; he was a reliever mostly and occasional spot-starter who had been pitching well down the stretch, but had only moderate success against Minnesota. Williams knew it was a chance to take, but he needed Lonborg for the final game if there was any hope of winning it all against an even-tougher Dean Chance.

The Twins went ahead 1–0 in the first inning. Kaat was pitching a strong game through the first two, striking out four Red Sox batters. But fate was on Boston's side as the big left-hander strained his left elbow while striking out Santiago in the top of the third. It was their "Kiss of Death," wrote a Minnesota sportswriter in the next day's paper. In the bottom of the sixth, a tie game, 2–2, George Scott greeted reliever Ron Kline, 7–0 on the year and historically tough on Boston, with a first-pitch home run, his 19th, well into the center-field bleachers. It was the eleventh homer off Kline in 73 innings pitched. As Rico Petrocelli said later the team was ecstatic and they nearly ripped Boomer's uniform off upon his arrival in the dugout. It was a dramatic breakthrough moment for the Red Sox who had been battling Minnesota nose-to-nose, and gave them a lift going into the home stretch of the contest. Carl Yastrzemski gave them the breathing room they needed in the seventh inning when he smacked his 44th home run, a three-run clout, that solidified the game for Boston, winning it 6–4.

It was up to Jim Lonborg now, who was 0–6 lifetime against Minnesota, and further help from California, who had split their doubleheader with the Tigers the day before. California simply needed to do it again — along with a Red Sox victory — for Boston to win the American League pennant. It was destiny about to happen, as 35,770 partisan Red Sox fans, the season's largest crowd, pressed into the little Fenway bandbox for the final showdown. All of Boston was glued to this game, and because it was getting national attention as well, NBC in an unprecedented move canceled the telecast of a scheduled pro football game to broadcast the Sox-Twins nationwide.

The Twins took an early lead by scoring a run in the first, and added to it with another run in the third when Yastrzemski, uncharacteristically, let Killebrew's single roll through his legs allowing speedy Cesar Tovar to score. Dean Chance was in command through five innings yielding but 4 hits and no runs. But everything unraveled for the Twins in the sixth when the Red Sox put together five runs on a combination of key base hits, misplays, wild pitches and an error by the usually sound veteran Minnesota club. They were the only runs they needed. Lonborg pitched the entire game yielding just one more Minnesota run, and won his 22nd when Rich Rollins lofted a soft fly to Rico Petrocelli at short for the final out. Red Sox 5, Minnesota 3. Pandemonium reigned in Boston that day.

But it wasn't over; winning the pennant still depended on the outcome of the California-Detroit twin bill. The Tigers won the first game; another win for them would mean a tie with Boston and the need for a playoff game. Destiny once again was on the side of the Red Sox. Detroit, trailing 8–5 in the ninth, put two men on base with one out with their reliable leadoff hitter, Dick McAuliffe, in the box against Angels' reliever, seasoned veteran George Brunet. McAuliffe, an All-Star and a dangerous hitter with a home run stroke, had already knocked in three of the Tigers' five runs. But he pounded a Brunet pitch into the dirt to Gold Glover Bobby Knoop at second who turned a double play, the first of the year hit by McAuliffe. It was all over, as the 1967 pennant flag was Boston's.

Without any stretch it was "The Year of Yaz," wrote Larry Claflin of the *Herald-Traveler* summing up the astonishing feats achieved by Carl Yastrzemski in 1967. He was indeed the progenitor of the September surge, the main reason why the Red Sox won the pennant. But, by any fashion it was not exclusive. It was not *all* Yaz — or the manager either — was the stern reminder issued by his teammate, Tony Conigliaro, critical of the press for their unrestrained — perhaps pardonable — indulgence in the accomplishments of Yastrzemski and Dick Williams. Amazing as Yastrzemski was in that September stretch run (he had 40 base hits including 9 home runs), there were others in that lineup that made the dream possible, he said. Among them was George Scott who struck 29 base hits in September, the second-most on the team, and whose fielding accomplishments were often extraordinary and vital to game outcomes.

Scott recalled the details of Yastrzemski's sensational month giving full credit to his teammate. "He had a phenomenal run, the best I've ever seen," said Scott. But he unhesitatingly stressed that he was close on Yastrzemski's heels in batting average throughout the year, and was having a pretty good run of his own in September. "You'll have to remember, I was batting behind him which was one reason why he was getting more pitches to look at, with him batting third and me fourth," said Scott.[25]

It was the closest race in American League history, and the first pennant for the Red Sox in 21 years. Larry Claflin of the *Herald-Traveler*, writing with boundless enthusiasm, proposed the Most Valuable Player award for Carl Yastrzemski, and as runner-ups George Scott and Jim Lonborg. Yastrzemski did indeed win the MVP, also the Triple Crown, and his third Gold Glove; Lonborg took the Cy Young Award.

George Scott won his first Gold Glove and received 12 percent of the MVP vote, placing him 10th among the 24 American Leaguers receiving votes. Scott finished the regular season batting .303 with 171 base hits, second on the Red Sox behind Yastrzemski (189), and tied with Jim Fregosi for third in the American League, behind Cesar Tovar (173). He was one of only four American Leaguers who hit for an average above .300, behind Yastrzemski, Al Kaline and Frank Robinson, all future Hall of Famers.

8

Nothing But Gibson

With the experience he is still gaining at a young age, Scott may go down as the greatest defensive first baseman of his era.— Ben Henkey[1]

The St. Louis Cardinals had overrun their opponents winning 101 games during the 1967 season, finishing 10½ games in front of the second-place Giants, and eased into the National League pennant on September 18 with hardly any fanfare. Some had conceded the pennant to them long before that. They were rich in baseball talent, a veteran ball club, and all of their regulars had World Series experience, having won it in 1964 in seven games over the New York Yankees. Cardinals pitcher Bob Gibson had dominated New York with 31 strikeouts in that Series, a record-setting performance.

The Red Sox finished with 92 victories and just a .568 winning percentage, the lowest winning percentage in the history of the American League. The oddsmakers, on paper, had the Cardinals 3 to 1 favorites over the youthful and inexperienced Red Sox, certainly far better odds than were given Boston to win the American League championship before the season began. The hunch was that even 3 to 1 odds may have been optimistic, since of the Red Sox regulars, only Elston Howard had any World Series experience.

There had been good-natured banter going on between the two teams in late August as they neared the home stretch, and it appeared they might meet in the Fall Classic, led by the Boomer himself, George Scott. George, learning of a traveler in his presence bound for St. Louis who apparently held some personal status with some of the Cards, called out to him as he was leaving to ask him to extend his well-wishes to two of their premier performers, Lou Brock and Curt Flood, both veterans of the 1964 World Series. "They know the Boomer," said Scott, spoken with the self-assurance that he was on the "inside" with both men. When the message was relayed to them in St. Louis, it was confirmed: they did indeed know the Boomer, and both broke out into big smiles when they heard of Scott's salutation to them. Brock spoke of knowing

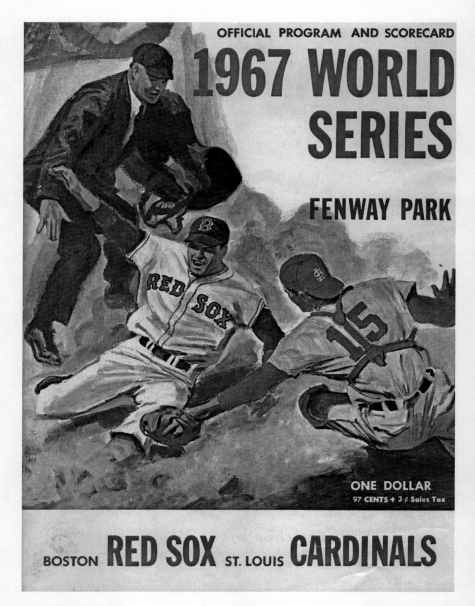

OFFICIAL PROGRAM AND SCORECARD

1967 WORLD SERIES

FENWAY PARK

ONE DOLLAR
97 CENTS + 3¢ Sales Tax

BOSTON **RED SOX** ST. LOUIS **CARDINALS**

1967 World Series: Boston Red Sox vs. St. Louis Cardinals (courtesy of Boston Red Sox).

George all through pro ball and mentioned, anecdotally, an occasion when he opposed Scott's team in the Florida Instructional League. Scott had hit three consecutive home runs in one of the games, and was walked by the same pitcher a fourth time. George had asked him why he didn't throw him any knockdown pitches, to which he smugly replied that he didn't play that brand of baseball. Scott's retort, according to Brock, who was more than amused by the exchange, was: "Well, just keep throwing them over, baby!" As the subject of the Red Sox first sacker broadened, Brock's mirth was not to be contained. He paused to reflect on Scott's inventive side mentioning his use of the home run term, "long taters," popularized by the Red Sox slugger: "He kills me," he laughed, every time he heard George using the term. Then, in a sobering afterthought, Brock spoke with a grimace, "Hope he doesn't hit any against us."[2]

In September scouts had begun to appear in the stands following the contending teams as they made their way around the leagues and into the stretch run. One such scout, a super scout, whose credentials were of the highest caliber, had been trailing the Red Sox. Though refusing to allow his name to be entered into print, he was nevertheless willing to share his thoughts with Bill Liston of the *Boston Herald-Traveler* who summarized the scout's analysis of Dick Williams' team. He described the Red Sox overall as a "tough ball club." Of George Scott he wrote: "He's a tremendous fielder—maybe the best," emphasizing the value of Scott to an infield that had weaknesses. Scott's range to his right was remarkable, he marveled, and, he was a master at executing the difficult 3–6–3 double play, and "frequently makes them," he reported. He made a curious opinion about the manager, Williams, suggesting that his team's allegiance toward him was possibly a marginal one; leaving the reader with the feeling it could even be fragile under any number of circumstances. "Players aren't exactly in love with him as a guy, but they play for him," he said. Those words had a ring of prophecy difficult to ignore.[3]

The two teams had played each other once during the spring Grapefruit League season, with the Red Sox coming out on top in a high-scoring game, 10–9. St. Louis got a good look at Boston's soon-to-be MVP, Yastrzemski, who knocked in six runs that day with two homers and six RBIs. The Cardinals portrayed a certain swagger about them from the outset of the Series, and the St. Louis press confidently published their elitist views—among these was the attitude that the Red Sox did not belong on the same field with the Cardinals—in spite of the risks and incentives it might have given the Red Sox. The St. Louis press was undeterred in lacing the sports pages with such folderol as the Series was approaching. The Boston players couldn't help but be inspired, cutting the articles out and posting them prominently on the clubhouse walls. It did them little good in their preparation for game one and a very confident Bob Gibson who would turn out to be the dominant force and the difference in the Series.

Despite their irritating bluster coming into the Series there was little argument that on paper the Cardinals were the superior team. They had good balance of power and speed among their regulars who were a mix of All-Stars and future Hall of Famers—four of them: Cepeda, Gibson, Brock and Carlton. They were led by their '67 MVP Orlando Cepeda, basestealing threat Lou Brock and their superstar pitcher Bob Gibson. Defense was solid led by Gold

Glover Curt Flood, two-time MVP Roger Maris, catcher Tim McCarver and slick infielder Julian Javier. Pitching was as formidable featuring a well-rested Gibson, who was injured for a good part of the season due to a leg fracture, but who still won 13 games, along with left-hander Steve Carlton, rookie Dick Hughes and Nelson Briles. They excelled in all areas, were aggressive on the basepaths and had good batsmen capable of advancing runners. The Cardinal regulars had an impressive .286 season batting average. The Red Sox had little with which to compare. Foremost was their superstar and Triple-Crown winner Carl Yastrzemski, who carried the team on his shoulders through September to a championship. After Yaz there was the Boomer, George Scott, the only other Red Sox player to hit above .300, and a defensive stalwart, too. Otherwise, they were a mix of front-end support and bit players who hit for a combined .244 average.

As the Series quickly approached, starting on Wednesday, just three days after the regular season ended on Sunday, Red Sox fans were in need of a pause to relish what their team had done, but there was barely enough time to celebrate. Harold Kaese of the *Globe* reinforced that feeling with his salute to the team the day after beating Minnesota: "And now for the great anti-climax — the World Series."[4] Dick Williams had his hands full with only two days to sort out a starting nine that typically depended on who was the hottest player at the moment. His top hurler, Jim Lonborg, who Williams would have preferred to kick-start Boston's chances, was unavailable having pitched on Sunday. He would have to go with Jose Santiago, he decided, to start the Series against the Cardinal ace, Bob Gibson. Santiago had pitched well in their stretch run and seemed to the young manager — who was to win the American League Manager of the Year award — his best alternative choice for the opener. An article in *The Sporting News* characterized the Red Sox manager as a bit of a magician: "A look at his lineup would convince anyone that he did it with mirrors."[5] "We'll take it in six" asserted a confident Carl Yastrzemski the day before the first game, pumping some confidence into his troops and reassurance to the Red Sox faithful, who had elevated the 28-year-old superstar to near demigod status after his incredible September performance.

The 64th Fall Classic opened on October 4, a balmy day in Boston before a standing-room-only crowd of 34,796 shirt-sleeved fans. But it was all Bob Gibson, setting the tone for the game by quickly dispatching the first two Red Sox batters, Adair and Jones, on strikeouts with his blazing speed, and then getting Yastrzemski on a weak foul popup, sending a groan through the Fenway crowd. George Scott broke the ice for Boston in the second inning with a clean single lined to left-center, raising hope among the Fenway folks that Gibson was hittable, but he was stranded there when the Cardinal hurler quickly got back to work by overpowering Rico Petrocelli and Reggie Smith on strikeouts. The St. Louis ace made one mistake on the day, trying to slip a curve by Sox

1967 Impossible Dream team. Opening game of 1967 World Series on October 4 with St. Louis Cardinals in Fenway Park, Boston (courtesy of Boston Red Sox).

pitcher Santiago who cranked the wayward pitch into the Fenway left-field net for a home run, tying the game at one-apiece in the third. He also had further trouble with a pesky George Scott — the one irritant in an otherwise masterfully pitched day — who, in addition to his single, stroked a Gibson fastball off the left-field wall for a double. Gibson, who had pinpoint control, became noticeably more cautious against a dangerous Scott, he now perceived, who represented the final out in the ninth inning. Even though there was no one on base and this was possibly his last batter, Gibson gave up his only walk to the young slugger, the first Red Sox batter to run the count to more than three balls, rather than risk giving up a crucial game-tying home run in the closely matched contest. He then dispensed with Mike Andrews on a soft fly to right and the game was his, 2–1.

It was clear, however, that in addition to the wizardry of Gibson there was also far too much Lou Brock, the National League's basestealing champion. The Redbirds' speedster was 4-for-4, all singles, tying a World Series record of four base hits in one game, the 32nd person to accomplish it. He also stole two bases (Petrocelli claimed he had tagged Brock out at second base before his hand reached the bag[6]) scoring both St. Louis runs, enough for them to win. Gibson's performance was a gem, fanning 10 Red Sox on six scattered base hits. After the game Gibson was indifferent to reporters when asked his opinion of the Red Sox and their superstar Carl Yastrzemski; he described Boston's left fielder as nothing more than a "decent batter," reaffirming the hauteur displayed earlier by the Birds and the St. Louis press.

George Scott, meanwhile, managed another base hit the next day, his third in two games, another walk, and scored a run. It was Red Sox ace Jim Lonborg's turn in Game Two before another sellout crowd of 35,188. Williams moved slugger George Scott — the only man with two hits off of Gibson — to his familiar cleanup slot behind Yastrzemski, forcing opponents to pitch to him. Its effect was almost immediate. Scott's presence behind Yaz gave Yaz better pitches to look at, so he erupted in a home run into the right-field bleachers in the 4th inning, and again in the 7th, a three-run blast — well over the visitors bullpen. Lonborg was nearly perfect: his first piece of business was to issue a roguish statement to the Cards' speedster, Lou Brock, who ran them ragged in Game One, by throwing his first pitch straight for Brock's right ear. A student of the Sal Maglie (Red Sox pitching coach) school of pitchers' acumen, Lonborg had hit 19 opposing batters on the season. Brock went sprawling, the Cardinal bench turned to howling and the Fenway fans were jubilant, erupting in robust cheering, as they sensed that this would be a much different outcome. Lonborg frankly admitted after the game that he did indeed throw at the Cardinal, saying, "What do they think I'm going to do — give them home plate?"[7] Brock was neutralized by Gentleman Jim on that pitch and he was not a factor in the game. Facing only 29 St. Louis batters, Lonborg took a perfect game into the seventh inning before walking Curt Flood. Altogether he threw a one-hit, 5–0, masterpiece, yielding a lone double to Javier with two out in the eighth inning. It was only the fourth one-hitter in World Series history, the last to do it was Floyd Bevens of the New York Yankees in 1947.

Later when Scott returned to his home in Greenville, Mississippi, after the Series, he reflected on the tone of play between the two teams. "There was bad blood between the clubs, no doubt about it," he said with resentment. "You should have heard some of the things that were said out there," he went on, in support of his view that Lonborg, "one of the meanest young pitchers in baseball," had to throw at batters to keep them off guard and in defense of his territory. Lou Brock was one of those batters; "You just gotta throw at him," Scott quipped.[8]

Any cordiality, strained to begin with, that may have existed between the two teams soon evaporated into vitriol following the second game, and it was directed at "Big Jim" Lonborg. Lonnie had stunned the St. Louis ball club and their fans with his aggressive and stunningly effective pitching style, yielding but one ineffectual base hit and all-but taking the bats from the hands of Redbird batters. The Cardinals' gamester and a team leader Lou Brock, who himself was shut down by Boston's 6' 5" hurler, reluctantly admitted that he had "good stuff"; but it was meant to be backhanded at best for he was quick to point out that Lonborg was not overpowering, like Marichal or Gaylord Perry. To a man the Cardinals tabbed Lonborg "Good, not great," appearing only to them — all of them — to have had a bad day at the plate. Cardinal Manager Red Schoendienst put things into perspective, however, squashing the flack surrounding Lonborg's performance with a sobering retort: "How do you pitch a bad one-hitter?"[9]

The Birds were back in their home court for Game Three, Busch Memorial Stadium, on October 7 before a crowd of 54,575 fans anxious to shed the numbing effect of Lonborg's stellar performance two days earlier. Several of the Cardinal players were still upset following the second game; Curt Flood, who was seething, vowed they would retaliate and not stop at just an average player; they would "get Yastrzemski." It was prophetic: upon Yastrzemski's first plate appearance Nelson Briles, the Cardinals' starting pitcher, struck him with a pitch on the back of the leg, bringing both managers out of their dugouts for a discussion with home plate umpire Frank Umont. But nothing came of it; Yastrzemski was quickly dispatched attempting a steal of second base, and the game settled into a non-event for the Red Sox. Pitcher Gary Bell was ineffective, giving up five hits in two innings and was taken out in the top of the third. Neither of the Red Sox top hitters, Yastrzemski or George Scott, could muster even a scratch hit and the Sox went down to defeat, 5–2.

Game Four was almost a repeat of Game Three, except this time it was the St. Louis ace, Bob Gibson, in the box looking for a repeat performance. And perform he did by striking out six Red Sox batters and yielding one less base hit — five — than he did in Game One. George Scott, who was one of Gibson's victims on three called strikes, said after the game that he never saw any of the balls thrown by Gibson, and turned to McCarver to ask him where they were pitched. Scott did manage a single in the fourth inning, however, his third hit of the Series off the hard-throwing Redbird pitcher. He also made a nifty fielding play in the fourth by taking a hard-hit ground ball off the bat of Maris, but instead of stepping on the bag for a second out which would have allowed Brock, the runner at third base to score, he charged Maris coming up the base line, tagged him — all the time with his eyes on Brock — and prevented Brock from scoring. Boston, however, went down to a 6–0 shutout defeat and was now down by two games to the Birds in the Series.

Curt Flood had more to say about the Red Sox and Lonborg who was scheduled to pitch Game Five, a crucial one for Boston and Lonnie if they had hopes of bringing the Series back to a friendlier Fenway Park. Flood and the Cardinals were certain Lonborg would not repeat his mastery of them in their cavernous stadium that had a better background in which to hit. "He won't be that tough," asserted the fleet St. Louis outfielder. Lonborg proved them wrong, this time pitching a three-hitter that mesmerized the Cardinal batters and their fans. The Sox were up against a tough left-hander, Steve Carlton, who was 14–9 on the year with a 2.98 ERA, identical to Gibson's. Carlton was nearly the equal to Lonborg, yielding only a single run through six innings with five strikeouts. But Lonborg was better, giving up no runs on only two hits until a Roger Maris home run in the ninth. The Sox had added a couple of more runs in the top of the ninth and the game ended in a Boston win, 3–1.

Once more George Scott went hitless but he scored a key run in the ninth inning after he walked, moved to third on a Reggie Smith double, and was driven in by Elston Howard's two-run RBI single that was the margin of victory for Boston. To the disappointment of the St. Louis fans, alarmed at the thought that the Red Sox may be capable of winning it all in Boston, it was now back to the Hub city and Game Six. Their champagne celebration would have to be put on hold.

Another standing-room-only crowd of 35,188 filled Fenway on Wednesday, October 11. Down three-games-to-two with their backs to the wall, there was hope again in Boston of another Red Sox clutch run, just like the one they made at the end of the regular season — and had been doing all year long — when they pulled out two must-have victories (combined with a Detroit loss) against a favored Minnesota club to seize the pennant. With just two more games, if they won the first one then it would be their big guy Jim Lonborg, the Redbird killer, in the final. It seemed like the perfect fit.

Dick Williams surprised everyone by inserting a relatively obscure pitcher, Gary Waslewski, into the lineup to start the critical sixth game, passing on his regulars Bell and Santiago. Waslewski had been up-and-down between Boston and Toronto, and was only added to the Series roster to replace an injured Darrell Brandon. He had pitched three perfect innings in relief of Bell in Game Two, fanning three Birds (Brock, Cepeda and Javier). Williams had a hunch to place his faith in the untested 26-year-old 6'4" right-hander, and it paid off, once again. Waslewski took the game into the sixth inning with a 4–2 Red Sox lead, before being replaced. After the Cardinals tied it up in the seventh on a Lou Brock home run off John Wyatt, who admitted he had thrown Brock a spitter. The Red Sox came right back with four more runs in their seventh to go ahead to stay, and win, 8–4.

With the Series all tied up, just the way it was scripted some believed, for a perfect ending to a Cinderella season, surely the Red Sox were about to win it all. The *Globe*'s Harold Kaese summed it up the morning of October 12, the day of the seventh and final game, self-assured after watching the Red Sox and their come-from behind performances of an extraordinary year: "This is a story that has to have a happy ending." [10] Dick Williams was even more confident;

when asked who he would pitch in the final game, his answer was, "Lonborg and Champagne." It made the front page — in large bold print — of the *Boston Record-American* the same morning and was all over the national newswires. It made Bob Gibson furious, said Cardinals catcher Tim McCarver. George Scott's self-assuring boasting probably didn't help; the *Herald-Traveler* boldly carried his grandstander remarks, "We'll KO Gibson in Five — Scott."

But it was not to be. Lonborg was called on to pitch on only two days rest, while his opponent, Bob Gibson, had three; Lonnie simply didn't have it. Red Sox reliever Dan Osinski's memories of October 12 were vivid: "He couldn't break a pane of glass," exclaimed Osinski, speaking about Lonborg's warm-up performance before the final game.[11] Pitching coach Sal Maglie informed Williams of Lonborg's apparent ineffectiveness but Williams, who did not get along with Maglie, shrugged him off. He was going with his ace no matter what. It turned out to be one of the few mistakes Williams made all year, but it was a big one, said Osinski. "All the while I was thinking how lousy it was for a manager to do that to his ace pitcher," said Maglie, after Williams left Lonborg in the game when he was getting shelled.[12]

It was all Bob Gibson and Lou Brock in Game Seven. Gibson, who was the World Series MVP, overpowered Boston batters in the seventh game by fanning 10, for a Series total of 26, and hit a home run of his own to cap his third victory, a three-hitter. One of those hits was the first off of him, in the fifth inning, a George Scott triple that was laced with authority 420 feet to the triangle in Fenway's center field, and scored the first of two Red Sox runs on Javier's misplay of the relay throw. He was also the final out and strikeout victim of the game and World Series, as St. Louis coasted to victory, 7–2.

"The only memory that anybody should have of that 1967 World Series is that if it wasn't for Bob Gibson we would have been champions," asserted a proud George Scott. "Everybody talks about how Bob Gibson had us intimidated, but that's not true. Gibson beat us but he never had anybody in that lineup intimidated." Analyzing the circumstances of the Series further, Scott said, "Nelson Briles and those guys shouldn't have got us out [the way they did]; we let one of those games get away [from us] and Bob Gibson went the rest of the way to win." Asked how he felt he fared personally in the Series, Scott answered: "Well I was probably a little off of where I would have wanted to be, [but] I felt that I swung the bat good against Bob Gibson." The Boomer did fare well against Gibson, batting .364 on four hits — the most of any Red Sox batter off the Cardinal hurler — including a double and triple. Only Jose Tartabull, used sparingly when Gibson was pitching, was better against the Redbird hurler with a .400 batting average with two hits in five at-bats. Yastrzemski was next at .273.[13]

The postseason culminated in a series of testimonials and tributes to Red Sox personnel for their remarkable season and the implausible achievement of ascending from the depths of being a ninth-place team to become the "Impossible Dream" American League champions. Carl Yastrzemski won the AL Most Valuable Player, Professional Athlete of the Year, and the *Sports Illustrated* Sportsman of the Year awards, and a Gold Glove; Jim Lonborg won the AL Cy Young Award; Dick Williams was named Manager of the Year by both major wire services and the *New York Times*; Dick O'Connell was honored as Major League Executive of the Year by *The Sporting News* and United Press International; and George Scott walked off with his first Gold Glove for fielding excellence.

What was even more dramatic about the '67 team and their season was what they had accomplished long-term for the franchise. They lifted the team from a morbid state of stagnation to a legacy of being a winner that has brought the city and organization together in somewhat of a symbiotic relationship that is affectionately referred to as "Red Sox Nation." On the occasion of Dick Williams' induction into the Red Sox Hall of Fame in 2006, he commented about the surge of his team and Fenway Park attendance in the second half of 1967. "And that started the whole thing rolling," he said, alluding to the current team's enormous partisan public appeal.[14] "That year was the dividing line in Red Sox history," wrote Bob Ryan of the *Boston Globe* on June 21, 2007.

Twenty-three-year-old George Scott, just five years out of high school and a scant four years in the minor leagues, returned triumphantly to his home in Greenville, Mississippi, following the Fall Classic as a proud member of the American League champion Boston Red Sox, one game short of being a World Series champion. He also would have a Gold Glove, symbolic of major league baseball fielding excellence, to his credit.

Not long after Scott's return to Greenville, and after picking up his World Series check, one of his first acts was a show of loyalty to his mother by fulfilling the pledge he had made to her when he first signed with the Red Sox — he bought her a new house, car, and furniture, and gave added assurance she would never have to work again. If nothing else came of his time spent in the big leagues, he thought, he was determined to keep his commitment to lift his mother from the ravages of poverty she had endured over her lifetime.

The irony, however, was that in spite of the newfound privileged status bestowed upon her by her son, she had few rights to speak of. Magnolia remained in the segregated south end of town where she and other Greenville blacks were consigned, not as a matter of choice, but of race. Greenville's white community had not changed their stripes a great deal from the accepted dogma —*separate but equal*— of the times that they knew and embraced. It was still a black and white town by anyone's definition. "There was never any equal; there was only separate," exclaimed Hodding Carter III on the legacy of the town and their implacable determination to preserve their established way of life in the face of the recent Civil Rights Act and national and regional pressure to integrate. It was always an incremental process for them, and "social mixing" was the hardest part, said the former editor of the *Delta Democrat-Times*.[15]

By his accomplishments and mere presence George Scott galvanized the town to coalesce into a working unit, even if it was only momentary. They formed an "interracial group," they called it, a committee of blacks and whites assigned, astonishingly, to cooperatively work together in a common cause — the celebration of a black man who was the toast of the town. It was unprecedented for Greenville, a town still reeling from the weight of segregation, still very much a white man's place, and they were about to honor Scott with a key to the city.

They came out in large numbers, both black and white, on November 16, to celebrate one of their own who had put their town on the national map. It started with a 38-vehicle motorcade, stopping at the city hall for Mayor Pat Dunne to honor the man "who has spread the name of Greenville and Coleman High across the American League and, finally, across the baseball world," declared Dunne.[16] It was perhaps the largest crowd ever to attend a parade in Greenville. Then it was on to his beloved Coleman High, where George excelled as an all-around athlete, and where, on this day, he was hailed by his teachers, coaches and their esteemed principal, G.P. Maddox. The ceremonies ended with a George Scott Appreciation Dinner at the National Guard Armory, where their featured speaker, Red Sox coach and Scott mentor Eddie Popowski, saluted George for being a superstar and "the greatest first baseman" in major league baseball.

Of the numerous dignitaries attending, one stood out. Scott's high school basketball coach, Andrew Jackson, spoke of the significance of the black and white community coming together to celebrate a black man. "This in itself holds powerful implications," he said with an expression of hope that segregation would become but a distant memory.[17] But it was only momentary; during an interview in 1973 he spoke sadly about his home town not having changed from what it was: "Everything is [about] race," he lamented.

9

Bewitched

It bothers some, but probably bothers (Dick) Williams not at all that players like John Wyatt, Jim Lonborg and George Scott have not taken his shots standing still, or that Tony C. and Mike Ryan spoke publicly in criticism of him, and that a former coach (Maglie) predicts his comeuppance. — Jerry Nason[1]

Within hours of George Scott's — and the Red Sox' — last at-bat of the 1967 World Series, manager Dick Williams was surrounded by zealous reporters eager to probe his brain on the why's and wherefore's of what had just happened at Fenway, and, more importantly, his long-range plans for the team. Williams' focus was unquestionably on "next year." Already he was laying the groundwork for 1968, in his mind filling holes in pitching and catching, and expressing confidence that with these changes they could repeat atop the league with the right players. Unlike Red Sox managers of the past who had little to offer their fans but hope after still another losing season, this time the gesture that they could win appeared genuine. There was good reason to trust the youthful manager's optimism after leading the team to its most successful season in twenty-one years. There seemed to be some magic in his touch.

But there was nothing enchanting about Williams' approach to his big first sacker, George Scott, who was but an anomaly to the enigmatic skipper. Williams wasted little time openly berating Scott to the press, a tactic he would engage in repeatedly during 1968 that would have enormous repercussions with the Red Sox first sacker, and the team. "I would have hated to put him on the scales during the World Series because his weight was way up again," said the crusty Williams to anyone willing to listen. Of course, there were plenty of reporters who were eager to listen.[2]

About to walk off with the Major League Manager of the Year award, Williams was now looking for a three-year contract which seemed to him commensurate with his 1967 accomplishments; in fact he thought the deal was practically in his back pocket since GM O'Connell favored the idea. Both men were startled that owner Tom Yawkey, peculiarly, did not share the same view; for whatever unimaginable reason Yawkey wanted just two years. In spite of Williams' colossal success in lifting a perennial loser to sudden and unexpected prominence, a would-be charm for most franchise owners, there was something definitely not clicking between the two men. There followed protracted discussion after which the Red Sox owner finally gave in, begrudgingly, agreeing to a three-year deal for $55,000 per season.

Despite coming to terms Williams was miffed, so much so that he even momentarily and unwittingly left his son at the ballpark that day after leaving Yawkey's Fenway Park office. Williams speculated that Red Sox VP of Player Personnel, Haywood Sullivan, was behind it, or possibly Yawkey was once again lining up one of his "steam bath" buddies for his job, he reasoned. He had had little contact during the season with Sullivan, whom he didn't trust, labeling him Yawkey's "office flunky," and was resentful of the Red Sox owner who displayed little interest in the team until the end of the 1967 season when they were winning. The feeling apparently was a mutual one. Neither said much to each other during the '67 stretch run. Since Yawkey's attention was on Williams' players, particularly his star Carl Yastrzemski, with whom he would kibitz and cavort daily in the clubhouse. "I wasn't in his social club," said Williams, deeply resentful of Yawkey's meddling and the undermining it might bring to his team.[3]

"He [Yastrzemski] was a powerful figure during those days of Mr. Yawkey; same way Ted Williams was," said Scott, supporting the view that the Red Sox owner had the ear of some of his players to the detriment of others. "I could fawn with Mr. Yawkey all I wanted to, but if I didn't play baseball I was gone," lamented Scott, implying that there were favorites among Red Sox players that began to split the team into groups and eventual dissension.[4]

Along with the disappointment he was feeling from the salary-dispute encounter with

Red Sox manager Dick Williams, who George Scott claims nearly drove him out of baseball (courtesy of Boston Red Sox).

Yawkey, Williams had additional reason for frustration when he learned of the Christmas Eve knee injury to his ace hurler, Jim Lonborg, who was hurt while skiing at Lake Tahoe. It was a major setback. Lonborg would return to pitch again, but never would he have another season like the one he had in 1967.

Lonborg's devastating injury began the "two-year nightmare" Williams described for himself in his 1990 autobiography, which wafted into the 1968 season and would have a crushing effect on 24-year-old George Scott. Already disturbed by the apparent loss of his number one pitcher, Williams became more upset when upon arriving in Winter Haven he first saw a "fat and sloppy" George Scott, he alleged, leaving him with the feeling he would be without a first baseman as well.

Then there was Tony Conigliaro trying to recover from the horrible injury of '67. Hitting well in spring batting practice things looked optimistic for him, but this soon deteriorated along with his vision; before long Tony C. was missing pitches by a foot or more, the obvious effect of his being beaned by Jack Hamilton. A highly spirited Conigliaro, desperate to make a comeback, found himself butting heads with the frustrated Red Sox skipper, adding to Williams' discontent as he watched his young superstar struggle and his intrepid team of '67 unravel.

Williams' pugnacious behavior began to catch up with him and his team as he strove for the perfect season — nothing less than a World Series win he insisted of himself— which he would soon learn he would not accomplish with his team of overachievers; now injuries and player behavioral issues were threatening even the possibility of another pennant. "I would forget my manners, my common sense, sometimes even that I was a human being," wrote a disconsolate ex-manager years later in his memoirs of that disappointing season.[5] His tension from dealing with a potentially disastrous situation in '68, especially after his instant fame the previous year, turned him literally to drink as a quick fix "to stay sane," he wrote, even if it "inevitably made me hateful."[6]

George Scott's year began on a high note when he married Malvina "Lucky" Pena of Falmouth, Massachusetts, on January 21, with Red Sox teammate Joe Foy as his best man. This was starting out to be an even better year for George, he was sure of, now with his new wife and the prospect of another winning season playing for a championship team. Improving on his .303 batting average, maybe winning another Gold Glove, but especially winning it all this time was definitely in the forefront of his mind. What could be more exciting than this: he was a top-flight athlete, an established professional ballplayer at 23 years of age, a premier defensive star, participated in a World Series after only two years of major league baseball, and was considered a valued and integral member of the AL Champion Boston Red Sox.

Dick O'Connell meanwhile went to work in the offseason dutifully seeking to fill Dick Williams' order for more pitching, picking up two proven starters from the National League, Ray Culp of the Cubs and Dick Ellsworth of the Phillies. The plan was to bolster a pitching staff, no better than marginal in '67, entirely around their Cy Young Award ace, Jim Lonborg. It could hardly have been anticipated that they were to become the principals of an otherwise mediocre pitching staff and that Lonborg wouldn't even join the staff until mid-season.

Baseball pundits and bookmakers could see the Red Sox no better than 6 to 1 odds to repeat in 1968; their money was on Detroit and Minnesota as 5 to 2 favorites to take the American League crown. A poll of members of the Baseball Writers' Association of America predicted the Red Sox would finish fourth behind Minnesota, Detroit and Chicago. It wasn't about to scare Dick Williams or his team who were famously and pessimistically charted for the second division in 1967 by the same group of writers and Las Vegas betting line.

Larry Claflin of the *Boston Herald-Traveler* reported on Dick Williams' initial assessment of his players' conditioning upon their arrival in spring camp, saying he was "very pleased" overall, but was surprised with the overweight condition of their new acquisition, Gene Oliver. Surprisingly, nothing was said at the time about George Scott who Williams was more than willing to publicly eviscerate at the slightest whim. Scott's weight, 227 pounds when he arrived in camp, was of primary concern to the Red Sox skipper, which he pointed out in his autobiography years later. In the meantime Ken "Hawk" Harrelson, in his first full year with the Sox and comfortably leveraged with a three-year $150,000 Boston contract was out to take the first base job away from Scott. Before his arrival in Winter Haven he spoke of the possibility he could be traded since Scott was a Red Sox fixture at first base: "I'll give Scott a battle. He's a great player, but I won't concede him anything," said Harrelson. It was a prophecy in the making.[7]

The exhibition season opened on March 8 in Sarasota, springtime home of the Chicago White Sox, before 4,515 fans, the largest crowd ever to attend an opener there. Fans were eager to see the AL Champion Red Sox tangle with a good Chisox club and their feisty skipper Eddie Stanky, who notoriously disliked Yastrzemski and the Red Sox. Boston lost the game and five of their first six contests as Williams shuffled players in-and-out of lineups, which would turn out to be his style the entire year. Big George Scott was ripping the ball at a .462 pace with 6 RBIs, 5 extra-base hits including two home runs, and a 1.353 slugging percentage for the first six games. His second home run on March 12 against the White Sox was a "tater" that would have left Boston's Logan Airport, claimed an exuberant Scott, speaking with considerable hyperbole. Things were looking good for George, but not for an agitated Dick Williams who, after a tough 10-inning loss the next day — the fifth in six days — against the Cincinnati Reds, was fuming despite his preseason promise that he would do a better job of "managing" his frustrations.

On March 14 Boston won its second game of the spring, 7–1, against the White Sox on a strong performance by their new hurler Dick Ellsworth. "Had Scotty been in the game the first bunt is an out," said the Red Sox manager, confident his Gold Glover would have caught the popup bunt that led to the single run, and meant a shutout for the left-hander.[8] He was back in the lineup the next day against the Houston Astros, whose pitching shut the Red Sox down for eight innings until the Boomer came to bat in the ninth. With two on and one out, and two strikes on him, Scott launched his third homer of the young spring season — his third hit of the game against a stiff crosswind that players had been wrestling with all day — that won it for the Red Sox 3–1.

Assessing the play of Red Sox players through nine games (in which the Sox were 3–6) Harold Kaese of the *Globe* provided a mere one-word explanation for George Scott — *outstanding*, he wrote on March 17. On the same day Dick Williams wrote a *Globe* byline article of his own in which he acknowledged how fortunate he was that none of his pitchers had arm trouble because of the unusually cold Florida weather. And just as quickly, as if self-inflicting some sort of poison on one of his starters, Gary Bell suddenly came down with a sore shoulder.

The jinx, if that's what it was, also extended to George Scott, who after Kaese's article could muster only five more base hits over the remainder of the Grapefruit League season. On March 26 after a game with the Pirates in which Scott hit a triple, he exclaimed to reporters while getting off the clubhouse scale that "I'm going to have a great year."[9] He was down to 214 pounds, a pound below the weight Dick Williams demanded he reach by Opening Day. Scott waxed philosophical with the press admitting, as was Williams' assertion, that when his weight was down he felt good and played better. But whatever the advantages he perceived were coming from his improved girth, it did him little good with the bat, finishing the spring season with an anemic .206 batting average after slugging 3 home runs and 9 RBIs in the first week of exhibition play.

The '67 MVP and Triple Crown winner, Carl Yastrzemski, didn't fare any better, batting only .243; of his 17 base hits only one was an extra-base variety, a double. The focus was clearly on 23-year-old Sox superstar Tony Conigliaro whose comeback attempt held center stage with the Red Sox and major league baseball. He made a fair start but by the third week of the spring season began to have trouble with his vision and was striking out regularly. On April 2 Tony C. played his last game of the 1968 season against the Senators, going 0-for-3, all strikeouts. In an April 3 interview with the *Globe* with teammate Carl Yastrzemski, Conigliaro revealed for the first time that he was having vision problems that began some ten days earlier, and planned to visit with an eye specialist while in Boston where he was heading that night for a military reserve meeting. He was hitting a paltry .125 with 22 strikeouts in 66 at-bats.

Neither Dick Williams nor trainer Buddy LeRoux said they were aware of Conigliaro's situation. Williams at first was irked by the news from Boston: "I don't think there's anything wrong with Tony's vision despite what he said when he got to Boston," said an irritated Dick Williams, who may have been upset that Conigliaro did not report the problem to him before leaking it to the press. "If Tony can't get the job done, we'll take it from there," said the apparently unsympathetic Red Sox manager. Conigliaro was furious upon hearing what Williams said about him, responding angrily: "Dick Williams is going to be sorry for what he said; and if he isn't, he isn't a man."[10] It was confirmed the following day after several extensive eye examinations that Tony Conigliaro would not play another game in 1968, and quite possibly his career was over. Although no apologies were issued by Williams, he recanted his earlier position of disbelief in Conigliaro's story, saying he was completely shocked by the news.

The Red Sox were in a sorrowful state having finished at the bottom of the Grapefruit League with a less than satisfactory 9–18 exhibition record. Williams had little to look forward to with two of his stars, Lonborg and Conigliaro, out for the long term, and Tony C. perhaps out for good. "We will be all right," declared Williams to the din of reporters' questioning of the second-year manager who now appeared to have his hands full. "Working as a unit," he said, as in 1967, would undoubtedly be the key to a successful season thought the pensive manager, in spite of the mounting player injuries. He had confidence in his team, especially his infield: "One of the biggest men, offensively, is George Scott," he said, explaining that he was the key man to "the best infield in the league."[11]

American League president Joe Cronin was even more effusive in his portrayal of the Red Sox first sacker: "It's worth the price of admission at Fenway Park just to see Scotty play first base. He is the best right-handed first baseman I have ever seen." Cronin proceeded to elaborate on the contradiction of such a big man, like Scott, whom you wouldn't expect to be so lithe, possessing cat-like qualities around the bag.[12] He has "hands like a card shark, quick and slick," wrote the *Globe's* Harold Kaese of Scott in his April 7 preview of the 1968 season.

Yastrzemski confidently predicted that Scott was going to have an even "better year than last year" because he was doing a better job of going with the pitch and hitting to right field, instead of always trying to pull the ball. Talk quickly shifted to whom of the Red Sox hitters would take over the cleanup spot made available by Conigliaro's absence; the obvious candidate was the Boomer according to most of the sports scribes. But Williams had other ideas preferring that Scott bat fifth where he felt he was more effective. "Every time you put him in there [cleanup] he thinks he's Babe Ruth," said Williams.[13]

They were looking for Scott to apply a shorter swing and home runs would just come naturally, explained former Red Sox hitting coach Bobby

Doerr, describing the goal they had in mind for Scott in 1968. "If the (Fenway Park) left-field fence had been in right field George would probably have been a .325 hitter," said Doerr with perfect confidence that Scott had the raw talent to be a Hall of Fame–type hitter provided he made adjustments in his hitting style.[14]

On the same day of Conigliaro's devastating news, national tragedy struck: civil rights activist and Nobel Peace Prize recipient Martin Luther King was struck down by an assassin's bullet, sending a pall over the entire nation. Major league baseball now had to contend with cancellations and the effect of racial riots that were arising in several major cities, including Detroit where Boston was to open their season; there was even talk about canceling all or some parts of the baseball season. The remainder of the spring season ended abruptly; Boston's April 7 final spring game with Washington was canceled as was the Tuesday regular season opener in all major league cities. Significant rioting was occurring in Detroit that threatened cancellation of the April 10 delayed-opener, due to Governor Romney's state of emergency proclamation and a curfew set by Detroit mayor Jerome Cavanagh, which was lifted in time for the Red Sox 1968 season to get underway.

Nothing could have been so unimaginable for 24-year-old George Scott than the nightmarish year he was about to experience under the strong-armed and peevish nature of one Richard Hirschfeld Williams. On Opening Day *Globe* columnist Jerry Nason, in a thoughtfully-written profile of the Red Sox skipper, compared him with Celtics all-time legend Red Auerbach, whom he described as ideologically similar. That is, except for one stylistic difference. "You have never heard of Auerbach being privately cut up by his own players, in or out of season," wrote Nason. It was telling and written with a foreboding twist to it that may have been as good a forecast on the season as even Nason himself couldn't have imagined.[15]

The season's first pitch hadn't been thrown yet when problems began for Boston, when their once fair-haired third baseman prospect, Joe Foy, wanted out. Dalton Jones had won the hot corner position from him in spring training, the second time Foy had lost a starting role in three seasons, and he could see no future for himself in the Hub city.

The Red Sox got off to a good start by winning their opener, 7–3, over the Tigers. Yastrzemski, who barely hit the ball out of the infield the entire spring, blasted two home runs. George Scott had some good-humored praise for the Sox superstar, wondering how anyone, namely Yastrzemski, could hit so anemically all spring and yet clout a couple of home runs right out of the gate when the money was on the line. But Yastrzemski adroitly shifted the spotlight from himself to place it squarely on Scott who had made a brilliant defensive play that stopped Detroit's momentum in the eighth inning. "But how many guys can make a play like *you* did on Horton today," said Yaz, speak-

Gold Glover George Scott reaches for a foul ball in the stands (courtesy of Boston Public Library).

ing about Scott's chasing of Willie Horton between second and third base — Horton had rounded second too wide after stroking a double — after a perfect throw from Yastrzemski to the first baseman who had covered second base on the play. "That's why you're the best first baseman there is," exclaimed the Red Sox left fielder.[16] Detroit's manager Mayo Smith said after the game, in which

Scott made several good defensive plays, that Boston's first sacker was the best he had ever seen, including Gil Hodges, repeating what Dick Williams had said earlier.

In spite of the opening day heads-up play, George Scott was off to a miserable start with only 3 base hits in his first 33 at-bats. Already Dick Williams was unhappy with his first sacker, with reports circulating that he might sit him down. Scott reacted to the rumor angrily, that the team was winning (they were 6–4), he was fielding well, and sitting on the bench was not going to cure his slump. He stayed in the lineup for another three games going 0-for-9; on April 28 Scott was benched, replaced by Norm Siebern.

By May 1 Boston was playing .500 ball (8–8) and in third place, 3½ games behind the leader, Detroit. Few of the Red Sox regulars were hitting: Scott .100, Howard .154, Jones .121, Smith .226, Harrelson .227 and Yastrzemski .246. Scott's confidence was shaken by the poor start and began to show in his usually sound fielding, missing a play at the plate in one game that drew the manager's ire. Reporters picked up on the emergent unpleasantness brewing between Scott and his quick-tempered manager, and looked for some indulgence from Williams while the young slugger regained his footing. "Shown patience and given encouragement ... the potential is there for sure," wrote the *Globe*'s Harold Kaese.[17]

Hitting was going to be difficult for all batters in 1968, given how dominant the pitching would be — described as the Year of the Pitcher — that produced an American League earned run average of 2.98, the lowest of any year since the Dead Ball era. This would prompt Major League Baseball to lower the pitcher's mound in 1969 to lessen the pitcher's advantage over the batter.

On May 17 the Red Sox dispensed with their ace reliever, John Wyatt, selling him outright to the New York Yankees and a grateful Ralph Houk who planned to use the right-hander as their "number one reliever." Wyatt, among others, had been in Dick Williams' infamous dog-house since the end of 1967 when he said he couldn't pitch because of a stiff arm. Over the winter Williams publicly discredited the pitcher debunking him in the press. Wyatt counterpunched with a letter to Larry Claflin of the *Record-American* complaining about the manager and asking to be traded; this sealed his fate with Williams. Asked *why* such a bewildering maneuver by the Red Sox, Vice President Haywood Sullivan would say only, "I can't say anything more than what happened." It seemed clear that Williams had washed his hands of Wyatt and didn't want him around under any circumstances.[18]

Amidst the rancor surrounding the Wyatt sale, the troubling story on Williams' disassociation with Tony Conigliaro came up again in an article by Clif Keane of the *Globe*. Keane raised serious moral questions about the manager's behavior in not contacting Tony C. after learning he might never play baseball again. Williams had disclosed that he had not seen his injured ballplayer since he had left spring camp early in April, and frankly seemed quite proud of it. It appeared, related Keane, that Williams was still holding a grudge for not being made aware of Conig's eye problem before he was examined. "That was quite staggering," said Keane.[19]

It wasn't until Boston had played their 30th game on May 15, against Washington, that the Boomer hit his first extra-base hit — a two-bagger. Five days later he hit his first home run of the season, against the Angels, and things were beginning to look better for George who put together 12 hits in 10 games, batting .316 during the streak. But after going hitless the next two games Williams wasted no time pulling Scott from the lineup and starting utility infielder Jerry Adair in his place; Adair had never played first base professionally. Ken Harrelson took over after that for a stretch of four games in which he collected 5 hits and 2 home runs. And in the next two games, playing right field, the Hawk hit two more home runs, reinforcing Williams' perception he was making all the right moves. By the end of May Scott was hitting an alarming .154, far beneath his capabilities, he insisted, and well below what Boston management expected from their 1967 .300 hitter. The Red Sox, hitting .238 as a team, was playing under .500, at 22–23, and in fifth place, 6½ games out of first and just one game better than sixth place.

Right about this time, just before Scott would once again enter Williams' doghouse, Harold Kaese of the *Globe* wrote a gripping article on the merits of a right-handed power hitter — a pure unabashed slugger type — in Fenway batting behind Yastrzemski. Yaz was not getting quality pitches anywhere around the plate following Conigliaro's departure and after the conversion by Williams of George Scott, a long-ball hitter, to nothing more than a non-threatening "base hits" man. Kaese used as foundation for his hypothesis Frank Howard, Washington's massive slugger, as a possible trade solution for the Sox. Like waving a carrot and then taking it away, he artfully dismissed the idea out of hand as not being the Williams brand, as his preference was "bat control" type players who could bunt, hit-and-run and hit to the opposite field. "But the Red Sox are not going to win the pennant hitting to the opposite field at Fenway Park," argued Kaese, stressing that they needed home runs to win, which they had plenty of in 1967, and they required reliable power behind Yaz to make him a more effective hitter. In pointed criticism of Williams Kaese questioned the manager's judgment in making Scott a "Dodger type" singles hitter when he had such raw natural power. Kaese's argument was well-founded and indisputable, the Red Sox could not survive the season without more power. Speaking for the Fenway following who sorely missed George Scott's big bat. "[We] grieve its loss," concluded Kaese despairingly.[20]

It was the "big swish" brand of baseball that was once highly favored by Red Sox brass, wrote Harold Kaese, reminding readers of Boston's penchant for the home run in their little ballpark and their long line of right-handed power hitters such as Jimmie Foxx, Dick Stuart, and Walt Dropo, whose job it was to smash baseballs against or over Fenway's alluring 37'2" high wall, designated the "Green Monster" (so-named in 1947). George Scott was one of those hitters. He had an extended type of swing, a massive batting stroke, a sweeping over-swing that Red Sox hitting instructor Bobby Doerr was attempting to "correct" inexorably as prescribed by the redoubtable Dick Williams. The Boomer was Doerr's number-one spring project. But there were concerns by some about changing this type of hitter with a natural swing designed for the long ball, into something much less; Doerr knew it. The outcome could be more daunting, something in-between, possibly, leading to problems with his timing, rhythm and more importantly, confidence.

"He's been analyzed more than teenage music," wrote the *Globe*'s Ray Fitzgerald in a critical essay on what was wrong with George Scott.[21] The consensus among the Red Sox players and manager Williams was that for the Red Sox to win the pennant they needed their big first sacker back in the lineup and hitting again. Scott agreed, of course, but felt the "big swing business" being advanced by the Red Sox was exaggerated. All he needed were a few base hits to bring back his confidence, which had already been seriously affected by the "new way" of hitting Williams wanted from him. Scott harkened back to what he had been told by "another Williams," Ted, which was in direct conflict with Dick Williams. Ted, who spent time with the young rookie slugger in Winter Haven and the Florida Instructional League in 1966 and again in '67, had taken a liking to George, and Scott respectfully sought Ted's advice, absorbing everything the Splendid Splinter had to offer him about the art of hitting. "He told me 'don't change your style,'" said Scott, plain and simple. Coming from one of the greatest hitters of all-time it was a message that resonated with the young slugger more than anything the Red Sox were trying to instill in him.[22]

A buzz was rampantly spiraling around Boston with one central theme: "What's wrong with George Scott?" One sportswriter even went so far to speculate that there can be no coincidence; it must be marital bliss since Scott was married just before the season started. On June 3 George broke out of his slump against Detroit with a three-hit performance, including two doubles and an important two-out base-on-balls, after being in the hole with a 0-and-2 count, that led to two more key runs and a Red Sox win. The game also marked the first Fenway Park appearance for Jim Lonborg since the World Series, a relief stint that helped preserve a win for Boston.

Scott continued to play well, going 2-for-6 in the next day's doubleheader split with the Tigers. "People keep telling him to hit the ball hard every time and the hits will come," wrote Bob Sales of the *Globe*.[23] He did just that in the first game, but was robbed by third baseman Don Wert who intercepted Scott's hard shot in the hole that was destined for left field in the second inning, and center fielder Stanley chased down his long drive to the left-center field wall in the fourth. But in the sixth inning George came up to bat with the bases loaded. Scott was looking for and laid into a Mickey Lolich fastball that sailed over Gates Brown's outstretched glove in left center and ricocheted off the scoreboard for a standup double; two runs scored, the only runs of the game on the only extra-base hit. The partisan crowd, which had had little to cheer about, bellowed their approval, especially because it was George, with whom they empathized and who had become a Fenway crowd favorite. Scott was asked somewhat obtusely by a reporter following the game if he was discouraged that he had not been hitting. His response, a solemn but sage reply for his years, was that there was no room for discouragement. "You can go but one way," he said, "and that's up."[24] And that's what he was determined to do.

It was noteworthy that for the first time in his career George Scott used a golf glove while batting, which he believed contributed to his successful day. It was of no small coincidence that teammate Ken Harrelson also used a golf glove; in fact he was credited with originating its use for a better grip of the bat that was later developed, manufactured and marketed for professional baseball and became popularly known as the "batting glove." Scott would use a batting glove — sometimes one on each hand — with every at-bat for the remainder of his professional baseball career.

Scott added two more base hits on June 5, stroking another double, this time with two men in scoring position, and an RBI single, knocking in three of four Red Sox runs against a dominant Dennis McLain, who that year would win 31 games. Scott hit safely in six straight games batting a hefty .450. But what followed were three games in which he went hitless; once again he angered Dick Williams who charged that George was "peeking" at the left-field wall. "So he is out of there," griped the irritated manager, replaced by Harrelson, a move that was rapidly evolving into Williams' tactic each time he banished the big first baseman to his most dishonorable but well-populated doghouse.

Not only didn't George Scott play, none of the Red Sox played for four consecutive days of rain-outs, tying them with the 1954 club for a team-record number of successive postponements. George was inwardly seething at the thought he was being benched again, just when he thought he was regaining his batting stroke that from the beginning of the season had abandoned him. After the June 11 rainout Scotty had a long batting practice session with hitting coach Bobby Doerr, and while swatting at baseballs, he complained he was confused over his manager's treatment of him and about not getting a chance to play. Doerr didn't have an answer for him; he just needed to be patient, he said, and he'd be in there. But he wasn't going to be. "The first baseman can't hit if he's on the bench," wrote Clif Keane of the *Globe*, with clear sympathies for Scott.[25] Williams reneged and played George in the first game of the June 13 doubleheader, but sat him down after that as he had originally promised, after the first baseman went hitless in three tries.

Following the final home game against California Yastrzemski, Petrocelli and Scott engaged in extra batting practice. The mood was relaxed and light-hearted as the three teammates put themselves through the paces hitting base-balls all over Fenway. George was particularly comfortable with Yaz and Petro, who were also his friends; no coaches were around, no manager, no advice to have to listen to time and again, just a few sportswriters in attendance who watched the three-man spectacle. Scott was the last to hit, with Yaz pitching. "The most awesome display of power I've ever seen," said Carl, describing the several blasts of George Scott that went far over the left-center field net and deep into the bleachers. "There's nothing wrong with that man," decried Yaz, except, he said, that he's become defensive instead of aggressive, and has lost his confidence. Yastrzemski seemed angry: "Why don't they leave him alone and let him swing?" he asked rhetorically.[26]

Ken Harrelson was having a stellar year, his best of a nine-year career in which he was to hit 35 home runs, win the American League RBI title, achieve All-Star status and nearly win the Most Valuable Player award. No sooner had Scott shaken the dirt from his cleats and found a spot on the Red Sox bench when Harrelson responded with a prodigious display of batting prowess in a string of five games clouting 5 homers — one a walk-off grand slam — and knocking in 15 runs. Of the Red Sox four victories in that span Harrelson almost single-handedly won three of them. It was like pounding a nail into the frustrated Scott, who seemed to be getting closer to the end of the bench with each home run launched by Harrelson.

But Dick Williams knew despite Harrelson's power display that it was purely one-dimensional; he realized that to have any chance for another pennant he had to have George Scott in the lineup, and his glove in the infield. Harrelson remained at first, however, for the next four games, continuing to pummel opposing pitchers, with 8 more base hits, another

George Scott returned to the Boston lineup on June 19, 1968, after spending time in manager Dick Williams' doghouse. Here he's sliding into home under tag of Detroit catcher Bill Freehan (courtesy of *Boston Herald*).

home run and 8 RBIs; but he also made three costly errors. He was adequate but he was no George Scott around the bag, lacking Scott's range and the confidence he brought to the entire infield.

On June 19 Scotty was back — but this time at third base. He went 0-for-4, striking out twice. He announced that evening he had had enough; he was going back to his "old swing" despite what manager Williams and Bobby Doerr had to say about it. "Just let me hit," he said, and he'd work himself out of the slump, he insisted. "His feelings are hardly acceptable to Dick Williams and Bobby Doerr," wrote Clif Keane of the *Globe*, reporting on the obvious displeasure Scott was about to encounter from his reluctant hitting coach and churlish skipper.[27] "That's really when the relationship took a different turn from there because I wouldn't make the change," said a reminiscent George Scott years later. Recalling that Williams also threatened him with being sent back to the minors because of his stubbornness, and that he had talked to owner Tom Yawkey about it, Scott's latent anger that was festering bubbled to the surface: "He lied," he ranted, remembering the unpleasant occasion. "I talked to Mr. Yawkey when we got home and he said he knew nothing of it, that he hadn't told him anything. So it was kind of tough [between us] from there," said Scott.[28]

Meanwhile Williams had made 31 lineup changes in 61 games. On June 22 he made still another switch, returning Scott to first base with Harrelson going back to right. There were immediate rewards, as Scott played a strong game defensively, won by Boston, including his inning-ending unassisted double play when he snatched a liner off the bat of Wayne Causey. Boston's most reliable pitcher that year, Jose Santiago, who was to make the All-Star team, developed arm trouble that day; he won that game, another one five days later, and then, as the arm became worse, never won another game in the major leagues. Jim Lonborg was struggling with shoulder problems of his own since spring training and hadn't won a game, and starter Ray Culp developed tendonitis in his elbow. Things were looking dire for Williams — his team wasn't hitting, the pitchers were going lame on him, and the media, who once lauded him their "super-shuffler," were now beginning to use more derisive terms such as "slump shuffler" because of his frequent lineup changes of a beleaguered team.

On June 20 Scott broke up Denny McLain's try for a no-hitter in the seventh inning, which the Sox ultimately lost, 5–1. It was the start of a string of ten games in which he hit safely in nine of them for a .278 average. When he was 0-for-5 the remaining two games in June, he was replaced by Dalton Jones — one of the Red Sox' big hitters in the '67 World Series — with whom Scotty would share first base the remainder of the 1968 season. Jones had no credentials for handling the first base bag; it was only the second time in his five-year stint with the Red Sox that Jones played the position.

Boston was moored solidly in seventh place at the end of June, thirteen games behind first-place Detroit. George Scott was still struggling at the plate, hitting .183. "Scott is killing us," ranted a frustrated Dick Williams after absorbing a tough extra-inning loss to Cleveland in which George was 0-for-2, and was removed by Williams in the sixth inning. Yastrzemski was slumping badly and neither Petrocelli nor Mike Andrews was doing much either. The manager felt that someone had to carry the burden under the circumstances; his sights were clearly leveled at George Scott. "Fair or foul, Scott has become the patsy in what may become the first of many lineup changes," wrote the *Globe*'s Neil Singelais.[29]

It appeared to be a brilliant move by Williams putting Jones at first, as Boston won 11 of their next 12 games, and the Red Sox moved into fourth place 9½ games out of first by mid–July. Scott got closer to the end of the bench with each Red Sox win. He was being used sparingly by Williams who shuffled him in and out of lineups, mostly using him defensively in late innings or in pinch-hit roles. On July 17 he started for the first time since the end of June and, batting third in the lineup, clouted a monstrous home run off of Twins ace left-hander Jim Kaat, 437 feet to dead center; he also made a couple of brilliant defensive plays. His reward was to be back on the bench the following day, collecting more of the proverbial splinters.

Before the July 26 game against Washington, in which he started at first base, Scott complained loudly to the press, and to anyone willing to listen, that he was disenchanted with how he was being treated by the manager, who showed no confidence in him, and therefore he was losing confidence in himself. No sooner would he have a good game, he said, and appear to be getting on track again, then he was pulled from the lineup. For the first time the 24-year-old slugger made overtures about playing for another club, which did not go unnoticed by the Red Sox brass. They were beginning to inwardly look at the manager with some reservations, since there were issues developing with other players as well.

In August freelance writer Leonard Shecter wrote a disturbing and quite controversial article for *Life Magazine* entitled "Baseball: Great American Myth," that caused a clamor throughout the Red Sox organization and their city. Shecter was traveling with the Sox in May of that year to do a story on the defending champions. What it in large part turned out to be was a misguided testimonial by several Red Sox players on their manager, and their dislike for the man, that came back to haunt them when the magazine hit the store shelves. Players scrambled to deny what they were alleged to have said; Shecter himself had to publicly defend what he wrote. Boston scribes were all over it, but, characteristicly the journalistic fraternity came to the defense of Shecter, whom the *Globe*'s Harold Kaese described as "an experienced and able writer."[30]

Ken Harrelson, who had not been performing well earlier in the season and was unhappy, was quoted by Shecter as saying about Dick Williams: "There's no way you can like that man. He doesn't give you a chance to like him." Harrelson was furious, denying he ever said that, but the Boston press gave their nod to Shecter as the most likely credible source. Don McMahon, traded by the Red Sox to the White Sox in 1967, was bitter over his former manager. "He got an expression on his face like I smelled or something and he had it all the time I was there," said McMahon.[31] After several interviews over a span of six weeks hanging around with the Red Sox, Shecter's summary view of Williams was particularly dispositive, and in his discourse he bluntly concluded about the Red Sox skipper that "Williams is not liked by his players" — period.

America's Olympic hero Jesse Owens was hired on July 3 by AL president Joe Cronin as his "special public relations director" to help with player relations, and "what's bugging them," said Owens. Although he was cautious about disclosing that his real purpose was to address racial problems that had been filtering through the leagues, it was generally believed that the black athlete was Owens' charge; it was indeed the black athlete that received his greatest attention. He pointed out problems with the White Sox' Tommy Davis as illustrative of the issue. Davis, who was an All-Star and reputed solid hitter, had been in an uncharacteristically bad slump, and "obviously something was bothering him," Owens said. The *something* was someone, Eddie Stanky, which was resolved when he was replaced by Al Lopez. On July 16 while he was attending a National League game, Owens mentioned that he planned to approach George Scott, "a great hitter who just can't seem to be able to do anything this year," he said.[32] Owens began his new role by meeting players in the first week of August; he paid his first visit to White Sox Park on August 6 to begin his troubleshooting with some of the White Sox and Red Sox players, among them Davis and Scott. It was the first night of another benching of George — this one for a stretch of six games — by Williams. Scott was 6-for-17 in the previous eight games, four of them doubles, and hitting at a .353 clip before being sat down.

He didn't start another game until August 11. On August 20 he was penciled in by Williams to face his old nemesis, "Sudden Sam" McDowell, of the Cleveland Indians. McDowell, who had a gun for an arm, was having another very good year; he would win 15 games and strike out a major-league-leading 283 batters. Before the game Cleveland manager Alvin Dark was talking to the sports scribes about the expansion draft that was due to occur in a couple of months, and which of the players on each team would be protected. He immediately brought up the subject of George Scott whom, he expressed, he would trade for anyway expecting he would be protected by Boston. Obviously critical of Scott's handling by the Red Sox, Dark stated, "I would tell him he was going to play and he would stay in there. He needs that kind of help."[33]

Then the Indians manager spotted George at the batting cage, broke up his session with reporters, and quickly walked over to him for a long chat.

As if he were confirming his value to the Indians manager, who expressed a definite interest in him, Scotty stroked his third and final homer of the year off the hard-throwing McDowell that went deep into Municipal Stadium's left-field seats. It was the only Red Sox run of the contest. "He (Williams) sent me up to bat against Sam McDowell thinking that McDowell was going to make me look bad," said Scott after his playing days were over. He was convinced that putting him in the lineup against McDowell was just another set-up by Dick Williams, who he claimed had it in for him after he refused to cooperate with the manager's effort to alter his batting style, and who, he felt, was trying to embarrass him. "(He wanted) in all situations to make George Scott look bad because he wanted to trade me," said Scott. "But he had to convince Mr. Yawkey and Dick O'Connell because they didn't want to trade me, but Dick Williams wanted to get me out of his hair. Then fortunately they fired him the next year."[34]

He was benched again for the next two games, and then on August 23, the start of a three-game series at Baltimore, Williams surprised everyone, including Carl Yastrzemski, by inserting Yaz at first base for the first time in his major league career. He was to become the seventh man to play first base for the Sox that season, and the third in succession who was not a first sacker. "Defensively, for a Siebern, Jones, Harrelson, Adair and Yastrzemski to replace Scott was like Tony Galento taking Dick Button's place on ice skates," wrote the *Globe*'s Harold Kaese.[35]

Why? was the querulous response from faithful Red Sox followers who were beginning to wonder if their manager had all of his marbles. Baseball pundits, including those of other ball clubs, were second-guessing Williams. Many were saying that the Red Sox were likely to have done as well, and maybe even better, if they had simply left Scott at first for the entire 1968 season. The odds were, however, he was not going to be with the Red Sox in 1969.

It had become a leading story on the Red Sox — the discontent of their 24-year-old first baseman and his treatment by his contemptible manager. "George Scott is storing up like Vesuvius, and somewhere near the end of the season he will erupt unless something is done to stop it," wrote Clif Keane of the *Boston Globe*. Maybe it was even a racial thing, said Keane, but deferred the thought because "where in major league baseball do you find any communication between white and Negro?" Williams had not even talked to George in two months. Keane suggested they were both at fault but placed a greater onus on the manager whom, he suggested, needed to talk to Scott behind closed doors. Keane's conclusion: "And — like we said — this guy can play the game. There is only one ballplayer on the Red Sox who can play it better — Carl Yastrzemski."[36]

George Scott's "Vesuvius" did indeed erupt as Keane had predicted. On Saturday, September 7, after a game against the Angels in California, Scott learned that Dick Williams was going to put Rico Petrocelli at first base the next day. He was to become the eighth Red Sox first baseman during the year, and the fourth to play the position without any previous experience there. It was a peculiar move by the manager, made less than two weeks after experimenting with perennial All-Star and Gold Glove left fielder Carl Yastrzemski at the position. He said the move was "to rest Adair and Gibson," and no doubt also to get Rico Petrocelli, who was suffering from an elbow injury, back into the lineup. Rico was reticent to take the assignment, feeling completely out of his element at the position, and it showed. He misjudged a Rick Reichardt pop fly in the third that fell behind him, and missed a tag play on Jim Fregosi at first that Scott, it was surmised, would have made. Scott was devastated and he exploded in a rage, blasting Williams and insisting it would be the last time he would be humiliated by the man. "All the guy is trying to do is kill everything I've got for the game," bellowed a very upset Scott, who promised he was not going to play for him again.[37]

It seemed clear to the Boston writers that Scott had burned his last bridge with the Red Sox and that he would be on the trading block in short order. "Unless, of course, Yawkey should see things his way," wrote the *Globe*'s Singelais, remembering how many times in the past Yawkey had sided with his players and the manager received the boot instead.[38] On Monday morning, September 9, the *Herald-Traveler* reported that Scott had approached GM Dick O'Connell about the matter and avowed he would also personally speak to owner Tom Yawkey when he got home from their western road swing.

Overlooking his promise not to play again for Williams, that night in Oakland against the A's Scott was in the starting lineup, at first base, his first starting assignment since September 3. Williams had him batting eighth. A brief moral victory for George said the sportswriters, but he was certain to be traded nevertheless. Feeling "strange" at the plate because of a loss of confidence, Scott took two called third strikes in his first two plate appearances. In the seventh he blasted a shot off of Chuck Dobson, chasing fleet-footed Rick Monday deep to the center-field wall, 410 feet away; Monday caught the ball against the fence with his glove hand fully extended. On Tuesday morning Dick Williams announced he was starting Dalton Jones at first; three hours later he changed his plans, announcing Scott would start there instead. His rather bland explanation to a band of eager sportswriters who knew they were onto a story was that he and his coaches had "talked it over" and simply decided it was best to start Scott. The writers, seeing it differently, felt there could be no other reason for the sudden change than the belief that someone in the Red Sox hierarchy called upon the manager to play Scott. Williams denied it.

As if defying the Red Sox brass Williams started Jones at first base the first game back from their road trip, on September 13. "It will depend on who's pitching," said the manager, suggesting he would use Scott only against left-handers.[39] He was back in the starting lineup on September 14 against the Twins' Dave Boswell, a right-hander.

The buzz was on in Boston and ramping up in major league circles on just who was going to win the war of nerves, Scott or Williams? An even bigger question was can the Red Sox keep both? "Not now," said Tim Horgan of the *Herald-Traveler*, explaining that to keep Scott would merely undermine the manager, and to keep Williams may just banish a player with the best potential "for years to come."[40] The decision was squarely in the lap of one Thomas A. Yawkey.

Although it was by far the most serious of the issues hanging over the Red Sox, the Scott-Williams conflict was not the sole problem with the team. There was dissension on the club, among the more notable their superstar Carl Yastrzemski who had an encounter with Williams on September 8 in California when Yaz was asked to take a pitch on a 3–0 count that he thought he should have hit. Then veteran Elston Howard was disgruntled because he was not playing much, nor had the manager spoken to him in a very long time, he said with great annoyance. Ken Harrelson, who was having the best year of any of the Red Sox players, spoke publicly to deny the accusation. "There is no dissension on this ball club that will hurt us on the field," he said, and then blamed "one or two writers" who he said were stirring up trouble.[41] Ironically he was the very man who was alleged to have complained earlier in the year in the *Life Magazine* article that Dick Williams was not a likeable guy.

George never regained his footing the rest of the way in 1968, switching frequently with Dalton Jones, starting one game at third base on September 25, and sitting out the final three games of a hopelessly miserable season. He finished with his worst career statistics in fourteen seasons of major league baseball: played in 124 games, hit an anemic .171 on only 60 base hits, and hit a meager 3 home runs, none at Fenway. The Red Sox as a team finished the season in fourth place, with an 86–76 record, 17 games behind the Detroit Tigers who ran away with the pennant, and then beat St. Louis in the World Series. In spite of a poor year at the plate, Scott repeated with defensive honors, acknowledged as the best first baseman of the American League by winning his second Gold Glove award, despite playing just 112 games at first base.

Whatever the motivational forces were that inspired a contemptuous Dick Williams to singularly take apart young George Scott in that forgettable season of 1968, one truth seems to stand above everything else. He may have had more to do with dismantling George Scott's spirit and the erosion of the young ballplayer's confidence than anything Scotty may have brought upon himself. Williams nearly psychologically destroyed Scott. Although few teammates were spared the insults of the irascible young field manager, a well-recognized fact,

George became a special target of Williams' derisiveness, which was a generally accepted view by many of his Red Sox teammates.

"For the first time in my life I let somebody get in my head," lamented Scott in retrospect. "All of my life from Little League ball all the way up I never let anyone get into my head. Dick Williams got into my head and he really messed up my mind. Williams had me that year [in a mental state] so I just could not stay focused; my concentration was not good. As a matter of fact, if I don't go to Puerto Rico and play winter ball under Frank Robinson I probably wouldn't have had a long career in baseball because I had lost my confidence. By the time I got to San Juan I had lost all of my confidence."[42]

10

Rehab

Maybe he [George Scott] gets too much advice on his hitting. — Dick O'Connell, Red Sox GM[1]

"Nobody wished me good luck," grumbled a disheartened George Scott as he stashed personal belongings into his duffel bag and picked out three bats to take with him to Puerto Rico to play winter ball for Santurce. The Red Sox had just lost their final game of the 1968 season to the Yankees before a Sunday Fenway sellout crowd, with it they lost their hold on third place and another $600 per man of World Series money that would now go to the Cleveland Indians. But as disappointing as it had been for the Red Sox after their sensational Impossible Dream performance of '67, with injuries and key players not performing well, they excelled at the turnstile in '68 by drawing an unprecedented number of nearly two million fans on the year.

George had been relegated again to the bench by Williams for all three games of the season-ending series against New York. He was miserable, his emotions palpable in the Red Sox clubhouse following the final game midst the clatter of teammates who were about to scatter and reporters mulling around zealously seeking scoops. He could find little solace to ease his disappointment and was troubled that no one seemed to care.

On Wednesday October 9 the Red Sox submitted their "frozen 15" list of protected ballplayers to the American League office in advance of the expansion draft scheduled to occur in six days. Two new teams, the Kansas City Royals and Seattle Pilots, were entering the league, which was breaking into two divisions, Eastern and Western, of six teams each. To the surprise of most fans and some sportswriters George Scott was on the protected list. Player Personnel Director Haywood Sullivan answered the critics with some unexpectedness of his own, along with a mild warning to Red Sox coaches and their manager: "We intend to keep George around and something has to be done about his present situation," said a critical Sullivan, who appeared to speak for more than just himself, but as a likely spokesman for owner Tom Yawkey, whose one desire above all others was to have a "happy" team.[2] It was not the kind of message Dick Williams, who "bends like a lamppost," wrote one Boston writer, wanted to hear.

On the following Tuesday, October 15, Kansas City wasted no time snatching up Joe Foy, their second pick in the first round, whom the Sox left unprotected. It was a surprise to just about everyone in Boston who felt Foy should have been at least worthy of a sharp trade than to be discharged in this manner, with nothing of value to speak of except cash for Red Sox coffers. Foy said he was glad to leave Boston lambasting not the organization, but Dick Williams, whom he despised, calling him "a two-faced sneak." Foy said the Boston skipper didn't speak to him all year. Fan reaction was immediate and furious: a Boston bartender asked rhetorically, "Who's goin' to play third?" The answer was just as immediate: Williams was giving the job to his leading doghouse resident, George Scott. This would allow his '68 batting star, Ken Harrelson, a first baseman by trade, to move back there full-time. Foy had made a league-leading 30 errors in '68. There was a strong need for improvement at the hot corner and Williams was confident the Gold Glove first baseman had the hands for the job, in spite of his oversized stature — all 220 pounds of him — atypical of a third sacker.

Meanwhile teams of both leagues were salivating at the thought of picking up Scott for some right-handed power, the Indians' Gabe Paul in particular, who already had former Red Sox discard Tony Horton at first base, but who wanted Scott's superior defense and his bat power. His manager, Alvin Dark, who felt George had been mismanaged, was high on the young slugger and anxious to have him in their fold. Paul knew the Red Sox needed a catcher and the Indians had two good ones in Duke Sims and Joe Azcue. This was about to become even more problematic for the Sox as their veteran catcher, Elston Howard, a defensive stalwart and a good handler of pitchers, announced his retirement on October 21. Howard's personal disenchantment with Williams was as likely a reason for his calling it quits when he did, as he was eager to get back to the Yankees and coaching; his parting words about the Red Sox manager: "I don't care to get involved with him. I've been taught too much class for that."[3] Howard was another of the Red Sox manager's infamous doghouse victims and didn't know why, claiming Williams had not spoken to him for "a long, long time." But as much as Boston had a need and yearned for good catching, they were reluctant to turn their backs on Scott, whom they felt held great promise and was likely to regain his batting skills with the right kind of leadership.

Humiliated over his performance, and feeling within himself a thoroughly beaten man after the '68 season, for the first time George Scott had doubts about his future in baseball. GM Dick O'Connell commented about Scott's bad year as, "One of those things you have to write off." It was clear, however, in spite of all the noise surrounding Scott and the Red Sox, and other teams vying for Scott through trade or purchase, that O'Connell and Yawkey had no intentions of dispensing with the big first baseman, by suggesting that he would be manager Williams' number one "rehab assignment." It was a direct challenge issued to the crusty manager to mend his ways with his players and restore their confidence, and foremost to work on the reclamation of George Scott to return him to the level of play and the ballplayer they knew he could be. The question looming was, would Dick Williams stay?

O'Connell had arranged for his troubled ballplayer to spend the winter in Puerto Rico with the Santurce Crabbers under their new manager, Frank Robinson, of the Baltimore Orioles. Robinson's managerial debut turned out to be a perfect match for Scott. It may have been the single most important decision George would make in his career, for Robinson worked closely with the young ballplayer, restoring in him his self-respect and the confidence that abandoned him under the caustic Dick Williams. Scott has credited Frank Robinson with turning him around, and his primary reason for staying in baseball. Robinson was particularly sensitive to the kind of pressure George was experiencing, which had earmarks of racial intolerance.[4]

Whether or not there was a racial element attached to Williams' treatment of Scott is subject to conjecture; there is no doubt, however, that George took the brunt of his skipper's wrath, and it was of a virulent kind. But it was also evident that of the Red Sox regulars who frequented the manager's doghouse, the greater numbers were black: Scott, Foy, Wyatt, Howard, and Santiago (Latino), and, sometimes, even Reggie Smith. Each received more than a proportional share of Williams' retributive nature. Coincidence? Maybe so, maybe not. It is difficult to say.

If there truthfully was racism at play it might well have been something that Williams himself was unaware of, but it nonetheless may well have occurred. Former major league pitcher and current Major League Baseball Players Alumni Association board member Jim Mudcat Grant, who played for Dick Williams in Oakland, had this to say: "People like Dick (Williams) and people like Solly Hemus, and other [white] people, they weren't the only ones... . We (black ballplayers) were titled as being lazy and don't work hard, and all that kind of stuff— black male. That could have some resonance to it in terms of how a manager or a coach may act towards you." Grant explained that it was a manifestation of the era. If managers were accused of being racist they would adamantly deny it; they didn't even know that they were, argued Grant. "It's really based on the way it was," he said.[5]

Scott arrived in Santurce in the early part of October to prepare for the winter league season scheduled to open on October 17. He was made aware of his impending shift to third base by Williams two days before. Frank Robinson, his manager, was a seasoned veteran, an MVP in both the American and National Leagues (the only player ever to accomplish it) and destined to be both a Hall of Famer and the first black major league manager (for 16 seasons, winning the AL Manager of the Year award in 1989). He was an inveterate leader who stood tall for the black ballplayer when circumstances called for it; he was a man of stature respected by his peers.

His timing couldn't have been any better; George thrived under Robinson's tutelage, batting .295 for Santurce with a league-leading 13 home runs and 46 RBIs, over the course of 69 winter league games. Importantly, he also led the league in walks, a sign that he had his batting eye back again. His performance made him an overwhelming choice by a vote of his peers as starting first baseman on the All-Star squad. Santurce won the pennant by 5½ games over second-place Ponce, but then lost the semi-final playoff series to their crosstown rival, San Juan, 4 games to 3. Scott hit two more home runs in the playoffs. It was a remarkable comeback for the 24 year old after such a miserable major league season. Drawing the attention of Red Sox brass, they now saw in him a rejuvenated youngster with a more positive state of mind, and a more confident ballplayer fashioned under Robinson's careful guidance.

Scott has good memories of his relationship with Robinson and of his time in Puerto Rico, and about maturing under Robinson's guidance and leadership. It was a career-defining moment for George who gives most of the credit for his rehabilitation and recovery, and about being a smarter and better ballplayer, to the two-time MVP and future Hall of Famer. "Having had a chance to play for Frank Robinson was the best thing that ever happened to my career, because not only did he help me mentally, but he also helped me physically, and I became a better player," said a respectful George Scott. "A lot of things probably I shouldn't have taken personally, but I did. He taught me a lot, and I always said that I had Frank Robinson to thank for the turnaround in my career."[6]

In December, prior to the opening of the 1969 spring training season, Major League Baseball hit a snag: a dispute had arisen between the players and owners over the owners' cutbacks to the players' pension plan. Unlike before when players often came up short with the owners under a loosely organized union arrangement, this time they were intransigent. A pivotal year, 1969 was to be the first of several key historical events between the parties, leading ultimately to the end of the *reserve clause* and the advent of *free agency*. The players overwhelmingly rejected the owners' pension proposal and voted not to sign their contracts until the matter was resolved. It was unprecedented and talk began to circulate that there would be a strike. Bowie Kuhn, recently appointed acting baseball commissioner by the owners, ultimately convinced the owners to meet all of the players' demands just prior to the February 26 reporting time, for all players, to ensure that the spring exhibition season would open on schedule.

The training camps, however, were to some degree impacted by the threat-ened strike; most pitchers and catchers failed to report on time, and the major-ity of players had not even signed their contracts before the official opening date. George Scott was among them but not for the same reason favored by his teammates. George did not sympathize with the union position, empha-sizing he could not afford to sit out unlike the more well-paid superstars like Yastrzemski, Mays, and Clemente. George's position was straightforward — he wanted a raise before he would play, he said.

There was little doubt George's confidence was restored after his Puerto Rico performance and he felt, in a moment of hubris, he was worthy of a "token" salary increase notwithstanding his miserable season of '68. As his

teammates were talking pen-sion, George was talking pay-raise. He hired attorney Bob Woolf, a noted pro athlete lawyer, to represent him — a good move, but bad timing — but even Woolf had no leverage to muster any further money from Dick O'Connell and the Red Sox. Scott's main argument with Boston rested in his not having been given a chance to play in 1968 — an affront to Dick Williams — proving to them that when given the opportunity, such as in Puerto Rico under Robinson, he was capable of great things. The argument fell on deaf ears. On February 28, two days after the Red Sox camp opened for the full squad of players, Scott, along with holdouts Reggie Smith and Ray Culp, signed their contracts and then took part in a workout. George, a shining paragon of the Puerto

February 28, 1969 — Scott's arrival in Winter Haven, Florida, for spring training, as a Red Sox holdout looking for a raise following a successful winter ball season in Santurce, Puerto Rico, notwithstanding a dismal 1968 season (courtesy of *Boston Herald*).

Rican League, hadn't lost his touch, clouting two practice home runs—one over 420 feet—out of Chain O' Lakes Park. He was feeling very good about himself and much more mentally prepared to deal with his '68 nemesis, Dick Williams.

Sportswriter Clif Keane reported in his spring column "Scott Solemn, Feels Sure at 3d" that George was tight-lipped but not content with the switch being made of him by Williams, but he was far more anxious to stay in the lineup. With a certain resignation he would make the best of the situation. Tension between the manager and his two-time Gold Glover was still palpable, as both shared a nearly pathological dislike for each other. Scott stated that he and Williams did not get together before the start of spring training to iron out differences: "I come to the park and say hello to him and he says hello to me," said Scott; it was strictly business. George was content with that as long as he was playing.[7]

It seemed clear to savvy Boston sportswriters that Dick Williams was working under some kind of mandate by the Red Sox brass to mend his ways with his players, as he was surprisingly mellow throughout most of the spring season. Astonishingly he even had good things to say about his new third sacker, Scott, whom he praised for George's slick play at the position. Scott showed good range covering ground balls hit in the hole with his long reach and making strong accurate throws to first. "I don't care how much he weighs, just look at him out there at third base and you can see what I mean about how he can field the position," Williams said with what seemed to be a sudden and quite unexpected change of heart over the matter of the big infielder's waistline.[8]

There was good reason why the Red Sox skipper was gushy about his team as on that day, his damaged right fielder, Tony Conigliaro, making a comeback bid against 1,000-to-1 odds, smashed his first home run

February 27, 1969—Unsigned George Scott standing next to Billy Conigliaro and Ken Harrelson at a batting cage. Scott had a miserable season in 1968 while Harrelson, who replaced Scott at first base much of the season, had a career year in '68 and nearly won American League MVP. Scott signed his 1969 Red Sox contract the next day, February 28 (courtesy of Boston Public Library).

Scott working out at third base in spring training, at the position where manager Dick Williams would play him for most of the 1969 season (courtesy of *Boston Herald*).

since his injury of August 1967. It gave the team a mental lift, most of all Conigliaro. Tony C. hit three more homers in the final five games of the exhibition season presenting the Red Sox with a pleasant surprise that their young superstar outfielder was back. Boston finished the exhibition campaign at 11–15. George Scott looked strong defensively and offensively, batting a solid .305 and stroking 25 base hits, 3 home runs and 16 RBIs. He and the Red Sox had every reason to believe he also was back to his 1967 form.

The 1969 season started with a bang when on April 8, Opening Day in Baltimore, a recovered Tony C., who miraculously was now seeing the ball well again, clouted a 10th-inning home run off Pete Richert to put Boston in front 4–2. He later scored the winning run in the 12th inning. All of Boston was ecstatic; Tony was back. The Sox won five of their first six games, and tied a 1935 American League record in the first three by playing consecutive extra-inning contests, a total of 41 innings.

George Scott was off to another slow start with one base hit in his first fifteen at-bats. Dalton Jones replaced him for one game on April 13, after Scott was beaned on April 12, but George returned to the lineup the next day and hit safely in three successive games, going 6-for-12 with 2 home runs, both at Fenway, his first home runs hit at Fenway since 1967. On April 19 the Red Sox startled their fans by trading Ken Harrelson to Cleveland in a six-player deal. Harrelson was a charismatic figure in the Hub, a mod, foppish kind of guy and regular fashion plate; there was an allure about him that appealed to young and old. Joining Harrelson were pitchers Dick Ellsworth and Juan Pizarro, in exchange for Cleveland's on-again, off-again, pitcher Sonny Siebert, pitcher Vicente Romo, and catcher Joe Azcue. Azcue had been a frequent name tossed around much earlier in a proposed deal for George Scott, which the Red Sox had steadfastly refused to do. The Indians were not going to release Azcue, however, without getting a quality Red Sox slugger in return. It came down to either Scott or Harrelson, and the Sox chose the "Hawk," once again declining to part with Scotty.

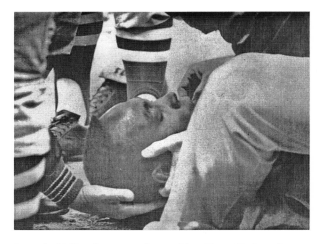

June 3, 1969 — Scott was beaned by Cisco Carlos of the White Sox. He missed one game, then was back in the lineup on June 6, tying the game against Kansas City with his fifth home run of the season (courtesy of *Boston Herald*).

By the end of April Boston was in third place, three games out of first behind Baltimore and New York. George Scott finished the month batting .208 with 3 homers, tying his home run mark for all of the 1968 season in just a dozen games. But he slumped again for most of May and by month's end was hitting under .200, a mere .193. This time Dick Williams stuck with Scott, unlike in '68 when he was moved in-and-out of lineups like a yo-yo. In the last week of May into early June, a span of ten games, he hit safely in eight of them for a .355 average. Then on June 3 Scott was beaned by Chicago's Cisco Carlos, striking him on the top of his helmet that resulted in a concussion. He missed one game, was back in the lineup on June 6, when he tied the game against Kansas City with his 5th home run, a towering blast on a two-strike count in the bottom of the 10th inning.

It was raining that night, there were two outs, and 29,438 fans were streaming for the exits at Fenway as it appeared Boston had lost to the expansion Kansas City Royals. Then a "wicked explosion occurred at home plate," wrote Clif Keane of the *Globe,* describing Scott's blast that rocketed halfway up the wall behind the center-field bleacher seats. It was "awesome," said Keane. And the 29,438 fans who were leaving came back to watch the Red Sox defeat Kansas City in the 11th on a Dalton Jones homer. They were "singing in the rain," said the Boston sportswriter.[9] Interestingly Keane reported that George saved his skin with that home run, as he was about to be benched by Williams, who for some inexplicable reason was on Scott again in spite of his recent performance. Scott stroked his 6th homer the following day.

On June 11 catcher Joe Azcue, who had come to the Red Sox on April 19 in the Harrelson trade, suddenly went AWOL because of his disenchantment with Dick Williams over not playing enough. An All-Star catcher in '68, and enamored that he would be the Boston manager's choice for Red Sox catching duties (Williams had picked Azcue for the '68 All-Star team), the Cuban back-stop came to the Hub confident of being the team's number one receiver. But it didn't work out that way. Azcue played six games in April, sparingly in May starting in just eight games, and was benched in June; he played a total of 19 games in which he batted .216. His complaint was that he was not given a chance by the Red Sox skipper, nor was he given the respect he felt he deserved. Williams had no intentions to ameliorate the situation with Azcue and made it plain to Red Sox brass to trade him. As far as he was concerned Azcue was nothing but a defector and he was in no mood to take him back, especially when the catcher went over his head.

In the long run the Azcue affair had cataclysmic consequences for Williams. Neither Dick O'Connell nor Tom Yawkey was happy with him over the matter, feeling he should have made an effort to reconcile with their newly acquired catcher, who had the potential to be a timely hitter with a little more patience. "I was just hoping to play one against the other man in there," said Williams explaining his tactics.[10] But it did not sit well with the Red Sox brass, which saw Williams as intransigent. On June 15, the trading deadline, Boston sent Azcue to California for Angels catcher Tom Satriano, which turned out to be a poor exchange for Boston. Williams exclaimed with a certain degree of pugnaciousness that he not only wanted to see Azcue leave Boston, but he was quite disappointed he wasn't traded out of the American League. All of New England was mumbling about the matter: why for heaven sake was Azcue pursued by the team — almost two years in the making — if they were not going to use him?

The Red Sox returned to Boston for a brief three-game homestand against Oakland, and were soundly trounced by the A's, losing all three, the last two by a margin of 22 runs. Reggie Jackson demolished Red Sox pitching by hitting 4 home runs on 9 base hits and 15 RBIs (ten in one game). Boston pitching was not about to stop him. Adding to the debacle were 9 Boston errors, a reminder of pre–1967 Red Sox teams. Pitching was bad, fielding was bad, and Dick Williams was furious. George Scott, meanwhile, batted .300 for the series and hit his seventh home run.

Batting at a torrid pace in a stretch of eight straight games stroking 14 base hits for a .424 average, George Scott was on a roll. On June 21 in a game against the Yankees Scott was responsible for three of the Red Sox' four base hits, and knocked in two of their three runs. In a June 24 doubleheader split with Cleveland, Scott was 6-for-8 with two home runs. He had reached base safely in 22 consecutive games, and 28 of his last 29. But he ran into more bad luck when on June 26 he was struck by a pitch thrown by the Indians' Horacio Pina, leaving him with a bad bruise on the heel of his right hand that benched him for the final four games of June and affected him for most of July. Scott batted .361 for the month with 5 home runs, raising his season average 57 points to .249; he led all Boston hitters in June.

By July 1 the Red Sox were in second place at 43–31, but a full 11 games behind Baltimore, who appeared to be pulling away from the Eastern Division teams. Williams was becoming apoplectic over his team's poor performance having seen them lose seven straight from the end of June into July. He showed little restraint in publicly criticizing his players, and that was never more evident than his tirade — openly shared with the press — directed at Tony Conigliaro on his misplay of a fly ball on June 29 against the Senators that contributed to their loss. Tony explained that he "lost it," apparently not seeing the ball for a brief moment, and then froze as the ball dropped; he was inconsolable. Williams was not of a mind to ask questions of his ballplayer, or confer clemency; he was enraged and benched Tony C. for the next two games.

George Scott stood out like a beacon that day by coming to the defense of his friend, as Conigliaro, near tears, sat frozen on the locker room bench. "There were several horrible mistakes out there, man. Yours was only one of them," exclaimed Scott, doing his best to lift the spirits of the devastated teammate and help him understand that he alone did not lose the ball game. Clif Keane, the Boston newsman, witnessed the herculean efforts of Scott, who knew the wrath of the manager better than any of the Red Sox players, and who did his best to aid the young slugger. Keane wrote in his next day's column what he had observed in the Red Sox locker room, and of George Scott: "And when I walked out, I thought more of George Scott than I ever did."[11]

The *Boston Globe's* July 7 morning edition contained a feature article by Ray Fitzgerald with a headline: "Mates Solidly Support Conig," reflecting the Red Sox players' unwavering solidarity for their fragile teammate. Once again Williams' non-communication with his players rose to the surface and was cast all over the newswires. Asked about the matter by a scrutinizing press, Williams tersely replied, "The players know my standards," as if by being indifferent to the situation — even when it involved Tony C., a fan-favorite coming back from a devastating injury — seemed the most sensible way for him to handle it.[12]

What followed thirteen days later was a column written by Keane that was headlined: "Is Dick Williams on Way Out?" with a subheading that read, "Yawkey Rates Sox Manager Only as 'Good.'" In an informal session with Yawkey and O'Connell, Keane had baited Yawkey by asking him on a four-part scale of "fair to outstanding" to rank the BoSox skipper, and was pleasantly surprised when he was rewarded with a response. It rocked the city and infuriated Dick Williams who demanded an immediate audience with the Red Sox owner, which occurred the following morning. According to Williams in his book *No More Mr. Nice Guy*, Yawkey's explanation to him was nothing more than an insipid "I just don't think you are doing good enough."[13] Whatever was said that day, coagulating underneath was Yawkey's personal distaste for the Red Sox manager and his readily apparent inability to communicate with his players, citing for Keane his displeasure of Williams' habitual public criticism of Tony Conigliaro, among other Red Sox players frequenting his doghouse. And the Azcue affair was still smoldering. "So you never can tell what will happen between now and October," blurted Yawkey, raising speculation the Red Sox manager was on a short leash.[14]

Remarkably the origins of what we now know as Red Sox Nation was taking form; in spite of the perceived lapse in Red Sox performance since the spectacular 1967 pennant-winning year, and disgruntlement stirring amongst players and the front office, the little bandbox known as Fenway Park was filling with fans. In their second year under Williams since the Impossible Dream, Fenway Park would draw over 5½ million fans in that span, an unprecedented number of enthusiasts, far exceeding the level of previous years, which certainly was to Williams' credit and could not be ignored by the Red Sox brass, no matter how Tom Yawkey felt about him.

On August 1 Boston was tied with Detroit for second place, 15 games behind a surging first-place Baltimore team; George Scott was batting .239. That night in the opener against Oakland, the eighth game of a long western swing of less than inspiring Boston baseball — the Red Sox losing 7 of 11 games — Williams clashed with Yawkey's beloved superstar Carl Yastrzemski. Unable to make a play at first on an infield grounder, third baseman Sal Bando threw a tentative Yastrzemski out at home plate for the final out in the first inning. It killed a Red Sox rally in which they had scored two runs. Williams was incensed and, in front of the entire team, confronted the three-time American League batting champion who appeared to be dogging it (Yastrzemski admitted later that he had occasionally loafed around the basepaths), declaring he was fining him $500. It was the first fine of Carl Yastrzemski's career. Williams offered no remorse or excuses for his conduct; he was content with the result no matter how publicly it was done. Rico Petrocelli did all he could do to refrain from openly criticizing the manager; "The man was screaming," said the frustrated shortstop, who found the entire episode baffling. Though the fine may have been justified, the manner in which it was executed may have been the final blow for Yawkey, leading to Williams' eventual downfall.

"There was an undercurrent of unpleasantness," on the ballclub reported the *Herald-Traveler*'s Larry Claflin in the first few home games following the Red Sox' return to Fenway. They seemed to be fading, said Claflin, instead of picking up the pace as they did so famously in '67. Williams was platooning and constantly juggling lineups in his frustrated attempt to find the right combination and to finally win consistently. But in spite of all the changes and shuffling of players, one thing was consistent — George Scott was almost always in the lineup. Through August 26 he had played in 118 of 125 games, second only to Yastrzemski who had played in all of them. In spite of the "intramural sniping," wrote Ray Fitzgerald of the *Globe* that was going on about the clubhouse, and proved more than confusing to the big infielder who saw no room for that, Scott was performing steadily. He made several sensational plays in the field, at third and first, had three three-hit and one four-hit game, and on August 18 in the tenth inning hit a walk-off double, a concussive smash off Fenway's center-field wall, beating the Twins. He was the top Boston hitter for the month of August with a .330 average, but the Red Sox were floundering in third place well behind the Eastern Division leader, Baltimore, trailing by a substantial 19½ games.

Toward the end of September during a three-game series in Detroit, Tigers manager Mayo Smith announced he would be happy to take the Red Sox' George Scott in a trade over just about anyone else on that team if offered, because "He's one guy who walks onto a field, runs around in fielding practice, tries to make every play. He likes the game; that's why I want him." Smith added that he was confident Scott would hit quite a few home runs in the Detroit ballpark. For the Boomer, Smith said, he was quite willing to give up his All-Star first baseman Norm Cash and future 20-game-winner Pat Dobson, which had to pique the interest of GM O'Connell.[15] At about the same time manager Ralph Houk of the Yankees joined an evidently widespread managers' push for Scott, vocalizing a similar interest in him. Sensing a trade for Scott was possible because of longstanding, well-publicized strained relations with his manager and because of viable trade rumors that had been ruminating for so long, Houk was optimistic this could be pulled off with the Red Sox.

The Red Sox were not of the same mind, however; to the surprise of many it was their manager, Dick Williams, who was expendable. On September 22, Dick O'Connell informed Williams that he was being discharged by the Red Sox effective at the end of the '69 season. O'Connell, who seemed not to be behind the firing, was a reluctant spokesman, said a stupefied Williams. O'Connell made it clear that he was being ordered by "the old man," who left town before the announcement, to notify Williams of the change. The following morning, the day of the official announcement, word had leaked out and reporters were clamoring for an interview with the 1967 Manager of the Year, who was the yet-to-be-announced deposed pilot of the Boston Red Sox. It was a done deal they learned; Williams was out.

It was like a breath of fresh air to George Scott who never liked Williams, and said so unhesitatingly after the firing: "I didn't like him and he didn't like me," ranted a rejuvenated Scott.[16] Coach Eddie Popowski, George's mentor and former minor league manager, was given the reins as interim manager for the final nine games of the season. "Pop" won the first three against New York and a fourth against Detroit, and looked as though he was going to sweep the remainder before being stopped by the Tigers in a 2–1 victory.

George Scott surged in the final nine games under Popowski, batting .367 on 11 base hits, including his 15th and 16th home runs, helping lift the Red Sox into a tie for second place with the Tigers on September 26. The team fell back to third again, however, where they finished the season with a 87–75 record in the newly formed Eastern Division, 22 games behind the first-place Baltimore Orioles. Scott's final numbers were modest but much-improved over his 1968 performance: a batting average of .253 with 14 doubles, 5 triples and 16 home runs.

Contrary to baseball pundit opinion, beginning with the *Globe*'s Harold Kaese in August 1968, who felt a troubled Scott would not survive the Red Sox, George Scott had endured, outlasting his nemesis skipper after all. In the eyes of the 25-year-old ballplayer, it was to be his just reward.

11

A Confident Boomer

Scott is happy because he is free from the restraint of the previous managerial regime in Boston. He did not like Dick Williams, and he makes no bones about it. — Larry Claflin, *Boston Herald-Traveler*[1]

"Well, Mr. Yawkey's toy is broken now; someone else can fix it," said a bitter Dick Williams in his farewell message to the Red Sox fans and listeners of his Boston-based radio program.[2] It followed the October 2 selection and announcement of the Sox' new manager, Eddie Kasko, a utility infielder who had played sparingly for Boston in 1966, and managed their Triple-A Toronto and Louisville affiliates. Kasko replaced Dick Williams as manager of Boston's Toronto farm club when Williams moved up to the parent club in 1967. Kasko became the sixth Red Sox manager in ten years.

There was an entirely different demeanor about soft-spoken Eddie Kasko from his predecessor as he stepped to the microphone that same afternoon, the day after the season ended, surrounded by a nearly overwhelming mass of newspaper people and their numerous microphones, clamoring to hear what he had to say. Many of them felt Williams unfairly and unceremoniously had the rug pulled out from under him. The new guy had a calming manner about him, a decided change from the irascible extroverted Dick Williams, which would have a settling effect on George Scott. It was clear from the outset of his first few words to the press that Kasko was called upon by the Red Sox brass to settle down the player ranks, and to stabilize a fragmented team. It was to be a tall order after three years of hardball tactics engaged in by the previous Williams regime. Yawkey, O'Connell and Sullivan were duly convinced, however, that Kasko had the talent and overall personal makeup for the job, and would bring calm to the team.

Kasko was candid, straightforward, and wasted no time suppressing rumor mills gone rampant, by announcing that he had no plans to trade front-line players, such as Carl Yastrzemski, Tony Conigliaro, Rico Petrocelli, Mike

Andrews, Reggie Smith or George Scott. He also announced that he would keep established players in their rightful positions instead of the switches and constant juggling that had occurred in previous years. Above all he would "treat them as men," answered Kasko carefully to a question from one reporter who asked him how he would deal with what he termed "Yawkey's pets." Kasko knew that Yawkey had his favorites, which had been a bone of contention between the Red Sox owner and Williams, and he was cautious not to stray into that territory with investigative reporters who would scrutinize his every move.

It was a message that was like a breath of fresh air to George Scott, who would adjust well to the new boss. After the Red Sox' announcement on Kasko, the beleaguered but revitalized 25 year old, with a renewed sense of optimism, departed for Puerto Rico for another season of winter ball with Santurce under Frank Robinson, scheduled for an October 23 opener of a 60-game winter season.

Once again Scott stood out, helping his Santurce Crabbers to the finals of the Puerto Rican Winter League playoffs before losing to a strong Ponce team that went on to win the Caribbean championship series. And he was once more selected for the All-Star team, in which he knocked in the only run of a 6–1 loss to an all-star squad of Puerto Rican "nationals." He was among the leaders on the year with a .285 batting average, fourth in home runs with 10 (he hit an 11th homer in a playoff game against Mayaguez; claimed he hit a

12th in another playoff match) and a team-leading 39 RBIs, 6th in the league. For his two solid seasons of all-star caliber baseball, George shares the spotlight with Bill White of being named to the Santurce Imports "Dream Team" as one of their all-time top first base-

Santurce, Puerto Rico, 1969 — Another good winter under Frank Robinson (center), pictured here with George Scott (right), and Tony Perez. Scott credits Santurce manager Robinson with saving his career after his dismal 1968 year under Dick Williams (courtesy of baseball historian Jorge Colon-Delgado).

men.[3] "You considered George Scott a threat at all times," said former major leaguer Merv Rettenmund, who played with Scott on the 1969 Santurce team. "He was a quality major leaguer because he had a zero fear factor; he went up there and he took those swings, and, the other thing he was such a fantastic defensive player, and he was a hard player. I don't think I've ever seen anyone work harder at the game; he was ready to go all the time," said Rettenmund.[4]

Not only did George Scott benefit from Frank Robinson's guidance, as he so often stated was the reason for his comeback in '69, but he enjoyed the mentorship of another celebrated future Hall of Famer, Roberto Clemente, who took Scott under his wing in the winter of 1969, and to whom George similarly credits for his recovery. Roberto had joined the San Juan team in late November; both clubs, San Juan and Santurce, shared the same stadium, Bithorn, for home games. One of the great hitters of the game, Clemente talked often and at length with Scott, taught him batting techniques, confidence-building, and, like Robinson, mentored him as no one else of that stature had ever done for him before. George embraced his leadership.

"He told me that if I started using a bigger bat like he does I'd make better contact with the ball and wouldn't have as many bad habits," said Scott to a crowd of reporters, on his communications in San Juan with Clemente. He took his advice to heart, wielding perhaps the biggest piece of lumber — a 38-ounce bat, like Clemente's — of any player in the American League, or even, possibly, in all of major league baseball besides Clemente. One other factor, added Clemente, was his observation that Scott had abandoned his aggressive batting style, and he needed to get back to that. This, of course, was a reflection on the Dick Williams regime, which, by attempting to change his swing, made him tentative and unsure of himself at the plate. "I'm doing it my way this year," declared the exuberant first sacker, flashing his familiar gold-mouth smile.[5]

The new manager had his sights fixed on 21-year-old shortstop Luis Alvarado to make the big club. Alvarado, who had played for Kasko in Louisville, Boston's Triple-A farm club, had good credentials; he was a slick fielder and had his best year in the minors in 1969, batting .292 with 166 base hits. Kasko, however, was not about to move his All-Star shortstop Rico Petrocelli, who had hit a phenomenal 40 home runs in '69. He felt there was a spot for Luis at third base, enabling him to move the best first sacker in baseball, George Scott, permanently back to first where he belonged. But he cautioned George it could be temporary if Alvarado didn't work out; it was a pleasant dilemma, but one Kasko was not taking lightly. What he didn't want was for Scott to be shuffled between positions like he had been in previous years, leaving him unsure and unsettled. He was concerned about that, wanting George to feel secure and stabilized in his infield assignments. Scott was receptive to the notion, especially when for the first time in three years he was being shown respect that he never experienced under Williams.

Scott arrived for his first day of spring camp on Thursday, February 26, with a fully signed contract and a demeanor of nothing but contentment. He began smashing line drives in all directions, and then, for the benefit of anyone who cared to listen — namely numerous Boston sportswriters mingling around the batting cage — spoke loudly about having no plans to listen to anyone, except himself, who wanted to give him hitting advice. "Having guys make suggestions is one thing," he said, "but changing a man's style is another. I don't think changing will get a man out of a slump," said Scott in nearly a boisterous manner, alluding to his contentious moments over hitting under Williams.[6] Scott had the assurance of his new manager Kasko that he would be left alone, which was like an elixir to him.

He was happy — everyone was happy on the Red Sox — and morphed his good feelings of a new lease on life into a phenomenal spring season. He was a "Red Sox terror," wrote Larry Claflin of the *Boston Herald-Traveler*, reporting on Scott's Florida performance.[7] He was on a hitting rampage the entire spring with several multiple-hit games, including four three-hit games, amounting to 34 base hits, 14 of them for extra bases. And he hit for power by stroking 6 home runs with 20 RBIs, for a .805 slugging percentage and an impressive .442 batting average. The Red Sox had one of their best springs in years, finishing with a 15–12 record, augering a good start for rookie manager Kasko.

Kasko was dumbstruck over the display put on by Scott. "No player could have any better spring than George has had," said the incredulous manager.[8] Besides his hitting, he was fielding magnificently, snatching up everything hit his way, and doing it with finesse that captivated Florida fans wherever he appeared. "You can't imagine how much Scott helps the rest of the infield by picking up those low throws to first," said Red Sox veteran journeyman infielder Dick Schofield on Scott's fielding prowess. He didn't just leave it there but elaborated on Scott's exceptional fielding skills and what they meant to the team. "You can hurry your throw on a slowly-hit ball and not worry about the ball going through for two bases. If you get it to George — even on the hard bounce — he will stop it," said the plucky little infielder admiringly.[9]

But there were some critics who were more skeptical, raising questions about the Boomer because of his past letdowns after a strong spring. "If the American League could squeeze 162 games between March 8 and April 1, George Scott might possibly be the greatest baseball player of all time," wrote the *Globe*'s Ray Fitzgerald in a tone of disparagement.[10] Larry Claflin of the *Herald-Traveler* offered his own views on the Scott situation: "Suffice to say that George feels free of bondage now. It is up to him to prove his point that he was mismanaged by Williams. The only way he can do that is by hitting the baseball."[11] And indeed, there was no doubt George Scott was hitting the baseball with a certain confidence he could not recall experiencing since the first few months of his debut year with Boston in 1966.

He was in an ebullient state of mind as the season drew closer, having just completed his best spring ever. And to boost his confidence further the new manager rewarded Scott for his performance by naming him his Opening Day cleanup hitter. Kasko himself was on a high, believing his team was solid and possibly capable of overcoming a strong Baltimore club. Not only did he have a rejuvenated George Scott, who appeared rehabilitated, but he also had one of the best outfields in major league baseball, Alvarado showed promise at third base, and new veteran southpaw Gary Peters, acquired from the White Sox during the winter, was nothing short of fabulous the entire spring, winning 4 games and throwing 32 consecutive innings of shutout ball.

The Red Sox opened the 1970 season on April 17 with New York in venerable Yankee Stadium. Scott was in the lineup batting fourth behind Yastrzemski, as promised by Kasko. On his first official at-bat (he walked his first time up) of the season he singled sharply to left, and later scored one of their first two runs. In the 5th inning he started a rally by slashing a triple past right fielder Curt Blefary that led to two more runs, enough for Boston to capture the opener, 4–3, for their new manager and newly acquired veteran left-hander Peters.

Scotty was trying too hard, said Kasko, who was taking some heat from Boston sportswriters to pull him from the cleanup slot. George was pressing and he knew it, said Carl Yastrzemski, who said that Scott was once again attempting to lift every pitch into the far reaches of left-field territory, and instead was hitting soft grounders and harmless fly balls to leave runners on base. By April 27, with the Red Sox at 7–8, and Scott hitting .211 with only 5 RBIs and 2 home runs, (his second, a mammoth blast above the Fenway left-field light tower on April 25), Kasko made his move, dropping George into the 6th slot in the batting order. With that strategic maneuver he began to make good contact with the ball again, rapping out 14 base hits (including five doubles, two triples and two homers) in seven consecutive games at a .519 pace. On April 30 in a wild game against the Oakland A's, won by the Red Sox, 8–7, Scott was a big factor in the win as he hit two 420-foot line shots off Fenway's center-field wall, his third home run, and made a phenomenal game-saving catch with two runners on in the eighth, flashing his glove to rob Don Mincher of a double hit sharply down the first-base line.

On May 1 he lofted his 4th homer into the Red Sox bullpen, then he repeated his extraordinary fielding in a losing cause the following day against California, taking two hits away from Roger Repoz, both unassisted plays on balls smashed in the dirt, cracked a triple, and by the end of the day had climbed to a .309 batting average. "I'm making them stay away from my kitchen," said Scott, a term he had popularized to describe an inside pitch, explaining how he was using better judgment, making the pitchers come to him instead of chasing bad balls. He launched three more homers in mid–

Scott, the defensive stalwart (courtesy of Boston Red Sox).

May, all long blasts, one into the right-field stands of Cleveland Stadium, and two well over Baltimore's center-field fence. But the Red Sox were in a swoon, losing 17 of 26 games in the month of May, falling to 20–25 and slipping into 4th place in the Eastern Division, 11½ games behind league-leading Baltimore. Since they were 9 games behind the pace of Dick Williams' 1969 team, rumblings began in Boston that Kasko was suspect, especially by the naysayers who had opposed the controversial switch to the new skipper.

On June 2 in a game against the Minnesota Twins, Scott made another phenomenal fielding play that pitcher Ray Culp declared preserved a victory for him. Scott was playing close to the bag holding the runner, Harmon Killebrew, with no outs. Left-handed hitter Rich Reese propelled a drive down the first-base line that seemed certain to clear the bag and go for extra bases. But Scott came from nowhere, snagged the bullet hit by Reese, and scrambled to touch first to double up a bewildered Killebrew. The play killed the rally as Boston went on to win, 5–1. The credit was being heaped on Culp after the game for allowing just one run, which had followed a 22–13 shellacking of the Red Sox on May 31 by Chicago, but he was quick to give the credit to Scott. "The guy is so darn good that you take him for granted until he comes up with a play like that. Then you wonder all over again how he does it," said the Boston pitcher.[12]

All was not sweet for the Red Sox, however, as they continued to stumble through June, struggling to rise above .500. Kasko's experiment at third, Luis Alvarado, was not working out, at the bat and particularly defensively, so on June 12 he was benched and Petrocelli went back to shortstop after 18 games at third. Quite unexpectedly the wheels were falling off the wagon of their pitching staff. "They ought to have an unlisted number in the bullpen," said one press box member remarking on the embarrassment of Boston hurlers. Jim Lonborg had come up with another sore arm, left-hander Bill Lee departed for the Army for the balance of the season, Gary Peters was a disappointment, and ace reliever Sparky Lyle was not doing the job. On June 19 Kasko moved Scott to third base to plug the hole left by Petrocelli. It would be his position for the remainder of the season. He responded by rapping 19 base hits in 45 at-bats at a .422 pace, concluding the month of June with a .282 average. But the Red Sox remained under .500 at 34–36 and in fourth place.

The Boston fans maintained an assault on Yastrzemski, booing him mercilessly as the apparent reason for the team's collapse — and certainly the reason for Dick Williams' ouster, they surmised — since the splendid season of 1967; this in spite of hitting close to .300, and eventually just missing the AL batting crown for the year by mere percentage points separating him from Alex Johnson of the Angels. Things were going so bad for him with Red Sox fandom that the *Globe*'s Neil Singelais interviewed the harried Sox superstar at the end of June just to get his perspective on the situation, and maybe attempt to set the record straight about his relationships with his managers; the subheading to his June 30 article was "[Yastrzemski] resents talk about relationships with Yawkey, Kasko."[13] George Scott was decidedly more candid about the circumstances of Yaz's association with the Red Sox managers, especially his relationship with owner Yawkey: "He discussed the team when he was with Mr. Yawkey. He was a powerful figure during those days of Mr. Yawkey; same way Ted Williams was," said George of the Red Sox superstar outfielder and Hall of Famer.[14]

On July 17 in a game against the Milwaukee Brewers, Scotty banged up his right hand sliding headfirst into second base attempting to steal. It was the same hand he had hurt in a May 16 game against the Indians that left him with a nagging injury for three weeks. On July 18 Boston's team doctor confirmed that George had fractured his hand — an oblique fracture of the fourth metacarpus — that would put him out of action for a month, a total of 32 games (he replaced Yastrzemski in late innings of one game on August 17 just before his full return). "This is a real bad day for me," said Scotty speaking in sorrowful tones, as if the world had just collapsed beneath him.[15] He was hitting a solid .283.

He returned to action full-time on August 19 against Chicago with his team firmly in fourth place, and saw a 5–2 Red Sox lead evaporate into a 13–5 defeat, with the White Sox scoring 11 runs in the ninth to prevent Ray Culp, the only steady Red Sox pitcher, from winning his 14th of the season. Scott hit .325 through the end of August and .319 in September, finishing the year just under .300 at .296, with 16 home runs. The Red Sox ended the year in third place with the same won-loss record as 1969, 87–75, an extraordinary 21 games behind the Eastern Division leader Baltimore Orioles, concluding an inauspicious debut for rookie manager Eddie Kasko.

During a mid–September series against the Yankees after losing three straight to Baltimore, when no one on the club was very happy about how the games were lost, Scott approached Haywood Sullivan in the clubhouse and confronted him directly about whether he might be traded. Rumors were circulating around the team and league that many of Boston's players were expendable; the Yankees' Ralph Houk made no secrets about his need for big men to improve on his light-hitting team, and George Scott would fit perfectly in his plans. But when Scott left to take batting practice Sullivan turned to the newsmen standing around and said, "I wish I had 25 more Scotts on my ball club."[16] It appeared that George was a Red Sox untouchable.

The offseason spelled a few surprises in Beantown, one that sent shock waves through the city when on October 11 Boston traded their beloved local boy, Tony Conigliaro, to the California Angels, the very team that had nearly killed him in 1967 due to a pitch by Jack Hamilton. It was a six-player deal sending Ray Jarvis and catcher Jerry Moses to the Angels along with Conigliaro for unknown utility infielder Doug Griffin, light-hitting reserve outfielder Jarvis Tatum, and the key player in the deal for Boston, ace reliever Ken Tatum. There were disturbing personnel issues emerging on the club with players breaking into factions, led by Conigliaro and Yastrzemski that distressed Yawkey; since Yawkey favored Yastrzemski, the die was cast and Conigliaro was expendable.

O'Connell knew they needed to improve their pitching for better balance, but also required more speed, quickness and a solid third baseman so that they could move the best first baseman in the league, George Scott, to his rightful spot across the diamond where the Red Sox felt he belonged. O'Connell wasn't done; in the grand scheme of things he still needed the premier infielder he was looking for, and went out and got him from the White Sox on December 1 in 36-year-old perennial All-Star and Gold Glover Luis Aparicio in exchange for Alvarado and Mike Andrews. Aparicio could go to short and they would move Petrocelli to third base. The question mark was Doug Griffin, whose credentials were immediately challenged by Boston fans and writers alike with their refrain, "Doug Who? Where does he play?"[17] It would make for an interesting winter in the Hub discussing and watching the evolution of a team once laden with power transform into one built upon "defense and speed," in the words of manager Kasko.[18]

For the first time since he broke into major league baseball George Scott did not opt to play winter ball. He was comfortable with his situation now, liked his new manager and felt confident about his and Red Sox' chances of having a good 1971 season. He was now a family man and a new father, anxious to spend some time with year-old George Scott III in the offseason.

"He was a players' manager. Eddie and I got along good ... he was a good manager," said Scott of Red Sox manager Eddie Kasko, reflecting on his short stint with Kasko in 1970 and 1971.[19] No doubt a view shared by other members of those Red Sox teams who looked upon their docile and all-too-obliging manager as a good guy — too good, perhaps, that eventually led to disorder and general discontent among the players who would squabble and openly bring their conflicts to a discerning and willing press.

The talk during winter meetings was about an improved Boston Red Sox team since the acquisition of Aparicio and relief-standout Ken Tatum, who had 39 saves the previous two years with California. Aparicio, or "L'il Looey" as he was known, was to be the fulcrum of major change to the Red Sox infield, moving All-Star shortstop Rico Petrocelli to third base and Scott to first, with Griffin manning second. Kasko would move Billy Conigliaro to center field, Reggie Smith to right, and Carl Yastrzemski from first base back to his accustomed left field, altogether seven position changes that potentially could be unsettling for any team. But O'Connell and Kasko knew they had to do something to improve their defense, which finished the year the worst fielding team in the American League. Yankee manager Ralph Houk, speaking at a Boston Baseball Writers' dinner that winter, directed what was intended to be a good-natured barb at the Red Sox situation, but struck at the heart of a Red Sox problem. "I see the Red Sox are practically claiming the pennant, but from what I can learn, nobody on the team knows where he is going to play this year," joked the Yankees pilot. The incautious remark would bear on what was to become of Boston's discordant 1971 season.[20]

Scott reported to spring camp overweight along with reliever Sparky Lyle, among some other Red Sox, and they were immediately assailed by the Boston media who relentlessly kept them in their spotlight while they maintained a vigil on manager Kasko to see what he would do. Since Kasko threatened his players with a $500 fine if they failed to meet his weight standards, it was shades of Dick Williams all over again for Scott, who labored under the stress and threats of the ex-skipper who ran his team like a Marine boot camp. George, who resented the sportswriters' insults, and made no bones about it, resorted to wearing a rubber sweat suit (two of them at times) to drop the pounds, and he succeeded in meeting Kasko's goal; no fines were to be imposed on the big first baseman and George was happy again. He promptly vent his frustration by hitting the longest batting practice homer of spring camp that cleared two outfield fences, off Kasko, who was pitching. Kasko later entertained the press with his own comical theory for the Scott blast: "That's my confidence buildup pitch," he said with tongue-in-cheek. Clif Keane of the *Globe*, persistent in his criticism of Scott, which seemed to be in fashion among the reporters looking for a good story, in one article described him as "a little heavy." In a few strokes of the keyboard he just as quickly shifted his essay from rebuke to praise of Scott for his impressive monster shot off Kasko, which clearly trumped matters of weight, reasoned the senior writer.

The Red Sox got off to a good start quickly by winning their first four exhibition games, and six of their first eight. George Scott was off to a good start of his own, hitting .368 with two home runs. When he missed the next two games due to illness, journeyman Mike Fiore, a lifetime .223 hitter whom the Red Sox had acquired from Kansas City in 1970, stepped in at first base and promptly hit two home runs, one in each game—his 3rd and 4th of the young exhibition season—in 11 trips to the plate. When asked by a probing Boston press if Fiore could be a starting first baseman, "I'd certainly have to consider it," said an impressed Kasko.[21] This raised journalistic eyebrows further amid speculation that this couldn't be making George any too happy. Fiore proceeded to hit his 5th homer two games later, reinforcing Kasko's delight in the upstart first sacker even more and provoking further speculation among newspaper people that Scott's starting job could be in jeopardy. It was a hot topic. Scott responded to questioning after Fiore had hit his 5th with, "No way it's going to happen."[22] Kasko wasn't as optimistic providing a one-word response, "Fiore," to a reporter's questioning on what he liked about the loss to Washington on March 16.

Any such feelings about Fiore taking over were soon vanquished as Scott began a torrid run against the Orioles, starting with a 3-for-4 day on March 15; in 18 games he produced 30 base hits at a .469 pace, with 5 home runs. In spite of this, rumor was hot that Boston would soon trade Scott for big Frank Howard of the Senators; Howard was a certifiable home run hitter, but couldn't hold a glove to Scott in the field. Scott dispelled that rumor as well by hitting two long home runs—his 6th and 7th—in a 5–3 win against the Tigers. The following day Kasko put Mike Fiore in left field, where he platooned him for the balance of the Grapefruit League season. Scott finished the spring with a .446 batting average, 7 home runs and 17 RBIs, tops on the club.

"You know I went to spring training every year like I was a rookie," recalled Scott, remembering his days in Winter Haven with the Boston club. "I would never sit around and say I'm the starting first baseman of the Boston Red Sox, because from year to year things change. You have to go to spring training every year questioning that there's somebody that can take your job from you. I kept myself humble. I think I kept myself working. So you see you have to come to spring training as if you are a rookie, you know, and win that job again."[23]

Things were not so promising, however, in the Red Sox camp. Elements of discord were beginning to show among the players that were seized upon by the Boston writers who raised it to gossip level of the daily sports section. The biggest problem was among the outfielders. Acrimonious squabbling between Tony's brother, Billy Conigliaro, and Joe Lahoud, described as "emotionally untamed youngsters," by Neil Singelais of the *Globe*, was still smoldering in spite of their claim that things were better. "We get along OK, we talk to each other now," said Billy C.[24] Billy was the odds-on favorite for the starting center field berth after two seasons of flip-flopping with Lahoud, each taking their turns of being sent down to the minors at the end of spring training. Their handling by the team did not sit well with either of the emotionally charged outfielders who appeased themselves of their frustrations by verbally assaulting each other that became abundantly rich fodder for team gossip for the newspapers.

Boston opened at home on April 6 against the Yankees before 34,517 Fenway-packed fans, winning 3–1 on the solid pitching of Boston's steadiest pitcher Ray Culp, a 17-game winner the two previous seasons. Scott was 1-for-3 knocking in the third Red Sox run on a sacrifice fly. But Opening Day elation quickly subsided when the Red Sox began their first road trip losing three straight to a weak Cleveland club; it was topped off by newly acquired right-hander Alan Foster, a lifetime 14–24 pitcher from the Dodgers, who in the final game stood George Scott and the rest of the Red Sox on their heads. He was just "waiving aimlessly" at the ball, wrote the *Globe*'s Clif Keane of Scott's sub-par performance.

Boston's next stop was a three-game swing with the Senators. On the bus trip from the airport to the D.C. hotel, an undercurrent was building amidst insinuating remarks by reporters questioning whether this would be another early season flop by Scott after his all-too-typical and very spectacular spring. The clamor reached the big first baseman, and he erupted in a rage. "The roof almost came off the bus," wrote *Globe* sportswriter Clif Keane, reporting on Scott's tirade that was aimed at the writers whom he felt were provoking controversy and inciting the fans. "And don't start judging me and the rest [of the players] until we finish this road trip and the long home stay and then ask what ails George," he said forcefully to his captive audience.[25]

He harbored concerns, however, admitting that he had not performed well in the months of April and May; but this time it would be different he felt, he was sure of it. But he was not feeling good about the Boston press who instead of encouraging him — as he believed they should — was assailing him with questions of doubt about his abilities and intimating he was not a reliable clutch hitter, diffusing their criticisms of him throughout the newspaper dailies. It was an eye-opener, raised doubts of his own as to their motives, and, perhaps for the first time moved him to a higher level of maturity than before, realizing he may have been a special derisive target of the local scribes. "I think the underestimating that was going on was being done by the media, especially the media in Boston. I don't know why, but I think I do. They never gave me the credit that I deserved. But when I didn't do well they were the first ones to jump on me," said Scott reflecting on his days with the media, hinting there was a possible racist element here among a few of the journalists.[26]

At the conclusion of the nine-game road trip the Red Sox were 5–5, and in third place. In the second game of a May 2 doubleheader against the Twins, the final of a twelve-game homestand, Scott ripped into a pitch on a 3–2 count off left-hander Ron Perranoski in the bottom of the ninth that quickly reached the 420-foot mark in center field, the deepest part of Fenway, for a run-scoring game-tying triple. George Thomas singled him home for the winning run and a sweep of the doubleheader, propelling the team into first place at 14–8, one game in front of Baltimore. It was Scotty's 27th base hit of the young season, giving him a .310 average, third-best of the Red Sox regulars behind Yastrzemski and Reggie Smith. The naysayers were about to turn into converts.

The big swish—Scott's outsized home run swing (courtesy of Boston Red Sox).

The Red Sox were on a roll, winning six straight games during May 2–8, and won 13 of 16 games by sweeping Chicago, Detroit and New York on the road, before losing to Baltimore on May 22. During this streak Scott hit his third home run into Comiskey Park's right-field bleachers on May 6 in a 10–1 Red Sox win. He strained his back two innings later trying to catch a wind-blown popup on Chicago's wet Astroturf, but against medical advice returned to action in five days. He was leading the Red Sox regulars with a .323 average. *Boston Globe* writer Will McDonough wrote a feature article on his return, which was headlined, "Scott's Ready, Eager; Sox Need His Bat." On May 17 Scotty was the difference in a 3–2 win against the Detroit Tigers: "He performed his customary brilliant job around first base," wrote the *Globe*'s Neil Singelais, describing Scott's fifth-inning theft of a certain double hit down the line by Jim Northrup, sure to score two, but instead ending the inning.[27] It was a fielding gem. Then in the bottom of the inning, with two outs, Scott stroked a two-run double off Dean Chance, knocking in the game-winning runs. It was his third game-winning hit of the season, second only to Yastrzemski who had four. On May 20 Scotty hit a tremendous blast, through the fog, six rows deep into Fenway's center-field bleachers in the eighth inning off Lindy McDaniel of the Yankees, securing victory for Boston, 5–2. He had told Yastrzemski before the homer that he was going to hit one into the Boston bullpen. He was wrong; it went much farther.

Then it was on to Baltimore for four games with a talent-laden Orioles team led by the Robinson boys, Frank and Brooks, and one of the best collections of pitchers in baseball in starters McNally, Palmer, Cuellar and Dobson, each 20-game winners that season. The Red Sox, who were to win 9 of 18 games against a Baltimore club that would win 101 on the season, were in first place by 3 games over the Orioles. Boston split the series but not before their key reliever, Ken Tatum, was struck by a batting practice line drive before their May 23 twin bill, fracturing his jaw in three places, requiring plastic surgery and keeping him on disabled status for a month. Losing Tatum was a bad blow for Kasko and the club.

Scott hit a long home run over Memorial Stadium's center-field fence in the first game, but ran aground with home plate umpire Bill Kunkel, who called Scott out on three quick strikes thrown by McNally, each one further outside the strike zone than the previous one, in a crucial moment of the second contest. The pitches were so wide of the plate visible to everyone in the stands and on the field that it had the appearance of partisanship, for whatever inexplicable reason, or something more personal. Scotty was enraged as was coach Eddie Popowski and Kasko who were promptly ejected. Remarkably George was not, but commented after the game, which the Red Sox won, 2–1, "He has no business being in this league; I couldn't reach those pitches with a broom."[28] He was booed loudly by the 48,856 partisan crowd after that to which he responded with raised fists — a Black Power gesture — inciting them even more.

The talk in the clubhouse after the Baltimore series was pennant. Beating the Orioles twice in their own ballpark was a morale booster, as the Red Sox maintained a hold on their three-game first place lead over the Birds; there was every reason to be confident. Their pitching looked better, Lonborg was optimistic after a strong game against the Orioles on May 21 won by Boston, and they were getting good support from the subs. Then they promptly lost two games to Washington at Fenway. They would have lost a third to them had not Scott made a gem of a fielding play in the 6th inning, perceived by many to have saved the game for Boston. The Senators had the bases full with two out, when Toby Harrah hit a routine grounder to John Kennedy at shortstop, who threw wildly to first. Scotty stretched his 6'2" frame to a full extension, face down on the infield dirt and caught the ball in his outstretched glove, maintaining contact with the bag with his left foot for the inning-ending putout. It was a sensational maneuver by the big first sacker that drew tumultuous applause from a small gathering of 14,995 Fenway fans.

The first-place Oakland A's of the Western Division, led, ironically, by their first-year manager and Boston Red Sox reject, Dick Williams, came to the Hub. The man who once captivated the city by his aggressive managing style, bringing Boston a pennant after 21 long years, was now wearing a different uniform. A huge crowd of 35,714 zealous fans filled the stands on Friday night, May 28, many just to cheer the man whom they felt was forsaken by the club, and others to ruthlessly boo the man they felt was responsible for his departure, Carl Yastrzemski. But there was another reason: young Oakland sensation, Vida Blue, their phenomenal left-hander with 10 wins already, who was to win the Cy Young and Most Valuable Player awards, and strike out over 300 batters, was scheduled to pitch.

George Scott spoke confidently about his upcoming encounter with the 21-year-old phenom, remembering a game in 1969 when he hit a home run off him. As it turned out he was to have a lot of success against the Oakland flamethrower through the years, hitting .382 on 21 base hits, with 5 home runs. The opener of the two-game series against the A's was no different: Scotty lined sharp singles off Blue the first two times up. With Boston leading 3–2 in the eighth inning, two outs and runners on first and second, and Scott coming to bat, manager Williams lifted Blue rather than let him pitch to the dangerous Scott. Scott promptly laced a run-scoring single, his third hit of the game, off reliever Locker that turned out to be the winning run, which was poetic justice perhaps for a once-tormented Scott after the seasons of anguish he endured under the acerbic Williams.

It was a turning point, however, for the euphoria of the club quickly and decidedly changed after a couple of consecutive losses. It was enigmatic; instead of rallying like Kasko felt they should have, bickering among a handful of players superseded what should have been a unified effort at winning and began to grip the team. Unable to handle the success they had enjoyed to that point by building a 29–15 won-loss record, the Red Sox began to crumble, losing five straight games and seven of their next nine, including a series sweep in Fenway by the expansion team Kansas City Royals, who would win 12 of 13 games from the Red Sox that year. The pitching was abysmal; as the *Globe's* Ray Fitzgerald put it, "Right now the Sox pitching staff consists of Siebert (who lost two games in the streak) and a set of rosary beads."[29] Lonborg, who had come back from his rehab stint at Louisville, lost two games. Aparicio, in the worst slump of his long major league career, hitless in 44 straight at-bats before getting a single on June 1, considered quitting.

On June 6, the final game of the Red Sox homestand, California pitcher Clyde Wright tripled off Siebert in the seventh inning scoring the fourth run for the Angels that concluded in a 5–2 California win. The hit drew gasps from a multitude of fans and reporters who saw the ball sail over center fielder Billy Conigliaro's head and strike the wall just four feet above the ground, a catchable ball most everyone thought. The press had no intentions to pass it up pursuing the matter of the apparent misplay rather aggressively in the clubhouse after the game that led to tension with reporters and squabbling among Red Sox teammates.

Not surprisingly a petulant Billy C. exploded in defense of his outfield play and over the distastefulness of the situation. George Scott, who was watching the matter unfold in the clubhouse and alarmed at what he was seeing with writers surrounding and appearing to bait Yastrzemski and Smith, for the good of a story, came to Conigliaro's defense pointing out to them that there were 25 players on that field and no one should take individual blame. He was disgusted with what was happening and with the appearance of reporters and certain players acting like a wolf-pack ganging up on the young outfielder. Eddie Kasko seemed to take it all in stride, however, surprising the local newsmen, leading to bigger questions of whether Kasko had control of his team. He soon found himself in the crosshairs of the media. The general feeling was that there were far more things amiss and objectionable about this team than met the eye: unhealthy cliques had formed since Dick Williams' departure, creating contending player factions. A hostile fan base that had not warmed to the new manager was in evidence and there was talk again of another Red Sox skipper being fired. It would lead to further problems.

"If you asked me today what I regret the whole while I was in the Red Sox organization is that they let ballplayers get into their own little groups. They let these guys — whichever group you were in — dictate what went on around Fenway Park. When I played guys like Yastrzemski, Lonborg, Foy, Reggie [Smith], they had their little group. [Tony] Conigliaro, Billy Conigliaro,

Mike Ryan, [Jose] Tartabull — we had our little group. And the pitchers had their little group. You lost the sense of team," said a mournful George Scott remembering those troubled years in Boston.[30]

The Red Sox meanwhile had slipped into second place 1½ games behind Baltimore. They would win a mere 6 of their next 15 games as well as become the victim of yet another three-game series rout by a surprisingly dominant Royals team; they would then recoup some of their losses with a seven-game win streak through July 1, bringing the Red Sox within 2½ games of the Eastern Division leading Orioles. Scotty put together 17 base hits, 11 RBIs and clouted five home runs over that span. One of those four-baggers, his 11th of the season, was a tremendous shot — reminiscent of one he hit there in 1966 — off Detroit's Joe Coleman on June 30 in Tiger Stadium that tied the game at 2–2 in the fourth inning. "The clout by Scotty kept rising, and landed in the second deck in left center. It might have carried 500 feet without exaggeration if it hadn't been obstructed while in flight," wrote the *Globe*'s Neil Singelais.[31] The Red Sox won the contest, 8–7.

Just before the All-Star Game break on July 10 in New York, following a 5–3 loss to the Yankees, another unfortunate Red Sox outburst occurred between teammates, this one more noteworthy and likely more damaging to team spirit and morale than the incident of the month before. Once again Billy Conigliaro, a peevish sort, was in the middle of it. He had just learned of his brother Tony's retirement announcement from the Angels due to failing eyesight of his previously damaged eye, and a feeling he was on the verge of "cracking up." It caught his brother Billy C. by surprise, and he became angry releasing his month-long pent-up emotions and hostility wholly on teammate Carl Yastrzemski, whom he blamed for Tony's being traded among other contentious and conspiratorial allegations. It was irrational behavior of the worst kind, catching manager Kasko and the Red Sox brass completely off guard and likely to threaten team unity, said GM Dick O'Connell. Outfielder Reggie Smith said he would not play with Conigliaro again. But cooler heads prevailed, apologies were made, and Billy C. (and Reggie Smith) appeared in Boston's lineup in the first game following the All-Star break, giving an appearance that things were settled and decorum restored. They weren't and wouldn't be, and O'Connell knew it.

There was a certain vicariousness to the tension he was feeling over the affair, and it was getting to George Scott, whose frustrations were starting to show like it was his own personal nightmare. He simply wanted to play baseball, continue unabated the quest for a pennant, and hope that the bickering that was fragmenting and polarizing his team would soon come to an end. But he was working on a short fuse himself these days. On July 12 after losing all three games to the Yankees he lashed out at a Boston reporter who, critical of Conigliaro's performance just a month before, was alleging that Billy C. should have caught Danny

Cater's game-winning single on Saturday that led to New York's 5–3 victory. The outburst made the news, placing him squarely in the front office's spotlight looking every bit like another one of those Red Sox malcontents poisoning the ranks.

Boston was playing mediocre baseball, with a 61–45 record through August 1, leaving them in second place, 5½ games behind Baltimore and 4½ games in front of third-place Detroit. No one was hitting, including Scotty. "Eddie [Kasko] is really too darn soft about all these players," wrote the *Globe*'s Clif Keane, highly critical of several Red Sox players and their manager.[32] After splitting a two-game series in Baltimore, the Red Sox came home for a long 15-game homestand, but were humiliated, losing 11 of them, including seven consecutive games. Not only were the losses disappointing, they were embarrassing. Four of them came against Dick Williams' Oakland team, and three were against the expansion Kansas City Royals. During the August 10 game against the A's the Fenway fans gave Williams a standing ovation after being ejected for displaying his moxie by arguing a couple of close calls at first base. Every cheer he received was matched by boos for Carl Yastrzemski each time he stepped to the plate, or jogged to left field. The booing was relentless; Yaz was a marked man. He was removed from the starting lineup for the final two games of the homestand for weak hitting. Red Sox pitching had collapsed; fielding was nothing less than atrocious and their hitting anemic. Boston committed 16 errors in the home stand leading to 13 unearned runs. Scotty, however, was playing well batting .327 with three home runs, upping his season total to 19.

By August 29, just before a three-game series with the Eastern Division leading Orioles at Fenway, the Red Sox were mired in third place 14½ games out of first. While Scott had hit .272 for the month with 20 home runs on the season, it was apparent, however, that Red Sox management already had changes in mind for 1972 and George Scott did not appear to be in their long-range plans. Kasko began to platoon him with Mike Fiore (batted .177 on the year) on occasion toward the end of August. On September 8, 23-year-old Cecil Cooper, called up from Boston's Double-A Pawtucket farm club where he was batting .343, made his first appearance in a Red Sox uniform as a pinch-hitter. Cooper, who went on to be a five-time All-Star and twice a Gold Glover, assumed a starting role at first base on September 13 and started 10 of the remaining 14 games of the season, finishing with a .310 batting average. Scott could see the writing on the wall that he was going to be trade bait, which he expressed to the Boston writers following his pinch-hit appearance against Washington on September 18.

The Red Sox finished the season in third place at 85–77, 18 games behind first-place Baltimore. Astonishingly they outdrew all other American League clubs with 1,678,732 fans in spite of their little ballpark, shoddy performance and unruly team behavior. George Scott finished the year with a .263 batting average, second only to Reggie Smith (.283) of the regulars, with 24 home runs and a .441 slugging percentage. He also walked off with his third Gold Glove award. A *Boston Globe* article ruminated on the team's strengths, one of them being George Scott:

> Those who crave the responsibility, who thrive on it — they are the ones you want on your team. ... It is rising to the challenge — oh, not, it's more. It's praying for the challenge, for the chance to excel.
>
> The Red Sox have a little of it. Carl Yastrzemski is one. George Scott is another. Scott has it in the field. Yastrzemski has it everywhere and that's why Tom Yawkey can call him "a complete baseball player." Scott wants every ball hit his way. He devours sharply hit balls, bad throws. He turns them into his stage.
>
> Yastrzemski wants the ball hit to him. He wants them to test his arm. And he wants to be at bat. He wants those men sitting on the bases — not merely for his individual statistics, but because that's what sports are all about. It's being there. If Scott could carry his instinct to be great in the field into the batter's box with him, he'd be one of the great players of all time.
>
> There may be other Red Sox players with this magic quality — but you don't sense it the way you do with a Yastrzemski or a Scott. Don't give me the men who merely thrive on pressure, give me the men who plead for it. They're always ready.[33]

On October 10 the Red Sox and the lowly Milwaukee Brewers, who finished last in the Western Division, pulled off a blockbuster 10-player trade, sending Jim Lonborg, Billy Conigliaro, Joe Lahoud, Ken Brett, Don Pavletich, and George Scott to the Brewers for speed merchant Tommy Harper, pitchers Lew Krausse and Marty Pattin, and a minor leaguer.

Owner Bud Selig and GM Frank Lane tabbed Scott as the "key" man in the deal. Scott was immediately enthusiastic about the trade feeling he would get a fresh start in Milwaukee with less pressure than in Boston. "In Milwaukee, I think I can be a team leader," said Scott. "I'll be given credit there, not overshadowed. I think they need a lift and I think I can be the guy to do it. I should have a shot at batting cleanup or third."[34]

With that George Scott, a popular Red Sox figure and a favorite among the locals, after six years of highs and lows in the Hub, where he had played his entire major league career, said his goodbyes to Boston.

12

The Key

Scott is visioning just what the Brewers had in mind last month when they made him the key man in their big trade with the Red Sox. The Brewers were looking for a home run hitter. Scott hopes he has at last found a town, a park and a team with which he can reach his full potential. — Larry Whiteside[1]

"I'm a good observer and I can tell when people change on me," said a resigned George Scott to hordes of Boston reporters the day after the announcement of his trade to Milwaukee. Scotty was made aware of the deal somewhat ingloriously when stopped by a local while jogging near his Cape Cod home. The news was not surprising but the way it was handled was, fueling his disappointment with the Red Sox front office for not being upfront with him in addition to not informing him of the trade. Any doubts he had about leaving the Red Sox were made less painful by the disrespectful manner of his exit. It was time to move on.

No one in the Red Sox organization, notably the front office, bid adieu to any of the six departing players, nor did they attempt to soften the situation with public relations mumbo jumbo to satisfy the inquisitive and numerous inquiries, with statements like "we hated to let them go." In fact it was the opposite. GM O'Connell acted with repugnance toward the players, saying he was "sick" of their complaints, which surprised Boston sports writers for the uncharacteristic enmity he displayed, indistinguishably, toward all six. No doubt Billy Conigliaro, a troublesome player, was the prime target of his spite, but Lonborg, Lahoud and Scott were also in his sights. Manager Eddie Kasko, who notoriously sat on the sidelines, took a familiar tact; he said nothing.

Newly appointed general manager Frank Lane of the third-year expansion Milwaukee Brewers and their manager Dave Bristol were delighted, however, to see such a contingency of quality major leaguers coming their way, especially a power-hitter like George Scott. Scott and pitcher Marty Pattin, who went to the Red Sox, were the key men in the deal. It was later learned that the sticking-point initially to any trade was Boston's reluctance to include Scott in the mix, but the Sox relented when Lane balked at reaching any agreement that didn't include the big infielder. Both Lane and Bristol, who had not always agreed on player transactions, had collaborated on the deal. They were in complete agreement that acquiring Scott, the big prize, was a priority. Lane, famously known as "Wheeler Dealer" and "Trader Lane" for his numerous and spectacular baseball player swaps, described Scott as a "high caliber of player" likely to immediately improve their chances of being a contender. The trade also would accelerate the timetable of making the Brewers a bona fide quality major league establishment, to shed the ragtag team label they inherited from the failed Seattle Pilots franchise.

Cedric Tallis, general manager of the Kansas City Royals, failing in his attempt to trade for big Frank Howard of the Senators, along with several other clubs, was eager to pick up Scott; learning of the blockbuster trade with Boston, Tallis immediately approached Lane to discuss a possible deal. He needed a first baseman of Scott's Gold Glove caliber and bat power. Scott had been Tallis' prime target before opting for Howard, but he couldn't work out a deal with Boston, who wanted pitcher Dick Drago in return. But Lane turned Tallis down also. He had his man. Scott was his lynchpin in the transaction; he was to be a Brewer.

There were repercussions felt among the Red Sox fan base over the loss of their big first baseman, who had provided them with so many sensational moments with his glove. When the Boston media polled Boston fans about the big trade, the response was generally the same: a trade was clearly needed, but of the six players who became expendable they hated losing the most their beloved first baseman with the slick glove and great baseball instincts. Unquestionably the finest first sacker of his era, Scott saved many a Red Sox infielder from errors on errant throws, and he was a master at digging out short-hop ground balls that could not be fielded by the average first baseman. "Milwaukee fans will delight in George's fielding, no matter what he hits," wrote one sportswriter, remarking that any kind of hitting Scott generates in Milwaukee will simply be a bonus.[2]

Feeling redeemed for his pursuit by other clubs and the appreciation of his skills being shown him by Bristol and Lane, Scott was in an ecstatic mood. "For me, it's like a new lease on life," said the new Brewer, who discounted any reason for concern created by the Brewers' intent to make him — a Gold Glove first baseman — their third sacker. But the *Milwaukee Journal*'s Larry Whiteside wasn't as optimistic about the change, feeling that it could be a strategically poor move to transition Scott across the diamond when he was a proven first sacker. "Of the six players Milwaukee acquired from Boston Scott holds the key to what success the young Brewers hope to enjoy," wrote Whiteside about Scotty's value to the organization.[3] GM Lane was more sanguine about the situation but, internally, he knew that he should have an established third baseman at the hot corner and keep Scott at first where he provided the greatest value to the team. When he failed to pick up the Angels' All-Star third baseman Jim Fregosi during the winter meetings, Lane became defensive, exclaiming "I don't know why everybody is so worried about Scott playing third base," adding that his coaches were supportive of the move.[4]

An 80 degree temperature and a clear sky greeted Brewers pitchers and catchers as they were welcomed on February 26 to their 1972 spring training site in Tempe, Arizona, by manager Dave Bristol. Among them, reporting four days ahead of schedule, were George Scott and Joe Lahoud, two of the six Red Sox *refugees*, proclaimed one Milwaukee scribe somewhat ominously, eager to get started and demonstrate their enthusiasm for their new team. Scott had undertaken a personal conditioning program during the offseason to keep his weight down that brought smiles to the face of his new manager. Sporting a sleek 197 pounds on his 6'2" frame and a fancy new mustache to go with it, he looked every part the slim rookie he was in 1966. The *Milwaukee Journal* found reason to highlight Scott's new appearance and early camp arrival in a headline, and a challenge: "New Brewer, Scott, Beats Teammates into Shape." For once he was safe from the fines threatened by teams for players reporting overweight; in the case of the Brewers it was $100-a-pound.

The Brewers lost their first two Cactus League games of the exhibition season, but then raked former Cy Young Award winner Denny McLain, a new arrival with the Oakland A's, for 8 hits and 10 runs in three innings on March 12, for a 14–4 Milwaukee victory. Scotty hit a 450-foot tater, a ferocious line drive that left the ballpark in a hurry, landing on a road some twenty feet behind the left-center-field fence, knocking in three runs on the day (amounting to 6 RBIs for the first three games). One writer suggested humorously that the ball was hit hard enough to kill even the indomitable Arizona rattlesnake. It would be his only home run of the spring, as Scott finished an abbreviated strike-shortened exhibition season respectably with a .291 average and 9 RBIs. The Brewers did almost as well by winning 11 of 21 contests.

On April 1 the first strike in the history of major league baseball occurred, based on a player vote of 683 to 10, to end the 1972 exhibition season and delay the start of the regular season. The owners were aghast at what had happened, believing that there was no unanimity in the player ranks and if they simply held their ground, as before, the players would soon fold; but this time they didn't. Instead it was the owners who buckled to the pressure of the work stoppage, unprecedented as it was, due to the great loss of revenue that would result from it. On April 12 they reached a compromise with the players by agreeing to add $500,000 to the pension fund for higher benefits, and a willingness to add salary arbitration to the collective bargaining agreement. The fallout from this for the 1972 season was that the 86 games lost during the 13-

day stoppage were never made up, because the owners refused to give the players back-pay for games missed while they were on strike. The Brewers lost six games from their 162-game schedule.

A special panel of baseball writers, broadcasters, players, field managers and general managers nominated George Scott as one of eight American League third basemen for the 1972 All-Star ballot. It was an extraordinary measure of respect by Scott's peers, who thought highly enough of his skills to nominate him for the position in spite of his limited play there, especially after a rough spring at the hot corner where he uncharacteristically committed seven errors.

The Brewers were moved from the weaker Western Division to a strong Eastern Division for the 1972 season, posing some disadvantages for a developing ballclub, which opened in Cleveland on April 15 and won, 5–1, on a well-pitched game by 1971 Rookie Pitcher of the Year, Bill Parsons. In spite of the win they were off to a slow start losing the next three, and won only three of their ten games in April, quickly and predictably finding themselves at the bottom of the division. It was a slow start as well for Scotty, who managed only four base hits and a .103 batting average.

On May 9 manager Bristol, in the first game of a County Stadium twin bill, started Scott at first base, where he was a Gold Glover, and the change seemed like an elixir to him. He hit his first home run of the year and went 3-for-6 in the doubleheader against Oakland. He explained later that he felt relaxed for the first time since arriving in Milwaukee. First base was like a charm to him; he was comfortable there, confident of his skills, and he could finally concentrate on his hitting. He had also made up his mind to abandon the notion that he had to carry the club by himself.

The Brewers were in last place, seven games out of first, on May 14 when the Red Sox came to town for a two-game series; it was the first encounter with them since the controversial, and in some circles, less-than-popular 1971 blockbuster trade. They lost the first game, 5–1, in ten innings to Ray Culp who went the distance for Boston. Bristol, clearly frustrated, having lost 15 of their first 21 games with a team batting average of .179, worst in the American League, held a rare meeting with his club before the second contest, using some not-so-sweet adjectives to emphasize a "time to win" theme. Some changes were needed, and he made them, putting George Scott back in his customary first base slot and moving Briggs, who had been playing first, to the outfield "where they play best," explained a harried manager. Scotty wasted no time rewarding the Milwaukee manager for his apparently brilliant decision, by belting a prodigious two-run bomb in the very first inning off Sonny Siebert, leading to a 4–1 Brewers win.

But the Brewers were anything but successful; they proceeded to lose 5 of their next 8 games, including two poorly played games May 26 and 27 against Boston, the first series in Fenway Park for Scott, and Milwaukee, since the trade, in which there were five Milwaukee errors. Bristol was on the ropes, with his job in jeopardy. Bud Selig, the Brewers owner, on the morning of May 28 announced to the press — curiously, with Bristol in attendance — that he was firing the field manager and replacing him with his Triple-A Evansville pilot, Del Crandall, a Milwaukee favorite who was a member of the city's only World Series championship team, the 1957 Braves. Crandall became the third manager of the young Brewers-Pilots expansion team.

Crandall's first statement to a zealous Milwaukee press was that he wanted his team to "have fun;" it was an offhanded remark, perhaps, but had the effect of critiquing the deposed skipper who was felt to be too rigid, an unremitting "taskmaster," complained GM Lane, who did not always get along with Bristol. Neither did George Scott, who had trouble adjusting to the unyielding style of Bristol, as well as with some of his teammates, who couldn't comprehend or find reason to embrace the querulous ex–Red Sox star, who sensed by now he was on a club bereft of its dignity and doomed to lose. Losing was not a part of Scott's vocabulary, or personality, and he chafed at the idea of this being his future, showing little patience for teammates who were willing to accept the status quo, and of an administration indifferent about winning.

Scott lamented that he didn't produce for Bristol, embarrassed with his .147 batting average at the time of Bristol's firing, but there was no mistaking that there was no love lost between them. To Bristol Scott was an anomaly; Scotty, meanwhile, was finding it hard to make adjustments to his new team and his intransigent manager. His "cultural deprivation" was to blame, wrote sportswriter Larry Whiteside — a pioneer award-winning black journalist — of the *Milwaukee Journal*, for Scott's communication breakdown with teammates. Bristol, a stickler for rules, was regularly on him for "policy" matters — his own personal ones — that rubbed Scott the wrong way. In one instance Bristol insisted Scott wear his socks a certain way; Scott viewed it as petty, refused to cooperate, and then brooded; Bristol fumed. When Scott threatened to take the matter to the Players Association, the matter was dropped. There were other "incidents," wrote Whiteside, including a dugout fight between Scott and the Brewers' new third baseman, Mike Ferraro, who did not take well to Scott's intensity and offbeat language. Just a "misunderstanding," they said later. But the presence of new manager Crandall and his "have fun" philosophy had a soothing effect on George, who declared he could play for the man, unlike how he felt about Bristol. While Scott saw hope with Crandall, this relationship, as well, was to erode in a series of perplexing events in the next few seasons.[5]

Years later, Scott offered an explanation that shed some light on his philosophy about the game and why he had run-ins with some teammates — it was all about winning: "I did not make a lot of friends in baseball, and the reason was because I was very serious about my job. I did not do a lot of talking at the ballpark. If you wanted to be my friend you had to wait until the game was over. Once I went into the clubhouse and put that uniform on, I was dead ready on beating your ass. That's the way I played. I kept my serious game face on; I knew I had to because that's what got me as long a career as I got in baseball. I stayed in that league because of my willingness to go out there and play to win. I went out there to play to win every game. When I look around and I don't see guys going at it the way I think they should, it [upsets me]. I went at it, and I went at it hard. I never took life for granted, and, you know, I did not make any friends on the field."[6]

It was a period of mutual adjustment, insisted writer Whiteside, between a typically conservative Midwestern city, like Milwaukee, and a churlish figure like Scott whose behavior, they believed, was inappropriate and out of place for their kind of town. But Whiteside came to Scott's defense, emphasizing his extraordinary athleticism and giving him a round of verbal applause, with these remarks: "The Boomer, as he still likes to be called, although thus far this season he hasn't hit many of the prodigious taters of other years, may be one of the last of a dying breed of ballplayers. He is an instinctive athlete who goes about every motion on the field as if he were born to it. To see Scott play first base is still one of the genuine treats left in baseball. It's no wonder that he owns three Gold Gloves, emblematic of three appearances on the AL All-Star Fielding Team of *The Sporting News*, at the position (1967, 1968, 1971)."[7]

On May 29, the Brewers avoided a four-game sweep by the Red Sox with an 11–3 rout. It was their biggest offensive assault of the year, more notable because of George Scott's display of open defiance of the Red Sox organization for trading him, and the Boston media — Scott's primary target — for their tireless heckling of him for his feeble batting average. Scotty wasted no time, clouting a first-inning run-scoring triple, and then launched a 420-foot home run in the seventh, both off ex–Brewer Marty Pattin, knocking in 4 of the Brewers' 11 runs. He trotted slowly, methodically and immodestly around the bases following his four-bagger, stepping forcefully on each base for emphasis, as if to symbolically insert a dagger into whomever in Boston felt culpable, and then for good measure leaped with a final flourish onto home plate. The Boston crowd, still upset with the Red Sox for trading their beloved first baseman, and of their spring trade of ace reliever Sparky Lyle to New York for Danny Cater, cheered Scott throughout the series; when he landed on home plate they shouted with mock approval.

Crandall stepped in officially as the new Milwaukee manager on May 30, a home game against the Yankees, and was rewarded in his debut with a 3–1 one-hit gem by Skip Lockwood. Scott was 2-for-4 driving in one of Milwaukee's three runs. On the same day of Bristol's dismissal by the Brewers, Scott began a nine-game hitting streak in which he batted .533 with 11 RBIs, followed by another run of 13 consecutive games amassing 20 base hits between June

16 and 28, raising his average propitiously to .255. But the Brewers, who as a team was batting .228, could not shed themselves of the Eastern Division cellar. By the All-Star break Milwaukee was 15½ games out of first.

By the third week in August Scotty was solidly in third place on the American League leaderboard with 64 RBIs, and rapidly moving toward Milwaukee's club record of 82 set by Tommy Harper in 1970. It was a great source of pride for George who was acutely aware of the Red Sox' unabashedly open assertion he was incapable of achieving RBI leadership with the Brewers. It was like a burr in his side that inspired him to perform at his very best against Boston: In the five years he was with Milwaukee, Scott batted just under .300 (.291) against the Red Sox, collecting 101 base hits, 58 RBIs, 20 home runs and a .524 slugging percentage. He became a nemesis to the Red Sox, not only because of his performance at the bat and in the field, but also because of the enormous following he had in Boston, who flocked to see their beloved Boomer flash the fancy glove he now called Black Magic around Fenway Park again.

A sequence of unpropitious events occurred toward the end of the 1972 season that was disturbing to the Milwaukee ballclub, and may have set the tone for the balance of the season. Still mired in last place, as they had been all year, Crandall made what appeared to be a rookie manager error on August 24 — five weeks before the end of the season — by letting slip that he would release three of his coaches at the end of the year. The timing was bad, creating a lame duck atmosphere between the players and the staff. Then on August 30 in a game against Kansas City umpire George Maloney called Scott out on strikes on a pitch that even the County Stadium fans knew was a ball. The pitch was a foot-and-a-half outside and enraged Scott, who was clearly upset with the umpire and feeling powerless for being taken out of a crucial situation with a runner in scoring position in a tightly contested 1–1 game; he was hitting .318 and had been knocking in baserunners with regularity. Scott continued with his rage at Maloney in the field after the at-bat, and was ejected for the third and last time of his major league career. It seemed obvious to everyone in the ballpark that it was because of the strikeout call, but it was learned later the reason for the ejection was that Scott had made an inappropriate gesture toward heckling fans that was seen by only a few, among them umpire Maloney and manager Crandall. "He took the bat out of my hand. If I walked away in that situation and didn't say nothing, I'd be cheating myself, cheating the fans and cheating the team," said a still-fuming Scott after the game.[8]

The matter was subject to debate in the Milwaukee papers whether Scotty would be fined, and GM Lane preferred to sidestep the controversy by deferring such a decision to his manager. Crandall showed less compunction by promptly levying a $500 fine on Scott, a particularly stiff penalty that enraged Scotty even further and led to a nagging coolness between them; once again Scott discouragingly found himself in conflict with a manager. "I'm not sure I can help the ball club in my present frame of mind," said the perplexed Scott. Though he was clear he was not complaining about the reason for the fine, he expressed frustration with the sizeable amount of money being taken from him, unusually high for the times. "This fine hurts me and I am very low," he said.[9]

The Brewers played mediocre ball the remainder of the season, finishing pitifully in last place in the Eastern Division with a 65–91 record, 21 games behind the leader, Detroit. George Scott, meanwhile, had a good first season with the Brewers. He was the team RBI leader with 88, breaking the old team mark of 84 set by Tommy Harper, placing him fourth among the American League leaders, which was a remarkable feat for anyone playing for a last-place club like the Brewers. He tied with John Briggs for second on the team with a .266 batting average with a club-leading 154 hits (33 more than his closest competitor), second-most of his major league career. He was also team leader in doubles (24), triples (4), runs scored (71), total bases (246) and placed second with 20 homers to Briggs' 21. He also had an impressive team-leading 19 game-winning base hits. He made but a scant 10 errors at his first base position, none in the last two months of the season, leading to his fourth Gold Glove award. He was the man around whom the franchise was to be built, exclaimed owner Bud Selig, commenting at the conclusion of the season on the big trade that brought Scott and five of his Red Sox teammates to Milwaukee. Scott was later honored by the Milwaukee baseball writers as 1972's Most Valuable Brewer.

"If there is such a thing as a respectable last place team, we would have to be it," remarked first-year manager Crandall, emphasizing the powerful one-two punch of Briggs and Scott in the middle of his lineup — perhaps the only high point of a bad Brewer season — as he sought solace from the rigors of dealing with a cellar-dwelling ballclub.[10] Then there was George Scott who experienced troublesome moments with two managers, teammates and an administration he claimed lacked a winning attitude, in his startup year with Milwaukee. "It was tough times for everyone concerned, especially Scott," wrote Larry Whiteside of the *Journal*.[11]

Another important Milwaukee offseason trade was made by new GM Jim Wilson with the Phillies on October 31. The key man in the transaction was the Phillies' Don Money, a sure-handed infielder, who would fulfill the Brewers' needs at third base. Money knew the value of having a Gold Glover like Scott at first base and wasted no time praising the legendary first sacker who was likely to keep many across-the-infield tosses — six of his ten errors in '72 were errant throws to first — from making the errors column. With Scotty handling chores at first base, that dubious statistic was likely to change for the better.

The Brewers opened their 1973 spring exhibition season on March 9 against the Oakland A's, beating them, 5–3. Scotty had his usual good spring start by rapping out 6 base hits in his first 13 at-bats, including three home runs, and feeling quite content as he readied himself for the upcoming season, knowing confidently he was to be in the Brewers' starting lineup on Opening Day. He had arrived a day earlier than he had to, at four pounds lighter than his 1972 playing weight. Without question he was the hardest worker in camp, including wearing a 15-pound belt around his waist for even further conditioning, as noted by his charmed manager. Scotty batted .327 over the 21-game spring span with 10 RBIs, and another strong spring showing to his credit.

The Milwaukee press was touting Scott as their key man to the success of the Brewers' 1973 season, featuring him on the front page of the *Journal's* April 1 edition, of the "Men's and Recreation Section" of the paper. "First baseman George Scott, the Brewers' top hitter last year, is looking for his best season ever in 1973," was emblazoned under an oversized photo of the Brewers' star player. It was particularly satisfying to Scotty who said that much of the previous year was spent "win[ning] the fans in Milwaukee," and so he felt personally vindicated after the troubles he encountered in the previous season. Del Crandall was doing some promoting of his own of the Brewers' superstar by lauding his leadership qualities as the spring season was drawing to a close. "He showed the last part of last year that he's going to be a leader; not a cheerleader, but the kind who can lead the team by what he does on the field," said the exuberant skipper as he proudly gazed out onto the field at his superbly talented first sacker going through the fluid paces of spring drills.[12]

But the Brewers were a magnificent flop on Opening Day, April 6, in Baltimore losing, 10–0. The game was marked by being the first of its kind to use a so-called designated hitter that was to become a staple of the American League. Ollie Brown established baseball immortality by being the first Brewer DH. George Scott was off to a miserable start himself, going 0-for-12 before getting his first base hit, a run-scoring single, off the Orioles' Doyle Alexander on April 14. But the Brewers as a team were soon becoming the surprise of the American League. On April 29 they slipped into first place, however briefly, when Baltimore lost its game that day to Oakland, but then relinquished the lead by losing that night to Texas. It was the first time in the history of the ball club, other than on Opening Day in 1971 and 1972, that they had ascended into first place. On May 1 "the astonishing Milwaukee Brewers," as reported by the Associated Press, had regained the lead by one-half game over Baltimore, by beating Oakland, 4–3. But Scott was languishing yet again in the early part of the season, batting .236 with 3 home runs.

The Brewers hovered among the leaders, tottering between first and third, in a densely congested pack of Eastern Division ball clubs barely separated from each other and the vaunted first-place spot. On May 12 they rose to the top again by beating the Tigers, 6–2, provoking their manager, Billy Martin, fuming at the idea of the Brewers in first place, to remark disparagingly: "If they [the Brewers] can win with that club, I'm a Chinese aviator."[13] For good measure the Brewers beat Martin's club the following day, as well.

Crandall, astonishingly, was winning with a team laced with a hodgepodge of veterans and rookies, with as many as four to five first-year men in the starting lineup, two of whom would place 2nd and 3rd in Rookie of the Year voting. The pitching began to crumble, however, and the Brewers lost their next eight of twelve games. On May 25 they had dropped into last place after a 5–3 loss to California. All was not bright with the club among some of the players, either. Ex–Red Sox outfielder Joe Lahoud was being used sparingly, mostly in pinch-hit roles, and was simmering over his lack of playing time. He finally lashed out at the Brewers' front office toward the end of August asking to be traded, saying angrily: "I don't enjoy playing for people I don't respect."[14] But the biggest disturbance was coming from their first sacker, Scott, who was still smoldering over the 1972 fine levied him by Crandall, of his treatment by the Brewers' front office, and for other instances in which he and his manager did not see eye to eye. At the very best their relationship approximated that of a wobbly dispirited truce.

It all came to a head on May 30 when Del Crandall levied his second fine on Scott, this one a whopping $1,000, after missing two games because of a groin injury. The reason for the fine was never disclosed by Crandall or Milwaukee management, but there was an implicit allegation of malingering. Scott was irritated that he had been unceremoniously demoted from his cleanup position in the batting order in the two previous games, May 26 and 28 against California. The ultimate indignity was foisted on him on May 29 when Crandall had him batting 7th. Scott said nothing to Crandall of his displeasure of being dropped in the order, but instead requested he sit out the game because of a nagging groin injury. He missed the May 30 contest as well, a second straight shutout loss to the Minnesota Twins, frustrating Crandall even more since he needed the big slugger's bat, and who may have felt Scott was "dogging" it. Following the game Scott openly complained about the indignity he was feeling over being slotted in the lower half of the batting order; it did not escape Crandall, and he imposed the fine (it was never revealed, however, until later when the matter was leaked to the press).

George Scott was enraged for not being believed by his manager. "I said I was hurt and the manager didn't believe me," he said later in the season. "He fined me $1,000. In his mind I was dogging it."[15] With a reputation for being one of the hardest-working athletes on the ball field, this slap-in-the-face assault on his pride and self-respect couldn't have been more insulting to Scott. Scott filed a grievance with the Major League Baseball Players Association on June 18. The repercussions of this were far-reaching, more so than simply being a franchise or an American League problem, but one that touched all of baseball. The fine was at the heart of one of baseball's "most discriminating practices," wrote journalist Martin Ralbovsky, which was the arbitrary fining of ballplayers for such alleged misdeeds as malingering, discontent and so-called "bad attitudes."[16] Baseball management was in complete charge of the process, as they were judge and jury — either a player paid the fine or ran the risk of suspension. The player had no say in the matter, and no opportunity to appeal. Not going to stand for it, Scott was prepared to file a civil suit and take it all the way to the U.S. Supreme Court, if necessary, he asserted.

The matter of the fine and grievance appeared to have an opposite effect on Scotty than one would have ordinarily expected of an athlete following such tumult. Instead of brooding, the fine invigorated him and he proceeded to play inspirational baseball for the balance of the season. Scott returned to the lineup on May 31, but Crandall, who would not yield, had him batting in the 7th slot. Scotty returned to the lineup with a vengeance, going 2-for-3 in a 4–2 loss against Minnesota. He was besieged by reporters, still unaware of the fine, afterwards sensing they were on the cusp of a good scoop. "I had pulled a groin [muscle]," responded Scott, answering their pointed questions. "Today was a warm day. I came in early today, took two whirlpools and had it wrapped real tight. It felt good. The warm weather helps," he said affirming for them that the injury was real. But he could not hide his distaste for the matter. He was clearly upset with his manager, and with GM Wilson, whom he felt should have spoken to him, mumbling some words to the reporters about being the only $80,000 salaried player in the league batting seventh. The rift between Scott and the club wasn't going to abate anytime soon.[17]

On June 1 Crandall had George back in the cleanup slot, and he cracked a mammoth home run off Chicago knuckleballer Wilbur Wood. It was the start of an impressive winning streak, historic for the Brewers, in which they won 15 of 16 games, ten in succession starting on June 8 and culminating in a 8–3 drubbing of the Red Sox on June 18, when Scott slugged two home runs. On June 10 in a game against the Angels, Scott banged his knee injuring it enough to come out of the game. But he was back in the lineup the next day, and games thereafter. "That shows character," exclaimed an opportunistic Crandall, whose Brewers had won six in a row, shrewdly showing support for his big first sacker with words that were meant for public consumption, after their blowup just two short weeks before. But just as suddenly the Brewers began a precipitous slide, losing nine of their next twelve games.

Scotty was having a solid month of July: For 21 games through July 20, going into the mid-season All-Star break, he was batting .350. But then another incident appeared to have occurred between Scotty and his manager, although no explanation was given, and Scott was benched for the final two games of a three-game series (July 20–22) in Kansas City, in which the Brewers lost all three. Alarmed by the mysteriousness of what was taking place, Scott's obvious unhappiness, and where he had been hitting so well, the Milwaukee scribes questioned the Brewers skipper, who responded blandly laced with a tone of sarcasm: "He doesn't feel well." Scott expressed another view, directing the questioners back to Crandall, with the comment: "There are two guys who know what's wrong," refusing to elaborate; the inference from this seemed to point to the manager and general manager, stemming perhaps from the fiasco of May 30.[18]

Dealing with his frustrations induced by Brewer management, Scott continued his July rampage by stroking 13 base hits in 29 at-bats, including the first grand slam of his career on July 29 off of the Yankees' Sam McDowell — the same man who struck him out three consecutive times in his rookie year of 1966 — hitting at a .448 pace. The four-bagger was a game-winner, Scott's 5th base hit and 6th RBI on the day, for a Brewers' doubleheader sweep of first-place New York.

McDowell, a left-hander, walked left-handed batter Dave May to fill the bases. Yankee manager Ralph Houk stuck with McDowell to face right-handed slugger Scott. It was a fatal decision, as Scotty launched a tremendous blast on an inside pitch to left-center that nearly left County Stadium, a feat that had never been done since permanent bleachers were installed in 1961. It remains uncertain whether Scott's homer on that day actually remained in the ballpark. It was reported that the ball landed two rows from the top of the bleachers. New York left fielder Roy White said it went over the bleachers and on one hop struck the metal chain link fence that surrounded the stadium, located 40 feet behind the bleachers.

"It was the greatest applause for a player I've ever heard at the Stadium. I can't recall one for Henry Aaron that was as loud as that," said Brewers owner Selig. Scott not only received resounding cheers immediately following the blast, to which Scott doffed his cap, but received even more, a standing ovation that grew to a deafening roar when he marched out to take his post at first base. It was a touching tribute for Scotty who at that extraordinary moment became the beneficiary of a special fan salute, a very personal one, knowing of his frustration with Milwaukee management.[19]

In spite of Scott's heroics, the Brewers won only 13 of 30 games in July, to be mired in 5th, six and one-half games behind the first-place Yankees. Scott continued to hit well through August finishing the month at .298 with 19 home runs and 81 RBIs, raising his own average 44 points since the middle of June. But once again controversy raised its loathsome head when on August 30 the *Los Angeles Times* leaked a story that Scott, Milwaukee's highest-paid player, was not a so-called "untouchable" to trade according to GM Wilson. It was another personal insult by the Brewers that stirred Scott even more; to him it was just another dagger thrust at him by the Brewers, adding to the already strained relations between them.

With his emotions now bubbling at the surface, Scott boiled over at Crandall and Wilson for the humiliation he was feeling, figuring he would be traded. Wilson became defensive, suggesting later on that the statement he made was taken out of context. The Milwaukee fans were in an uproar over the matter, suggesting that the club get their act together and come up with a way to retain their beloved superstar. By the time of the World Series in October, in the face of numerous trade offers for Scott by other clubs, who were eager to wrap their arms around such a gem of a complete ballplayer, Wilson declared Scott a definite untouchable.

On September 6 the *Milwaukee Sentinel* broke the story of the May 30 debacle, the punitive action by the Brewers and the grievance brought by George Scott; it came as a complete surprise to the city of Milwaukee. The *Sentinel* learned that the executive director of the Major League Baseball Players Association, Marvin Miller, was directly involved, announcing that the hearing on the grievance was to be heard on September 14. The pressure was bearing down on the Brewers who, confronted with lasting consequences and a damaging legal battle, wavered for the first time by suggesting they might rescind the fine. Miller and Scott continued their plans to pursue the grievance, even into the civil courts, if necessary, threatened Scott. Things were beginning to look ominous for the Brewers, and for baseball.

On September 8 Milwaukee officially dropped the fine, hoping to douse the action once and for all and allow them to slip away silently and unblemished from the public spotlight. Scott, once content to adjudicate, softened his stance. Astonishingly, he expressed satisfaction with the result, remarking that he got his "justice" after all. He could have made far more of the situation, as possible legal precedent, but he chose not to. His pride was intact, and he had regained his self-respect, which at the time was of greater personal value to him than anything else he could have achieved through litigation. He was now ready to focus on baseball.

Oakland A's outfielder Reggie Jackson once remarked that black ballplayers were often suspected of malingering by white managers — which appeared to be the central issue in the Scott case. "White players get hurt, they sit out. Black players get hurt, they're expected to play anyway. It's like we're animals or something," said Jackson. "As soon as a black player says he's not feeling well, the manager says, 'Get it X-rayed.' If nothing shows up on the X-ray, the reaction is automatic. He's dogging it. That kind of thinking has been around baseball for years. It's unconsciously racist."[20]

Relieved of the burdens of a frustrating year and the effects of a weighty grievance matter hanging over him, Scotty had another strong month, batting .345 in September. He finished the season in grand style in Boston, playing in his favorite park in front of adoring fans, who still loved the big fellow from Greenville. In a four-game series that the Brewers lost every game, Scotty put on his own show by rapping out 7 base hits in 13 at-bats, a .538 pace, including 3 home runs, 1 triple, and 7 RBIs. His 24th four-bagger of the year was hit in the season-ending game, September 30, as a pinch-hitter. The Brewers finished the year firmly in 5th place at 74–88, 23 games behind division-leader Baltimore.

Scott compiled impressive year-end statistics, with a team-leading .306 batting average and 107 RBIs, breaking the Brewers club record he had set the previous year (he was second in the American League in both categories). He was club leader with a .487 slugging percentage, tied for fourth in the league; he tied with teammate Dave May and Oakland's Sal Bando for total bases (295); was team leader in runs scored (98); and was second on the team in game-winning hits (14) and home runs (24). He also claimed his 5th Gold Glove, garnering the second highest vote count (33-of-44) of all the candidates. He was listed among the American League's Most Valuable Player candidates by the Baseball Writers' Association of America, and was voted by the Milwaukee chapter of baseball writers as their MVP selection, which he shared with teammate Dave May.

13

Mentor

When I go in and negotiate, I don't negotiate on the basis of Dick Allen or Reggie Jackson. I negotiate on what George Scott had done. I achieved my life's ambition. When I was a kid, I wanted to be like Willie Mays or Mickey Mantle. Both were $100,000 players and now so am I. That's why I've got a lot to be thankful for. — George Scott[1]

"Brewers' Great Scott Enters Champagne Class," the *Milwaukee Journal* headlined Lou Chapman's reporting on the Milwaukee star first baseman, who had just entered the superstar payroll class after signing his new contract with the Brewers in late December 1974. He had signed for a reported $100,000, but it was later learned the figure was actually $110,000, making him the third-highest paid athlete in Milwaukee sports history, behind Kareem Abdul-Jabbar and Oscar Robertson of pro basketball fame. Even superstars Hank Aaron and Warren Spahn of the great Braves teams of the '50s failed to pull down that kind of money in Milwaukee.[2]

Scott was a study in affluence, reported the media, as he strode exultantly from the County Stadium executive offices into the parking lot, wearing a fur-collared coat and black-and-white turtleneck sweater, and beaming a countrywide smile. "I believe in first class and will continue that way," he said to reporters as he got into his Cadillac parked smartly outside the stadium.[3] It was a grand moment for the 29-year-old major league standout from the Delta, who once picked cotton near the banks of the Mississippi River at $1.75 per hundred-pound satchel, and who was all too familiar with the life of poverty.

Quite unexpectedly Brewers Manager Del Crandall, of all people, began to speak of Scotty's latent "leadership" qualities and how these traits could benefit the club. He had been a "take-charge" guy the previous two years, said Crandall of Scott, something Scott had assumed on his own, which, Crandall pointed out, by his usual hard work and dedication would be exemplary for his youthful ball club. The average age of the Brewers' important middle-of-the-infield and center field — upon which managers customarily build their teams — in 1974 was approaching 21 years, and some of the pitchers slated to make the team were just as youthful and inexperienced. "He's on the verge — if not there already — of being the team leader," said the Brewer skipper of his new $110,000 man.[4] Crandall, however, was not quick to back his words of prophesy with any captainship appointment, reserving that decision for much later.

The Brewers were now training in a new spring location in Sun City, Arizona, which Bud Selig had negotiated for his team for the next ten years. But their exhibition season was about as inglorious as the previous year with the Brewers winning 10 of 23 games. Scott, true-to-form, did assume his usual spring leadership role by hitting with gusto, a .396 average, a spring-best 22 RBIs, and 5 home runs, his last a grand slam off Oakland's Bob Locker.

But it was largely a disappointing 1974 season for the Brewers, who started well by gaining first place on April 13, where they remained for six games, then dropped precipitously to fifth place on May 7. They then climbed back into a four-way tie for first on May 13 before bouncing between there and second until a month later, June 13, when they dropped to third. They had held first place, either solely or shared, a total of 20 games. But then they began a descent reaching the bottom of the East Division on June 18–20, spent parts of August there, finally concluding their season in the same spot they finished the year before, in fifth (76–86) at 15 games out of first place.

The 1974 season was marked by a series of events that still resonate today for George Scott, which he believes may have been his greatest disappointments on the playing field. They were

The Brewers' first $100,000 man, George Scott, being touted to the Milwaukee fan base along with their new rookie, 18-year old Robin Yount, who would go on to a Hall of Fame career (courtesy of George Scott Collection).

named the "Beanball Wars" by the press because of their intensity and the extraordinary nature of the three-day event that began on July 14 on a sweltering 92-degree Sunday in Milwaukee's County Stadium in a doubleheader with manager Billy Martin's Texas Rangers. Martin, a man with a feisty reputation and a militant nature, was upset with what had occurred the previous day when his shortstop, Toby Harrah, was knocked down by Brewer pitching, he claimed. Martin felt it was intentional and complained in earnest to the umpires and to Crandall, whom he disliked, while at home plate exchanging lineups. He openly threatened he would order his hurlers to throw at their 18-year-old rookie shortstop phenom, Robin Yount, with head-high brushback pitches. It was an ominous gesture disturbing to the umpires and to Crandall, who suspected the angry Texas manager just might carry out his threat. He was right. In the sixth inning, Texas reliever Pete Broberg, who had a sizzling fastball, began throwing dusters to young Yount, knocking him down twice. In the sixth, he did the same to Scott, who had 5 RBIs on the day including a homer off Broberg, sending him sprawling to the dirt. Martin, who had been warned, was summarily ejected by umpire Ron Luciano. Broberg was tossed a few innings later for continuing his beanball assault on Brewer players and for his part in the matter. Martin was later fined for his indiscretions by the American League and suspended for three games.

This led to a "basebrawl" two days later with the Twins, as described by a reporter about the even more troublesome Minnesota event that made the Texas affair seem more like a "tea party," he maintained. The Brewers had control of the contest with a 5–2 lead through six innings and appeared to be coasting toward a win. In the seventh Ray Corbin of the Twins came on in relief and with pinpoint control struck out both Yount and Don Money. The next batter, Bob Coluccio, who was 3-for-3 on the day, was struck on the side of the head by Corbin's first pitch, a fastball, and staggered to the ground; he got up, began to walk toward the pitching mound, and then fell again. There appeared little doubt what was intended by that pitch. Scott had been standing near the dugout waiting to hit after Briggs, who was in the on-deck circle. What he saw enraged the big Brewers slugger, who led the charge to the infield and Corbin where Brewers and Twins players congregated. Twins manager Frank Quillici soon joined them and the battle began. Scott led the skirmish by knocking Quillici to the ground which was followed by several small clashes all around the infield. It was later reported to be the wildest ever brawl noted by a consensus of players and writers, lasting a good ten minutes before it was brought under control.

Recounting the events "like it was yesterday," said Scott in a much later interview, the importance of protecting the young Brewer players was paramount to him. "All those kids were babies. Most of the managers tried to intimidate them," said George. "Frank Quillici came to the back of the dugout and pointed to the head of Coluccio," said a still-raging Scott speaking with an indelible memory of that day; Quillici denied ordering a bean ball. "Coluccio was never the same ballplayer after that," said Scott. There's merit in what he claims: Coluccio was hitting .260 at the time, but finished the year at .223. The following year he batted .202, was sent to the minors, bounced between major and minor league ball the next two years, and then left baseball for good.[5]

The 1974 All-Star Game was held on July 23 in Pittsburgh, and was won by the National League, 7–2. How the players got to be elected and the reserves chosen was nothing but a "farce," wrote sports writer Bob Wolf of the *Milwaukee Journal*, who was critical of the process and particularly of the All-Star managers. Dick Allen, the 1972 AL MVP, was the fan selection for starting AL first baseman. But when it came time to name the backup players for the AL team, many of the clubs, the Brewers among them, were stunned at the choices. The American League manager, Dick Williams, historically a George Scott antagonist, made two choices for his reserve first basemen. One was future Hall of Famer Carl Yastrzemski, the Red Sox part-time first baseman, with which few could be critical. But far more startling was Williams' second choice: Kansas City's John Mayberry, an adequate fielder batting just .260 compared with George Scott and his .297 batting average, who was the superior first sacker.

It was a supreme snub of Scotty that enraged Bud Selig, who appealed the matter, along with Williams' snub of his third baseman, Don Money, to American League president Lee MacPhail. Selig was seething, calling it "disgraceful" in his formal letter to MacPhail; the effort by Selig was of no avail, however, but to the city of Milwaukee Selig's actions at the least brought into the open the injustice of Williams' initiatives. Money later was named as a reserve when Sal Bando, Williams' crony and backup selection from Oakland, came down with an injury. But in spite of his good bat (among the AL leaders) and being the hands-down best fielding first baseman in the American League, if not all of major league baseball, Scott remained off the AL All-Star team.

Del Crandall was upset, too, and ranted about the Scott snub shortly after the All-Star Game. "He's been underpublicized," said Crandall of his spectacular first sacker. "It's about time he gets the recognition he merits," he said, rating him with the six or seven best players in the league. Boston writers, in town for the Brewers-Red Sox four-game series, agreed with Crandall, complaining further that the trade sending Scott to Milwaukee had been a bad one. Scott was hitting .304 at the time, positioned firmly among the ten top hitters in the American League.[6]

He was rewarded with his 6th Gold Glove, 4th consecutive, and named co-recipient with Don Money for the "Magic Glove Award," Milwaukee's own team award for fielding excellence. Fifty-five American League managers and

coaches made George Scott a near-unanimous pick as best fielding first baseman. Of the 13 ballots not cast for Scott, five of them were by the Milwaukee
staff that was precluded from voting for their own players. He had an American
League best 1,345 putouts for first basemen and a major league best 114 assists,
helping his team tie with the Orioles as the best-fielding team in the league.
Only Joe Torre of the St. Louis Cardinals approached his assist total with 102.
He named his glove "Black Magic," which he had stained black, at a time
when the conventional major league baseball glove was brown or tan in color.[7]
His range, reflexes and instincts around first were far-and-away superior to his
peers; he had a take-charge attitude chasing pop flies and scooping balls hit
into the hole, and "better than any," said one sports scribe, coming in on bunts
and whipping the ball to second base to start double plays. He was every bit
the consummate first baseman.

Scott also took leadership in a few other important Brewer statistics. He
led the team with 82 RBIs, 36 doubles, a .432 slugging percentage, and .777
OPS (on-base + slugging). He finished second to teammate Don Money's .283
and .346 batting and on-base averages with .281 and .345, respectively.

One of the more striking moments in Milwaukee Brewers history was the
1974 offseason acquisition of home run king Hank Aaron from Atlanta, which
would turn out to be one of the most fortuitous and meaningful moments in
George Scott's professional baseball career, as well. Aaron, who had surpassed
the legendary Babe Ruth's home run record of 714 that season, signed a contract
on November 2 to come back to Milwaukee. It was there as a member of the
Braves that he cut his teeth as a pro ballplayer and excelled for 12 years, winning
a World Series (1957), and becoming a Milwaukee and baseball legend. He
and his team were beloved by the city, making their 1966 departure to Atlanta
a crushing blow, some Milwaukee fans declaring they would never return to
the game of baseball again. It was a brilliant move by Bud Selig to woo the
celebrated superstar back to the city from his waning days with Atlanta, and
drawing on a fan base that would surely respond well to the memorable slugger's
return. His instincts proved to be flawless. Brewer mania had set in with Aaron
triggering season ticket sales in the fall and winter at a pace 20 percent ahead
of the previous year. The Brewers would set a team record by drawing 1,213,357
fans in the 1975 season, nearly a 27 percent increase over 1974. Aaron became
Scott's mentor. It was the perfect union according to Scott, who stated that it
was the only occasion in his major league career that anyone "at that level"
spent time with him to explain the finer points of hitting.

> My locker was next to [Hank Aaron's] and he used to get in early, and I would
> get in early [also] and we'd sit around and just talk baseball. The reason that
> Hank was able to do that for me [be a mentor] was that when I grew up as a
> young boy playing baseball in the backyard I was Hank Aaron or Willie Mays.
> And here I am in the major leagues in the same locker room, on the same team

with this guy. It was unbelievable. You know Hank Aaron helped me out over there [Milwaukee]. He helped me out a lot. I will always say that the 1975 season was a direct tribute to Henry Aaron, because Hank used to sit and talk to me about hitting, about pitchers, about setting pitchers up, and all of that. If I had had him with me for four or five years there's no telling what I would have done in baseball.[8]

One of the first acts by Del Crandall as players arrived for 1975 spring training in Sun City was to abide by his promise to fine anyone who reported to camp overweight. He wasted no time by meting out the first of such penalties to George Scott, assessing him $700—$50 for each extra pound—for his over-the-winter imprudence. Scott, whose coffers were more amply lined than in previous years, saw some humor in this and began bantering with Brewers newly appointed general manager Jim Baumer, while both were standing around the batting cage. "See, Jim, that's why I argued with you for the extra $2,000 on my contract. For things like this," joked an obviously contented Scotty. Said Baumer: "We always get it back somehow."[9] A moment of unconscious nascent prophesy, perhaps, that would soon surface and lead to friction between Scott and the rookie Brewer general manager, who appeared intolerant of their star first baseman.

On March 12, the day before the Brewers' exhibition opener with the Cubs, Crandall appealed to Aaron to give his team an impromptu closed-door talk on hitting and the mental preparation required of a good hitter. What better man for that than Aaron, thought the Brewer skipper; it lasted over an hour. When it ended and spilled out onto the clubhouse floor, an informal session began with the young Brewer players huddled around Aaron and Scott, spellbound as they listened intently to the two accomplished ballplayers exchanging words of wisdom about hitting. It was a profound moment as well for Scotty, a conscientious student of the game and of hitting, with whom Aaron appeared to identify like a kindred spirit. They were rooted in conversation with each other at times, as if alone, yet in the presence of others as they embellished on answers to the questions that were being raised by the Brewers youngsters. A bond was about to manifest itself between the two that would raise Scott's confidence and overall performance level to never-before reached heights for him as a major leaguer.

Once more Scotty led his teammates in yet another successful spring exhibition season for the big first baseman by hitting an even .400 on 22 base hits. The Brewers, with a modicum of disappointment expressed by Crandall for not coming up with a better showing, finished at 12–12.[10] The day following the final spring game the Brewers traveled to Boston for their April 8 opener with a formidable Red Sox team. It was a chilly day in Boston, which did not deter a Fenway throng of over 34,000 fans who came out for the festivities. It was not only Opening Day, but also Tony Conigliaro's comeback attempt after a 3½ year absence from baseball, as well as the American League inaugural for the new Brewer, "Hammerin Hank" Aaron. It had a storybook crowd-pleasing ring to it. The Brewers were keyed up before the game, anticipating the introduction of Aaron and all the hoopla surrounding it; George Scott was in high-spirits as he unveiled his new first baseman's mitt, a manufacturer-issued black model. "Here it is, here it is," he hollered, "Black Magic," appealing to his teammates to take a look.[11] But the game fell flat for the Brewers who couldn't overcome the four-run deficit they were dealt in the first three innings, and lost, 5–2. Scott, who was accustomed to hitting well against Red Sox hurler Luis Tiant, was 1-for-3, a double. The next day the Brewers turned the tables on Boston by winning, 7–4, behind Milwaukee newcomer Pete Broberg's pitching and clutch hitting by Scott, precipitated by a four-pitch walk to Aaron, loading the bases. Scotty promptly followed with a hard-hit two-out single to knock in the first two runs of the game. It was to be the start of an extraordinary season for the big first sacker from Mississippi leveraged by the presence of a certifiable slugger, Hank Aaron, batting in front of him.

The Boston Series set the stage for the long-awaited home opener in Milwaukee on April 11 against the Cleveland Indians. Over 48,000 fans, undeterred by the 40-degree football weather temperatures, filled the stands to welcome Hank Aaron back to their city, and they were rewarded with a 6–2 Brewers win, putting them into a tie for first place. The Brewers drifted between first and second through April, and then on May 1 went into first place where they remained for most of the month, in spite of weak bats and injuries soon to follow. By the end of May only George Scott and their young shortstop, Robin Yount, of the regulars, were getting base hits with any kind of consistency, helping to keep the Brewers in contention. Scott was hitting .272, Yount .322; Hank Aaron was struggling at .187. The rest were languishing. "Scott Hot, Brewers Not," was the May 9 headline of a *Milwaukee Journal* article highlighting George Scott's runs-batted-in streak of eight consecutive games that was approaching the major league record of twelve held by Joe Cronin and Ted Williams. Scotty would fall short, however, knocking in runs in nine consecutive games before being stopped on May 10 against Kansas City; he amassed 14 RBIs in that span.

In spite of being among the leaders there were problems developing on the club with key injuries and a serious player behavioral issue involving their talented but temperamental second baseman, Pedro Garcia, who could not get along with Del Crandall, alleging, among his numerous complaints, that the manager was interfering in his personal life though that was never explained. Their dislike for each other bordered on pathological. Crandall benched Garcia on May 14 with an eye to sending him back to the minors, but owner Bud Selig reinstated him a week later despite his promise he would not interfere with the decisions of his field manager. The entire fiasco with Garcia did not set well with the rest of the Brewer players, several who lost their respect for the manager, assuming he had caved in.

Underlying all of this was an apparent issue with Crandall and hitting coach Harvey Kuenn, about trying to change Garcia's batting style, according to former Brewer captain, George Scott. "That's why I got angry when Del Crandall and all those guys [coaches] tried to change Pedro Garcia, and started messing with his head," declared Scott many years later. It struck a nerve with Scotty, whose earlier dealings with his former nemesis, Dick Williams, had left him with lasting emotional scars from the Red Sox manager's dogged attempts to change his own swing. "If he loses his aggressiveness [with the bat] he may become a worse player," exclaimed the former slugger, still frustrated with the situation confronting Garcia and remembering his own personal struggle with Williams. "They messed him up," decried Scott still harboring vivid memories.[12]

Yount and Money went down with injuries, Yount with an ankle sprain on May 9 that benched him for ten games and Money, the Brewers 1974 MVP, who underwent hernia surgery on May 28 that disabled him for nearly a month. It would have an effect on the team. From May 17 to the end of the month the Brewers lost 10 of 12 games—five by one run—putting them into a tailspin and into second place, 2½ games behind the Red Sox. During that same period Scott, unlike the rest of his teammates, was hitting well; he was 14-for-43, a .326 pace, with 2 home runs and 11 RBIs.

The good pitching that held up the Brewers earlier in the year, led by Bill Champion and Pete Broberg, soon faded, and by the first week of June Brewer pitching had regressed to a 4.06 ERA performance level, near the bottom of the American League. The bats were nearly as bad. On June 5 they were hitting a mere .238 as a team, third from the bottom. But while the Brewers were struggling George Scott was building his own personal momentum, by stroking 34 base hits—including an eleven-game streak—22 RBIs, 7 home runs and a .496 slugging percentage in the month of June. His RBI total of 53 was second only to Boston's Fred Lynn who had 56.

By the first of July the Brewers had crept back into second place, tied with the Yankees, one game behind the Red Sox, and about to play three important games with Boston in Milwaukee, starting with a doubleheader on July 2. Rick Wise, a 19-game winner for Boston that year, was on the mound in the first game, and was pitching a no-hitter through eight and two-thirds innings. He had walked Bill Sharp (only his second of three) with two outs, and George Scott came to bat. "I was trying to jam him. He's just a good hitter, that's all," said Wise.[13] Scotty proceeded to launch the ball well over the center-field fence to break up Wise's no-hitter, which would have been his second in the major leagues. "He crushed it," said teammate Bobby Darwin, the on-deck hitter, who followed with a home run of his own off Wise. Boston won the game, 6–

3. Scott severely sprained his ankle sliding into first base in the second game, and was carried from the field on a stretcher. But the Brewers managed to take two of three in the series, tying them with the Red Sox for first place.

Ordinarily an injury like Scott's should have kept him from the lineup for days, but Scotty was back in there after missing only one game, but limping decidedly, returning as the designated hitter in the first game of a doubleheader with Detroit. He had trouble keeping his weight back on breaking balls due to the pain, and was 0-for-8 in the next two games. But on July 6 he began a streak of five games in which he hit his 15th and 16th home runs, had 9 base hits at a .474 pace. By the All-Star break he was hitting .281 with a .842 OPS and 58 RBIs.

Once again there was controversy surrounding fan All-Star selections, and "perhaps the worst slipup of all," wrote *Milwaukee Journal* columnist Bob Wolf, was banishing George Scott to sixth place in the voting behind inferior players who were not performing at his level. Gene Tenace of Oakland, the fans' selection to start at first base, was hitting .275 with 14 home runs. Baltimore's Lee May, hitting .244, placed fourth. None of the players voted in front of Scott approached his runs-batted-in mark, except for May, who also had 58 RBIs. Scott led the others with 16 home runs — Tenace was next with 14 — and he was far-and-away the best defensive first baseman in the league, if not both leagues. All-Star manager Alvin Dark, who knew the true measure of the big first baseman who had been playing at an All-Star level, selected Scott as his primary backup along with Mike Hargrove of Texas and Boston's Carl Yastrzemski.

It was a frustrating moment for Scotty when he first realized he had not been honored by the fans, and he vented to the press and anyone else who would listen that he couldn't understand the injustice of the fan balloting. "You can't tell me the fans are voting right when I finish seventh [6th actually]," complained Scott, frustrated over the lack of recognition of his skills and year-to-date accomplishments.[14] Based on the consensus of other reporters and baseball minds Scott had made a reasonably sound inference; he was robbed yet again. The 1975 All-Star Game was played, fittingly, in Milwaukee, and became as much a celebration of Hank Aaron, promoted theatrically by Bud Selig, as it was an All-Star event. Aaron was also an alternate selection along with Scott to represent the Brewers. When Gene Tenace was announced as the American League starting first baseman the Milwaukee crowd reigned boos down on him as if the balloting had been his contrivance. Dark did, however, put George in the game playing first base in the top of the 7th with the American League down, 3–0; it was not a memorable occasion for Scotty who struck out in his two plate appearances, in an American League losing cause, 6–3. "I think I was just too keyed up," said Scott following the game. "I wanted to hit one for my fans."[15]

Reporters, eager for something provocative, interviewed several AL players willing to discuss the embarrassment of what had just happened to them. Among them was Reggie Jackson who was 1-for-3 on the day. He was bitter about the loss, rambled on about their reasons for losing, and then proceeded to list his favorite team and players. "My favorite player in baseball is George Scott, and my favorite National League player is Johnny Bench" said the future Hall of Famer and incomparable baseball superstar, making the Brewer first sacker his preeminent choice of a long list of notable ballplayers.[16]

Chuck Johnson of the *Journal*, reporting on events surrounding the July 15 classic, wrote about Milwaukee's local hero Scott, declaring that he "is something," reflecting on a question asked of the big first baseman by one of the newspaper people probing him on why he was wearing "beads" around his neck. It was actually a puka shell type of necklace he wore that he began to use that year, made up of various kinds of shells and beads that gave the menacing appearance of shark's teeth. Turning on his humorous side, Scott's quick-witted reply was: "Those are second basemen's teeth," without further explanation. This, of course, morphed into a variety of interpretations. Though the popular belief was that these were supposed to be Scott's mementos from his hard take-out slides of second basemen, he later explained it was symbolic of the rocket-like line drives he customarily hit to the right side of the infield, displacing infielders' teeth because of their inability to protect themselves.

The Brewers continued to be plagued by injuries. Pedro Garcia, their slick but moody second baseman, went down with a back injury on July 5 and remained out for over a month, playing sparingly after his August 11 return. Pitcher Bill Champion developed arm trouble and saw limited action the second half of the season. It was another blow to an inept pitching staff that had trouble surviving the early innings. Then one of their sluggers, Bobby Darwin, fractured his hand on August 2. And on the same day, and the day following, their promising 22-year-old outfielder Sixto Lezcano, another Latino like Garcia, ran aground with Del Crandall, who fined the young rookie a total of $150 for the two-day "temper tantrums," and benched him for a few games. Lezcano insisted it was unjust and he wouldn't pay the fine, whereupon the club took the money from his paycheck, according to their normal practice.

In the midst of what was happening to the team, losing 19 of 31 games in July, Crandall, who had hinted more than a year before about designating George Scott a team captain, appointed him to be the Brewers' on-field team leader on July 23. He was the Brewers first captain in the six-year history of the team. Scott had just clouted his 19th homer driving in his 62nd and 63rd RBIs the day before the announcement, and was on a streak of 8 games that continued to 14 consecutively in which he hit safely, including 5 home runs in that span. He hit .313 in July with 36 base hits, 8 home runs, 67 RBIs, a slugging percentage of .574 and an OPS of .929.

The Brewers, however, were sliding further toward the bottom. On July 30 they were one game below .500, firmly in fourth place, ten games behind first-place Boston whom they had just beaten two-out-of-three games. Rumor was beginning to circulate that Crandall's job was at risk, causing the *Journal's* sports columnist Mike Gonring to write of the preposterousness of such a thought, choosing to place the blame with the players not the manager. He pointed out the many problems on the club, the worst being inconsistent pitching, that would finish dead last in the American League, and a leaky defense, that would finish next to the bottom. And, for a team that was hitting just about as poorly (.249; third from bottom in AL), to be just one game below .500 meant "Somebody's doing something right," exclaimed the sportswriter. That "somebody" was George Scott, who not only was hitting well but fielding in his usual Gold Glove manner.

The Brewers went into a losing spiral that spanned the final two months of the season, losing 41 of 57 games. On August 25, after losing 20 of 25, Crandall exploded and ordered a closed-door clubhouse meeting to scold his players on their shoddy performance. George Scott also held the floor over his teammates, charging them with being "the laughing stock of baseball."[17] Scott was himself seething, sensing that an underlying reason for the Brewers' collapse was a lack of self-discipline with too much partying and general unpreparedness, which he loathed. "The players have to play harder, the coaches have to coach harder, the manager has to manage harder and the owner has to own harder," he said to a bevy of reporters only a few weeks before when Brewer defeats were becoming commonplace.[18]

Crandall's days with the Milwaukee Brewers were numbered when on September 22 in a game with Cleveland, rookie outfielder Sixto Lezcano once again locked horns with his manager by refusing to go into the game as a pinch-runner, a game in which George Scott was 4-for-5 and hit his 32nd and 33rd home runs. Lezcano was immediately suspended for the remainder of the season. It was also discovered that Pedro Garcia had unilaterally decided not to make the road trip because of his bad back. It was apparent Crandall was losing control of his club.

But while the Brewers and Crandall were falling apart "Scott Keeps Booming," was the headline of the September 25 *Milwaukee Journal* article following Scott's personal 10–3 demolition of Frank Robinson's Cleveland Indians by stroking his 34th homer and 4 RBIs. Losing manager Robinson threw up his hands, overwhelmed by Scott's performance. "He's something," he said of Scott. "He can carry a club when he's right."[19] The following day against Detroit Scotty provided all that was needed to defeat the Tigers, 3–0, knocking in all of the runs with two long home runs, the second (his 36th) a two-run shot that sailed high and long against the wind into the center field bleachers. He was awarded *The Sporting News* Player of the Week in which he was 10-for-27 with 5 home runs and 13 RBIs.

The Brewers finished the 1975 season rooted in fifth place again, 28 games behind first-place Boston at 68–94, Crandall's worst managerial performance since coming to Milwaukee. He was fired on September 28 before the final game of the year against the Tigers. There were mixed reactions among the players and media, typical for a manager who has just been released. Milwaukee Pitcher Jim Colborn was the harshest critic blaming Brewer management for failing to back their manager.

It was a stellar year for Scott, however, perhaps the only bright light of a forgettable year for baseball in the city of Milwaukee. Scotty led his club in practically every category: 36 home runs, 176 base hits, 109 RBIs, 86 runs, 9 game-winning hits, and a .515 slugging percentage. He hit safely in 115 of his 158 games played. More significantly, he was the American League RBI and total bases leader (318), tied Reggie Jackson for most home runs, and finished fourth in slugging percentage. He topped it off by winning his 7th Gold Glove-5th consecutive — by a near-unanimous 23-of-24 possible votes, as the best defensive first baseman in the league.

14

I'll Never Quit

If there was a better player [than me] in baseball last year I want to see him. There isn't another player who led the league in three categories like I did. I drove in more runs than anyone in the league and the Brewers never got anyone on base for me. Now you tell me how anyone could be more valuable than a guy who drives in all the runs for a fourth [fifth] place team. — George Scott[1]

Barely had the ink dried on the final lineup cards of the 1975 season and equipment packed and stored for another year, and the Brewers rewarded Scotty with a new two-year contract through 1977 for an estimated $150,000-$160,000, placing him among the elite top 10 highest-paid major league ballplayers. In essence he was the lifeblood of, if not actually, *the franchise*.

But trade rumors were circulating during the World Series that George Scott might be on the block in exchange for the California Angels' All-Star strikeout artist Nolan Ryan. Remarkably, and quite unexpectedly, strong interest in him was being voiced from manager Dick Williams, and their GM Harry Dalton. Brewers GM Baumer, who admitted their only "untouchable" was young Robin Yount and who was anxious to do some meaningful trading, in the next breath declared that clubs would have to "overwhelm me," if he were to give up his Brewer MVP first baseman, the bread-and-butter of the team.

Trade talk became even more intense during the winter meetings in Hollywood, Florida, among the Angels, Red Sox and Brewers; they were working on a three-way deal that would have sent Scott to California, but it never materialized. The Red Sox tried to negotiate a separate deal for Scott, but that fell through as well. Scotty was to remain a Brewer. "Nobody's going to drive in runs like George," exclaimed the Brewers' new manager, Alex Grammas, who was the Brewers' second choice after Hank Aaron, who rejected their offer, in an ebullient sigh of relief over the Brewers' retention of their big Gold Glover and slugging first sacker.[2]

Despite his remarkable season George Scott was in for disappointment;

this one at the hands of his own peers. By a thin margin of 11 votes (95 to 84), closest of the balloting among the candidates, the 214 players who participated selected the Kansas City Royals' John Mayberry as their choice for American League All-Star first baseman on *The Sporting News* all-star team. To Scott it was another snub, who, in the foremost categories of player performance, essential to team performance, outperformed every other first baseman. He drove in the most runs, hit the most home runs, and hit for the most total bases of any other American League player, and clearly carried the Brewers throughout their miserable season; his value to the team based on fielding performance was unsurpassed. Scott, by his exploits in the field, was by far the best defensive first baseman — for which he was honored with his 7th Gold Glove — executing many game-saving plays that never reached a statistical spreadsheet, or, for that matter, that were even capable of being translated into a statistical measure. But Mayberry, whose batting statistics were similar in several areas to Scott's, was on a team that finished second; Scott played for a team that finished next to last.

Even Mayberry's new skipper, Whitey Herzog, whose team had won 41 of 66 games following his mid-season appointment as Royals manager, equivocated about Scott not being chosen when doing an assessment of player balloting. "I guess maybe Scott could feel that he should have been the [all-star] first baseman," said Herzog, who then neutralized any possible controversy by suggesting that his first baseman had a "fine year," too and, besides, the "vote was close."[3]

Then there followed the most distinguished baseball post-season award, the Most Valuable Player, which added to Scott's disappointment. Rookie of the Year award recipient Fred Lynn of the Boston Red Sox was also honored as the American League MVP, the first rookie in either league to do so; he received 22 of 24 first-place votes from the Baseball Writers' Association voters. Scott finished eighth in the voting and was clearly frustrated, feeling he had been overlooked. "I drove in more runs than anyone in the league and we [Brewers] never got anyone on base for me," said a disheartened George Scott. But George's dignity was restored when he was honored by the Milwaukee writers on January 25 at their annual Diamond Dinner event by designating him the Brewers' 1975 MVP. He was also the Associated Press' pick for their all-star team, distinctively composed of American and National League players. Scott was one of only four American Leaguers among the ten players selected, and the only American League infielder.

Among the many awards George Scott received for his outstanding 1975 performance, perhaps the most curious, if not intriguing, was the one he received from Boston scribes at their annual writers' dinner. On January 29, four days after the Milwaukee Diamond Dinner ceremonies, the Boston writers toasted George with a so-called "special achievement" award "for fashioning his most productive major league season." This was unadulterated sentiment, perhaps, for Scott's remarkable achievements in that year that largely went unrecognized, yet plaudits for a man who remained a New England media and fan-favorite, who after more than four years still begrudged his absence from Boston.

Once more the spring season was interrupted by labor disputes between major league baseball owners and the Players Association. Toward the end of October 1975, executive director Marvin Miller had received a terse written notice from the owners that as of December 31, 1975, they were terminating the Basic Agreement they had reached earlier, and also their funding agreement for the pension plan, effective March 31, 1976. It was a significant blow to accomplishments achieved earlier between the two parties, and nothing but a "hostile act," declared Miller. But before all of this was fully digested or acted upon there came the historic *Seitz Decision* on December 23, 1975, which effectively granted free agency to major league ballplayers one year after expiration of their contracts. Seitz was summarily fired by the owners, but the die was cast in favor of the players. The owners appealed the Seitz decision twice, and lost both times, leaving them with the singular decision of negotiating for the best deal they could muster with the players. But the owners were still holding to some form of reserve clause language in any of their so-called bargaining, in spite of the legal decisions favoring the players, and the spring camps were shut down.

Commissioner Bowie Kuhn, realizing the risk to major league baseball by not opening the season, invoked his authority; on March 17 he announced the opening of spring camps, even while negotiations were still being worked on and no new contract had been reached. It was like a message from heaven for George Scott, who had been critical of the Players Association for not taking the owners' eight-year offer, a far cry from anything the players had just won in the courts. He chose to admonish them. "I think the players should stop crying about slavery and worry about playing baseball. If they'd play as hard as they complain, they'd all be superstars," said a frustrated Scott, thrusting his own principled argument of how he viewed some players.[4] Scott already had a two-year $160,000 contract tucked away, so he was eager to get started. No doubt his views did not sit well with his teammates.

Start they did with drills on March 20 and with exhibition games underway four days later, more than three weeks after camps should have opened. But all was not contentment in the Brewer camp. Bud Selig, who was one of the recalcitrant owners refusing to negotiate with the Players Association, and his GM Jim Baumer had chosen to play hardball with the thirteen unsigned Brewer players. Baumer invoked the renewal clause of the uniform player's contract and cut several players' salaries by the maximum allowed of 20 percent. It was unsettling to the Brewer players, especially pitcher Jim Colborn who cried foul. Baumer was already feeling the heat by being a principle in the firing of the popular Del Crandall, and not accomplishing any trades in the offseason. Now he was bearing the wrath of his players, many who found him too tough at contract time, one who even labeled him "nasty."

The Brewers finished an abbreviated spring season at 6–8; Scott played sparingly but still led the team with a .321 batting average, hit two home runs and 8 RBIs, second only to Darrell Porter who had 13. They opened the 1976 regular season on April 8 in Milwaukee in 44-degree weather, in front of a crowd of 44,868, and won 5–0 behind Jim Slaton's 4-hit pitching, and proceeded to win 8 of their next 11 games, slipping into first place on April 29. But it was downhill from there; the Brewers had fallen precipitously into 5th place three and a half weeks later. On May 27 in a tightly pitched game against Boston, Pete Broberg made an errant pickoff throw in the dirt to first base that Scott couldn't handle, leading to the winning run. Broberg later made the comment that it was a "catchable ball." That aroused George Scott who responded angrily that he didn't make alibis and he saw no reason why Broberg, a 1–4 pitcher with a "four point ERA," should either. Broberg was stunned claiming he didn't mean it the way a vexed Scott had interpreted it. It was apparent that the labor unrest and salary disputes of the spring, leaving players rankled and very unhappy with Brewer management, were now expanding into a whole other territory; Grammas, whose club was still in 5th and a full six games out of first, realized he now had his hands full. "He's playing no matter who's pitching," said Grammas responding to Scott's suggestion that maybe another first baseman should play when Broberg was on the mound.[5] Scott's displeasure continued into another game three days later when he complained to Grammas about being taken out for a pinch-runner. "Hell no, I don't like it," raged the big first baseman, who scoffed at Grammas' actions which he thought insulting.[6] Scott, who had two hits on the day and was batting .242, was clearly embarrassed.

On June 1 the Brewers reached the bottom of the division, 8½ games out of first, where they were to languish between fifth and sixth for the balance of the year, by losing a doubleheader to the last-place Tigers, each loss by one run on ninth-inning rallies. It was their third consecutive one-run loss to Detroit, losing in the final innings of come-from-behind victories. George Scott, who was 4-for-8 in the doubleheader, exclaimed: "Either they're the '27 Yankees or we're the Bad News Bears."[7] Manager Grammas saw no humor in the matter, however, after the twin bill debacle and chided the players unmercifully. "He said we were all rotten," said one Brewer player. Further troubles ensued the next day when the Brewers lost their fourth straight to Detroit on another late-inning Tiger rally, when pitcher Jim Colborn, who was 2–6 and still fuming over the treatment he had received from Jim Baumer in the spring, balked at Grammas' instructions to intentionally walk a batter. Grammas dashed to the mound and gave Colborn a tongue-lashing in full view of the crowd and television audience. Nothing was going right for the frustrated rookie manager. After the game, both Colborn — who was accused of throwing bean balls at Detroit batters — and George Scott, who was nearly beaned by Detroit's Vernon Ruhle and had to leave the game, received threatening telegrams. Three times the normal amount of Detroit policemen were at the next and final game of the series, but nothing came of it.

Baumer, who was criticized for not making any offseason trades on a club that was going nowhere without new blood, picked up 28-year-old Von Joshua on June 2 from the Giants for a player-to-be-named, and on June 3 traded relief pitcher Tom Murphy and outfielder Bobby Darwin to Boston for 1975 World Series hero Bernie Carbo. Darwin and Murphy were the happiest men after learning of the trade, gloating about it in the Brewers clubhouse among their teammates, many whom approached them with congratulatory remarks on how very lucky they were to be leaving a Brewers' sinking ship. On June 10 Milwaukee unloaded their troubled second baseman Pedro Garcia in a trade for another second baseman, 31-year-old Gary Sutherland, who was hitting .205. "Pedro was floundering, you might say," said Grammas.[8]

But it wasn't over: Just before the June 15 trade deadline rumors were swirling that California's Nolan Ryan was about to be traded to Milwaukee for the Boomer, George Scott. This fell through, however, when Ryan, looking like his old self, shut down the Brewers on a two-hit, 1–0, shutout on the same day of the proposed trade. Baumer was also working on trading for Oakland's great reliever Rollie Fingers, and talented All-Star outfielder Joe Rudi. This also fell through when the A's eccentric owner Charlie Finley sold them outright to Boston for $1 million each. Commissioner Bowie Kuhn later voided the deal as not being in the "best interests" of baseball.

Clearly frustrated at not accomplishing the swaps, and buried in last place 13 games from the top, Baumer began to rant after a June 22 shellacking by the Tigers, their fourth straight loss. It was a game of numerous mental mistakes, missing cut-off men, misjudged fly balls, infield errors and horrific pitching. But the blame for losing generally was laid at the feet of his big guy and Brewer MVP, George Scott, and their catcher Darrell Porter, who was hitting .216. They are "killing us," complained Baumer, who did not spare any words to criticize his first baseman and catcher; it was a trait of his according to one scribe of being "too straightforward" that would eventually lead him into trouble. And trouble it turned into, from one George Scott, who was outraged at being Baumer's target, and for Grammas' intent, possibly as a reaction to Baumer, of moving him to sixth in the batting order. "That's only an alibi for his own shortcomings," he said accusingly of Baumer.[9] He chided them both by pointing out that there were others on the team just as upset as he was, but chose not to speak up. "You hear them mumbling," he said.[10] "This is purely murder," moaned Grammas after a June 27 Sunday doubleheader loss to the Yankees, the Brewers' 8th loss in their last 9 games. The *Journal*'s Mike Gonring described them as "that traveling carnival," who were firmly mired in 6th place 16½ games out of first, and six games behind 5th-place Boston.[11]

Not long after Scott's verbal tirade with management the Milwaukee throng, weighing Jim Baumer's harsh and intemperate critique of the Brewer slugger, and searching for a fall guy upon whom to lay the blame for the Brewers' demise, suddenly turned on him. It was a natural fan reaction, as if it was sanctioned by the club, after their general manager's public evisceration of their highly paid first baseman. On July 2, in a shutout loss to the Red Sox, Scott, who was hitting .261 and now slotted third in the order, couldn't seem to do anything right — hitting into two double plays, fanning twice and failing to advance runners, two from scoring position. The County Stadium crowd demonstrated their disapproval by booing him derisively, like a scoundrel, more loudly with each at-bat. Scotty was miffed at his performance, stating it was one of his worst, but was surprisingly conciliatory when asked how he felt about being rebuked so badly by his hometown fans, who only a year ago had cheered him so approvingly. "That's part of the game," he said. "That's life, man. Fans forget in a hurry," promising he'd get even; "I'll produce," he said.[12] It probably was a turning point for George in how he viewed the club and the city who never let up on him after that game.

The Brewers rallied by winning 8 of their next 10 games including an astonishing five-game sweep of Texas, topped off by doubleheader come-from-behind victories, sending the Milwaukee fans into a state of euphoria, like they had won a championship, remarked one reporter. They hadn't seen anything like this all year. "You couldn't have any more thrills than this," exclaimed Grammas.[13] Scott was productive with 12 base hits for a .316 pace in the 9-day span. Nonetheless the Brewers remained in last place, 14½ games behind first-place New York.

July 20 turned out to be a historic day in baseball, not because of anything the team had accomplished, since the Brewers were solidly in last place going into the game, having lost the last 5-of-6 since returning from the All-Star Game; it was the occasion of Henry Aaron's last major league four-bagger, the 755th "tater" of his long and illustrious career. George Scott, batting fourth, fittingly, preceded Aaron's blast with one of his own, lifting a 3–0 delivery by California's Dick Drago deep into County Stadium's left field bleachers, so deep (well over 400 feet) that he stood at home plate watching its trajectory until the ball smashed into the stands. It was a mammoth shot. Barely had he sat down in the dugout when 42-year-old "Hammerin' Hank" followed with his ripping into a Drago hanging curve, lofting it into the left field stands.

With two months left in the season no one could have imagined it was to be Aaron's last. Pitcher Jim Colborn related afterwards that his wife mused over dinner that evening that it could have been the last home run they would see from Henry Aaron. "We could have seen history," she said. What a ridiculous thought he retorted. How right she was.[14] Six days later George Scott made some of his own personal history by breaking up a no-hitter for the fourth time in his major league career, when he hit a single in the ninth inning off Detroit's left-handed reliever Jim Crawford. The remarkable coincidence was that three of the four who were victimized by Scott's timely hitting were Detroit Tiger pitchers.[15]

On August 5 after Scott had led the Brewers to a 9–3 win in New York over the Yankees with a 3-for-3 performance and 3 RBIs, hitting his 11th homer and 53rd RBI, tops on the team, he sulked, not saying a word to reporters. Reporters being reporters, of course, drew their own conclusions, speculating that Brewer front office criticism of him, which was frequent, and the incessant booing by the Milwaukee crowd, disgusted at losing and looking for a reason and a culprit, finally caught up with the big first baseman. The booing seemed to take on a life of its own, no matter how well Scott was playing, which seemed to drive a nail into him further each day. "It's a shame," said Brewer Mike Hegan who sympathized with their first sacker for what was now becoming ritualistic behavior among the Milwaukee fans who sided with Brewer management.

On August 8 during a rainout in Boston, after the Brewers had lost two games there, Grammas ranted openly—"Pitiful," he called the team—about the poor performance in a 3–0 loss the day before. Scott could hold back no longer. Once more he displayed his pent-up rage to anyone who would listen about Baumer and Grammas for being the main protagonists behind his misery, inculcating beliefs readily embraced by the fan base provoking their hostility toward him. It couldn't have helped that earlier in the year Grammas had stripped him of the captaincy, and maybe his dignity as well, with which he had been rewarded by Del Crandall. His criticism of his manager was even finite, finding fault with him for not listening to his scouting reports on the Red Sox hitters, whom he knew well. It was the utmost of indignities, he perceived, to be ignored by his manager who not only took his title away, but who now shunned his advice. "I'm sick of playing in Milwaukee," said the angry Scott, stating he wanted to go back to Boston where he was appreciated.[16]

Following a late August three-game Brewers sweep of the Rangers in Texas, in which Scott was 6-for-10 and hit his 13th homer, reporters swarmed around Grammas to probe him on Scott's tirade about wanting to leave Milwaukee. Grammas dismissed it as just more poppycock. Scott later lamented that he was misquoted, but reporters were not going to buy it, concluding that he was not long for Milwaukee. "There seems to be little doubt that this is his last season as a Brewer," wrote the *Journal*'s Mike Gonring on August 27.

Scotty continued to play solid baseball, receiving the American League

Player of the Week honors in mid–September hitting .500 on a 14-for-28 hit performance, 8 RBIs and 3 home runs. But his team was not playing well losing all but one in that same span. During his hot streak all of Milwaukee turned out for a "Salute to Hank Aaron" night honoring him in his final year as a major leaguer. It ended up on a low note, with another Brewer loss, their 10th of the last 11 games, marked by an 11th inning Yankees' comeback victory, and another chewing out by Grammas following the game. Of the 7 Brewer hits Scott had 3 of them including his 18th and last homer of the season on that memorable day in Milwaukee, attended by a huge turnout of 40,383 Milwaukee fans who came to applaud a baseball hero who was one of their own. Sadly the next day's attendance was just over 6,000, a reflection of a Milwaukee attitude about their team that continued to the end of the season.

The Brewers ended the year losing 26 of their final 34 games in September-October, and finished dead last in the Eastern Division at 66–95, 32 games out of first. Scott was the anomaly on a club of generally poor performers. On the year he led the club in about every important production category among the regulars with 77 RBIs, 18 home runs, 166 hits, 73 runs, and a .414 slugging percentage. He batted .274, second among the regulars. And he walked off with his 8th Gold Glove award, 6th consecutively, which was to be his last. "Again, he was a source of teammate confidence by just being there," wrote the *Journal*'s Lou Chapman, summing up his reasons for Scotty being the best of the American League's first basemen.[17]

But the numerous disagreements with management and the rancor of the fans exhibited toward Scott and the club had taken its toll; changes were going to be made and Scott appeared destined to be one of them. Among them was a personal matter that confronted the slugger; the trouble he had been experiencing throughout the year with the Brewers seemed to have spilled over into his domestic life. On October 19 he was ordered to make temporary support payments in a pending

December 1976 — George Scott speaks to press about his trade back to his "Garden City," Boston and the Red Sox (courtesy of *Boston Herald*).

divorce action filed by his wife, Lucky, that did ultimately end in divorce. "I thought it was supposed to be for life," said Scott in a much later interview on the matter of his marriage.[18]

Several clubs from both leagues were in hot pursuit of the slugging first baseman, who made various pitches to the Brewers during and after the World Series. But the Brewers held their ground looking for "a front line player," said Baumer, for a player with the dynamics, production capabilities and overall baseball skills of a George Scott. It came as a surprise when on December 6 it was announced that Scott had been traded, along with the outfielder Bernie Carbo, to the Red Sox in exchange for their promising young first baseman Cecil Cooper. "I don't understand it," said a frustrated Frank Robinson of the Indians, who expected to work a three-way deal with the Yankees to acquire Scott. "How could they give up Scott and Carbo for Cooper?" said Robinson.[19] Scotty was delighted, saying he was returning to his "garden city," and that he felt like he was coming out of exile after five years in Milwaukee. He later said, however, that his decision to go back to Boston turned out to be a terrible mistake:

> The only thing I was unhappy about [in Milwaukee] was the commitment that the team had to winning. At that time I just didn't feel that the team was committed to winning. I wanted to be out. It turned out to be the worst thing in the world for me. I could have stayed in Milwaukee and probably done some good things. I got out of Milwaukee and Yount and Lezcano, Gorman Thomas, and all those guys came of age, and they went to the World Series, and they started to win. I regret going back to the Red Sox in '77. I was very excited about going back. I don't think the Red Sox were that excited about having me back.[20]

Larry Whiteside, the black ex–*Milwaukee Journal* sportswriter, who had seen Scott play for the Brewers and was now a reporter for the *Boston Globe*, pointed out that Boston might not be getting the player they think they were, for the benefit of those harkening back to their memories of Scott in the Hub: "That will take some getting used to, for he is no longer the scared, backward kid out of Greenville, Miss."[21] Scared he was not and he proved it quickly by surprising everyone, especially Red Sox brass, when he balked at the deal by demanding more money and a contract extension to play in Boston. He was miffed that once again he had been insulted by baseball management for not advising him, a 10-year major leaguer with 5 years with one club, whose contractual right it was to be consulted of any trade proposals. He later explained he was never unhappy at the thought of leaving Milwaukee; he simply wanted some security through a longer-term contract with the Red Sox, and he knew there were several Boston players who had them. On June 9 Scott consummated a deal with Boston. He did it himself, going around his agent Gary Walker, whom he had hired in the interim, and negotiated a multiple-year contract for $175,000 annually.[22] Things were definitely looking up for George Scott.

15

A Garden City

It was very depressing looking at guys on our club who didn't want to play. We
had guys who'd come into the clubhouse laughing when we'd lose. You'd see
some guys who got scared when their names were in the lineup. There were guys
who were happy when they didn't see their names in the lineup. — George Scott[1]

The personal attacks made on George Scott continued to emanate from
Milwaukee even as the 1977 spring camps were about to open and teams were
beginning to focus on the arrival of new players and the business of a new season. It was as if he had perpetrated some sort of willful offense in the city,
having the nature of a crime, causing Milwaukee brass and a few former teammates to seek reprisal.

Bill Travers, the Brewers top pitcher in 1976 and a Massachusetts native,
was overheard speaking to fans disparagingly of Scott, saying he is now "your
headache." He later explained when pressed by reporters that Scott should
have been more discrete about his feelings while in Milwaukee. This was followed by the incautious words of Brewers general manager Jim Baumer at the
annual Milwaukee writers' Diamond Dinner, where George Scott frequently
had been rewarded for his meritorious service with the Brewers.

Known for his impolitic nature, having apologized to Scott once for being
too direct, Baumer rapped his former slugging first baseman in front of 700
guests by saying he now had a first baseman — Cecil Cooper — who speaks in
terms of "we." It was an obvious dig at Scott; for that brief moment Baumer's
personal desire to be more of a diplomat and decorous general manager had
been abandoned. Cooper, who attended the affair, spoke later of Scott as being
a bona fide superstar and one whose shoes would be difficult to fill; he acknowledged he bore the burden of carrying a Brewers team on his shoulders.

Jim Slaton, another Milwaukee pitcher, chose not to jump on the Brewer
bandwagon that was ganging up on their departed first baseman: "One guy
can't ruin a ball club. It takes a team effort," he said.[2] Red Sox shortstop Rico

Petrocelli, a former teammate of Scott's, who overheard the clatter about George, refuted what was being said. "People who talk like that just don't know Scotty," he said, emphasizing Scott's fierce competitiveness and his determination to win, and how it was natural for him to complain when he's losing. Losing was not in his vocabulary.[3]

Stunned by the vitriol that followed him from Milwaukee, Scott said simply that he would deal with the Brewers in the best way he knew how and that was on the playing field. "Any guy who tells you he's putting personal goals ahead of winning is full of baloney," said the new Boston arrival.[4] The Red Sox spring camp opened for the full roster on March 1. Scott made his appearance sporting mutton chop sideburns, a mustache of the makings of a Fu Manchu and looking several pounds overweight. He was at no loss for enthusiasm in making his presence known and immediately declaring that his nickname, "Boomer," had as much to do with his tongue as it did his bat.

The Boston press quickly sized up a possible conflict between Red Sox superstar Carl Yastrzemski and Scott, who both played first base. Manager Don Zimmer, in his first full year as their skipper, dismissed the matter out-of-hand by saying there was no conflict at all. Scott was the best first baseman in the league and "that's where he'll play," he said.[5] What followed was described by one Boston sportswriter as the "Great Left Field Sweepstakes," an extravaganza between two future Hall of Famers, Yastrzemski and Jim Rice, who were vying for that position or be assigned as the DH, while Scott would contentedly reside at first base.

Scotty proceeded to knock the cover off the ball with 7 base hits in his first five exhibition games at a .500 pace, including a 410-foot homer. He continued to hit well throughout the spring season finishing at .371 with 17 RBIs, 6 home runs, most of them of the prodigious variety, and a .710 slugging percentage. The club did just about as well winning 17 of 27 contests; their last win was on the last day of the exhibition season, a 4–2 victory over the St. Louis Cardinals on Scott's two-run homer in the eighth. The team was laced with power hitters like Fred Lynn, Butch Hobson, Carlton Fisk, Yastrzemski, and Rice, who were to set numerous home run records during the 1977 season. They had slugged their way to 34 spring home runs, the most since 1971 when they hit 36, and a team batting average of .285.

But there were concerns. Larry Whiteside of the *Boston Globe* wondered if the Red Sox had purchased "the proverbial bacon slab in the plastic pouch," in describing Scott who looked nothing like he did when he played previously for Boston.[6] Scott assured them he'd be ready when the opening day bell rang, and to just let him work off the poundage and work out the kinks on his own. He was ebullient over the prospects of playing on such a power-laden club like the Red Sox, which he called "awesome," feeling it was the best major league team he had ever played for.

The 1977 season for the Red Sox opened on April 7 in Boston's Fenway Park, on a chilly day before a crowd of 34,790 hopeful fans. Carl Yastrzemski was playing right field for the first time in his career. Hardly anyone could get warm said catcher Carlton Fisk, defending their pitcher, reliever Bill Campbell, who had just lost the save and the game, 5–4, to the Cleveland Indians in the 11th inning, and who bore the brunt of catcalls from Fenway fans who displayed their disapproval of Boston's $1 million man. Fenway was filled with its share of harsh critics, a "howling mob of perfectionists," wrote the *Globe*'s Whiteside, which would set the tone for the coming season. The Red Sox, who were picked to be a pennant contender, lost their first four games. Not only was the pitching faulty but they committed 10 errors, three of them, astonishingly, by their Gold Glove first baseman, George Scott. By the third week in April they were in 5th place.

On April 24 Boston won only their fifth game, shutting out the new expansion Toronto franchise, the Blue Jays, 9–0. Scott, who had been pressing, was hitting only .222, but achieved a landmark of sorts in that game by being the first Red Sox player to hit a home run in a regular season game on Canadian soil. It was George's first homer of the season, a seventh-inning shot off Jays starter Bill Singer. On April 26 the Red Sox were in Milwaukee, Scotty's first

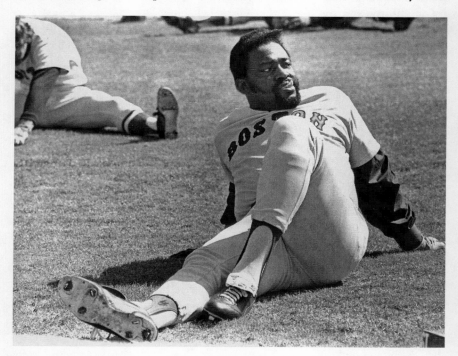

Scott sweating it out in Winter Haven (courtesy of Boston Red Sox).

trip back to the city that once cheered but then reproved him. A goodly sum of the 12,676 Milwaukee partisan fans jeered Scott. At one point someone threw a roll of toilet paper at him as he came to bat. He took it in stride until their pitcher, Jerry Augustine, made an ugly remark to the big Red Sox slugger as he ran out a grounder. It was "extremely uncomplimentary," wrote the *Globe's* sportswriter Bob Ryan suggesting there may have been racist content in what was said. "He knows what he said," observed Scott to the questioning of reporters. "Why should he want to do that?"[7] When he took the field Scott shook a disapproving finger at the Milwaukee dugout, aimed at Augustine, prompting even louder taunting of him that exploded from the crowd.

The Red Sox returned home on April 29 and swept three games from Oakland in which Scott was 5-for-8, including a home run blast that cleared Fenway's center field wall and struck the back of the bleachers, well over 430 feet. It was his fifth base hit of 14 in a twelve-game hit streak. On May 7 he broke up a no-hitter in the fourth inning off California's Frank Tanana, who had set down 14 consecutive batters, with an RBI triple. On May 16 the Red Sox, who had won 8-of-12 and were gaining momentum, won their fourth straight by beating the Angels, 8–7. Scott powered the Red Sox to the win with two home runs in consecutive at-bats, raising his OPS to .864, as they slipped into a tie for first place with the Baltimore Orioles.

Milwaukee was in town on May 20 for a three-game series; the teams split the first two. Ex-Boston first baseman Cecil Cooper was 5-for-10 including a homer, his 6th, prompting the Boston press to inquire of Grammas, the Brewers manager, what he thought of his new first sacker. Grammas was effusive, capping his comments with a personal

Scott working the pounds off in Winter Haven (courtesy of Boston Red Sox).

reference that had the bite of a back-handed slap to the departed George Scott. "Everybody around here loves the guy," said Grammas excitedly, and in as many ways as he could.[8] Scott, who was 2-for-7 with a home run, provided some excitement of his own. On the 22nd he belted a game-winning grand slam home run into the Boston bullpen, the second of his major league career, breaking up a 10–10 tie, in the eighth off a screwball thrown by lefthander Rich Folkers, which launched the Red Sox to a 14–10 win over Grammas' Brewers. The game was marked by 11 home runs, tying an American League record for two teams set by the Yankees and Tigers in 1950.[9] Scott couldn't contain himself, taking a shot at his old Brewer manager who failed to bring in a right-hander to pitch to him. "Alex must think I'm a lousy hitter," chortled Scott reprovingly over Grammas' presumed mistake.[10]

In June the Red Sox, who were in third place the first few games of the month, began to break out, moving into second on June 8 one game behind the Yankees. Pitching that was perfectly miserable in May, the laughing-stock of AL clubs some quipped, was allowing fewer runs, and the hitting continued to soar at a pace that was near the top of the league. But the Boston fan base, fueled by a local sports radio talk show, *Clif-n-Claf*, hosted by the *Globe*'s Clif Keane and the *Herald-American*'s Larry Claflin, seemed always to have something to grumble about in a rather vexatious manner, frequently acting like rabid animals not content with mere winning, but who went for the jugular for any reason they could muster. There were complaints about the pitching, the coaching, the manager, the front office, to the point of ad nauseam. But most of the griping was centered on George Scott, undeserving as it was, who had made 11 errors and was "too heavy," complained the cultural milieu of Boston sports fanatics who would accept nothing less than a slicker, younger 23-year-old George Scott. The fan outrage toward Scott boiled over around the same time he appeared on the *Clif-n-Claf* show, which immediately dissolved into horseplay and an embarrassing mockery of blacks depicted eating watermelon and fried chicken. Keane, whose reputation on race had been spotty, and Claflin were terribly insulting of blacks that day at Scott's expense, who, surprisingly, seemed content to go along with the racial stereotypical nonsense that had deteriorated into laughter. It was a racist moment that neither of the two journalists seemed to comprehend and who were shocked at the accusation, Claflin in particular, who staunchly defended his actions as simply good-natured teasing, as the story burst onto the local television and radio audiences.

A year or two later Keane was heard bantering with players and sportswriters in the Red Sox clubhouse and was overheard by *Herald-American* reporter Marie Brenner referring to George Scott as a "bush nigger." Don Zimmer heard it as well and went into a defensive rage, knowing if this got out — especially at a time of racial unrest in Boston — it would blow the lid off of what little calm had been restored in the city. He accosted Brenner, demanding that she not write the story. George Scott heard it as well but refused to talk to Brenner since at the time he was apprehensive about his own status on the team.

The *Globe*'s Ray Fitzgerald, who characterized the Boston fans as malcontents, rose to Scott's defense quoting Don Zimmer who remarked that it wasn't Scott's weight that was the reason for his unusual number of errors; he was simply pressing too hard to do well for the Boston crowd, reminding the fans that Scott was a leading hitter in the spring season, and had made some sensational plays in the field. He would be back like he was in the spring said the Red Sox manager, once he rids himself of the jitters. Whereupon Fitzgerald summed it up: "I'll take Scott even at 33, and enough already with the tired chicken wing and racist watermelon jokes."[11] Scott was hitting .268 at the time of the story with 12 homers and a .874 OPS, and was on a five-game hit streak, 7-for-16, and a .438 pace. On June 5 he broke up a scoreless tie in the 6th inning off the Twins' Tom Burgmeier with a run-scoring single leading to a 5–1 Red Sox win. He was 3-for-3 on the day including his 1,700th major league base hit.

On June 14 Scott and his teammates began a record-setting home run rampage, which established many major league records and, with them, a string of victories leading the Red Sox into first place in the AL East. Scotty was a big factor in that assault on opposing pitchers, and established for himself a personal record that had been achieved by only three other Red Sox players. Between the 14th and 19th he clouted homers (6) in 5 consecutive games, tying him with Jimmie Foxx (6/1940), Ted Williams (6/1957), and Dick Stuart (5/1963). Jose Canseco eventually also accomplished the feat in 1995 with 5 homers.

After the June 14 game, in which Scotty blasted two homers, one that rocketed off the back wall of Fenway's center field bleachers — a tremendous clout, over 430 feet — and the other into the Red Sox bullpen, he went silent on the media, declaring he would not talk to them because of the unnecessarily harsh criticism and rude treatment he had been receiving. Though he deigned to explain, the vitriol he was hearing over sports radio talk shows, and particularly the brazen effrontery he experienced from Clif Keane and Larry Claflin, who in an instant made him their public pawn, had to have been behind his decision. Feigning silence was nothing new in the sports world; it had been the remedy of numerous sports stars through the ages as their way of stemming controversy and avoiding untruths.

On June 17, the start of an important three-game series against the second-place Yankees, who trailed Boston by a half-game, the Red Sox blasted four home runs in the first inning off Catfish Hunter to tie a club record for homers in one inning. Scott's was the fourth, a lengthy blast over everything in left field that made the first two homers look "undernourished," wrote one reporter. They proceeded to annihilate the Yankees by clubbing 16 home runs and sweeping the series. It was devastating, embarrassing to anyone who was a Yankee, or who followed them. "Sixteen times a Yankee outfielder started back. Sixteen times he searched the heavens, seeking the elusive bunny ball," wrote the *Globe*'s Ray Fitzgerald.[12]

During the second game Yankees manager Billy Martin, who had all he could do to not implode himself as he watched the debacle in utter frustration from the dugout, got into it with his superstar right fielder, Reggie Jackson, by nearly coming to blows. Martin embarrassed Jackson by pulling him from the field in front of a national television audience and 34,603 screaming Fenway fans, accusing him of loafing. It upset Yankees owner George Steinbrenner who nearly fired the pugnacious manager, but later relented. It was nothing but a "Circus Maximus," declared Sox pitcher Bill Lee, who did not endear himself to Billy Martin or the New York team with some of the things he said. The Red Sox outscored (30–9), out-homered (16–0), outslugged (.917), out-fielded with several defensive gems, and altogether completely outplayed the Yankees, who, ironically, would ultimately come back to win the 1977 American League pennant and World Series. Scott clouted three home runs in the series, passing teammate Jim Rice for the club lead with 18. "I haven't seen hitting like that since junior high and we were scoring 18 runs in the cow pasture," exclaimed a jubilant George Scott, who, at least for the moment, had broken his vow of silence to respond to a reporter who asked him if he had heard the Fenway cries of "Boomer, Boomer."[13]

The Red Sox were in the midst of a consecutive ten-game home run assault in which Scott played a major part, hitting 9 of the team's 33 taters during the period June 14–24. Yastrzemski hit for the next highest number (5). Thirty-three home runs in ten consecutive games set a major league baseball record, since tied by the Atlanta Braves, who accomplished the feat in 2006. In a four-game road sweep of the Baltimore Orioles, the first two by shutouts, Scott hit his 19th and 20th home runs, tops in the league. On the 21st, a 7–0 Luis Tiant win over the Orioles, Scott was nearly beaned by a Dennis Martinez pitch in the ninth hitting him in the hand. It appeared to be retaliatory by the Oriole hurler who had given up 4th-inning homers to Scott and Rice, and was soundly being beaten by the Sox. Scott didn't hesitate leaping to his feet and began to chase the young Nicaraguan left-hander who "fled for the nearest friendly embassy," wrote the *Globe*'s Bob Ryan.[14] "Did you see the look on the kid's face? He must have thought the Schlitz bull was coming after him," laughed Sox pitcher Reggie Cleveland.[15] The two homers established a major league team record for most homers (26) in a 7-game span. Boston hammered 5 more home runs the next day, including Scott's league-leading 20th off of Jim Palmer. By the end of the series they had a full five-game lead over second-place New York, had won 16 of their last 18 games, and had out-homered their two closest rivals, the Yankees and Orioles, in a six-game span by a margin of 24 to 1. They had also set numerous other major league and American League records for consecutive game home runs: 3 games [16–MLB record], 4 games [18–AL record], 5 games [21–AL record], 6 games [24–MLB record], 8 games [29–MLB record] and 9 games [30–AL record].

They appeared invincible. The pitching was strong and the hitting was next to outrageous with Red Sox batters burning up the American League with base hits, like a "reign of terror," said one sportswriter, and lofting home runs out of ballparks in an unprecedented manner. It seemed like it was not going to end; one reporter even suggested they were beyond human for their prodigious power display. And then it was on to New York and the cavernous Yankee Stadium where the Bronx Bombers and their defiant manager, who promised that the Red Sox would crumple before the season ended, lay in wait.

Inexplicably they did just that, like a house of cards over the next nine games. On June 24 they battled the Yankees into the bottom of the 9th inning, leading 5–3, George Scott having broken up a tie in the 4th with his league-leading 21st homer off Catfish Hunter. It was the third home run of the game hit off Hunter and seventh off him by Red Sox batters in just over a week. But the Yankees tied it with a Roy White homer in the ninth, hit off a usually reliable Bill Campbell, and they won it in the 11th on Reggie Jackson's run-scoring single. The Yankees followed up with

Greeted by Carlton Fisk after hitting another home run, Scott hit 33 homers in 1977 on a team that set many home run records (courtesy of *Boston Herald*).

two more wins over Boston, returning the favor of a sweep, the second game by a 5–1 score that brought an end to their incredulous home run streak. "The most breathtaking home run tear in baseball history was over," wrote Thomas Boswell of the *Washington Post*. The Red Sox had hit a few balls, one by Rice that was estimated at 430 feet that came close to going out, but were caught in the big Yankee ballpark. "This place is like Death Valley," snorted a disappointed George Scott.[16] They continued to unravel by losing their next three in Detroit and, shockingly, three straight to the Orioles in Fenway Park, where they had humiliated Baltimore, Texas, Chicago and the Yankees in the previous homestand. On July 2 they slipped into second place one-half game behind New York.

There was a kind of cultural cancer emerging through the ranks of the Red Sox pitching staff, unsettling to the team and particularly manager Don Zimmer that became a distraction to the psychology of winning. Zimmer was a product of old-school Dodger baseball, a purist who simply did not understand nor tolerate any form of player behavior that was not of the straight-and-narrow, or was in any way a departure from unadulterated baseball tradition.

Fundamentally, Red Sox pitchers disliked Zimmer and did not try to hide their feelings about their manager. Bill Lee, a nonconformist of the highest order and a dissenter type who had been struggling on the mound, was a principal among the group, who complained that he was simply misunderstood. He once said that if he were not a ballplayer he would be living in a Napa Valley commune and stomping grapes. Lee and Zimmer's relationship was a tempestuous one. In a moment of annoyance, Lee anointed Zimmer with an uncomplimentary title: "the gerbil." It immediately caught on with the Boston press and talk radio shows, and eventually the Red Sox fan base who seemed to revel in maligning the Sox skipper, was now known, disparagingly as "the gerbil."

Rick Wise, another Sox hurler who was struggling, felt he was being mishandled by Zimmer, as did Ferguson Jenkins and Luis Tiant. They began to gravitate toward each other as they sought common ground, confidants of a counter-culture they were, a bunch of iconoclasts who found strength in their own unity to effectively — and derisively — deal with Zimmer. Jenkins named the group, of which he was a self-appointed member, the "Buffalo Head Gang"— changed later to be the "Buffalo Heads"— comprised of Bill Lee, Jim Willoughby, Wise and free-spirit Bernie Carbo. Jenkins reasoned that Buffaloes were the personification of ugliness and that Zimmer looked every bit the part of a buffalo; plus they were dumb. It fit perfectly. And their torment of Zimmer began.

On July 4 the Sox erupted against the visiting Toronto Blue Jays by smashing 8 home runs, setting and tying all matter of major league home run records in the process. George Scott hit two of them, after suffering through a 0-for-24 drought, lofting one into the center field bleachers, and the other a tremendous blast rocketing high over the left field screen and bouncing off the facing of a building across the street from the ballpark. It was hit so high and far wrote one reporter, with obvious hyperbole, that it was likely to have landed "six hours later" at the Esplanade three miles away. Of the eight homers four of them were hit in just one inning, only the 10th time that had been accomplished in major league history, the 5th time the Red Sox had done it, and the second time they did it that season. The eight home runs in one game also tied a major league record with five other teams; and the Red Sox set a major league record of five or more home runs in a game for the 7th time in one season; the old record of six was held by the 1947 Giants. Seven of them were solo shots, also a major league record.

What had not reached the record books was Scott's performance the game before, on July 3 against Baltimore, when he clouted three long blasts that were caught sensationally by Oriole outfielders to rob him of home runs each time. One of them was caught by center fielder Al Bumbry, who chased Scott's drive to the 420 foot Fenway triangle in center and leaped over the high wall of the Red Sox bullpen to snag the home run ball. In each case the runner on first, Carlton Fisk, advanced to second base, a rare maneuver that in most cases would end up with the runner being thrown out. "All of them were out of the park," said Oriole right fielder Ken Singleton on Scott's drives. Both outfielders conceded they had no chance to catch Fisk going into second base because of the distance the balls were hit.[17]

Three Red Sox were elected by a vote of the fans for the American League All-Star team: Carl Yastrzemski, a perennial All-Star in his 11th midsummer classic, Carlton Fisk, his fifth All-Star appearance, and shortstop Rick Burleson, his first. Rod Carew of the Minnesota Twins was the unanimous choice to play first base with over 4 million votes. George Scott, who had 25 home runs, finished third to New York's Chris Chambliss in the fan balloting. He railed at the thought that the best American League players were not starting, such as Boston's Jim Rice and Larry Hisle of Minnesota, who were having better years than Richie Zisk or Reggie Jackson. And he couldn't hold back his objection for coming in third by over a million votes behind Chambliss, who had hit only 8 homers. "You've got to blame the fans," he said. "We had 90 taters sitting on the pine."[18] Scott credited American League All-Star manager Billy Martin with making things right by picking him, Scott's third and last All-Star appearance, as a reserve over Martin's own man, Chambliss, along with Rice, Fred Lynn and Sox reliever Bill Campbell. It was another win for the National League, 7–5. Scott replaced Carew in the 7th inning, flied out his first time up against Tom Seaver, but in the bottom of the 9th launched a 385-foot home run into the right-center-field Yankee Stadium bleachers off of Rich Gossage. It was the only American League home run of the game, and only their second extra-base hit. Scott's point was made.

Boston continued to keep pace with first-place Baltimore until July 31, when they slipped back into first by a half-game on the stellar pitching of their new rookie pitcher, Don Aase, who had been called up from Pawtucket, their Triple-A farm club. Pitching, however, was still a main worry of Zimmer's, and Bill Lee continued to be his biggest personal nightmare. "You guys ask him a baseball question, and in two minutes he's talking about life in China," complained the irritated Red Sox manager, who was as ready as anyone in the organization to wield the axe to the left-hander.[19] But there were other issues also; Scott had not hit another home run since the All-Star Game, and he had made an uncharacteristic 20 errors in the field.

The Red Sox, however, began to surge again behind Aase, and a rejuvenated Fergie Jenkins, winning 13 of 15 games through August 18 and holding a 3½ game lead over Baltimore. But it unraveled from there, the Red Sox losing five straight and falling into second place on August 23. On September 3, with Boston in second, 4½ games off the lead, Don Zimmer dropped Scott—one of Boston's top run producers (82) with 31 homers—to 7th in the batting order. It hit him like a bolt of lightning; nothing had been said to him, and his pride was hurt. He played a couple of more games in the 7th slot, and then on September 5 engaged in a sit-down, announcing to Zimmer he was "not mentally prepared to play." He said that he might have been more receptive to the idea if the manager had simply come to him to explain what he was planning to do, and why. "But he didn't," said Scott. At about the same time the problem between the pitchers and Zimmer manifested itself once again. Zimmer's peculiar fiddling of his staff from day to day did not sit well with them, particularly Wise, Jenkins and Lee who lost any remaining respect they had for the man. Scott sat out two games, and then returned batting seventh. Zimmer returned him to his regular 6th position in the order on September 15, where he remained for the balance of the season. The Red Sox finished in second place tied with Baltimore at 97–64, two games behind the Yankees. Astonishingly, the third-place team, Detroit, finished well behind the leaders, 25 games in back of New York.

George Scott had a solid first year back in Boston, hitting a respectable .269, crunching 33 home runs (as the team set a club record of 213 home runs in one season), 157 base hits, 95 RBIs and a .500 slugging percentage, the second highest of his career.[20] He had an uncharacteristic year in the field, however, committing 24 errors, the most he made in the majors in one season. In spite of that he was a sentimental favorite for another Gold Glove, but he fell short, edged out by the White Sox' Jim Spencer, 13 votes to 9. Once again reporters were speculating that Scott was on the chopping block. One Chicago reporter announced with certain conviction that any team looking to get the big first baseman had to accept Scott's remaining two years of his contract and pick up his "$450,000 salary that goes with it," which was a tall order for most clubs when the ballplayer was about to turn 34.

16

Bricks and Bats

I have a lot of respect for George Scott, a man who, I feel, never has been portrayed accurately in this town. He certainly is not sophisticated, and he has a talent for malapropism perhaps beyond compare. As a rural southern black who actually does eat and enjoy both chicken and watermelon, and who takes no pains to hide it, he is an easy target for tasteless media attackers who find it easier to perpetuate a stereotype than to work at presenting the whole man. George Scott deserves better treatment.... George Scott is just an honest ballplayer, and the team will be better off when he's back in the lineup.— Bob Ryan[1]

A year after owner Tom Yawkey's death in July 1976, his venerable and beloved institution — the Red Sox — that he nurtured and over which he had reigned since he established ownership in 1933, was put up for sale. Several suitors pursued the opportunity, but Jean Yawkey, Tom's widow, who had assumed ownership of the team after her husband's death, favored the group led by ex–Red Sox trainer, Buddy LeRoux. Haywood Sullivan, the Red Sox' former VP of Player Personnel, who had a close personal friendship with the Yawkeys, had joined the group. Sullivan's presence in the deal was persuasive for Jean Yawkey, who accepted the LeRoux-investor–led offer, even though it was not the highest bid. After the American League rejected the proposal initially, they relented when Jean Yawkey joined as the third general partner with LeRoux and Sullivan. The deal was consummated on May 23 for $20.5 million.

When Jean Yawkey announced the sale of the Red Sox she also fired their general manager, Dick O'Connell, architect of the 1967 Impossible Dream Red Sox and long-time favorite of her husband, Tom; she promptly elevated Haywood Sullivan as O'Connell's replacement. Sullivan, to the enormous pleasure of Don Zimmer, began dismantling the band of Buffalo Heads, one rogue member at a time. The immediate effect was positive, but ultimately it may have proved more of a disservice to the organization than anything they had hoped to gain in the transactions, losing bench strength, weakening the farm system and forfeiting pitching depth.

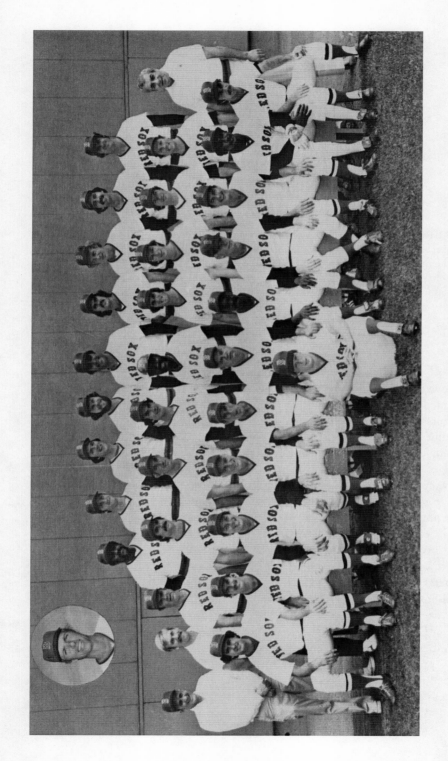

The 1978 Boston Red Sox. George Scott is in middle row, seventh from left (courtesy of Boston Red Sox).

Sullivan, in his new role as general manager, took immediate action over the winter by signing free agent pitchers Mike Torrez of the Yankees, Baltimore's Dick Drago and Minnesota's Tom Burgmeier. He shamefully practically gave away Fergie Jenkins to the Texas Rangers for little-known pitcher John Poloni, and cash. Jenkins would win 18 games in 1978; Poloni never made the Red Sox roster. Boston's promising hurler Don Aase was traded to California, along with cash, for speedy infielder Jerry Remy. And the biggest acquisition of all came on March 30, 1978, toward the end of spring training, when Boston traded four players, including a Don Zimmer antagonist, Rick Wise, for Dennis Eckersley. Surprisingly Zimmer's main nemesis, Bill Lee, who Zimmer more than once tried to convince the Red Sox to trade, remained on the team.

Manager Don Zimmer was not on sturdy ground with the Boston media and fan base that often ripped him to shreds, especially on the radio talk shows. He made the comment as the spring season was about to get underway that in 1977, after making a pitching change and walking back to the dugout, that the only person cheering him was his wife. "Everybody else was booing," he said.[2]

On March 1 as 1978 spring camp officially opened for all Red Sox player personnel, George Scott arrived having shed 20 or more pounds, he claimed; he had been wearing a rubber sweat suit whenever he exercised in the offseason, which he continued to use in spring training. Sensitive about his weight, often deriding reporters who dared ask him about it, this time Scott openly acknowledged that weight was indeed an issue for him in 1977 and the problem needed to be corrected. But in spite of his personal training efforts he turned up with a cranky back when he first arrived in camp that was to be more problematic for him early in the season; a sign that the years of major league baseball were beginning to take its toll. It failed, however, to hold him down. On March 7 in an intra-squad game he wasted no time with the bat ripping two impressive homers, one of them a 415 foot grand slam. Their new left-hander, Poloni, acquired for Fergie Jenkins, was pummeled. "We were just tuning up," said an ebullient Scott of his homers and of his teammates who crunched some of their own.[3] Not long into the spring season Peter Gammons of the *Globe* declared that Scott was a "hefty problem," well over his 215 pounds listed in the *Red Sox Media Guide*, and may be trade bait, but that no one was interested. He ran steadily around the ballpark every chance he got "in that red sweat-suit" wrote Gammons, and managed to shed possibly 25 pounds, they thought. When performance projections were being made for each Red Sox player, "George Scott's weight" was front and center of every sportswriter's note pad.

The Red Sox had a decent spring, winning 15 of 26 exhibition games. George Scott fared well hitting .320 with 3 home runs, second best to Dwight Evans, 24 base hits, also second best, and 11 RBIs. But there were racial overtones brewing again with the Red Sox: *New York Times* journalist Gerald Eskenazi, in his April 10 article "'Yes We Can,' Red Sox Say," spoke of the "tight little island" of a team the Red Sox were, who grew their own, to explain why they only had two blacks — George Scott and Jim Rice — and only two black players on the top two Red Sox farm clubs. It was a startling statistic, one that would be noticed and written about again by other baseball and newspaper critics as the season progressed, particularly as the Hub's spotlight fell on their budding — yet black — superstar Rice, who resisted any effort by the media to put him in the middle of issues surrounding Boston and race. He had doubts about Boston, a city still simmering in racial unrest and its little ballpark "where racist behavior still percolated and epithets could be heard wafting from the stands," chided the *Washington Post*. *Providence Journal* sports columnist Bill Reynolds touched on some of this in his 2009 treatise on the '78 season and its effect on the city following four years of anti-busing rallies and racial violence in Boston. It was a "welcome escape," he wrote, from the ravages that had divided the city; at least for awhile.[4]

Before the start of the 1978 season the Commissioner's office issued a list

of active players with "glittering career statistics" that were worth watching as they approached certain career milestones. George Scott was one of the notables: 192 base hits short of reaching 2,000 and 52 RBIs short of reach-ing 1,000, certainly impressive career numbers among a mix of 10 still active veterans with such credentials. But as promising and as hopeful as things were from the outset for both the Boomer and the Boston ball club, with the latter performing as well in the first half as any Red Sox team in modern memory, there was a ghastly downside to the events of that season. Scott struggled with chronic injury for the first time in his career.

April 18, 1978 — Some things in common. Milwaukee Brewers and ex–Red Sox Cecil Cooper holds George Scott on first after he had walked in a game won by Boston, 7–6. Cooper was traded by the Red Sox in 1976 to Milwaukee for Scott and Bernie Carbo (courtesy of *Boston Herald*).

The Red Sox, who appeared unbeatable at first just crushing the opposition, had found another way to disappoint their success-starved fans, by losing again, but the manner in which it was done this time seemed almost surreal.

Boston lost three of its first four games but quickly gained their footing by winning eight in a row, and slipped briefly into first place on April 21 by a half game over the Tigers. Zimmer had George Scott batting 7th, which he had more than once objected to in prior years when placed there, but this time he offered no resistance. The Red Sox were loaded with power all up-and-down the lineup, and Scott's productive bat was one Zimmer was depending on, with 33 homers in '77, as well as his defensive strengths that made the infield well-balanced. Scott started slow by hitting .233 through the first nine games, but then surged with a six-game hit streak in which he was 12-for-26, raising his average to .339, third-best of the starting nine. But on April 23 after a strong 6-for-10 performance in a doubleheader against the Indians, his back went into spasm and he was sidelined for several games; with the exception of one DH appearance he missed 17 games, the longest period he had ever been away from the action. On May 15 he had happily returned to the lineup, but ran into more hard luck on that day in Kansas City. In the fourth inning Amos Otis hit a Texas leaguer pop fly down the right field line hotly pursued by second baseman Remy, right fielder Evans and Scott. The ball, blown back by the wind, bounced off Scott's outstretched bare hand. Two innings later the middle finger of his right hand swelled and he was removed from the game; it was a hairline fracture. It was to be his personal nightmare for the rest of the season. He was out again for another 12 days, returning as a pinch-hitter on June 4, and then as a DH for five games, finally returning to the lineup on June 12 at home, against the Angels.

The *Globe*'s Bob Ryan wrote a particularly flattering if not eulogistic article in the midst of Scott's extended absence in which he apologized for himself, and others, in taking the talented first baseman for granted, and who, he noted, was clearly missed. Carl Yastrzemski, who replaced the Boomer at first base, was simply not in Scott's class, said Ryan; nor did anyone stop to think why third baseman Butch Hobson was making so many errors after Scott had left. Was it mere coincidence that he was getting worse at his position? Ryan emphasized Scott's dedication to duty, his loyalty to the game and the team, and the value of not being one of those athletes who whined, but who came to play every day. "I submit that the personification of that trait is George Scott," wrote Ryan.[5]

The Red Sox were burning up the league by setting a club record 23–7 in May, 34–16 through the end of May and in first place three games ahead of the second-place Yankees; by the end of June they were still in first place, 8 games in front. Scott, however, was struggling at the plate, affected by the injured finger that was healing all too slowly, preventing him from getting his accustomed grip on the bat, and causing him to make adjustments in his swing leading to bad habits at the plate. Don Zimmer was not about to put him on the DL. "Right now we're not going to do it. Who would we bring up?" moaned the Red Sox skipper.[6] Unlike the month of April when he was making good contact with the ball and went days without striking out, when he returned in June strikeouts began to mount, as many as 5 in one game against the Yankees. He finished the month hitting .244. July wasn't much better for the Boomer. He batted .196 with only two home runs, getting his first hit in a string of 26 at-bats on July 31 against Chicago. He looked as bad at the plate as the numbers indicated; with each out the Fenway crowd became more restless, booing him mercilessly. Dwight Evans appealed to the media to soften their criticism of Scott, a sensitive man who was clearly affected by the crowd; it was blistering at times, and hopefully with the aid of the Boston scribes it would inspire the fans to ease up as well. The more they booed him the tighter he got. It seemed to work: on July 31 upon singling in the 7th the Fenway crowd roundly cheered. "Sooner or later things are going to come my way, they've got to," chanted the ever-optimistic Red Sox slugger.[7]

Scott and the Red Sox put up some pretty fair numbers in August, Boston winning 19-of-29 and Scotty hitting .281 on 25 base hits. In the last nine games of the month he was 13-for-35, hitting at a .371 clip, including three homers, topping it off on August 29 — a Jimmy Fund promotion night before 34,393 fans — with his third career grand slam off of Seattle's Glenn Abbott, sealing a Red Sox victory. Scott crushed Abbott's first pitch which "was sent soaring somewhere near the site for the nuclear power plant in Seabrook," wrote the *Globe*'s Peter Gammons.[8] Center fielder Rupert Jones never moved. Neither did Scott until he watched it disappear into the night's sky. It was a "so there" moment for Scotty who had been extremely frustrated with himself, the media, and the hometown fans who were relentlessly razzing him. After his slam the fickle fans called him out hoping for a bow, just like old times, all the time chanting "Booma — Booma — Booma" for their beloved Boomer. He never moved. Luis Tiant poked his head above the dugout instead, fooling some that it was Scott. He reverted at once to silence as he had done in '77 when confronted with the same treatment and the embarrassment of the radio show racial debacle. "I'm mad at everyone," which was all he would say, aiming somehow to return the punishment he had absorbed for four long months, and maybe restore some of his pride that had been shattered.[9]

By September 1 the Red Sox still had a fairly comfortable 6½ game lead over New York, who, on August 9, had vaulted over Milwaukee into second place. The Red Sox, meanwhile, were having pitching problems: Only Dennis Eckersley was throwing well; Torrez, Tiant, and Jim Wright were ineffective, and Bill Lee had been banished to the bullpen by Zimmer. Right fielder Dwight Evans, an important Red Sox cog on offense and defense, was beaned on August

Another bomb hit by the Boomer (courtesy of Boston Red Sox).

28, suffered dizzy spells and was not effective after that. And the defense generally fell apart, particularly Hobson, a Zimmer favorite, who would commit 43 errors on the season.

Under contract for just one year, Zimmer pressed Haywood Sullivan and the Red Sox for a multi-year deal. But Sullivan refused to give him an extension, insisting that any contract discussions would take place once the season had ended. It made him uneasy and he began to press his players to improve performance in his attempt to run away with the division title, proving his point to management that they should reconsider. He wore out his team, stubbornly stuck with original rosters, questioned injuries and fidgeted with his pitching staff constantly.

What seemed highly improbable, actually happened: in July just before the All-Star Game the Red Sox were 57–26 and up by 9 games over Milwaukee. The Yankees were 11½ games back. It was a very comfortable lead, and the team was playing almost flawlessly. Baseball pundits exclaimed that a division title was nearly in the bag for Boston; they could play the balance of the season at a .500 pace and win. The Yankees needed to play at a .700 pace to catch them.

George Scott slides into second base against Kansas City.

Catch them they did, surging at a .730 pace. The Red Sox played under .500 ball after the All-Star break, at 24–26, while the Yankees were 36–18 during the same period.

New York rode into Boston on September 7 for an important, and as it evolved, a decisive four-game series, having won 12 of their last 14 games and now only 4 games behind the first-place Red Sox. It turned into a disaster. The journalists labeled it the "Boston Massacre" because it was so one-sided. The Yankees outscored the Red Sox 42–9, winning the first two with scores of 15–3 and 13–2, and sweeping the series, to land them in a tie for first place. The Red Sox committed 12 errors, three of them by Hobson, who removed himself from the lineup two weeks later for the good of the team after committing his 43rd. George Scott was having miseries of his own, stuck in the middle of another prolonged slump, and was 0-for-11. It continued through September 13, an agonizing 0-for-34. NBC color commentator Tony Kubek made an amusing but sage comment during the series, epitomizing what was taking place: "This is the first time I've seen a first place team chasing a second place team."[10]

The Red Sox trailed New York in second place, but closed the gap between them and the Yankees by one game on September 23. They then matched them win-for-win the next six games, until October 1, when the Yankees lost 9–2 at the hands of the Cleveland Indians. Luis Tiant and the Red Sox shut down Toronto, 5–0, that day; the two teams were suddenly tied. It seemed predestined to Red Sox fans; there was hope and joy, and a certain confidence once again in the Hub. It was now all up to one playoff contest to decide who was going to be the AL East champion.

What is best remembered about that day, October 2, is that a light-hitting nondescript shortstop named Bucky Dent, a banjo hitter used primarily for his defense, with a lifetime record of only 22 home runs, and hitting a mere .243 at the time (.140 in his last 20 games), became an instant Yankee hero. Hurler Mike Torrez, a Yankee himself in 1977, and the Red Sox played a solid game leading into the sixth inning. Yankee bats were silent. Torrez had given up just two base hits, and the Red Sox enjoyed a 2–0 lead. It was beginning to look quite favorable for Boston. But in the top of the seventh, with one out, Chambliss and White reached on singles. Manager Bob Lemon, who replaced Billy Martin in July, pinch-hit Jim Spencer for sub Brian Doyle, and he flied out.

It was then Bucky Dent's turn. Torrez got two quick strikes on him, the second pitch he fouled off onto his ankle that sent him hobbling for several minutes. There was a serious question whether he would stay in the game; but he did. The next pitch by Torrez was history. With one infamous swing, Dent's hands lodged well up on the bat handle to poke a single somewhere, he lofted a soft fly — harmless-appearing at first — that settled just over the wall into Fenway's left field screen for a three-run homer, a Fenway Park homer that would not have gone out in most ballparks. He took the life from the ballpark with that hit; it went silent. It took awhile for the fans to come to grips with what had happened. After the Yanks scored two more in the 8th, the Red Sox rallied in the ninth, pulling within one run of tying the game, but Goose Gossage shut the door, forcing Yastrzemski to pop up to end it. Boston lost, 5–4, and the "Curse of the Bambino" remained intact.

"We really should have won the game. It was nothing but a pop-up," exclaimed Scott of Dent's home run, still carrying some of the frustration of that day during a much later interview. But when on the subject of manager Don Zimmer, he showed less tolerance. "Well any time that you lose [the division title] when you're 14 games up, and you're caught with a month left to play in the season, you can't just sit back and blame the players [entirely]," said Scott, making a strong statement that Zimmer should have taken most of the blame for that disastrous season. "Don Zimmer was probably one of the most over-rated of baseball people that I've ever seen," raged Scott in increasing decibels with each spoken word.[11]

Adding to his frustration of a bad season in which he played in just 120 games, batting .233 with 12 home runs, his wife, Lucky, filed for divorce a second time, in December. His world seemed to be coming apart.

17

Arriba King Kong

I was born poor, I was born black, and I was born in Mississippi. When you've been through that, you can deal with anything. The only thing I was ever taught was survival. The name of the game for me is survival. I'm not making big money, but I'm learning how to teach, how to manage. This is where my heart is. You can see I'm loose and free and easy. It's the first time since 1979 that I'm at peace with myself.—George Scott[1]

"I know I've got a job of redeeming myself," announced George Scott as he prepared for the 1979 season, jogging every morning, doing calisthenics, and wind sprints, and working hard to drop the extra weight gained during the offseason.[2] He was a virtual health fanatic wrote one scribe, while rumors still percolated that he was washed up and the Red Sox were anxious to find a suitor for their $200,000 previous-season's bust.

He showed a dramatic weight loss; by the time he arrived early at spring training camp, he was a svelte 216 pounds, down from 240 pounds, in a return to form that he displayed when he was a rookie. He expounded to willing reporters on the miseries of his previous year with first his back injury, and then the broken finger, and how he tried to come back too soon, which contributed to his poor hitting. He had little ability to grip the bat properly affecting his swing and also his power, he said. As it began to heal toward the end of the '78 season he noticed how much more bat control and power he had regained. "I know what people have said about me this winter and I also know those same people are unwilling to accept the truth," said Scott. "The truth is that I had a bad season because I had a broken hand."[3] This year it would be different, he claimed. He proved that by hitting over .400 during the spring exhibition season. But it didn't last.

Forty-one games into the 1979 season, with the Red Sox in second place, 1½ games behind the first-place Orioles, Scott was benched, beginning with the May 26 game in Toronto. He had been hitting .260 on May 16 but began a hitless streak over a span of the next 25 at-bats, dropping his average to .219. Carlton Fisk, who had been injured in spring training and was having elbow trouble, was sitting, making only three appearances to that point. Zimmer needed his bat, and with Scott struggling as he was, the decision was easy — put Fisk in as a DH and move Yastrzemski to first. "He [Scott] had a great spring training and he worked hard," said Zimmer. "He did a great job. But if you've got a hitter like Fisk on the bench, why not put him in there?"[4]

Scott was relegated to substitute duties, pinch-hitting twice at the end of May, and two more times in early June. He was hitting a meager .224. The writing was on the wall and Scott could see it. He asked to be traded. "Don Zimmer never came and talked to me about nothing," raged Scott in an interview many years later. "I don't think we had fifty words [between us] from a positive aspect."[5] On June 13 the Red Sox traded for Houston first baseman-outfielder Bob Watson, who would hit .337 for the Red Sox in '79, complicating things even further for Scott. But that was quickly resolved when on the same day, an hour after the Watson deal, they dealt George Scott to Kansas City for Tom Poquette. Poquette was a cut-from-cloth fair-haired Midwestern boy from Eau Claire, Wisconsin, and a fan favorite in Kansas City. He had been with them during the Royals' recent division championships, and had good seasons in '76 and '77 when he batted .302 and .292, respectively.

The move caused a furor within the Kansas City community; for days the local papers carried fan response questioning the deal of giving up on a young player for a 35-year-old .224 hitter near the end of his career. It was a risk Royals manager Whitey Herzog was willing to take; Herzog wanted Scott for added punch in the lineup — he was a proven right-handed power hitter — and for improved defensive measures. "George Scott is the best defensive first baseman in both leagues. And he is in excellent shape," said Herzog, who was the brains behind the Royals' three successive Western Division championships from 1976 to 1978, and who was looking for that extra snap he needed in his team to finally bring them a pennant. Herzog was confident that with the big Gold Glove first baseman he had his man.[6]

The Red Sox were in Kansas City at the time so everything happened very quickly. Scott donned his new number 29 Royals uniform (later changed to "0"), then sat on the bench for his first game, with time to think, and watched his replacement, Poquette, go 2-for-4 in his debut with the Red Sox. Poquette's strong performance, in front of a skeptical Kansas City crowd, did not make the prospects of George Scott's debut any easier, as the Red Sox fashioned an 11–3 win. There were other issues, too; dissension among the ranks developed with Pete LaCock and John Wathan, who had been platooning at first base until Scott's arrival. LaCock, a .271 hitter and a good first baseman, was not happy and made it known, while Wathan, a .244 hitter and sometimes used as a catcher, was more philosophical.

Scott made his KC debut on the road in Milwaukee, on June 15, and was promptly productive, knocking in two runs on a 2-for-5 day in a 14–11 Royals victory. On June 20 he had a three-hit game, increasing his number of base hits to 10 since joining the Royals, and was hitting .400. But it was what he did on the basepaths that impressed his manager even more. Not known for speed or running skills, Scott advanced to second from first on a long Amos Otis fly ball to left-center. Then in a heads-up play, he scored all the way from second on a long sacrifice fly by Darrell Porter. It got Herzog's attention; following the game he announced that until further notice George Scott, who had performed some third base duties, would be his permanent first baseman. During this surge by Scott, sportswriter Dick Young commented, "Too bad George Scott had to be 35 before he got in shape. He could have set records."[7]

On June 26 Scott made his first appearance before the home crowd after a ten-game road trip. It was an impressive one to the delight of 24,550 Kansas City fans, who were beginning to feel ebullient about Herzog's acquisition. Scott rapped another three hits — his 9th in 14 at-bats — including the game-winner in the 10th by stroking a bases-loaded walk-off single for a Royals

Scott swings away in a 1979 early-season game (courtesy of Boston Red Sox).

them within one game of the first-place Angels. Scott wrapped up the month of June hitting .382, to the delight of Herzog. But in spite of his great pleasure in having the big first baseman, it was not enough. Whitey was looking for the big hit from Scott — the home run ball. It was one of the main reasons the Kansas City skipper had traded for him. Herzog actually had movies made of Scott's at-bats for him to study to reacquire his old touch and relearn how to once again hit the long ball. Scott sensed the pressure, responding: "I just want to hit the ball and let power take care of itself," he said, brushing off Herzog's ambitious program of re-indoctrination.[8] It would prove to have negative consequences, bringing matters between them to a boil later on.

The Royals' pitching was not holding up, however. After a six-game win streak in late June, they went into an extended swoon by losing 14 of their next 15 games and falling precipitously into 4th place on July 14, 10 games out of first. Herzog was frustrated and feeling the heat while Kansas City fans were beginning to heat up themselves writing to the local newspapers and filling their fan columns with their own complaints, some about Scott, but most pointing fingers at Royals' brass — including Herzog for choosing Scott over much-needed pitching — for not making a smart trade. The *Kansas City Star* posted this sports page headline on July 15: "Despite Slump, Herzog Won't Change."[9] It was in reaction to Herzog's statement that in spite of it all he was still sleeping well, and there was nothing he felt he could do but to keep managing the way he always had. Scott also slumped in July, hitting his first and only Royals' homer on July 31, after which he received a standing ovation from the Royals' crowd to change their frequent boos of him to cheers; the homer followed an eight-game span in which the Royals were 5–3, and he was 7-for-22 hitting at a .318 pace. Scott later lamented that he was frustrated that Herzog would not play him more consistently.

Teammate Amos Otis vented his frustrations on July 23, publicly ripping the front office for sitting on their hands, complaining they needed a power hitter and pitcher to fill the breach. It was a scathing indictment of the Kansas City brass and no doubt sent them scurrying along with Whitey Herzog, who was feeling the pinch himself because of his choice of George Scott as that certain power hitter. It spilled over into the clubhouse. According to Scott in a later interview Whitey Herzog, who clearly was frustrated, held a clubhouse meeting during their series with Chicago in late July in which he openly berated Scott in front of the entire Kansas City team. "He said, 'the reason that we're not winning is because of George Scott,'" exclaimed an angered Scott, who still seems tormented by the accusation, explaining that it was largely the pitching that had broken down, and that Herzog was looking for an easy target because of the pressure he was feeling.[10] When Herzog was approached years later for an interview, his response to the question about the clubhouse incident was a resounding, "No comment," as the effects of that ugly moment obviously still lingered in his subconscious mind.[11] Fred Patek, the Royals shortstop, explained it differently, saying it wasn't a formal meeting, it was clubhouse banter going on as they prepared for the game after practice that led to an informal session, a spontaneous moment, when Herzog appeared in the clubhouse. "He [Herzog] kind of accused George of not doing his job.... It was just a big shouting match from what I can remember," said Patek.[12]

Scott played sparingly in August, and then on August 17 he was put on waivers by the Royals. No team claimed him — the $200,000 contract no doubt having something to do with it — and Scott became a free agent five days later. He remained confident he was not washed up, and began working out at the Royals' multi-sport complex as he waited on word from other clubs. Baltimore, San Diego and the Cubs were after him, but they were outbid by Billy Martin's Yankees, who signed him on August 26 — with no commitment beyond the '79 season — and placed him on their roster immediately. He started as a DH on August 28 in Texas and was 0-for-2 in the game; he followed that with a three-run homer in the next game off Dave Rajsich, his 271st career tater, and the last one he would hit in the major leagues. He tormented Herzog and the Royals in their final series of the year with a 4-for-9 performance in which Kansas City and the Yankees split the four games. After that he was used sparingly playing in 11 more games in pinch-hit and DH roles, finishing the season hitting .318 for New York, and .254 for the three clubs.

A man of eternal optimism, Scott was confident Billy Martin would take him back for the 1980 season. In the fall of '79 he received a letter from Yankee owner George Steinbrenner, who was engaged in a rebuilding effort, saying that Scott's services were no longer needed, releasing him officially on November 1. Steinbrenner and his club were still mourning the loss of their All-Star catcher and team leader, Thurman Munson, who had died that year in a plane crash. It was a year that was "symbolically and actually draped in black," wrote sportswriter Phil Pepe.[13] Wholesale changes were about to be made in the Yankee organization, and they did not include an aging first baseman named George Scott. Writer Bruce Markusen penned an article for *The Hardball Times* in May 2010, in which he commented that he was optimistic the Yankees were planning to bring Scott back in a platoon role in 1980. "I distinctly remember Scott's 1979 appearance in Yankees pinstripes as one of the few positive memories of an otherwise dismally tragic season," wrote Markusen.[14] In fact he had played so well in that last month that Topps actually printed a baseball card for him for the 1980 season, convinced the Yankees would bring him back. But it was not to be. He was now a free agent.

On November 2, 1979, Scott was picked by the Texas Rangers in the 14th round of the re-entry draft. It was the only team that showed any interest, and it was merely a fringe role at best. Texas announced their plans to use him strictly as a "utility player" to back up their established first baseman Pat Putnam. George, whose pride was hurt and who felt he still had a few good years in front of him, balked at the idea of a demotion, and got an agent. The Rangers did some balking of their own, and saw little need or interest in getting into negotiations with an agent. They made Scott a "take-it-or-leave-it" offer of a minor league role with their Triple-A Charleston farm club. Scott declined it, called it an "insult," and left the major leagues.

In the spring of 1980 Scott was still agitated about his dealings with Royals' manager Whitey Herzog, and the manner in which he was released by the Kansas City club. He bitterly accused him of messing up his career, feeling he had provoked other managers into blocking his chances of being picked up by another team. His indictment of Herzog got back to the ex–Royals manager, who had been fired by the team at the end of the 1979 season. He shot back at Scott's charges: "I wonder if it ever occurred to him that George Scott might be the reason I'm out of baseball."[15] Marital problems that had plagued him throughout the '79 season were still afflicting him, ending in divorce in 1980. He had sat by the phone all winter waiting for that phone call that never came.

Red Sox coach Tommy Harper, who would have his own racial problems later on with the club, and who would sue them for discrimination on his being wrongfully fired, urged Scott to make an appearance at the spring camps; he would never get an invitation, said Harper, who told him he had gone through the same experience. Scott took his advice and was seen traveling throughout Florida in his rented red Mustang, making appearances at several spring training camps. He tried the Tigers, but manager Sparky Anderson said they had two first basemen. With the White Sox, Tony LaRussa said he would pass Scott's message on to his boss, Bill Veeck. Then it was on to the Twins, and maybe, his best shot, he felt, the Rangers would reconsider. Or, maybe he'd try Billy Martin, who had just latched on with Oakland. Martin thought highly of the Boomer, thought George, and would surely give him a try in Oakland. And if this didn't work, then maybe it would have to be Japan.

Charley Lau, a New York Yankees coach, and a highly revered major league hitting instructor who had written articles and a prized book on the subject, in a 1980 article compared George Scott with Reggie Jackson, two aging superstars who needed to drastically adapt their hitting styles to survive in the big leagues. Lau said Jackson made the adjustments; Scott did not. He faulted him for his stubbornness, such as his unwillingness to use a lighter bat or listen to expert coaching advice. "Even after everybody else told Scott he needed to change, he wouldn't. But before anybody said anything to Reggie, he already had," said Lau.[16] Scott lamented in a later interview: "The pitching stopped me and I just wasn't able to do it [anymore]."[17]

On May 2, 1980, just over a month into the season, and still reeling from the shock of his rejection by all major league clubs, 36-year-old George Scott signed with the Yucatan Lions of the Mexican League, which was designated

Triple-A, although a brand of ball probably closer to Double-A. Only three days before he had been vetoed by the league because of his asking figure, 750,000 Mexican pesos per month (about $58,000 American dollars). But the team convinced the authorities that signing him would be in the best interests of the league, raising its competitive level, and so the deal was made and approved. He made more money in Mexico that season than any amount he could have made still playing major league baseball in the states. "Somebody told me, 'you never DH'd, you're still young enough. Go to the Mexican League and show people you can [still] play and maybe somebody will invite you to spring training,'" said Scott.[18]

It was a whole new way of life for the ex–big leaguer who was accustomed to major league luxury of first-class travel, posh hotels, fancy restaurants and first-rate playing fields. Instead he found shabby shanty towns and cities with houses crumbling, sweltering heat, rat-infested hotels and restaurants, lunatic fans (known to throw rattlesnakes into dugouts), and poorly lit and badly conditioned ball fields. Then there were the oppressive 18-hour bus rides, some as much as 22 hours, to neighboring cities after which they were expected to immediately play nine-inning ball games. The league consisted of 16 teams in four divisions and a 128-game schedule, more or less. He played in his first game for Yucatan on May 6 and stroked a double in his debut at-bat. But it was a shortened season due to a player strike, with all play suspended on July 3. Scott played in 41 games, mostly at first base, some DH, and hit .292 including 3 home runs, one a grand slam.

He went to Los Mochis of the Mexican Pacific League toward the tail end of their winter season as player-manager of the Caneros, replacing former major leaguer and Mexican legend Benjamin Papelero Valenzuela. It was George's first managerial assignment, brief as it was, in which he posted a 10–9 record. He also played in 18 games for them hitting .254 (17-for-67) with one double and 10 RBIs. The Caneros finished 8th in a ten-team circuit at 37–45.

Scott signed for the 1981 season with the Mexico City Tigers, owned by Mexico City businessman Alejo Peralta, and managed by their president, who was also their field manager, Chito Garcia. It was there that Scott caught on with the Mexican people by developing his own following and his own peculiar identity. He became somewhat of a celebrity, residing in a local hotel — the Hotel California — not far from the Tigers ballpark, the El Parque del Seguro Social (Social Security Park), in a $32-a-day suite that included a television, two beds and a phone. Mexican Baseball Hall of Fame sportswriter Tommy Morales befriended Scott, and gave him a nickname that stuck with the media and fans — they called him "King Kong." "In the U.S. it means black and ugly," said Scott, offended at first but softened when he realized the appellation was a compliment among Mexican citizens, who viewed him as big and strong, a giant among men. Each time he made a tough play the fans gave him a standing ovation, yelling "King Kong en acción!" He had found his niche, as "King Kong in action."

Gene Martin, a former major leaguer who played for the Poza Rica Oilers that same year, had fond memories of George Scott in Mexico. Martin said that each time the Tigers came to the city they would stay at the Hotel Poza Rica, and he and Scott and other American ballplayers would get together. Martin explained that because of the extreme tropical conditions they were playing in, with burdensome humidity, "heavy air," he said, it was difficult to hit home runs; but not so with Scott. "He hit it like we were playing in Denver." Martin recounted some of Scott's home runs that year that cleared the light towers of Social Security Park. Mexico City had purchased the towers from the old Houston Colts' stadium and had them put into their park. "They were tall; I mean they must have been two-hundred fifty feet high. I'd seen George clear them towers. I mean them balls just disappeared into the jungle," said Martin admiringly.[19]

Scott had an exemplary year pounding the ball game after game and leading the league in just about everything. He played in the Mexican League all-star game and was 2-for-4. He finished the season batting .355, third-best behind Willie Norwood of Reynosa, who led the league at .365, and Bobby Rodriguez of the Mexico City Reds, who batted .363. Scott hit 18 home runs on the season and two more in the playoffs won by Campeche, a second-place team in the regular season. "I wanted to go down there to prove to the major league owners that I could still play," said Scott, who became disillusioned when once again none of the major league teams sought him after such a splendid year in Mexico. "So I said 'something is wrong,' and I said 'the heck with it, I'm going to go into the coaches part of it.'"[20] He was beginning to realize that the Mexican League was nothing more than the major league's graveyard.

Garcia liked what he saw in Scott, liked the way he got along with his young ballplayers and the leadership qualities he exhibited, and a bond was formed between the two. Garcia was planning to move up into the team's front office and recommended to Peralta that Scott replace him as full-time field manager. He got the job for the 1982 season. It seemed like a perfect fit, but it wasn't. Scott had trouble with his players right from the beginning, making demands on them that they perceived as unreasonable, and not adjusting well to the culture of the league which involved long bus rides accompanied by drinking as the players' only way, right or wrong, to appease their boredom and help them tolerate the arduous travel. Scott was opposed to it and made no bones. Ex-major leaguer Doug Ault and Scott got into a swearing match on one occasion when Ault took beer onto the bus. The incident got back to management; Scott was fired suddenly before the regular season was even underway and shipped off to Poza Rica where he wound up playing for the Oilers.[21]

He had another good year at the plate batting .333 on 110 base hits and finishing third again on the leaderboard, but his home run production had fallen off to only 7 taters. He was voted a second time as the starting first baseman for the South squad all-star team, won by the North team, 4–3, on June 14 before 15,000 Merida, Yucatan, fans. Scott was the cleanup hitter and was 1-for-3. He played 83 games for Poza Rica in 1983, and then shifted to Veracruz where he finished the season, between the two teams batting .223 with just 5 homers. In his final season, 1984, with Veracruz he played in 86 games, mostly as a DH, batting .305 on 92 base hits. He assumed managerial duties for Veracruz part-way into the season, but left before it ended when Mexican League teams were struggling to pay their players because of the Mexican economy and the rapid devaluation of the peso. Mexican teams had to pay their American imports in U.S. dollars, which made it even more difficult. Scott said that Veracruz still owed him $4,000 of a $15,000 manager's contract at the time he left. "They just couldn't afford to pay me," said Scott.[22] He went back to Greenville, Mississippi, to be with his mother there, in the house that he had built for her, and where it all began for George Scott; his playing days were now over.

The marital difficulties that beset him in 1979–1980 that ended in divorce, his leaving baseball and the lucrative salaries he had earned in the major leagues, plus some likely mismanagement of personal funds, led to hard times for George Scott. In 1985 Scott sold two of his Gold Gloves for $600 apiece to someone who Scott later realized had snookered him into thinking they would be placed in a "hall of fame" somewhere. He was crushed that he had been so deceived. He later also put up for sale his Kansas City Royals game-worn shoes. Then he hooked up with a major New York memorabilia dealer, in a partnership, he said, and in 1986 spent his time poking around major league spring camps enticing players, many of them his friends, to participate with him in autograph and collectors shows in the offseason. It was a humbling experience for a man of such indomitable pride, but he persevered; it was just another episode of yearning for survival for the ex-major league slugger, All-Star and eight-time Gold Glover, who was all too familiar with hard times.

Jay Acton, a lawyer, New York literary agent, and an early pioneer that led to the incarnation of independent league baseball, was instrumental, along with Eric Margenau, in forming the Empire State League on Long Island in 1987. Miles Wolff, who developed independent professional baseball in 1993, forming the highly successful Northern League in 1993 and later the Can-Am League of which he was commissioner, and co-authored *The Encyclopedia of Minor League Baseball*, credits Acton with paving the way for this distinctive brand of pro ball that has since found its niche throughout the U.S. and parts of Canada. Acton's new league, which played its 50-game schedule at Hofstra University in Hempstead, New York, was comprised of four teams made up of players who had exhausted their collegiate eligibility, but were not drafted by major league clubs; in effect, the league gave them a second chance at being noticed by the big leagues.

George Scott, paid $2,000 to join the league, was one of three black managers; it was his first managerial role in the U.S. He had been desperately trying to hook on with a major league club as a coach or minor league manager, writing letters to them for several years since he left major league baseball, but none of them gave him the time of day. Matt Sczesny, a longtime scout and minor league manager himself, made a point to visit Scott in Hempstead that year, and was impressed. "He's a good baseball man, George. I guess he could manage. He knows the game, and it says a lot that he's here working in these conditions," said Sczesny, noting the Spartan conditions of the playing field: no lights, no dugouts, no scoreboards, and a "crowd" of 20–30 scattered across a small open-air grandstand.[23] Jay Acton, believing Scott was being given the snub by the Red Sox and other clubs, was more emphatic about how he saw the matter. "He's in first place, and with a team that has about the third-best talent in the league. If you're telling me he can't be a minor league manager or a big league coach, then there's something wrong somewhere," said Acton.[24]

The league MVP was George's oldest son, Dion, who played first base on his father's team, the Diggers. "He was the best player by far," said Acton, who shared an anecdotal story about father and son that year as the playoffs were approaching. Scott was in need of pitching. His solution: he traded his son, Dion, to one of the other teams to get what he needed. Dion was completely dumbfounded, as was Acton and others in the league. It was the quintessence of the expression, "to win at all cost," and, by his actions, the personification of a man who would do just that.[25] But the league, a no-frills enterprise, collapsed after two years of operations. Scott managed only the one year.

From 1988 through 1992 Scott worked for Premiere Auto Body, an automobile repair shop in Allston, Massachusetts, once known as Geneva Auto Body, that was physically located next to Fenway Park. It was the same place where Tommy Harper worked after he was dismissed — wrongfully, alleged Harper — by the Red Sox at the end of 1985, leading to his racial-discrimination complaint filed with the Equal Employment Opportunity Commission, who ultimately sided with Harper. Stan Block, the owner of the establishment, considered his workplace a refuge for former Red Sox black players, George Scott among them, to earn some kind of steady income and a place where they could land on their feet. Block noted that it was where the local newspaper scribes congregated and actually interviewed Harper in 1986 after he had filed his suit, and later after the EEOC upheld his action. Block, who was particularly close to Harper, felt that Haywood Sullivan was intolerant of blacks and lurking in the shadows of the debacle surrounding Harper's termination with the Red Sox. "She was a little bit tougher toward the black ballplayers," than

Tom Yawkey was, said Block of Jean Yawkey, who was closely aligned with Sullivan. Harper eventually settled his suit with the club.[26]

Scott was also doing some autograph peddling at the time, noted Block, visiting major league clubhouses and soliciting autographs and arranging shows. But this was not a successful venture. "They were friendly towards him, but none of them really helped him…. Hawk Harrelson promised him a job with the Chicago White Sox and he never came through," said Block. "The Red Sox never did anything for him at all, they never really recognized him. I felt bad for him because he was always sitting home waiting for some team to call him." Reggie Jackson helped Scott out "once or twice" when money was getting tight for him, but "that was about it," said Block.[27] During this time and before, Scott coached amateur baseball in Boston's inner city during the summer with Brannelly's Café in the Junior Park League (currently the Tom Yawkey Baseball League) comprised of collegiate and ex-minor leaguers.

In 1993 George was hired by Ernest Austen, the athletic director of Roxbury Community College, a Boston inner city school, to organize and initiate RCC's first baseball program. Scott was its first coach, and designed the uniforms that are still being used today. "George came and started the [baseball] program with his own money. He put the program on his back and got it started," said Edsel Neal, Scott's successor, of George's trailblazing work with the college and his personal financial investment in RCC baseball. In 1996 Scott took RCC to the National Junior College Athletic Association state championship with only a nine-player team, and lost against powerhouse Quinsigamond Community College of Worcester, Massachusetts. "He almost pulled off winning the state championship with [just] nine guys, and five of them were pitchers … and it was a one-run game," chuckled Neal admiringly over what Scott had nearly accomplished with a bare-minimum of players.[28] Scott's last year coaching RCC was 1997; after that he participated in some assistant coaching duties with them into 2000.

In 1994, during George's tenure at RCC, he signed on to manage the Minneapolis Millers, an independent league club of the newly formed four-team Great Central League started by Minnesota businessman Dick Jacobson. There were problems from the beginning. Jacobson, whose league owned all four clubs, was working on a shoestring budget and ultimately could not support the payroll. To complicate his ambitions he was competing for business with three other local ball clubs: the major league Minnesota Twins, a well-supported St. Paul club of the highly successful independent Northern League, and another startup club, the Minneapolis Loons of the independent six-team North-Central League. Then in August a member of a singing group, who had been staying in an Augsburg College dormitory in the Twin Cities while on tour, complained she had been raped by one or more members of the Millers baseball team who were staying at the same facility. Things rapidly deteriorated from there, with Jacobson canceling the final four games of the season to end his ill-fated venture with independent baseball and the Great Central League. George Scott, whose ambition was to get a foothold on managing in the newly charted and burgeoning independent leagues, got, instead, nothing but disappointment and a lesson in how not to run a business.

In 1995 Scott took yet another chance with independent baseball, joining a Saskatchewan, Canada, club, the Saskatoon Riot, in the newly formed Prairie League, made up of eight teams, four American and four Canadian. Scott became discouraged with the ownership, the Ferguson brothers, right from the outset who weren't committed to winning, he said. "I had never been nowhere where the owners can look out [on the playing field], see that they don't have talent, and still not be willing to spend some money [for players]," said Scott, complaining that they had a $55,000 salary cap yet a payroll of around $20,000. Asked to name some of his players, Scott retorted: "I don't care to remember them because they were lousy."[29] The Riot posted a 9–21 record under Scott, who became disenchanted and left the organization on July 13, midway into the season. "If I knew then what I know today, I never would have got involved [with Minnesota or Saskatoon]," said Scott. "Because I wanted so bad to try to get me a job in the United States in somebody's minor league system, okay, and I was out to just do about anything to show people that I was a good manager."[30]

His third attempt finally proved to be a positive experience. In 1996 he latched onto the Massachusetts Mad Dogs, an expansion team in the second-year independent North Atlantic League, made up of six clubs from New York State, New Jersey, New Hampshire, Pennsylvania and Ontario, Canada. Jonathan Fleisig, a 31-year-old trader of energy futures on the New York Mercantile Stock Exchange, and a successful businessman with ownership of two minor league hockey teams, owned the Mad Dogs, which were located in Lynn, Massachusetts. Scott had a successful year by winning 56 of 77 games and finishing 13½ games in front of Catskill, the second-place club. However, they lost the league championship in a two-game playoff sweep to Catskill's Cougars.

Mike Babcock, the Mad Dogs general manager at the time, recounted, on a disturbing note, how they lost the final game of the championship to Catskill. Mad Dogs ace hurler Jay Murphy, who had dealt with Catskill handily during the regular season, took his team into the ninth with a 2–0 lead. But it unraveled from there. The Catskill hitters started delaying tactics of stepping out of the box to distract Murphy. It did upset him; he proceeded to hit a batter, then the next batter "hit the weakest little duck fart" bloop single that scored a run, and ultimately the game was tied. The Mad Dogs then lost, 4–2, in 12 innings. According to Babcock it seemed to take the air out of the ballpark, losing to a team they were supposed to beat easily, and then watch Catskill celebrate their victory on the Mad Dogs' home field to make matters worse. Babcock said that he went to work for the Catskill team a year after that as their GM, when going through the desk drawers of his predecessor, he found a DVD tape *Gaylord Perry's Dirty Tricks of Baseball*, which assumedly was seen, believed Babcock, by the Catskill team in preparation of that championship game. "Everything on that Gaylord Perry tape is everything they did. They must have watched it on the way to the damn ballpark," said Babcock, still outraged at the thought they might have been beaten because of an opponent's contemptible tactics.[31]

George Scott was named Manager of the Year, and three of his players were picked up by major league clubs at the end of the season. Not only was the team successful on the diamond but they also drew the most fans (52,394), leveraging them for another season, if not in the North Atlantic League which was in jeopardy because of failing franchises, then somewhere else. The North Atlantic League collapsed as expected, but Fleisig's Mad Dogs shifted to the third-year Northeast League in '97, one of several independent leagues in a flourishing market, joining seven other clubs, including Catskill of the defunct North Atlantic League. Scott had another good year winning 45 of 82, finishing third in the first half but tying for the second-half lead at 23–17. Once again, however, they lost in the playoffs, 2-games-to-1, to Albany, who lost to Elmira for the league championship. The Mad Dogs had even greater attendance than the year before, drawing 72,681 fans, second only to Albany's 72,985. While things were looking financially very promising for the Mad Dogs, it didn't last. Repairs were needed at Fraser Field where the Mad Dogs played, and interest began to dwindle as the 1998 season wore on; by its end the Mad Dogs had the third lowest attendance (47,123) — a decline of over 25,500 fans — of the eight-team league. They fell to 39–45 on the year and failed to make the playoffs.

At the conclusion of the '98 season Miles Wolff, commissioner of the thriving and quite profitable Northern League, took an unprecedented step by merging with the eight-team Northeast League, establishing two divisions (Central and Eastern) with the 16 teams. It was his desire to enter the Northeast market where there were rich prospects for establishing a foothold, already proven by the success of the Northeast League, notwithstanding the poorer performance of the Massachusetts entry. But the Mad Dogs were assimilated nevertheless with the rest of their league, and joined the Eastern Division. They began the '99 season setting a milestone by signing a woman, Tammy Holmes, to their roster; she became the first female positional player of an all-male professional baseball team. Holmes had played for two years with the all-female Silver Bullets pro team before it folded. She played in two games with the Mad Dogs, was hitless (five strikeouts) in seven at-bats, with an on-base percentage of .222, and then left the team on June 13. The Mad Dogs were 21–22 in the first half of division play, one game behind the North's Division Adirondack. But in the second half they fell to last place at 20–23, and their attendance was the worst in the league at 38,528. It was the last season for the fiscally struggling Mad Dogs who succumbed at the end of the year.

Tragedy befell George Scott in 2000. His mother, Magnolia, died in September, and his significant other, Edith Lawson, of Randolph, Massachusetts, with whom he had a relationship of some 20 years, died suddenly on December 19, of a heart attack while going to work as a nurse at the New England Medical Center. It was a personal blow of immense magnitude for the Boomer; first his beloved mother, then his fiancée whom he was about to marry, died suddenly within three months of each other. Bereft with enormous grief he picked up the pieces of a life severely shattered, and moved on. He knew no other way to deal with it; George Scott knew what it was to survive. He moved into the home he had built for his mother in Greenville, back to his Mississippi roots, along with his teenage son Brian born of George's relationship with Edith.

Old friend Mike Babcock, who was then the GM of the Rio Grande Valley WhiteWings of Harlingen, Texas, of the independent Texas-Louisiana League, pursued Scott that winter to manage the WhiteWings. It was only a few months after Scott's personal tragedy, but because of their friendship Babcock knew it might be the perfect situation for George to lift him up by the bootstraps during some very dark days. The WhiteWings were a stable team, one of the 1994 charter members of the league, and had won the league championship in 2000 under manager Eddie Dennis who left the team after that. "That left me looking for a manager ... he [George Scott] was the first guy to pop into my head," said Babcock. It was not a good season for Scott, who had to deal with an undisciplined team, incidences of drugs among the players, and a wholesale bad experience. They finished well down the ranks of the seven-team league at 40–56. "The cast of characters we had in Rio Grande weren't the best character type guys, and I think that took a lot out of George that season because of that. It's all about the love of the game with George," said Babcock.[32]

Opportunity knocked once again, however, at season's end when old friend Jonathan Fleisig approached Scott with a proposal to start another independent club in 2002, the Berkshire Black Bears of Pittsfield, Massachusetts, that would join the Eastern Division of the powerful Northern League. It represented a return to a city steeped with numerous personal memories, and a venerable ballpark, Wahconah, where he first made a name for himself as a 21-year-old Red Sox prospect who tore the league apart in 1965 to dramatically carry Pittsfield to an Eastern League championship. The offer to manage again, especially there, was a no-brainer; he jumped at the chance. But once again he ran into disappointment with a team of players who seemed less than dedicated, nor willing to perform in a manner to which he was accustomed. "It was almost euthanasia ... because he's not a quitter," said Fleisig about the decision he had to make to relieve his friend, George Scott, of the indignities

Red Sox Hall of Fame induction ceremonies on November 9, 2006. Left to right: Dick Williams, Joe Morgan, George Scott, Dick Bresciani and Jerry Remy (courtesy of Boston Red Sox and Julie Cordeiro).

he was experiencing with a young ballclub of malcontents that ended in his firing. "It used to be 70% coaching and 30% recruiting; now it was 40% recruiting, 50% babysitting and 10% coaching; that wasn't George's personality," said Fleisig. Speaking about the caliber of the new young ballplayer that Scott was encountering, Fleisig added: "They were all state all-stars, or all-county; they were the stars of their high school team, they had been prima donnas and had their asses kissed since they were probably ten years old; they had it all ... they had a chip on their shoulder ... all the women love me, my mom loves me ... when you talk to somebody like George when it's about team, that's tough," said Fleisig, expounding on the reasons behind Scott's disenchantment with the 2002 year in Pittsfield, that concluded in a dismal 24–65 season.[33] Scott did not return in 2003. It was the end of his long and exemplary, sometimes turbulent, baseball career, 30 years professionally and 5 years of college and amateur baseball. George Scott was inducted into the Red Sox Hall of Fame in November, 2006, and the Mississippi Sports Hall of Fame in July, 2007.

On June 1, 2006, Boston sports radio talk show host Bob Lobel and his guest, journalist Mike Barnicle, were discussing the all-time best defensive players in Red Sox history. With each position they discussed, sauntering

between names of memo-
rable Red Sox players such
as Ted Williams, Yaz and
Ramirez in left field, Malzone and Vern Stephens at
third, Doerr, Andrews and
Loretta at second, and so
on, when the subject of first
base came up, it was George
Scott, hands down. They
went no further; end of discussion. In 2007 Rawlings,
commemorating 50 years
since the inception of the
Gold Glove awards, pro-
moted an event in which
the fans were to select the
all-time Gold Glove team

George Scott and Dick Williams at the 2006 Red Sox
Hall of Fame ceremony (author's collection).

at each position. The surprise was choosing former Dodger Wes Parker for first
base. Nick Cafardo of the *Boston Globe* cried foul, begging the question in his
April 15 article "Was there anyone as skilled with a first baseman's mitt as
George Scott?" It was a striking omission, he insisted.[34] Not only was he flashy
around the bag, a genius of a first baseman said many of his contemporaries,
but of the few first basemen who were multiple Gold Glove recipients, Scott,
14 years a major leaguer, was among the lifetime leaders in the all-important
"assists" category with 1132, placing him fourth behind Eddie Murray (1865),
Keith Hernandez (1682) and Mark Grace (1665). Murray had 21 years in the
big leagues, Hernandez 17, and Grace 16.

On May 19, 1990, at age 46, George Scott participated in a Red Sox old-
timers game against former Twins players, and a few other old-timers mixed
in. On one play Johnny Logan, a former Boston-Milwaukee Braves infielder,
hit a ground ball to former Red Sox third baseman great Frank Malzone, who
threw the ball to first with the ball landing well in front of the Boomer. He
flashed the glove he once called Black Magic and scooped up the errant throw
never missing a beat, like 1967 revisited. The *Globe*'s Bob Ryan, who wrote
the story, added a sentimental line at the end by making reference to a father
and son in the stands, with the father nudging his son and saying, "Didn't I
tell you? Nobody ever dug 'em out like the Boomer."[35]

Chapter Notes

Chapter 1

1. Will McDonough, "Scott's Dreams: Be a Mays, Cash for Ma," *Boston Globe*, May 10, 1966, p. 27.

2. Anthony Walton, *Mississippi: An American Journey* (New York: Vintage, 1996).

3. "Mississippi — The Eye of the Storm," Civil Rights Movement timeline, http://www.crmvet.org/tim/timhis61.htm, 1961; "Welcome to African American History," "The Civil Rights movement (1955–1965)," "Mississippi and Freedom Summer," www.watson.org.

4. Ibid.

5. Beatrice Scott interviews: May 3, 2006, and January 27, 2009.

6. George Scott interviews: January 21 and 23, 2006.

7. The *Shotgun House*—also known derisively as the *shotgun shack*— is an African American house design originating in the American South, often found on plantations. Typically long and narrow and consisting of two to three rooms, one behind the other, some say it's so-named because one can fire a shotgun through the front door with all the shot exiting the back door without ever touching a wall. Though no basis can be found for this description, one black Greenville resident explained the likely origin for this description: "Because we lived under the gun. I mean that's not a stretch."

8. Richard Annotico, "The Mississippi Delta: The Race War and Italians," *The Annotico Report*, January 14, 2007.

9. James C. Cobb, *The Most Southern Place on Earth: The Mississippi Delta and the Roots of Regional Identity* (New York: Oxford University Press, 1992), p. 306.

10. Ibid.

11. Hodding Carter III interview: February 6, 2009; Ann Waldron, *Hodding Carter: The Reconstruction of a Racist* (Chapel Hill, NC: Algonquin, 1993). Considered *moderate* by Northerners, yet starkly *liberal* by Southerners, Greenville's background and character between the 1940s and 1960s was formed largely by three elements: The Percy Tradition; Hodding Carter, Jr., and the *Delta Democrat-Times*; and the Industrial initiative.

12. Dorothy Ann Williams, "Growing Up Black in Segregated Greenville: A Candid Perspective," unpublished manuscript, written January 19, 2008.

13. Willie Richardson interview: December 21, 2007; Richardson and George Scott both went to Coleman High School, Richardson graduating in 1959 and Scott in 1962. They played as teammates on sandlot teams around Greenville.

14. Based on various interviews of Greenville citizens, "Mag" was the popular abbreviated name for Magnolia.

15. Beatrice Scott interviews: May 3, 2006, and January 27, 2009.

16. Leonia Collins Dorsey interview: October 11, 2008.

17. Rico Petrocelli interview: October 17, 2008.

18. McDonough, "Scott's Dreams"; "Scott: Little League Refugee with a Big Stick," *Los Angeles Times*, May 24, 1966, p. B4.

19. Leonia Collins Dorsey interview: October 11, 2008.

20. John Hawkins interview: February 10, 2009.

21. McDonough, "Scott's Dreams."

22. Greenville's white citizens, enabled by the influence of its Citizens' Council, resisted integration of their school systems following the 1954 Supreme Court decision *Brown v. Board of Education*, which ruled that racially segregated educational facilities were intrinsically unequal, and in violation of the Fourteenth Amendment. The town reacted to the decision by building a new state-of-the-art school, Coleman High, for black students which they hoped would pacify black residents and avoid integration they so feared. Integration of Greenville's schools did not occur until 1970. George Scott attended Coleman High during the period 1957–1962, a typical six-year span for black students of Greenville.

23. Frank Sanders interview: March 6, 2009.

24. Scott believes the origin for his nickname *Pee-tuck* comes from *Tucker*, the surname of Luther Tucker who played for the Greenville Bucks, a minor league team in the Cotton States League, in 1953 and who was player-manager there in 1955, the last year of the league. Neither Scott nor others close to him know the origin of the *Pee* attached to the name. Scott states that he is recognized even today by former Coleman High teammates, high school opponents and Greenville friends by the nickname *Pee-tuck* instead of by his given name George or his nationally popular moniker, "Boomer." The name has also been spelled as *Petuck*, but the more accepted form, *Pee-tuck*, is found in Coleman High's official school paper, *The Tiger Gazette*. Scott's school teammates abbreviated the name to *Tuck*, which he wore on the back of his football practice jersey.

25. Roger Birtwell, "Sidearm Pitcher Saved Scott for Sox," *Boston Globe*, May 23, 1966, p. 28.

26. Ron Anderson, "George Scott," in *The 1967 Impossible Dream Red Sox*, ed. Bill Nowlin and Dan Desrochers (Burlington, MA: Rounder, 2007*)*, p.100.

27. E.T. Davis interview: April 20, 2006.

28. Davis Weathersby interview: July 24, 2006.

29. John Hawkins interview: February 10, 2009. Hawkins was a co-captain on Coleman's 1961 football team with George Scott and A.C. Thomas. Thomas went on to play pro football briefly with the Atlanta Falcons.

30. The Etheridge boys, Bobby and Jimmy, were members of the all-white Greenville High School baseball team that won a state championship. Bobby Etheridge was signed by the San Francisco Giants baseball club and played at the major league level in 1967 and 1969.

31. "George Scott Day Named," *Delta Democrat-Times*, October 20, 1967, p. 9. Frank Barnes played at times with the St. Louis Cardinals from 1957 to 1960. He was the first athlete from Greenville to make it to the big leagues.

32. Elijah Moore interview: February 29, 2008.

33. Ed Scott interview: August 3, 2006.

34. Andrew Jackson interview: April 20, 2006.

35. Chuck Prophet interview: December 14, 2007.

36. Betty Jo Boyd interview: July 31, 2007. Boyd is a "social justice" activist from Greenville, Mississippi, who has worked the majority of her adult life in politics and political campaigns, starting with presidential candidate Adlai Stephenson to Mike Espy of Mississippi who became a U.S. Representative and then Secretary of Agriculture in the Clinton administration.

37. Hodding Carter III interview: February 6, 2009.

38. George Scott by all accounts gave birth to the baseball term *tater* that was popularized and is commonly used today to describe the home run. According to teammate John Hawkins of Coleman High, Scott used the term in the 1950s playing sandlot ball and on into high school in the early 1960s, and then the major leagues. Hall of Famer Joe Morgan also credited Scott with the term, though somewhat inaccurately referring to "another of George Scott's nicknames" as *Long Tater*, summarizing with "that's beautiful." [*ESPN Sunday Night Baseball*, August 28, 2005]. George's coach, Davis Weathersby, relates that the word *tater* means sweet potato in the Delta.

39. Rick Cleveland, "5 Legends Give Us Reason to Smile," *Clarion Ledger*, July 28, 2007, p. 1C.

40. Beverly Gardner interview: August 23, 2008.

41. Troy Treasure, "Mississippi Sports Hall of Fame Class of 2007: Power and Grace," *Delta Democrat-Times*, July 29, 2007, p. B4.

42. *Separate but equal* is a term from the 1896 U.S. Supreme Court decision *Plessy v. Ferguson,*

which declared that racially separate facilities, if equal, did not violate the Constitution. Segregation, the court said, was not discrimination.

43. Dave Distel, "George Scott's Boyhood: It's Right There in Black and White," *Los Angeles Times*, June 9, 1973, p. D1.

Chapter 2

1. Clif Keane, "'Scott Will Get Better 'n' Better,'" *Boston Globe*, May 10 1966, p. 27.

2. High school baseball programs were just emerging throughout the Delta and southern sections of Mississippi in the early 1960s, so there was no formal state tournament or official title awarded at the time. The strongest teams — such as Jim Hill and Lanier — were in the capitol city of Jackson, which Coleman dominated in 1962, among numerous Delta teams, thus emerging as a school with the best record.

3. Robert Young interview: January 16, 2009; Beverly Gardner interview: August 23, 2008; Davis Weathersby interview: July 24, 2006. By all accounts coach Elbert Foules was Scott's ultimate mentor and strived to prepare him for professional sports. His connections with former Negro Leaguers and major league baseball facilitated George Scott's opportunities of exposure to big league baseball. Foules coordinated a tryout for members of the undefeated Chicago Mill team with Dr. Noble Frisby of Greenville and with Cardinals scout Buddy Lewis, in July 1961. He also arranged a tryout held in Greenville for local black youth with Pittsburgh Pirates scout Bob Zuk, held in October 1961; George Scott attended both tryouts.

4. Birtwell, "Sidearm Pitcher."

5. Howard Bryant, *Shutout: A Story of Race and Baseball in Boston* (New York: Routledge, 2002), p. 72.

6. George Scott interviews: January 24, 2006, and March 3 and 23, 2006.

7. Glenn Stout, "Tryout and Fallout: Race, Jackie Robinson, and the Red Sox," *Massachusetts Historical Review*, 2004, pp. 12–13 and 18; Bryant, *Shutout*, p. 48.

8. Ed Scott interview: August 3, 2006.

9. Ibid.

10. Ibid.

11. Keane, "Scott Will Get Better."

12. Ed Scott interview: August 3, 2006.

13. Various interviews of Greenville's black residents affirm the practice of housing black ballplayers barnstorming through their town. This was particularly true during the 1940s and '50s when barnstorming was common; such players as Brooklyn's Don Newcombe and Roy Campanella and Cleveland's Larry Doby played and stayed there.

14. George Digby interviews: January 18, 20, and 29, 2007.

15. Ed Scott interview: August 3, 2006.

16. Keane, "Scott Will Get Better."

17. Larry Claflin, "Great Scott! Big George Opens Bosox Eyes With Swat Spree," *The Sporting News*, April 16, 1966, p. 44.

18. Birtwell, "Sidearm Pitcher."

19. Milt Bolling interview: October 16, 2006; Ed Scott interview: August 3, 2006; George Digby interviews: January 18, 20, and 29, 2007. Media typically reported Scott receiving a "$10,000 bonus," which may have been based upon how Scott, himself, represented the money. Digby thought it was $6,000 but was certain it was not $10,000: "No, he didn't get $10, 000," said Digby. "I think he got $6,000, is what he got, because I okay'd everything." Both Ed Scott and Milt Bolling were sure it was $8,000, which likely was the base amount.

20. Ed Scott interview: August 3, 2006.

21. Milt Bolling interview: October 16, 2006.

22. George Scott interview: January 2006

23. Bob Davies, "They Came To See, and Bob Hit No. 7," *Olean Times Herald*, June 9, 1962, p. 8.

24. David Condon, "In The Wake of the News," *Chicago Tribune*, May 14, 1966, p. B1.

25. George Scott interview: January 2006.

26. Bobby Doerr interviews: October 16, 2006, and June 5, 2007.

27. George Scott interview: January 21, 2006.
28. Bobby Doerr interview: October 16, 2006.
29. George Scott interview: January 21, 2006.
30. Bill Slack interview: June 8, 2009.
31. Hy Hurwitz, "Pesky Pegs Conigliaro Hub's Prize Slugging Prospect," *The Sporting News*, November 30, 1963, pp.15–16.
32. Keane, "Scott Will Get Better."
33. Bob Cole, "The Cage & Chorus," *Winston-Salem Journal*, June 23, 1964, p. 12.
34. Ibid.
35. Bill Slack interview: June 8, 2009.
36. Bill Slack recalls trying Scott at first during his recovery period. It most likely was during informal practice sessions since the record does not show Scott starting or playing any games at the first base position.
37. According to official recordkeeping, Winston-Salem finished the regular season with an 82–57 record. In fact they actually finished 83–56. The June 8 game against Greensboro — a tie game — was called due to curfew and replayed on July 22, when Winston-Salem lost, 2–1, but filed a protest. After the league upheld Winston-Salem's protest, the team won the makeup game, 1–0. The protest makeup game was not recorded in official standings.
38. Frank Spencer, "W-S Sox Are Almost Set," *Winston-Salem Journal and Sentinel*, April 5, 1964, p. B5.
39. Bill Slack interview: June 8, 2009.
40. E.T. Davis interview: April 20, 2006.

Chapter 3

1. Arthur Daley, "Great Scott!" *New York Times*, July 7 1966, p. 58.
2. Roger O'Gara, "Pittsfield Gives Warm Welcome to Buzas' Move," *The Sporting News*, June 12, 1965, p. 37.
3. George Scott interview: May 20, 2006.
4. Peter Golenbock, *Red Sox Nation* (Chicago: Triumph, 2005), pp. 225–226.
5. Bryant, *Shutout*, p. 8.
6. George Scott interview: May 20, 2006.
7. Rogelio Alvarez of Estrellas hit 15 homers but dropped out of competition before the end of the season.
8. George Scott interview: January 23, 2006.
9. Daley, "Great Scott!"

Chapter 4

1. Larry Claflin, "Big or Small, A.L. Parks Look Easy to Bosox Bombshell Scott," *The Sporting News*, May 21, 1966, p. 18.
2. Charles Pierce, "The Dead Zone," in *Red Sox Century*, ed. Glenn Stout and Richard A. Johnson (Boston: Houghton Mifflin, 2004).
3. Bryant, *Shutout*, p. 8.
4. Golenbock, *Red Sox Nation*, p. 279.
5. Ibid., p. 275.
6. Larry Claflin, "Rookie Foy Winterbook Choice to Nab Malzone's Post in Hub," *The Sporting News*, December 4, 1965, p. 30.
7. Sam Bernstein, "Legendary Hitter Created a Stir during His Six-Minute Induction Speech," *Memories and Dreams*, 2006.
8. Pres Hobson, "Red Sox Feel They're Not Above Self Criticism," *Quincy Patriot Ledger*, March 9, 1966, p. 21.
9. Claflin, "Rookie Foy."
10. "Foy, Helms, Murcer Rated Tops," *Quincy Patriot Ledger*, April 4, 1966, p. 24.
11. George Scott interview: January 21, 2006.

12. Larry Claflin, "Bosox Needlers Goading Flashy Joe Foy," *The Sporting News*, March 26, 1966, p. 5.

13. George Scott interview: May 20, 2006.

14. Pres Hobson, "Double Trouble Comes to Red Sox," *Quincy Patriot Ledger*, March 24, 1966, p. 31.

15. Larry Claflin, "Great Scott! Big George Opens Bosox Eyes With Swat Spree," *The Sporting News*, April 16, 1966, p. 44.

16. Tim Doherty, "Mississippi Sports Hall of Fame: Wait Worth It for Gregarious Slugger 'Boomer,'" *Clarion Ledger*, July 22, 2007.

17. Hobson, "Double Trouble."

18. George Scott interview: November 30, 2009.

19. Hy Hurwitz, "Red Sox Rookie Scott Refuses to be Second Best." *Boston Globe*, April 10, 1966, p. 59.

20. Ibid.

21. George Bankert, "Boston 'Oldtimers' New Sox Leaders," *Quincy Patriot Ledger*, April 12, 1966, p. 15.

Chapter 5

1. Harold Kaese, "Scott off Mark, Like Ted, Ruth," *Boston Globe*, May 6, 1966, p. 45.

2. By all accounts George Scott is the original "Boomer" of the professional sports world, including in Paul Dickson's *Baseball's Greatest Quotations* (New York: Harper-Collins, 2008). Norman "Boomer" Esiason of pro football fame actually acquired the nickname before he was born, but it was not known nationally until he entered the pro football ranks in the 1980s ("Boomer Esiason," en.wikipedia.org). Others such as sports announcer Chris Berman and baseball pitcher David Wells shared the nickname "Boomer," but they too followed Scott. Berman described how he got his nickname: "I worked at ESPN at the beginning in '79, I'm a loud, boisterous guy and one of the techs, who's now one of the vice presidents, said, 'You're a Boomer.' It's descriptive and it came from my co-workers, which I like" ("A Quick Chat with ESPN's Chris Berman," beyondrobson.com/sports/2008, March 2, 2008). Wells claimed his nickname began "in my rookie season" of 1987 ("History, Trivia & Memorabilia," posted November 18, 2001, at forums.nyyfans.com/showthread by "Gehrig," citing original posting by "Jersey Yankee" based on his interview of David Wells).

3. Bud Collins, "Sin for Sox Not to Hustle," *Boston Globe*, April 12, 1966, p. 51.

4. Ibid.

5. George Scott interview: March 3, 2006.

6. Ibid.

7. Ibid.

8. Ibid.

9. Larry Claflin, "Red Riding Hood Had Nice Trip Compared to Red Sox Disaster," *The Sporting News*, April 30, 1966, p. 20.

10. Ray Fitzgerald, "Herman Calls Sox Meeting," *Boston Globe*, April 18, 1966, p. 43.

11. George Scott interview: January 23, 2006.

12. Ron Hobson, "Ford's Strategy to Walk George," *Quincy Patriot Ledger*, April 27, 1966, p. 23.

13. Daley, "Great Scott!"

14. Rico Petrocelli interview: October 17, 2008.

15. Hobson, "Ford's Strategy?"

16. Studies conducted by *Hit Tracker*, a home run tracking and distance measurement group (www.hittrackeronline.com). Latent details of Scott's Yankee Stadium home run matched with present-day scientific measurements comprised of observed data and atmospherics places the *true distance* of the home run between 500 and 505 feet.

17. George Scott interview: January 21, 2006.

18. Jim Gosger interview: January 9, 2009.

19. Claflin, "Big or Small."

20. Studies conducted by *Hit Tracker*.

21. Jim "Mudcat" Grant interview: January 22, 2009.

22. Claflin, "Big or Small."
23. Ibid.
24. Jerry Nason, "Cronin Certain All Scott Needs Is 'Book' on Pitchers," *Boston Globe*, May 29, 1966, p. 31.
25. Troy Treasure, "Better Late Than Never," *Delta Democrat Times*, July 25, 2007, p. B1.
26. George Scott interview: March 23, 2006.
27. Clif Keane, "Benched Scott Feels Low, Pleads For Help," *Boston Globe*, July 19, 1966, p. 21.
28. Bob Sales, "Slumping Scott Gets Advice from Maglie," *Boston Globe*, July 20, 1966, p. 43.
29. George Scott interview: March 3, 2006.
30. Ibid.
31. Bill Nowlin, *Red Sox Threads* (Burlington, MA: Rounder, 2008); "Twins, Angels Slowed," *Chicago Tribune*, August 10, 1984, p. C6. Scott's AL rookie record for intentional passes was broken in 1984 by Seattle's Alvin Davis.
32. George Scott and Jim Fregosi of the California Angels were the only two American League ballplayers to appear in all 162 regular season games; *The Sporting News*, December 17, 1966, p. 33.
33. "Strike Zone Eludes Scott; Winter Ball May Be Cure," *The Sporting News*, October 1, 1966, p. 26.

Chapter 6

1. Rico Petrocelli and Chaz Scoggins, *Rico Petrocelli's Tales from the Impossible Dream Red Sox* (Champaign, IL: Sports Publishing, 2007), p. 50.
2. Ed Rumill, "Keep an Eye on Bosox Beauts," *The Sporting News*, December 3, 1966, p. 54.
3. Horacio Ruiz, "High-Quality Play Likely; Stars Inked," *The Sporting News*, October 8, 1966, p. 52. Marv Throneberry held the previous salary high of $1,200 a month when playing for Cinco Estrellas.
4. Eduardo Moncada, "Player Salaries Will Be Probed by Government," *The Sporting News*, December 17, 1966, p. 41.
5. Dick Williams and Bill Plaschke, *No More Mr. Nice Guy* (San Diego: Harcourt Brace Jovanovich, 1990), pp. 77–78.
6. Harold Kaese, "Scott Treated Badly by Sox," *Boston Globe*, August 25, 1968, p. 55; Clif Keane, "Scott Boiling at Treatment," *Boston Globe*, August 27, 1968, p. 27.
7. Will McDonough, "Scott's Dreams: Be a Mays, Cash for Ma," *Boston Globe*, May 10, 1966, p. 28.
8. Golenbock, *Red Sox Nation*, p. 296.
9. Will McDonough, "Red Sox' Scott —'Won't Be Dumb Swinger in '67," *Boston Globe*, February 11, 1967, p. 40.
10. Ray Fitzgerald, "Umps Warn Sox About Balks," *Boston Globe*, March 3, 1967, p. 28.
11. "Red Sox Explode for 5 Runs in 4th," *Boston Globe*, March 13, 1967, p. 25.
12. Ken Coleman and Dan Valenti, *The Impossible Dream Remembered: The 1967 Red Sox* (Lexington, MA: Stephen Greene Press, 1987), p. 22.
13. Will McDonough, "Williams' Shift Rankles Scott," *Boston Globe*, March 22, 1967, p. 44.
14. John Ahern, "Scott Plays RF, Stirs Trade Talk," *Boston Globe*, March 22, 1967, p. 50.
15. Petrocelli and Scoggins, *Rico Petrocelli's Tales*, p. 49.
16. Ibid., p. 50.
17. Harold Kaese, "Is Yawkey Back of Scott Shift?" *Boston Globe*, March 24, 1967, p. 19.
18. Harold Kaese, "Williams Uses Surprise Attack," *Boston Globe*, March 27, 1967, p. 21.
19. John Ahern, "Jubilant Scott Quits Fishing," *Boston Globe*, April 3, 1967, p. 23.
20. The *Boston Globe* reported the unofficial final spring statistics on April 10, 1967, which showed George Scott with 26 base hits and a .333 batting average. In fact Scott had 27 base hits and finished at .346. He was also credited by the *Globe* with 6 RBIs; he actually had 11 RBIs.

Chapter 7

1. Rico Petrocelli interview: October 17, 2008.
2. Jerry Crasnick, "Unyielding, Gruff Williams Was an Innovator," ESPN.com, July 26, 2008.

3. "Two Red Sox Enrolled in Exclusive Club," *Washington Post,* April 21, 1967, p. D2.
4. Larry Claflin, "Bosox Slumpers Feel Pilot's Wrath," *The Sporting News,* May 6, 1967, p. 12.
5. George Scott interview: January 23, 2006.
6. Rico Petrocelli interview: October 17, 2008.
7. Ray Fitzgerald, "Slugger Scott Turns Artist," *Boston Globe,* May 15, 1967, p. 27.
8. Nick Cafardo, *Boston Red Sox: Yesterday and Today* (Akron: West Side Publishing, 2007).
9. Ray Fitzgerald, "Baseball Still White Man's Game," *Boston Globe,* May 17, 1967, p. 1.
10. Larry Claflin, "Red Sox Boss Wins Weighty Argument with Slugger Scott," *The Sporting News,* September 2, 1967, p. 9.
11. Bill Nowlin and Dan Desrochers, eds., *The 1967 Impossible Dream Red Sox* (Burlington, MA: Rounder, 2007), p. 334.
12. Petrocelli and Scoggins, *Rico Petrocelli's Tales,* p. 79.
13. George Scott interview: January 23, 2006.
14. Petrocelli and Scoggins, *Rico Petrocelli's Tales,* p. 93.
15. Harold Kaese, "Bat Mightier than Glove," *Boston Globe,* June 28, 1967, p. 57.
16. Harold Kaese, "Sox Will Use Siebern at 1B," *Boston Globe,* July 17, 1967, p. 17.
17. Ben Henkey, "Kaline a Gold Glover for Tenth Time," *The Sporting News,* November 11, 1967, p. 27.
18. Roger Birtwell, "Siebern, Adair Start; Lonborg Flies to Hurl," *Boston Globe,* August 9, 1967, p. 49.
19. Claflin, "Red Sox Boss Wins."
20. Petrocelli and Scoggins, *Rico Petrocelli's Tales,* p. 130.
21. Glenn Stout and Richard Johnson, eds., *Red Sox Century* (Boston: Houghton-Mifflin, 2004), p. 324.
22. George Scott, "Beating That Stanky Is Just Great, Baby," *Boston Herald-Traveler,* August 28, 1967, p. 19.
23. Jack Clary, "Scott Spurs Lonborg," *Boston Herald-Traveler,* September 8, 1967, p. 41.
24. Ray Fitzgerald, "Tighter Fielding Saves Pitchers, Keys Sox Drive," *Boston Globe,* September 14, 1967, p. 51.
25. George Scott interview: April 20, 2010.

Chapter 8

1. Henkey, "Kaline a Gold Glover."
2. Jack McCarthy, "Cards' Brock, Flood Remember 'Boomer,'" *Boston Herald-Traveler,* August 31, 1967, p. 43.
3. Bill Liston, "Red Sox 'Tough Club' Super Scout Reports," *Boston Herald-Traveler,* September 25, 1967, pp. 29–30.
4. Nowlin and Desrochers, *The 1967 Impossible Dream Red Sox,* p. 355.
5. "Williams the Wonder," *The Sporting News,* October 21, 1967, p. 8.
6. Petrocelli and Scoggins, *Rico Petrocelli's Tales,* p. 185.
7. Stout and Johnson, *Red Sox Century,* p. 337.
8. John Carr, "Words Were Said in the Series," *Delta Democrat-Times,* November 3, 1967, p. 9.
9. Lowell Reidenbaugh, "Lonborg Blisters Cards, But Blister Spoils Gem," *The Sporting News,* October 21, 1967, p. 7.
10. Stout and Johnson, *Red Sox Century,* p. 339.
11. Dan Osinski interview: March 12, 2006.
12. Sal Maglie and Robert Boyle, "Baseball Is a Tough Business," *Sports Illustrated.* April 15, 1968.
13. George Scott interview: January 24, 2006.
14. Bill Ballou, "Williams Lit the Fire for Sox," *Worcester Telegram & Gazette,* November 10, 2006.
15. Hodding Carter III interview: February 6, 2009.
16. Leroy Morganti, "Scott Says His Day Is 'Greatest,'" *Delta Democrat-Times,* November 17, 1967, p.1.

17. Andrew Jackson, "High School Coaches Praise George Scott," *The Tiger Gazette*, December 1967, p. 4.

Chapter 9

1. Jerry Nason, "Dick Employs Psych Tactics," *Boston Globe*, April 10, 1968, p. 63.
2. Larry Claflin, "More Hurling Tops Bosox '68 Needs," *The Sporting News*, October 28, 1967, p. 16.
3. Williams and Plaschke, *No More Mr. Nice Guy*, p. 99.
4. George Scott interview: October 15, 2007.
5. Williams and Plaschke, *No More Mr. Nice Guy*, p. 108.
6. Ibid., p. 110.
7. John Crittenden, "Worries Gone — Harrelson Easy Winner on Links," *The Sporting News*, March 9, 1968, p. 21.
8. Clif Keane, "Ellsworth Lacks Stuff But Not Mound Savvy," *Boston Globe*, March 15, 1968, p. 25.
9. Will McDonough, "Scott at Playing Weight, Predicts His Best Year," *Boston Globe*, March 26, 1968, p. 28.
10. Clif Keane, "Angry Tony C. Blasts Williams," *Boston Globe,* April 4, 1968, p. 27.
11. Dick Williams, "What Williams Expects and Will Tell His Players at Meeting," *Boston Globe*, March 31, 1968, p. 51.
12. Larry Claflin, "Scott a Terror with Light Bat," *The Sporting News*, March 30, 1968, p. 9.
13. Will McDonough, "Scott Finds That a Little Swing Goes a Long Way With the Boss," *Boston Globe*, April 7, 1968.
14. Bobby Doerr interview: October 16, 2006.
15. Nason, "Dick Employs Psych Tactics."
16. Will McDonough, "Yaz, Baby, You Can Do It All...," *Boston Globe,* April 11, 1968, p. 49.
17. Harold Kaese, "Slump Shakes Scott's Poise," *Boston Globe*, May 3, 1968, p. 29.
18. Clif Keane, "Why Did Red Sox Sell Wyatt?" *Boston Globe*, May 19, 1968, p. 56.
19. Clif Keane, "Sox Manager's Many Moods," *Boston Globe*, May 21, 1968, p. 29.
20. Harold Kaese, "Sox Could Use Howard's Bat," *Boston Globe,* May 23, 1968, p. 53.
21. Ray Fitzgerald, "'Just Need a Few Hits,' Scotty Assures Analysts," *Boston Globe*, May 31, 1968, p. 24.
22. George Scott interview: May 7, 2006.
23. Bob Sales, "Scott Staying 'Hot' By Swapping Gloves," *Boston Globe,* June 5, 1968, p. 38.
24. Ibid.
25. Clif Keane, "Scott Returns Against Lefty Brunet," *Boston Globe*, June 12, 1968, p. 57.
26. Bob Sales, "No Flag for Sox Without Scott," *Boston Globe*, June 18, 1968, p. 41.
27. Clif Keane, "'Just Let Me Hit'— Scott," *Boston Globe*, June 20, 1968, p. 45.
28. George Scott interview: May 7, 2006.
29. Neil Singelais, "Slumping Scott Benched; Jones Gets 1b Chance," *Boston Globe,* July 1, 1968, p. 25.
30. Harold Kaese, "Quotes in 'Life' Probably Valid," *Boston Globe*, August 8, 1968, p. 25.
31. Leonard Shecter, "Baseball: Great American Myth," *Life Magazine*, August 9, 1968.
32. George Langford, "Owens Toils for A. L. as 'Watchdog,'" *Chicago Tribune*, July 17, 1968, p. C2.
33. Clif Keane, "Cleveland Likes Scott, Might Trade Catcher," *Boston Globe*, August 21, 1968, p. 52.
34. George Scott interview: January 23, 2006.
35. Harold Kaese, "Scott Treated Badly by Sox," *Boston Globe*, August 25, 1968, p. 55.
36. Clif Keane, "Scott Boiling at Treatment," *Boston Globe,* August 27, 1968, p. 27.
37. Neil Singelais, "Scott Demands Sox Trade Him," *Boston Globe*, September 9, 1968, p. 27.
38. Ibid.
39. Clif Keane, "Sox Troubles Grow: Yaz, Williams Feud," *Boston Globe,* September 13, 1968, p. 26.

40. Tim Horgan, "Scotty Gets to Play First, but for Whom?" *Boston Herald-Traveler,* September 10, 1968, p. 37.
41. Tim Horgan, "Hawk: Scott Wrong, Dick Right; Club Sore at Feud Talk," *Boston Herald-Traveler,* September 19, 1968, p. 41.
42. George Scott interview: January 21, 2006.

Chapter 10

1. Larry Claflin, "Great Scott! What Will Bosox Do With Poor George?" *The Sporting News,* September 21, 1968, p. 29.
2. "Sox to Protect Scott," *Boston Globe,* October 10, 1968, p. 51.
3. Bob Sales, "Yankees to Name Howard to Coaching Staff Today," *Boston Globe,* October 22, 1968, p. 35.
4. Gordon Edes, "Harper Finally at Home," *Boston Globe,* February 1, 2006. This article is based on an interview with former Red Sox player and coach Tommy Harper, who spoke about racist issues in the '60s with the Cincinnati Reds. It was Reds teammate Frank Robinson, facing the "same outrages" as Harper "that tested Robinson's mettle and manhood," who confronted the club to convince them to change.
5. Jim Mudcat Grant interview: January 22, 2009.
6. George Scott interview: January 23, 2006.
7. Clif Keane, "Scott Solemn, Feels Sure at 3d," *Boston Globe,* March 3, 1969, p. 18.
8. Larry Claflin, "Tony C's First Homer Since '67: What a Tonic for the Red Sox!" *The Sporting News,* April 12, 1969, p. 9.
9. Clif Keane, "Jones HR Wins in 11th, 4–2," *Boston Globe,* June 7, 1969, p. 19.
10. Clif Keane, "Sox Eye A's Catcher Roof," *Boston Globe,* June 14, 1969, p. 8.
11. Clif Keane, "Williams Angry, Sox Glum, Conigliaro Benched," *Boston Globe,* June 30, 1969, p. 17.
12. Ray Fitzgerald, "Mates Solidly Support Conig," *Boston Globe,* July 7, 1969, p. 21.
13. Williams and Plaschke, *No More Mr. Nice Guy,* p. 114.
14. Clif Keane, "Is Dick Williams on Way Out?" *Boston Globe,* July 20, 1969, p. 88.
15. Clif Keane, "Other Teams Eye Scott," *Boston Globe,* September 21, 1969, p. 75.
16. Clif Keane, "Players Divided Over Williams," *Boston Globe,* September 24, 1969, p. 1.

Chapter 11

1. Larry Claflin, "Awake or Asleep Scott Swinging Bat as Red Sox Terror," *The Sporting News,* April 11, 1970, p. 33.
2. Larry Claflin, "Yaz and Yawkey's Pets to Stay, Kasko Says," *The Sporting News,* October 18, 1969, p. 35.
3. Thomas Van Hyning, *The Santurce Crabbers* (Jefferson, NC: McFarland, 1995).
4. Merv Rettenmund interview: June 4, 2010.
5. Will McDonough, "Scott Batting Program—'I'll Just Do It My Way,'" *Boston Globe,* March 16, 1970, p. 24.
6. Ray Fitzgerald, "Scott on His Own At Bat—and Happy," *Boston Globe,* February 27, 1970, p. 27.
7. Claflin, "Awake or Asleep."
8. Ibid.
9. Larry Claflin, "How Good Can Reg Be? Bosox Ask." *The Sporting News.* March 31, 1970. P. 10.
10. Ray Fitzgerald, "Sox Display Flag Potential," *Boston Globe,* March 17, 1970, p. 29.
11. Claflin, "Awake or Asleep."
12. Ray Fitzgerald, "Culp Difference in Sox About-face," *Boston Globe,* June 3, 1970, p. 53.
13. Neil Singelais, "Boo If You Must, Yaz Will Take Hub," *Boston Globe,* June 30, 1970, p. 41.
14. George Scott interview: October 10, 2007.
15. "Scott Out 3 Weeks with Broken Hand," *Boston Globe,* July 19, 1970, p.79.

16. Clif Keane, "Add Scott to the Red Sox List of Untouchables," *Boston Globe*, September 16, 1970, p.70.

17. Larry Claflin, "'Am I Next to Go?' Andrews Wonders," *The Sporting News*, November 7, 1970, p. 47.

18. Larry Claflin, "Will Deals Buttress Porous Defense?" *The Sporting News*, February 27, 1971, p. 33

19. George Scott interview: July 1, 2010.

20. Larry Claflin, "Operation Big Switch — Will It Boost the Red Sox?" *The Sporting News*, February 13, 1971, p. 38.

21. Will McDonough, "Fiore, Petrocelli Belt Long Homers," *Boston Globe*, March 15, 1971, p. 20.

22. Will McDonough, "Scott, Fiore Scramble for 1st," *Boston Globe*, March 17, 1971, p. 35.

23. George Scott interview: April, 2006.

24. Neil Singelais, "Conigliaro, Lahoud Kiss and Make Up,." *Boston Globe*, April 1, 1971, p. 43.

25. Clif Keane, "Stung by Barb, Scotty Promises King-Sized 'Tater,'" *Boston Globe*, April 12, 1971, p. 23.

26. George Scott interview: January 21, 2006.

27. Neil Singelais, "In Field or At Bat, Scott's 'Where It's At,'" *Boston Globe*, May 18, 1971, p. 29.

28. Clif Keane, "Umpire Leaves Scott with Bad Taste at Plate," *Boston Globe*,. May 24, 1971, p. 21.

29. Ray Fitzgerald, "Pitching Woes Give Sox That Flat Look," *Boston Globe*, June 1, 1971, p. 27.

30. George Scott interview: October 10, 2007.

31. Neil Singelais, "All's Well With Yaz and That's Good News," *Boston Globe*, July 1, 1971, p. 51.

32. Clif Keane, "Benched Yaz Claims He's Over-concentrating," *Boston Globe*, August 1, 1971, p. 77.

33. Francis Rosa, "Red Sox Lacking 'Hit-It-to-Me' Guys," *Boston Globe*, September 2, 1971, p. 27.

34. "'I Was Prepared,' Says New Brewer Scott," *Boston Globe*, October 11, 1971, p. 55.

Chapter 12

1. Larry Whiteside, "Scott Aiming to be Brewer Bomber," *The Sporting News*, November 27, 1971, p. 52.

2. Larry Claflin, "Yastrzemski and Scott," *The Sporting News*, November 30, 1971, p. 40.

3. Larry Whiteside, "Scott Aiming to be Brewer Bomber," *The Sporting News*, November 27, 1971, p. 52.

4. Larry Whiteside, "Bristol Sees Davis as a Big Plus on Defense," *The Sporting News*, December 18, 1971, p. 58.

5. Larry Whiteside, "Adjustment Over, Scott Blooming as Brewer," *The Sporting News*, July 22, 1972, p. 18. Whiteside was a preeminent black journalist starting out at a time when black writers were neither fashionable nor well-accepted. He began his career with the *Kansas City Kansan* in 1959, then moved on to the *Milwaukee Journal* where he covered the Braves, then the Brewers, and numerous civil rights matters occurring at the time. From there he went to Boston in 1973 to join the *Boston Globe* staff, becoming the only black journalist covering major league baseball for a major newspaper. He was distinguished by his peers, receiving a lifetime achievement award in 1999 by the National Association of Black Journalists. He was honored by the Baseball Writers' Association of America with the 2008 J.G. Taylor Spink Award, for writing excellence, the third African American writer to receive the award.

6. George Scott interview: February 16, 2008.

7. Larry Whiteside, "Adjustment Over, Scott Blooming as Brewer," *The Sporting News*, July 22, 1972, p. 18.

8. Larry Whiteside, "Costly Gesture by Scott," *Milwaukee Journal*, August 31, 1972, p. 13.

9. Larry Whiteside, "Scott, $500 Poorer, Does Slow Brewer Burn," *The Sporting News*, September 16, 1972, p. 23.

10. Larry Whiteside, "Brewer Improvements Seen by Crandall," *Milwaukee Journal*, October 8, 1972, p. 3.

11. Larry Whiteside, "Scott Adjusts to His Job as a Brewmaster," *The Sporting News*, November 25, 1972, p. 53.

12. Tom Flaherty, "George Scott Fired Up for Season," *Milwaukee Journal*, April 1, 1973, p. 9.

13. Lou Chapman, "Hungry Brewers Feasting on May's Home-Run Bat," *The Sporting News*, June 2, 1973, p. 5.

14. Lou Chapman, "No Flag, But Brewers Gained Respect in 1973," *The Sporting News*, September 15, 1973, p. 14.

15. Lou Chapman, "Brewers Back Off, Forget About Scott's Fine," *Milwaukee Journal*, September 29, 1973.

16. Martin Ralbovsky, "Scott Calls Brewer Bluff; Case Closed?" *Milwaukee Journal*, September 10, 1973, p. 15.

17. Tom Flaherty, "Twins Make a Conformist of Colborn," *Milwaukee Journal*, June 1, 1973, p. 18.

18. *The Sporting News*, August 11, 1973, p. 24.

19. Larry Whiteside, "Scott's Slam Completes Sweep," *Milwaukee Journal*, July 30, 1973, p. 8.

20. Ralbovsky, "Scott Calls Brewer Bluff."

Chapter 13

1. Lou Chapman, "Superb Fielding and Hitting Make Scott 'Money' Player," *The Sporting News*, April 20, 1974, p. 7.

2. Lou Chapman, "Brewers' Great Scott Enters Champagne Class," *The Sporting News*, January 12, 1974, p. 30; Lou Chapman, "Brewers Report: Long on Foam, Short on Body," *The Sporting News*, October 4, 1975, p. 17.

3. Ibid.

4. Lou Chapman, "Turn-Around Brewers Turn Deaf Ears to Scott Offers," *The Sporting News*, November 3, 1973, p. 20.

5. George Scott interview: March 23, 2006.

6. Lou Chapman, "Brewers Point the Spotlight at Scott," *The Sporting News*, August 24, 1974, p. 23.

7. Lou Chapman, "Rudi Only New Face Among A. L. Defense Elite," *The Sporting News*, November 23, 1974, p. 52; "Crowd Pleasers Please Boston Crowd," *Milwaukee Journal*, April 9, 1975, p. 12.

8. George Scott interview: January 24, 2006.

9. Mike Gonring, "Scott Finds Offseason Appetite Not So Fine," *Milwaukee Journal*, March 7, 1975, p. 10.

10. The *Milwaukee Journal* reported Scott's spring statistics as batting .415 on 53 at-bats and 22 base hits. *The Sporting News* data and *Milwaukee Journal* box scores, however, show Scott with 55 at-bats on 22 base hits.

11. "Crowd Pleasers Please Boston Crowd," *Milwaukee Journal*, April 9, 1975, p. 14; Scott later changed the name of his glove to "Black Beauty."

12. George Scott interview: January 24, 2006.

13. Mike Gonring, "Scott Hurts Wise and Self," *Milwaukee Journal*, July 3, 1975, p. 8.

14. Mike Gonring, "Scott Sees Stars Over Baseball Fans' Taste in Balloting," *Milwaukee Journal*, July 13, 1975, p. 1.

15. Bob Wolf, "AL Talks a Good Game, NL Plays a Good One," *Milwaukee Journal*, July 16, 1975, p. 16.

16. Mike Gonring, "All-Stars Find It's Still a National Game," *Milwaukee Journal*, July 16, 1975, p. 13.

17. Lou Chapman, "Seething Pilot Crandall Blasts Brewers," *The Sporting News*, September 13, 1975, p. 16.

18. Ibid.

19. "Scott Top Boomer, Brewers Win," *Milwaukee Journal*, September 25, 1975, p. 18.

Chapter 14

1. "Fred Lynn Was Named the Most Valuable Player," *Los Angeles Times*, February 11, 1976, p. E2.
2. Lou Chapman, "Brewers Shedding No Tears Over Swap Shutout," *The Sporting News*, December 27, 1975, p. 50.
3. Joe McGuff, "Brett's All-Star Omission a Disgrace — Herzog," *The Sporting News*, December 13, 1975, p. 49.
4. "Morning Briefing," *Los Angeles Times*, March 5, 1976, p. D2.
5. Mike Gonring, "Fan of Broberg's? Not George Scott!" *Milwaukee Journal*, May 29, 1976, p. 14.
6. Mike Gonring, "Brewers ... Guess You Had to Be There," *Milwaukee Journal*, May 31, 1976, p. 7.
7. Mike Gonring, "Brewers Show Nothing, Grammas Shows Anger," *Milwaukee Journal*, June 2, 1976, p. 11.
8. Mike Gonring, "Brewers Unload Pedro, Problems," *Milwaukee Journal*, June 11, 1976, p. 12.
9. Lou Chapman, "Irate Boomer Fires Back at Baumer, Grammas," *The Sporting News*, July 17, 1976, p. 16.
10. Mike Gonring, "Playing 1st and Hitting 6th ... George Scott?" *Milwaukee Journal*, June 24, 1976, p. 14.
11. Mike Gonring, "Brewer Carnival Drops 2," *Milwaukee Journal*, June 28, 1976, p. 10.
12. Mike Gonring, "Dark Night for Scott, Brewers," *Milwaukee Journal*, July 3, 1976, p. 13.
13. Terry Shepard, "Shutout Caps Brewer Sweep," *Milwaukee Journal*, July 12, 1976, p. 9.
14. Richard Sandomir, "A Confluence of Coincidence This Weekend in Milwaukee," *New York Times*, July 20, 2007.
15. The games in which George Scott foiled no-hit bids were June 4, 1968, vs. Detroit, in the 6th inning; June 20, 1968, vs. Detroit, in the 7th inning; July 2, 1975, vs. Boston, in the ninth inning; and July 26, 1976, vs. Detroit, in the ninth inning.
16. Lou Chapman, "'I'm Sick of Milwaukee,' Declares Slugger Scott," *The Sporting News*, August 28, 1976, p. 12.
17. Lou Chapman, "Brooks' Long Fielding Award String Broken," *The Sporting News*, December 4, 1976, p. 56.
18. George Scott interview: March, 2006.
19. Murray Chass, "Red Sox Deal Cooper for Scott and Carbo," *New York Times*, December 7, 1976, p. 63.
20. George Scott interview: January, 2006.
21. Larry Whiteside, "Returning Scott Dubs Boston His 'Garden City,'" *The Sporting News*, December 25, 1976, p. 47.
22. "George!" *Black Sports*, September, 1977; varying reports ranged from a contract extension of two to five years, with the most probable being two years.

Chapter 15

1. Lou Chapman, "Housecleaning Gives Brewers Five New Regulars," *The Sporting News*, December 15, 1976, p. 48.
2. Lou Chapman, "Brewers Rap Departed George Scott," *The Sporting News*, March 26, 1977, p. 10.
3. Larry Whiteside, "Rico Happy to Be Red Sox Spare Part," *The Sporting News*, January 29, 1977, p. 34.
4. Larry Whiteside, "The Boomer," *Boston Globe*, April 6, 1977, p. 25.
5. "Phils Favored in NL," *Delta Democrat-Times*, March 6, 1977, p. 14.
6. Larry Whiteside, "Scott Down 10 lbs., Now Has 10 to Go," *Boston Globe*, March 21, 1977, p. 18.
7. Bob Ryan, "Fans Don't Bug Scott, but Young Lefty Does," *Boston Globe*, April 27, 1977, p. 58.
8. Larry Whiteside, "Cooper Has No Axe to Grind," *Boston Globe*, May 22, 1977, p. 101.

9. Lyle Spatz, ed., *The SABR Baseball List & Record Book* (New York: Scribner Publishing, 2007); The record of 11 home runs by both teams in a game has since been broken by the White Sox and Tigers in 1995, and again in 2002 by the same two teams, both times with 12 homers.
10. Lou Chapman, "Rodriguez Leaves Brewer Doghouse With a Rush," *The Sporting News*, June 11, 1977, p. 15.
11. Ray Fitzgerald, "Complaining's Name of Sox Fan's Game — But Why Pick on Scott?" *Boston Globe*, June 7, 1977, p. 27.
12. Ray Fitzgerald, "Martin: 'We Should Have Played Our Fielders in the Screen,'" *Boston Globe*, June 20, 1977, p. 18.
13. Larry Whiteside, "Boston Leaves Yankees with a Severe Case of Shell-Sox," *Boston Globe*, June 20, 1977, p. 26.
14. Bob Ryan, "Tiant Wins 2-hitter, 7–0, but Scott Steals Show," *Boston Globe*, June 22, 1977, p. 59.
15. Larry Whiteside, "Third Battle of Bull Run," *Boston Globe*, June 22, 1977, p. 21.
16. Larry Whiteside, "Zimmer Looks at the Bright Side," *Boston Globe*, June 26, 1977, p. 84.
17. Francis Rosa, "Scott Robbed Three Times," *Boston Globe*, July 4, 1977, p. 30.
18. Alan Richman, "AL: No One to Fear But Fans Themselves," *Boston Globe*, July 20, 1977, p. 21.
19. Ray Fitzgerald, "Is It Spaceman's Last Ride?" *Boston Globe*, July 25, 1977, p. 17.
20. Scott hit a ball in the bottom of the 7th off Dyar Miller of the California Angels on August 10, 1977, in Fenway Park, "that all reasonable men except the four umpires" agreed was a home run, wrote the *Boston Globe*'s Jack Craig; but the umpires ruled that it remained "in play." The ball struck the center field wall to the right of the yellow vertical line designating *out-of-play* [home run] territory. Second base umpire Russ Goetz, however, called the ball in-play. Scott shouted at Goetz as he rounded second twirling his arm symbolizing it was a homer. He easily legged out a triple but might have had an inside-the-park home run if he had not slowed his gait while protesting to the umpire.

Chapter 16

1. Bob Ryan, "Scott Earns his Keep," *Boston Globe*, May 22, 1978, p. 22.
2. Leigh Montville, "Williams Casts a Shadow, But Zimmer Not Worried," *Boston Globe*, March 7, 1978, p. 27.
3. Whiteside, Larry. "Poloni Shelled as Peskys Tumble, 26–5," *Boston Globe*, March 8, 1978, p. 23.
4. Bill Reynolds, *'78: The Boston Red Sox, A Historic Game, and a Divided City* (New York: New American Library, 2009).
5. Bob Ryan, "Scott Earns His Keep," *Boston Globe*, May 20, 1978, p. 22.
6. Larry Whiteside, "Scott Out for Three Weeks," *Boston Globe*, May 18, 1978, p. 42.
7. Steve Marantz, "George Scott: Despite Bricks and Bats, He Always Bounces Back," *Boston Globe*, August 1, 1978, p. 23.
8. Peter Gammons, "Drago Starts It, Scott Finishes Off Mariners, 10–5," *Boston Globe*, August 30, 1978, p. 21.
9. Ibid.
10. Stout and Johnson, *Red Sox Century*.
11. George Scott interview: April 2006.

Chapter 17

1. William Nack, "George Scott Is Alive and Well and Playing in Mexico City," *Sports Illustrated*, August 17, 1981, p. 44.
2. Larry Whiteside, "Scott Striving for Comeback with Red Sox," *The Sporting News*, January 13, 1979, p. 32.
3. Larry Whiteside, "Slimmed-down Scott Vows to Make Up for Bad Year," *The Sporting News*, April 1, 1979, p. 6.

4. Larry Whiteside, "Scott (0–25) Benched, Yaz Moves to First Base," *Boston Globe*, May 26, 1979, p. 21.

5. George Scott interview: October 2007.

6. Sid Bordman, "Royals Obtain Boston's Scott," *Kansas City Times*, June 14, 1979, p. 7E.

7. Dick Young, "Young Ideas," *The Sporting News*, June 30, 1979, p. 54.

8. Mike McKenzie, "It's a Battle Royal for Regular First Base Job," *Kansas City Times*, June 27, 1979, p. 5C.

9. Sid Bordman, "Despite Slump, Herzog Won't Change," *Kansas City Star*, July 15, 1979, p. 9S.

10. George Scott interview: March 2006.

11. Whitey Herzog interview: May 25 and 31, 2007.

12. Fred Patek interview: January 2008.

13. Phil Pepe, "Tragedy, Discontent Mark Yanks' Comedown Season," *The Sporting News*, October 20, 1979, p. 41.

14. Bruce Markusen, "Card Corner: George Scott," *The Hardball Times*, May 28, 2010.

15. "Bunts and Boots," *The Sporting News*, April 12, 1980, p. 46.

16. Thomas Boswell, "Losing It: Careers Fall Like Autumn Leaves," *Washington Post*, September 26, 1980, p. D1.

17. George Scott interview: March 2006.

18. Ibid.

19. Gene Martin interview: February 28, 2008.

20. George Scott interview: March 2006.

21. *The Sporting News* article of April 24, 1982, and former teammates' interviews support the view that Scott had a run-in with Doug Ault that led to his dismissal. George Scott, however, does not recall a specific incident with Ault; he does remember objecting to player drinking on the bus, and being let go in the spring by the Tigers. Scott believes his problems were with pitching coach Dick Pole, who he fired for "undermining" him, he alleges, with Mexico City's management.

22. Michael Madden, "He Is Still Trying to Make a Living in Baseball; But Business Isn't Booming for the Boomer; Now Pitching, Scott," *Boston Globe*, March 23, 1986.

23. Kevin Paul Dupont, "George Scott Is Managing in a Small-Time League, Hoping It'll Be … Boomer's Showcase," *Boston Globe*, July 24, 1987, p. 45.

24. Ibid.

25. Jay Acton interview: May 15, 2007.

26. Stan Block interview: October 8, 2008.

27. Ibid.

28. Edsel Neal interview: September 23, 2008.

29. George Scott interview: February 2008.

30. Ibid.

31. Mike Babcock interview: April 29, 2008.

32. Ibid.

33. Jonathan Fleisig interview: October 28, 2008.

34. Nick Cafardo, "Baseball Notes: Fielding Error," *Boston Globe*, April 15, 2007, p. C8.

35. Bob Ryan, "Old-timers Keep the Spirit Fresh," *Boston Globe*, May 20, 1990, p. 52.

Bibliography

Books

Anderson, Henry Clay. *Separate, but Equal: Images from the Segregated South*. Cambridge, MA: Perseus, 2002.

Baldassaro, Lawrence, and Richard A. Johnson. *The American Game: Baseball and Ethnicity*. Carbondale, IL: Southern Illinois University Press, 2002.

Bryant, Howard. *Shutout: A Story of Race and Baseball in Boston*. New York: Routledge, 2002.

Cafardo, Nick. *Boston Red Sox: Yesterday and Today*. Akron: West Side Publishing, 2007.

Cisneros, Pedro Treto. *The Mexican League*. Jefferson, NC: McFarland, 2002.

Cobb, James C. *The Most Southern Place on Earth: The Mississippi Delta and the Roots of Regional Identity*. New York: Oxford University Press, 1992.

Coleman, Ken, and Dan Valenti. *The Impossible Dream Remembered: The 1967 Red Sox*. Lexington, MA: Stephen Greene Press, 1987.

Dickson, Paul. *Baseball's Greatest Quotations*. New York: First Harper Perennial, 1992.

_____. *Baseball's Greatest Quotations: An Illustrated Treasury of Baseball Quotations and Historical Lore*. New York: Harper Collins, 2008.

Gentile, Derek. *The Complete Boston Red Sox*. New York: Black Dog & Leventhal, 2004.

Gillette, Gary, and Pete Palmer, eds. *The Ultimate Red Sox Companion*. Hingham, MA: Maple Street Press, 2007.

Golenbock, Peter. *Red Sox Nation*. Chicago: Triumph, 2005.

Grant, Jim Mudcat, with Tom Sabellico and Pat O'Brien. *The Black Aces*. New York: Aventine Press, 2007.

Jacks, Beth Boswell. *Grit, Guts & Baseball*. Cleveland, MS: Lee Sanford, 1996.

James, Bill. *The Bill James Guide to Baseball Managers*. New York: Scribner, 1997.

_____. *The New Bill James Historical Baseball Abstract*. New York: Free Press, 2001.

Johnson, Lloyd, and Miles Wolff. *The Encyclopedia of Minor League Baseball*. 2nd ed. Durham, NC: Baseball America, 1997.

Keating, Peter. *Dingers*. New York: ESPN Books, 2006.

Koppett, Leonard. *The Man in the Dugout*. New York: Crown, 1993.

Lowry, Philip. *Green Cathedrals*. New York: Walker, 2006.

Neft, David S., and Richard M. Cohen. *The World Series*. New York: St. Martin's, 1990.

Nowlin, Bill. *Day by Day with the Boston Red Sox*. Cambridge, MA: Rounder, 2006.

_____. *Red Sox Threads*. Burlington, MA: Rounder, 2008.

Nowlin, Bill and Dan Desrochers, eds. *The 1967 Impossible Dream Red Sox*. Burlington, MA: Rounder, 2007.

Nowlin, Bill and Jim Prime. *The Boston Red Sox World Series Encyclopedia*. Burlington, MA: Rounder, 2008.

Petrocelli, Rico, and Chaz Scoggins. *Rico Petrocelli's Tales from the Impossible Dream Red Sox*. Champaign, IL: Sports Publishing, 2007.

Reynolds, Bill. *'78: The Boston Red Sox, a Historic Game, and a Divided City*. New York: New American Library, 2009.

278 Bibliography

Riley, Dan, ed. *The Red Sox Reader*. Boston: Houghton Mifflin, 1991.
Siwoff, Seymour. *The Elias Book of Baseball Records*. New York: Seymour Siwoff, 2008.
Smith, Frank E., and Audrey Warren. *Mississippians All*. New Orleans: Pelican, 1968.
Snyder, John. *Red Sox Journal*. Cincinnati: Emmis, 2006.
Spatz, Lyle, ed. *The SABR Baseball List & Record Book*. New York: Scribner, 2007.
Stout, Glenn, and Richard A. Johnson. *Red Sox Century*. Boston: Houghton Mifflin, 2004.
Sumner, Benjamin Barrett. *Minor League Baseball Standings*. Jefferson, NC: McFarland, 2000.
Thorn, John, and Pete Palmer. *Total Baseball*. 4th ed. New York: Penguin, 1995.
Van Hyning, Thomas. *The Santurce Crabbers: Sixty Seasons of Puerto Rican Winter League Baseball*. Jefferson, NC: McFarland, 1999.
Waldron, Ann. *Hodding Carter: The Reconstruction of a Racist*. Chapel Hill, NC: Algonquin, 1993.
Walton, Anthony. *Mississippi: An American Journey*. New York: Vintage, 1966.
Williams, Dick, and Bill Plaschke. *No More Mr. Nice Guy: A Life of Hardball*. San Diego: Harcourt Brace Jovanovich, 1990.
Wolff, Miles, and David Kemp. *The History of Independent Baseball Leagues 1993–2002*. Sioux Falls, SD: Mariah Press, 2003.
Zimmer, Don, and Bill Madden. *Zim: A Baseball Life*. New York: Total Sports Illustrated, 2001.

Articles

Adams, Doug. "The Boomer and Me." *Life in the Delta,* July 2007.
Ahern, John. "Jubilant Scott Quits Fishing." *Boston Globe,* April 3, 1967.
_____. "Scott Plays RF, Stirs Trade Talk." *Boston Globe,* March 22, 1967.
Anderson, Ron. "George Scott." In *The 1967 Impossible Dream Red Sox*, edited by Bill Nowlin and Dan Desrochers, 100–107. Burlington, MA: Rounder, 2007.
Annotico, Richard. "The Mississippi Delta: The Race War and Italians." *The Annotico Report,* January 14, 2007.
Ariff, Mitch. "George Scott Singing 'Down Mexico Way.'" *Delta Democrat-Times,* September 29, 1982.
Birtwell, Roger. "Scott Hopes Slump Over." *Boston Globe,* September 20, 1967.
_____. "Sidearm Pitcher Saved Scott for Sox." *Boston Globe,* May 23, 1966.
_____. "What Can Scott Bring Red Sox?" *Boston Globe,* September 5, 1968.
"Brewers George Scott Thinks He's a Superstar." *Chicago Defender,* August 18, 1973.
Carr, John. "Sox Had Desire." *Delta Democrat-Times,* November 1, 1967.
Chapman, Lou. "Brewers and Scott Unhappy, Both Ready to Part Company." *The Sporting News,* November 6, 1976.
_____. "Brewers Back Off, Forget About Scott's Fine." *The Sporting News,* September 29, 1973.
_____. "Brewers Disagree as Scott Downgrades Their Bullpen." *The Sporting News,* June 22, 1974.
_____. "Brewers' Fadeout Doesn't Include Slugger Scott." *The Sporting News,* September 20, 1975.
_____. "Brewers' Great Scott Enters Champagne Class." *The Sporting News,* January 12, 1974.
_____. "Brewers Point the Spotlight at Scott." *The Sporting News,* August 24, 1974.
_____. "Brewers Rap Departed George Scott." *The Sporting News,* March 26, 1977.
_____. "Chesty Scott Accepts New Role as No. 2 on Brewers." *The Sporting News,* March 29, 1975.
_____. "'Great,' Beams Scott Over Flop of Swap Talks." *The Sporting News,* January 17, 1976.
_____. "'I'm Sick of Milwaukee,' Declares Slugger Scott." *The Sporting News,* August 28, 1976.
_____. "Irate Boomer Fires Back at Baumer, Grammas." *The Sporting News,* July 17, 1976.
_____. "Judge Scott Tossing Book at Enemies of Brewer Court." *The Sporting News,* May 31, 1975.
_____. "Scott: Best I Don't Stay with Brewers." *The Sporting News,* September 8, 1973.
_____. "Scott Fires Opening Salvo in Bid for $120,000 Pact." *The Sporting News,* December 22, 1973.
_____. "Scott Stays Aloft as Brewers Go Flat." *The Sporting News,* August 9, 1975.
_____. "Superb Fielding and Hitting Make Scott 'Money Player.'" *The Sporting News,* April 20, 1974.

_____. "Unhappy Scott Makes Rivals Feel Worse." *The Sporting News,* August 18, 1973.

Claflin, Larry. "Awake or Asleep, Scott Swinging Bat as Red Sox Terror." *The Sporting News,* April 11, 1970.

_____. "Big or Small, A.L. Parks Look Easy to BoSox Bombshell Scott." *The Sporting News,* May 21, 1966.

_____. "In Boston Book, Dick Williams Still Rides a White Charger." *The Sporting News,* October 11, 1969.

_____. "Red Sox Boss Wins Weighty Argument with Slugger Scott." *The Sporting News,* September 2, 1967.

_____. "Scott a Terror with Light Bat." *The Sporting News,* March 30, 1968.

Collins, H.J. "'Boomer' Here for the Love of the Game." *Lynn Item,* June 6, 1996.

Daley, Arthur. "Great Scott!" *New York Times,* July 7, 1966.

Dearmond, Mike. "Scott Wins Game, Fans with Homer." *Kansas City Times,* August 1, 1979.

Distel, Dave. "George Scott's Boyhood: It's Right There in Black and White." *Los Angeles Times,* June 9, 1973.

Duerson, Adam. "George Scott." *Sports Illustrated,* July 12, 2004.

Dupont, Kevin Paul. "George Scott Is Managing in a Small-Time League, Hoping It'll Be ... Boomer's Showcase." *Boston Globe,* July 24, 1987.

Finnigan, Bob. "Great Scott, What a Game!" *Boston Globe,* September 22, 1977.

_____. "Scott Drops Out." *Quincy Patriot Ledger,* September 7, 1977.

Fitzgerald, Ray. "Complaining's Name of Sox Fans' Game — But Why Pick on Scott?" *Boston Globe,* June 7, 1977.

_____. "Great Scott! A Raise, Yet!" *Boston Globe,* February 28, 1969.

_____. "Scott: From a Zero to a Hero with One Swing of the Bat." *Boston Globe,* June 20, 1978.

_____. "Should Scott Try Catching?" *Boston Globe,* March 25, 1967.

_____. "Slugger Scott Turns Artist." *Boston Globe,* May 15, 1967.

_____. "Switching Tough on Scott." *Boston Globe,* March 13, 1969.

Flaherty, Tom. "Injured Scott Proves Painful to A's." *Milwaukee Journal,* August 16, 1975.

Frau, Miguel. "Invincible Cuellar? Scott Has to Laugh." *The Sporting News,* December 13, 1969.

Gammons, Peter. "Scott's Game — Are They?" *Boston Globe,* July 23, 1985.

"George!" *Black Sports,* September 1977.

"George Scott Happy with Lowly Brewers." *Los Angeles Times,* May 6, 1972.

"George Scott Involved in BoSox, Brewer Trade." *Delta Democrat-Times,* October 11, 1971.

"George Scott Seen as Key Man." *Delta Democrat-Times,* March 29, 1972.

Gonring, Mike. "Fan of Broberg's? Not George Scott!" *Milwaukee Journal,* May 29, 1976.

_____. "Great Scott! Brewers Wheeling, Dealing." *Milwaukee Journal,* December 7, 1976.

_____. "Playing 1st and Hitting 6th ... George Scott?" *Milwaukee Journal,* June 24, 1976.

_____. "Scott Finds Offseason Appetite Not So Fine." *Milwaukee Journal,* March 3, 1975.

_____. "Scott Hot, Brewers Not." *Milwaukee Journal,* May 9, 1975.

_____. "Scott Sees Stars Over Baseball Fans' Taste in Balloting." *Milwaukee Journal,* July 13, 1975.

_____. "Scott Thanks God, Selig." *Milwaukee Journal,* March 24, 1976.

_____. "Scott's Gold Glove Tough on Hitters." *Milwaukee Journal,* March 26, 1975.

_____. "Scott's Life More Than a Game." *Milwaukee Journal,* August 31, 1975.

Greene, Daisy. "An Interview with Dr. Noble R. Frisby." *Mississippi Department of Archives and History and the Washington County Library System Oral History Project: Greenville and Vicinity,* April 28, 1977.

Halloran, Paul. "Great Scott!" *Lynn Item,* March 8, 1996.

Herbers, John. "A Different Dixie; Few but Sturdy Threads Tie New South to the Old." *New York Times,* March 6, 1988.

Hurwitz, Hy. "Red Sox Rookie Scott Refuses to Be Second Best." *Boston Globe,* April 10, 1966.

Jackson, Andrew. "High School Coaches Praise George Scott." *Tiger Gazette,* December, 1967.

Kaese, Harold. "Is Yawkey Back of Scott Shift?" *Boston Globe,* March 24, 1967.

_____. "Scott Treated Badly by Sox." *Boston Globe,* August 25, 1968.

Keane, Clif. "Benched Scott Feels Low, Pleads for Help." *Boston Globe,* July 19, 1966.

_____. "Just Let Me Hit — Scott." *Boston Globe,* June 20, 1968.

_____. "Scott Boiling at Treatment." *Boston Globe,* August 27, 1968.

_____. "Scott Spotlights Hitting Success with Golden Smiles." *Boston Globe,* March 14, 1969.

_____. "Scott Will Get Better 'n Better." *Boston Globe,* May 10, 1966.

Krider, Dave. "Legends of HS Football: Willie Richardson." NFLHS.com, 2002.

Lamb, Kevin. "Lack of Support Cuts Scott's Production." *Milwaukee Journal,* September 4, 1974.

Livingstone, Seth. "Lynn Has the Mad Dogs, and George Scott, Too." *Quincy Patriot Ledger,* August 5, 1998.

Madden, Michael. "He Is Still Trying to Make a Living in Baseball; but Business Isn't Booming for the Boomer; Now Pitching, Scott." *Boston Globe,* March 23, 1986.

_____. "The Priceless Now Has a Price." *The Sporting News,* June 2, 1986.

Marantz, Steve. "Despite Bricks and Bats, He Always Bounces Back." *Boston Globe,* August 1, 1978.

Markus, Robert. "Aaron Inspiration to Brewers' Scott." *The Sporting News,* April 3, 1976.

McCarthy, Jack. "Cards' Brock, Flood Remember 'Boomer.'" *Boston Herald-Traveler,* August 31, 1967.

McDonough, Will. "Scott at Playing Weight, Predicts His Best Year." *Boston Globe,* March 26, 1968.

_____. "Scott Batting Program: I'll Just Do It My Way." *Boston Globe,* March 16, 1970.

_____. "Scott Finds That a Little Swing Goes a Long Way with the Boss." *Boston Globe,* April 7, 1968.

_____. "Scott Sure Hits Will Come." *Boston Globe,* April 25, 1970.

_____. "Scott's Dreams: Be a Mays, Cash for Ma." *Boston Globe,* May 10, 1966.

_____. "Trials and Tribulations of George Scott." *Boston Globe,* April 21, 1977.

_____. "Williams Praises Scott's 3b Play." *Boston Globe,* March 31, 1969.

_____. "Williams Shift Rankles Scott." *Boston Globe,* March 22, 1967.

McHugh, Eric. "Inclusiveness Milestone Reached with '67 Team." *Quincy Patriot Ledger,* August 7, 1967.

Megliola, Lenny. "Boomer's Lament.," *Boston Sports Review,* July 2006.

Monahan, D. Leo. "The Trouble with Scott." *Boston Globe,* August 1, 1978.

Montville, Leigh. "Boots Bug Boomer." *Boston Globe,* July 28, 1977.

_____. "Seventh? How Could They Do It?" *Boston Globe,* September 8, 1977.

Murphy, Mark. "New Dogs, Old Tricks Manager George Scott Won't Stand for Bush League Attitudes." *Boston Herald,* June 23, 1996.

Murray, Chass. "Scott, Jackson Key Yanks' Rout of Royals." *New York Times,* September 1, 1979.

Nack, William. "George Scott Is Alive and Well and Playing in Mexico City." *Sports Illustrated,* August 17, 1981.

Newhall, Jeff. "The Boomer Is Back with More 'Dogs.'" *Lynn Item,* May 22, 1998.

Ortiz, Carlos. "Scott Grates After Royals Waive Him." *Boston Globe,* August 18, 1979.

Peters, Gil. "Scott Beats His Own Drum as AL Player of Year." *Los Angeles Times,* February 12, 1976.

Petraglia, Mike. "Where Have You Gone, George Scott?" *Boston Red Sox News,* January 18, 2002.

Pierce, Charles. "The Dead Zone." In *Red Sox Century,* by Glenn Stout and Richard A. Johnson. Boston: Houghton Mifflin, 2004.

Post, Paul. "The Boomer." *Sports Collectors Digest,* August 1, 1997.

Powers, Scott. "The St. Louis Cardinals of the Sixties and Their Effect on Black/White Relations in St. Louis." www.SABR.org.

"A Quick Chat with ESPN's Chris Berman." *Beyond Robson.com.* March 2, 2008.

Ralbovsky, Martin. "Scott Calls Brewer Bluff; Case Closed?" *Milwaukee Journal,* September 10, 1973.

Reynolds, Bill. "Red Sox Crossing the Color Line Even More." *Providence Journal,* September 11, 2000.

Roberts, Ernie. "Scott Keeps Pace with Foxx's Homer Pace." *Boston Globe,* July 16, 1977.

Rosa, Francis. "Scott: 'We Need to Win a Couple—and We Will.'" *Boston Globe,* July 3, 1977.

Ryan, Bob. "Scott Earns His Keep." *Boston Globe,* May 20, 1978.

_____. "Scott Thumbs Down on Seventh Up." *Boston Globe,* September 7, 1977.

_____. "Tiant Wins 2-Hitter, 7–0, but Scott Steals the Show." *Boston Globe,* June 22, 1977.

Sales, Bob. "No Flag for Sox Without Scott." *Boston Globe,* June 18, 1968.

_____. "Scott Staying 'Hot' by Swapping Gloves." *Boston Globe,* June 5, 1968.

_____. "Scott Wants to Play Baseball — If Not Here, Somewhere Else." *Boston Globe,* July 27, 1968.

_____. "What Two-for-Four Will Do, Scott Happy, Relaxed at .134." *Boston Globe,* May 16, 1968.

Scott, George. "Beating That Stanky Is Just Great Baby." *Boston Herald-Traveler,* August 28, 1967.

_____. "Stanky Makes Him Just Play Harder." *Boston Herald-Traveler,* August 27, 1967.

"Scott Left Off UPI All-Star Team." *Milwaukee Journal,* October 10, 1975.

"Scott Mum on Reason for Streak." *Boston Globe,* May 19, 1970.

"Scott Top Boomer, Brewers Win." *Milwaukee Journal,* September 25, 1975.

"Scott's Also Proud of His Fielding." *Delta Democrat-Times,* March 21, 1974.

Shecter, Harold. "Baseball: Great American Myth." *Life Magazine,* August 9, 1968.

Singelais, Neil. "Scott Accepts Demotion, Says He'll Get Hot." *Boston Globe,* April 28, 1970.

_____. "Scott Demands Sox Trade Him." *Boston Globe,* September 9, 1968.

_____. "Scott Hard Man to Keep Down.," *Boston Globe,* May 7, 1971.

_____. "Scott Hitless — But Relaxed." *Boston Globe,* September 10, 1968.

_____. "Slumping Scott Puts Sox in Hole." *Boston Globe,* April 21, 1970.

"Sound Off: Former Red Sox Player George 'Boomer' Scott." *Delta Democrat-Times,* January 22, 2009.

Stout, Glenn. "Tryout and Fallout: Race, Jackie Robinson, and the Red Sox." *Massachusetts Historical Review,* 2004.

"Talk: George Scott." *Bullpen, Baseball-Reference.* August 28, 2005.

Treasure, Troy. "Better Late Than Never." *Delta Democrat-Times,* July 25, 2007.

_____. "'Boomer' Scott." *Delta Democrat-Times Magazine; Delta Living,* Spring/Summer 2006.

Walcott, De. "Scott Is 'Not Bitter.'" *Delta Democrat-Times,* October 13, 1971.

"What's Wrong with the Red Sox?" *Sport,* March 1993.

Whiteside, Larry. "Adjustment Over, Scott Blooming as Brewer." *The Sporting News,* July 22, 1972.

_____. "Bat Silent, but Scott Isn't — He Fumes on BoSox Bench." *The Sporting News,* June 16, 1979.

_____. "A Bitter Loss for Red Sox ... a Bitter Twist to Scott Controversy." *Boston Globe,* September 8, 1977.

_____. "The Boomer." *Boston Globe,* April 6, 1977.

_____. "Moody Scott Now Brewer Cheerleader." *The Sporting News,* March 10, 1973.

_____. "Returning Scott Dubs Boston His 'Garden City.'" *The Sporting News,* December 25, 1976.

_____. "Scott Adjusts to His Job as a Brewmaster." *The Sporting News,* November 25, 1972.

_____. "Scott Aiming to be Brewer Bomber." *The Sporting News,* November 27, 1971.

_____. "Scott Booms." *Boston Globe,* March 14, 1978.

_____. "Scott Down 10 lbs., Now Has 10 to Go." *Boston Globe,* March 21, 1977.

_____. "Scott $500 Poorer, Does Slow Brewer Burn." *The Sporting News,* September 16, 1972.

_____. "Scott Lowers Weight, Lifts Sights." *The Sporting News,* January 28, 1978.

_____. "Scott Makes Sure Boston Won't Forget." *Milwaukee Journal,* May 30, 1972.

_____. "Scott Striving for Comeback with Red Sox." *The Sporting News,* January 13, 1979.

_____. "Scott Waiting by Telephone." *Boston Globe,* August 26, 1979.

_____. "Slimmed Down Scott Vows to Make Up for Bad Year." *The Sporting News,* April 21, 1979.

Williams, Dorothy Ann. "Growing Up Black in Segregated Greenville: A Candid Perspective," unpublished manuscript, January 2008.

Interviews

Acton, Jay. May 2007.

Babcock, Mike. April 2008.

Barthell, Joseph. April 2009.

Beene, Fred. October 2008

Block, Stan. October 2008

Bolling, Milt, October 2006.

Boyd, Betty Jo. July 2007.

Brandon, Darrell. May 2010.
Carter, Hodding, III. February 2009 and May 2010.
Davis, E.T. April 2006 and August 2008.
Dennis, Eddie. October 2008.
Digby, George. January 2007.
Doerr, Bobby. October 2006 and June 2007.
Dorsey, Leonia Collins. October 2008
Fleisig, Jonathan. October 2008.
Gardner, Beverly. August 2008.
Gordon, W.C. November 2007.
Gosger, Jim. January 2009.
Grammas, Alex. November 2007.
Grant, Jim Mudcat. January 2009.
Green, Lenny. October 2007.
Harper, Tommy. September 2008.
Hawkins, John. February 2009.
Haynes, Mary. October 2008.
Herzog, Whitey. May 2007.
Jackson, Andrew. April 2006.
Kardamis, Mike. January 2008.
Kelly, Zelma. September 2008.
Martin, Gene. February and March 2008.
McDowell, Sam. August 2008.
Mele, Sam. June 2007.
Moore, Elijah. February 2008.
Neal, Edsel. September 2008.
Osinski, Dan. March 2006.
Patek, Fred. January 2008.
Pattin, Marty. August 2007.
Petrocelli Rico. October 2008.
Prophet, Chuck. December 2007.
Provenza, John. September 2008 and March 2009.
Rettenmund, Merv. June 2010.
Richardson, Gloster. October 2008.
Richardson, Willie. December 2007.
Sanders, Frank. March 2009.
Scott, Beatrice. May 2006.
Scott, Ed. August and October 2006; March 2007.
Scott, George. January 2006 — October 2010.
Scranton, Bob. August 2008.
Segui, Diego. July 2008.
Slack, Bill. June 2009.
Thomas, A.C. April and October 2006.
Thomas, John. September 2008.
Tiant, Luis. January 2009.
Veale, Bob. March 2007.
Viegas, Clark. October 2008.
Ware, William. December 2007.
Wathan, John. May 2007.
Weathersby, Davis. July 2006.
Williams, Dorothy. October 2007.
Young, Robert. January 2009.

Archival Sources

Boston Public Library, Boston, Massachusetts.

Dartmouth College Library, Hanover, New Hampshire.
David A. Howe Public Library, Wellsville, New York.
Forsyth County Public Library, Winston-Salem, North Carolina.
Mississippi Sports Hall of Fame and Museum.
National Baseball Hall of Fame, Cooperstown, New York.
Olean Public Library, Olean, New York.
Saskatoon Public Library, Saskatoon, Saskatchewan, Canada.
William Alexander Percy Memorial Library, Greenville, Mississippi.

Newspapers

Berkshire Eagle
Boston Globe
Boston Herald
Boston Herald-Traveler
Boston Record-American
Chicago Defender
Chicago Tribune
Christian Science Monitor
Clarion Ledger
Delta Democrat-Times
Kansas City Star
Kansas City Times
Los Angeles Times
Lowell Sun
Lynn Item
Milwaukee Journal
New York Times
Olean Times-Herald
Quincy Patriot Ledger
Providence Journal
The Sporting News
StarPhoenix (Saskatoon)
Tiger Gazette (Coleman High School)
Valley Morning Star
Washington Post
Wellsville Daily Reporter
Winston-Salem Journal
Winston-Salem Journal and Sentinel
Worcester Telegram and Gazette

Other Sources

Ancestry.com.
Baseball-Almanac.com
Baseball America's Almanac (1994–2002)
Baseballprospectus.com
Baseball-Reference.com
Emerald Guide to Baseball (2007–2010)
Hardballtimes.com
Hittrackeronline.com
Retrosheet.org
SABR Baseball Encyclopedia
The Sporting News Baseball Guide (1981–1985)
Sports Collectors Digest

Index

Numbers in **_bold italics_** indicate pages with photographs.

Kuenn, Harvey 212
Kuhn, Bowie 163, 219, 221
Kunkel, Bill 185

LaCock, Pete 247
Lahoud, Joe 183, 190–193, 200
Lake Ferguson 14
Lane, Frank "Trader" 190–193, 195, 197
Lanier High School 19, 25
LaRussa, Tony 251
Lau, Charlie 251
Lawson, Edith 259
Lee, Bill 179, 232, 234, 236, 239, 242
LeMoine, Hank 34
Lemon, Bob 245
Leon Melenudos (Nicaraguan Winter League
  team) 49–50
Leoni, Raul 89
LeRoux, Buddy 97, *112*, 145, 237
Levee 14
Lewis, Buddy (St. Louis Cardinals scout) 26
Lezcano, Sixto 214–215, 225
Life Magazine 154, 158; *see also* Shecter, Leonard
Liston, Bill (*Boston Herald-Traveler* journalist)
  131
Little League 12–13, 33, 159
Lobel, Bob 260
Lock, Don 65
Locker, Bob 186, 206
Lockwood, Skip 196
Logan, Johnny 261
Lolich, Mickey 76, 124, 151
Lonborg, Jim 88–89, 102, 107–108, 110, 121,
  123–124, 126–128, 132, 134–138, 140, 142–
  143, 150, 153, 178–179, 186–187, 190–191
long taters *see* taters
Longwood, Mississippi 6–7
Lopez, Al 155
Loretta, Mark 261
Los Angeles Angels 25
Los Angeles Dodgers 97, 183, 261
Los Angeles Times 23, 202
Los Mochis *see* Los Mochis Caneros
Los Mochis Caneros (Mexican Pacific Winter
  League team) 252
Louisiana State University 23
Louisville *see* Louisville Colonels
Louisville, Kentucky 20
Louisville Colonels (Triple A International
  League team) 173, 187
Luciano, Ron 207
Lucy Webb Elementary School 10–11
Lyle, Sparky 179, 181, 196
Lynn, Fred 212, 218, 227, 235
Lynn, Massachusetts 257

MacPhail, Lee 208
Mad Dogs *see* Massachusetts Mad Dogs
Maddox, G.P. 16, 139
Mag *see* Scott, Magnolia
Magic Glove Award 208

Maglie, Sal 77–78, 82, 134, 137, 140
Magrini, Pete 47
Mahoney, Neil 28–29, 34
Major League Baseball Players Alumni Association
  (MLBPAA) 162
Major League Baseball Players Association (MLBPA)
  195, 200, 203, 219
Maloney, George 197
Malzone, Frank 43, 46–47, 55, 70, 81, 91, 102,
  261
Man of La Mancha 110; *see also Impossible Dream*
Managua, Nicaragua 49, 88
Mantle, Mickey 75, 81, 112, 123, 205
Maravich, Pete 23
Margenau, Eric (co-founder Empire State League)
  254
Marichal, Juan 135
Mariners *see* Seattle Mariners
Maris, Roger 132, 135–136
Markusen, Bruce (author *The Hardball Times*)
  250
Martin, Billy 199, 207, 232, 235, 245, 250–251
Martin, Gene 253
Martinez, Dennis 232
Massachusetts Commission Against Discrimination
  (MCAD) 27
Massachusetts Mad Dogs (independent North
  Atlantic League; independent Northeast
  League; independent Northern League) 257–
  259
May, Dave 202, 204
May, Lee 213
Mayaguez Indians (Puerto Rico Winter League
  team) 174
Mayberry, John 208, 218
Mays, Willie 5, 10, 38, 80, 83, 91, 164, 205, 209
McAuliffe, Dick 108, 118, 127
McCarver, Tim 132, 135, 137
McCraw, Tommy **60**
McDaniel, Lindy 185
McDonough, Will (*Boston Globe* journalist) 11,
  27, 74, 85, 91, 98, 102, 185
McDowell, "Sudden" Sam 71, 108, 155–156, 202
McGlothlin, Jim 117
McInnis, Stuffy 115
McLain, Dennis "Denny" 105, 118, 124, 151, 153,
  193
McMahon, Don 109, 155
McNally, Dave 111, 185
Memorial Stadium (Baltimore Orioles ballpark)
  185
Memphis Red Sox (Negro League team) 14, 17
Meredith, James 6
Merritt, John 23–24
Metropolitan Stadium (Minnesota Twins ballpark)
  77–78
Mets *see* New York Mets; Williamsport Mets
Mexican League (Triple A) 251–254
Mexican Pacific (Winter) League 252
Mexico City Reds (Triple A Mexican League team)
  253